Human–Computer Interaction Series

Editors-in-chief

Desney Tan, Microsoft Research, USA

Jean Vanderdonckt, Université Catholique de Louvain, Belgium

HCI is a multidisciplinary field focused on human aspects of the development of computer technology. As computer-based technology becomes increasingly pervasive—not just in developed countries, but worldwide—the need to take a human-centered approach in the design and development of this technology becomes ever more important. For roughly 30 years now, researchers and practitioners in computational and behavioral sciences have worked to identify theory and practice that influences the direction of these technologies, and this diverse work makes up the field of human-computer interaction. Broadly speaking it includes the study of what technology might be able to do for people and how people might interact with the technology. The HCI series publishes books that advance the science and technology of developing systems which are both effective and satisfying for people in a wide variety of contexts. Titles focus on theoretical perspectives (such as formal approaches drawn from a variety of behavioral sciences), practical approaches (such as the techniques for effectively integrating user needs in system development), and social issues (such as the determinants of utility, usability and acceptability).

Titles published within the Human–Computer Interaction Series are included in Thomson Reuters' Book Citation Index, The DBLP Computer Science Bibliography and The HCI Bibliography.

More information about this series at http://www.springer.com/series/6033

Judy Robertson · Maurits Kaptein
Editors

Modern Statistical Methods for HCI

 Springer

Editors
Judy Robertson
Moray House School of Education
Edinburgh University
Edinburgh
UK

Maurits Kaptein
Donders Centre for Cognition
Radboud University Nijmegen
Nijmegen
The Netherlands

Additional material to this book can be downloaded from http://extras.springer.com.

ISSN 1571-5035
Human–Computer Interaction Series
ISBN 978-3-319-79984-1   ISBN 978-3-319-26633-6   (eBook)
DOI 10.1007/978-3-319-26633-6

Printed on acid-free paper

This Springer imprint is published by SpringerNature
The registered company is Springer International Publishing AG Switzerland

Foreword

These two popular quotes vividly capture the necessity and misuse of statistical methods in research and argumentation in general. HCI is no exception.

The goal of the human–computer interaction field is to invent, design, develop, and understand effective means to delight users of computing devices, apps, and services. But unlike typical engineering and computer science problem solving, the solutions we devise in HCI rarely have a simple and deterministic measure of efficacy. Any measure we come up with, such as the usual time to completion, error rate, learning speed, subjective preference and ratings, tends to vary from trial to trial, task to task, and one individual user to another. Statistics, the art of making sense of fluctuating data, is a common method, among others, of moving our research, design or invention beyond a personal belief.

Most HCI researchers, particularly those coming from computer science and engineering backgrounds, did not usually have formal training in statistics. Even those who do often also struggle with deciding on the most appropriate statistical models, tests, data processing techniques, and software tools for each project because the underlying logic, assumptions and exceptions of each statistical method are complex and often debated by specialists. Statistical issues are often contentious in HCI publications. Paper reviewers often take issue with sample size, power, model assumption such as normality, and the statistical tests used. The reviewers' criticism of statistical methods often frustrates authors who follow other published papers on the same subject. Often neither the reviewers nor the authors have enough training in statistical methods to debate the chosen method's validity to a convincing level. Even if they do, research results, paper writing, and reviewing are just not the right forum for statistical method discussion.

Furthermore, even if one rigorously followed all the classical inferential statistics, the research conclusion and its reliability may still not mean the same to everyone. Ever since null hypothesis significance testing (NHST) became the dominant quantitative research method, its validity has been regularly questioned and challenged in empirical sciences such as experimental psychology. In recent years, such criticisms, and the advocacy toward alternative methods, particularly Bayesian methods, intensified in many fields. Resorting to simple descriptive statistics from larger samples, one psychology journal recently banned inferential statistics all together. However, no other journals have taken such an extreme position.

Unhappy with how statistics were interpreted and practiced in HCI Maurits Kaptein and Judy Robertson took their discussion formally by publishing their CHI 2012 paper "Rethinking statistical analysis methods for CHI." The paper drew great interest from researchers like me who are interested in and frequently apply statistical methods in our research, invention, product design, and development work. Knowing one conference paper is not enough, Judy and Maurits decided to take the subject to the next level, first by writing a journal paper. As the editor-in-chief of *ACM Transactions On Computer-Human Interaction* at the time, I ran an extensive board discussion of their journal submission. Many of my esteemed associate editors are enthusiastic and knowledgeable about the topic. Their views, however, are as varied as in the field. Some think most of what Judy and Maurits recommended was what they already taught their students. Some think science by nature is very much driven by community culture or prevailing norms. Some think criticisms of NHST are cyclic and may fade away once again. Most agree with the spirit of the Bayesian approach because it allows knowledge and hypothesis to be updated and improved with each new experiment, but they also acknowledge in practice the first novel study of a specific idea, design, or UI method, is always most valued. Subsequent studies which can give stronger Bayesian analysis benefiting from a prior estimated from the previous studies are less valued by academics and hence rare. There are also HCI researchers who do not think statistics are worthwhile and believe their best work did not rely on or use statistics at all. But none denied the need to educate the field to a much comprehensive level of understanding and practice of statistics in HCI. Several associate editors spontaneously suggested a book presenting the best practices of statistical methods from more than one school of thought. Everyone loved the idea of having such a book for their teaching and research. Having also served on the editorial board of Springer's HCI book series since its beginning, I knew academic publishers like Springer would welcome such a book proposal.

But having a wish or desire is easy. Many others in HCI have wished such a book, but they could not devote the large amount of time required to prepare, write, or edit such a book. Fortunately, Judy and Maurits did it, and they did a remarkable job. They reached out to an impressive set of knowledgeable authors in and outside the HCI field with different approaches and background in researching and practicing statistics. Judy and Maurits gave them a common set of hypothetical HCI data that researchers could easily relate to. The common dataset also allowed different statistical approaches be compared and contrasted. Judy and Maurits also wrote introductions to each section of the book, and multiple chapters of their own.

So finally, the HCI field has a comprehensive statistical methods book of its own for researchers and students. It may not resolve many of the explicit or implicit debates in statistical methods. Instead, the book supports a less rigid, procedural view of statistics in favor of "fair statistical communication." The book should become a common reference for empirical HCI research. Those who are interested in even deeper understanding of a particular statistical method can follow many of the references in the end of each chapter. I will certainly keep the book among the most reachable books on my shelf.

December 2015   Shumin Zhai

Preface

For those of us who are passionately interested in research, the methods we use are at least as important as our findings. We need to have confidence that our quantitative methods give us more than just an illusion of rigor; they should provide genuine insight into the problems which interest us. This book is a tool to assist researchers in making sense of their quantitative data without confusion, bias, or arbitrary conventions.

A few years ago we wrote a critical examination of statistical practice in Human–Computer Interaction which was presented at CHI 2012. Due to the lively discussions that surfaced at the conference, we thought there was more to "statistical methods in HCI" than could be conveyed through a conference paper. Initially, we set out to work on a journal paper which would both examine current practice, as well as introduce a number of statistical methods that are not covered in introductory research methods and statistics lectures but could, in our view, strengthen the field. The article then became lengthy, and we really wanted it to be hands-on. It spiraled out of control: we started involving both experts in different methods, as well as users of "a-typical" methods in HCI, and discussed their possible contributions to the article. Hence, mid 2014, we decided, in collaboration with Springer, to turn our article into a book. And here it is.

About the Authors

We confess to the reader at the outset that our own statistical practices are not perfect. In fact, over the years, both of us have committed about all of the potential errors identified in this volume (and they are there in the literature for you to sorrow over). These less than perfect analyses stem from ignorance of the pitfalls of null hypothesis significance testing—honestly!—rather than an intention to deceive the reading public. On occasion however, we have consciously used "traditional" methods rather than their more recent counterparts in order to tailor the analyses to the reviewers' expectations. It would be better for our field if authors didn't have to do this. You can help by leaving your copy of this book on coffee tables in HCI conference venues, with Part V of Chap. 14 helpfully highlighted.

Maurits

I am a social scientist and researcher primarily interested in persuasion, quantitative research methods, and optimal design. After doing my master's in (economic-) Psychology at the University of Tilburg, and doing a post-master program in User–System Interaction at the Eindhoven University of Technology, I received my Ph.D. with honors from the Eindhoven University of Technology, Eindhoven, the Netherlands. Next, I worked as a postdoctoral researcher at the Aalto school of Economics, Aalto, Finland. Afterwards, I worked for 2 years as assistant professor of Statistics and Research Methods at the University of Tilburg. During my Ph.D. I also worked as a research scientist at Philips Research, Eindhoven, the Netherlands and as a distinguished visiting scholar at the CHIMe lab of Stanford University, Stanford CA, USA.

Currently I am assistant professor in Artificial Intelligence (AI) at the Radboud University Nijmegen. Also, I am the track leader of a master track called "Web and Language." I (amongst other courses) teach a course on AI techniques on the web called "AI at the Webscale." You can find the website of the research lab that I run right here: www.nth-iteration.com.

At the end of 2012 my first "popular" (Dutch) book called "Digitale Verleiding" which, since 2015, is also available in English under the name "Persuasion Profiling" was released. I am also a founder of PersuasionAPI, "pioneers in persuasion profiling" (see www.sciencerockstars.com). The company is now owned by Webpower b.v.

My prime research interest are:

- Persuasive technologies. I focus on the real-time adaptation of the use of distinct persuasive principles in interactive technologies.
- Research methods. I study both parametric and non-parametric statistical methods, hierarchical models, and time-series.
- Online/streaming learning. I work quite a bit on how to fit hierarchical models online.
- Bandit problems. I have worked on policies for multi-armed bandit problems.
- Dynamic Adaptation. I have been involved in several attempts to model, in real-time, consumer behavior and adapt e-commerce attempts accordingly.

Obviously, my interest in research methods drove me to start editing this book. I have, throughout my studies and work, been interested in quantitative methods in diverse fields, ranging from social science, to computer science, to physics and engineering. And, I think the social sciences can broaden their views on their methods by looking around, and by keeping a close eye to modern developments. In this book we are trying to alert readers to methods that they might not have covered in their introductory stats course, but which are of use for their research and practice.

Judy

I am a computer scientist by training, although I am now a professor in the School of Education at the University of Edinburgh. I managed to graduate from two university degrees without ever taking a course in statistics; everything I know about statistics is self-taught. This is why I ended wandering down the path of editing this book—I kept innocently searching for answers to questions which should have been simple but weren't (such as "how do you analyse Likert data?"). It's quite easy to fall down a statistical rabbit hole if you don't start with the "traditional" knowledge about which statistical techniques to use in particular cases. I first became aware that null hypothesis significance testing (NHST) was a crumbling edifice when I listened to a podcast interview with Eric-Jan Wagenmakers who used Bayesian methods to demonstrate why experimental results from a series of PSI studies were flawed. While mildly disappointed that PSI doesn't really exist, I had a new rabbit hole to explore. But although I understood the criticisms of NHST and was interested to try new analytic techniques, I couldn't find many examples of such analyses in the HCI literature. I teamed up with Maurits, and we set out to draw together a book that would help other HCI researchers like me to apply appropriate statistical techniques to the sort of research problems we encounter daily. This is the book I wish I had beside me when struggling with countless analyses. I can attest to the fact it is useful: since getting initial chapter drafts from the authors, I have referred to them on many occasions already. I hope it is useful to you too.

Who Is This Book For?

This book is for Human−Computer Interaction (HCI) researchers who want to get better at making sense of quantitative data in a rigorous and thoughtful way. It aims both to critically reflect on current statistical methods used in HCI, and to introduce a number of novel methods to the HCI audience. Throughout the book HCI examples are used. However, we sincerely hope the book will be of use to a wider audience: this book, as far as we know, is one of the first attempts to bundle together non-introductory-course methods in a critical yet usable fashion.

It is not an introductory textbook—we assume you have a basic grasp of probability and commonly used NHST techniques such as t-tests, analysis of variance, and regression. We also assume that you have enough of a background in programing (or motivation to learn it) not to be intimidated by [R] code.

The Structure of the Book

The book opens with our own introduction which explains why the statistical methods we choose matter so much, and how researchers in other fields have moved away from blind reliance on the familiar null hypothesis significance testing (NHST) framework. It identifies some of the most common misunderstandings about NHST and often encountered misapplications of these methods. These themes are picked up again in the discussion Chaps. 13 and 14 at the end of the book.

In Part I (*Getting Started With Data Analysis*), the authors introduce the [R] environment (Chap. 2), explain how to visualize data to gain an intuitive understanding of your dataset before embarking on further analysis, and to illustrate your argument clearly in publications (Chap. 3). In the initial stages of the analysis, it is sensible to consider what to do about missing data—Chap. 4 explains how. Hint: you will always have more missing data than you expect and the solution is not to sweep it under the carpet.

Part II (*Classical Null Hypothesis Significance Testing Done Properly*) takes the pragmatic view that as many researchers will continue to use NHST, we might as well focus on applying such methods correctly and them interpreting them meaningfully. The issues of effect size and power are discussed in Chap. 5, highlighting the inconvenient truth that you generally need more participants than you want to find and that the size of an effect is more useful for interpreting the real-world significance of your results than a gloriously small p-value. Chapter 6 covers techniques for handling time with repeated measures analysis of variance and event history analysis. The importance of checking the assumptions underlying the tests you employ is emphasized in Chap. 7, along with a useful guide to the appropriate use of non-parametric tests.

We venture into the world of *Bayesian Inference* in Part III. Chapter 8 introduces the concepts of Bayesian reasoning and how they can be usefully applied to help us interpret data, while Chap. 9 illustrates how to quantify the strength of evidence for multiple competing hypotheses. This will equip you with the tools to weigh up the merits of alternative substantive hypotheses rather than examining the rather weak and watery hypothesis that the means of two groups are identical.

In Part IV we address some techniques for *Advanced Modeling in HCI*. Chapter 10 introduces latent variable analysis and structural equation modeling which can be used to infer properties of variables which cannot be directly measured. Chapter 11 discusses generalized linear mixed models, link functions and how to deal with data with a nested structure. In Chap. 12, techniques for latent class analysis and mixture models are explained with running examples.

Part V is a reflection on *Improving Statistical Practice in HCI*. Chapter 13 is a clear and well-argued call to use estimation methods to support fair statistical communication. The author offers many tips that researchers can follow to improve the clarity of their reporting. The concluding chapter by the editors draws together the chapters in the book and how the techniques presented here—and other novel techniques which we did not have the space to cover—could address some of the problems pervading the use of statistical methods in social sciences. To allay any doubts of those who believe that HCI is immune to the methodological failings of other fields, we critically analyze the methods used in eight case studies of top cited quantitative studies in our field. We consider changing attitudes to quantitative methods in HCI and conclude with some recommendations for authors, reviewers, and journal editors which we hope will help in improving the clarity and fairness of statistical reporting in our field.

The Sample Dataset: The Mango Watch

We decided that it would be helpful to have running examples relating to HCI, as presently this is hard to find in the literature. A shared dataset would provide some continuity between chapters and a link to topics of interest to HCI researchers. We were unable to find an open-source dataset which suited this purpose, so we provide a simulated dataset from the following hypothetical scenario:

> A company has recently invested in smart watches (known as the Mango) for all sales executives. They have tasked the world famous UX expert Professor Houdini and his team to evaluate the impact of the Mango on productivity among the sales staff. They firmly believe that having email on one's wrist[1] will cause faster response times to customers, and therefore more sales. The professor, at long last unfettered by constraints on resources imposed by measly academic research grants, has come up with the following data collection plan.

> Data will be collected for Sales Team A over a period of 3 months after the introduction of Mangos. Control data will be collected from members of Sales Team B over the same period—this group will not yet be equipped with Mangos. However, they will receive their Mangos in month 4, giving the researchers both between subjects (A compared to B) and within subjects (pre-Mango B compared to post-Mango B) data.

The measures used are:

- A 7 point SUS-like usability scale about experience of using Mango (ordinal).
- Average response time to answer customer emails (ratio/interval).
- Sales Team A and B staff are distributed over several geographical regions:
- Sales Team A: Aachen, Abik, Aberdeen,
- Sales Team B: Babol, Bakersfield, Barrie.

More details of the [R] code which generated the dataset can be found in the supplementary materials to Chap. 2. You will find that the chapter authors have extended and changed the scenario to better illustrate their techniques. For most of the chapters online supplements are available (http://extras.springer.com). If the authors deviate from, or extend the initial Mango watch dataset they either use [R] code—presented in the chapter text—to generate their data, or their datasets are

---

[1]It is company policy that Mangos must be worn at all times, even in bed.

available in the supplementary materials. As the code generates the data randomly, the data sets used by different authors will differ.[2] For this reason, we don't recommend trying to make sense of the experimental findings across chapters. Sadly, this book will tell you nothing of value about the impact of fruit-based smart watches on the performance of sales executives. However, the Mango watch scenario does offer a context that is shared between all chapters which saves the authors the effort (and space) to introduce novel settings. Needless to say, the editors remain open to funding offers from such companies who do wish to investigate fruit-based smart watch performance.

Our Approach

We chose to use [R] as the language for conducting the analyses in the book because it a widely used, free, open-source platform which evolves fast enough to keep up with new techniques as they emerge. We realize that [R] will introduce a learning curve for some readers (but in Judy's recent personal experience it is worth investing the time to make the switch from a graphical package). We have asked the chapter authors to explain the statistical concepts in plain language, and to introduce the supporting mathematics where necessary. You will find the finer mathematical details in footnotes from time to time, in places where Maurits' mathematical conscience has been sufficiently troubled. Above all, the authors have made a real effort throughout to help the reader to interpret the numerical results in the context of a research problem, as you will need to do yourself when making sense of your data for publication.

This book might be disappointing for some of you: in many ways the book will lead to more questions than answers. However, this is inherent in our subject: there is no single best method to use to analyze your data. Many methods could be considered, tried, and possibly combined. You may notice that the authors contradict each other from time to time, and that different analytical techniques lead to quite different interpretations of the data. This is a wider point of the book: we must choose the techniques we use wisely, and report it wisely so that other researchers in the future are aware of our assumptions and are informed to make their own interpretations.

It will become obvious as you read through the volume that the method of analysis really does matter. The decisions made by the analyst make a difference to the results and how they are interpreted. Interpreting quantitative data is more prone to subjectivity than you might think. It is better to acknowledge this fact and deal with it sensibly, than to hide it in a clutter of procedural use of "accepted" statistical methods.

---

[2]Some authors explicitly mention their seeds for reproducibility. Others provide their dataset in the supplementary materials.

Acknowledgements

We sincerely thank the chapter authors for all their patience, effort, and generosity in making this book work. We would also like to thank Shumin Zhai for his comments on our earlier writings and suggesting that we should edit a collection on the topic.

Contents

Contributors

Niall Anderson Centre for Population Health Sciences, Usher Institute of Population Health Sciences and Informatics, University of Edinburgh, Edinburgh, UK

Mark Andrews Division of Psychology, Nottingham Trent University, Nottingham, UK

Thom Baguley Division of Psychology, Nottingham Trent University, Nottingham, UK

A. Alexander Beaujean Baylor University, Waco, TX, USA

Pierre Dragicevic Orsay Cedex, France

Deborah Fry Moray House School of Education, University of Edinburgh, Edinburgh, UK

Lianne Ippel Department of Methodology and Statistics, Tilburg University, Tilburg, The Netherlands

Maurits Kaptein Donders Centre for Cognition, Radboud University Nijmegen, Nijmegen, The Netherlands

Matthew Kay Department of Computer Science and Engineering, University of Washington, Seattle, WA, USA

Grant B. Morgan Baylor University, Waco, TX, USA

Joris Mulder Department of Methodology and Statistics, Tilburg University, Tilburg, The Netherlands

Daniel Oberski Department of Methodology and Statistics, Tilburg University, Tilburg, The Netherlands

Judy Robertson Moray House School of Education, Edinburgh University, Edinburgh, UK

Michail Tsikerdekis School of Information Science, University of Kentucky, Lexington, KY, USA

Kerri Wazny Centre for Global Health Research, Usher Institute of Population Health Sciences and Informatics, University of Edinburgh, Edinburgh, UK

Jan Wessnitzer The Scientific Editing Company Ltd., Edinburgh, UK

Jacob O. Wobbrock The Information School, University of Washington, Seattle, WA, USA

Koji Yatani University of Tokyo, Tokyo, Japan

Joanna Young The Scientific Editing Company Ltd., Edinburgh, UK

Chapter 1
An Introduction to Modern Statistical Methods in HCI

Judy Robertson and Maurits Kaptein

Abstract This chapter explains why we think statistical methodology matters so much to the HCI community and why we should attempt to improve it. It introduces some flaws in the well-accepted methodology of Null Hypothesis Significance Testing and briefly introduces some alternatives. Throughout the book we aim to critically evaluate current practices in HCI and support a less rigid, procedural view of statistics in favour of "fair statistical communication". Each chapter provides scholars and practitioners with the methods and tools to do so.

1.1 Introduction

Why do statistical methods matter in the first place? Is it just dry academic pedantry about obscure statistics? The premise behind this book is that methodology—however dry it might seem—matters. The quality of our experimental design(s), statistical analysis and reporting makes all the difference to what we collectively believe about the design and use of interfaces. Statistics and quantitative research methods often fuel our understanding of how humans interact with computers. Misuse of statistics enables us to delude ourselves now and confuse our colleagues in the future, thus wasting resources in pursuing fruitless areas of research. Erroneous interpretations of collected data risk some of the most important conclusions in the field and misinform future research efforts. A combination of lack of statistical power through small sample sizes, and inattention to the consequences of multiple comparisons can lead to misleading conclusions that are almost impossible to interpret. And, even if the research findings in a published paper *are* true, because of the general lack of effect size reporting, we do not tend to address the question of *how much* of a difference they actually make. Papers within the field often report whether an

J. Robertson (✉)
Moray House School of Education, Edinburgh University, Edinburgh, UK
e-mail: Judy.Robertson@ed.ac.uk

M. Kaptein
Donders Centre for Cognition, Radboud University Nijmegen, Nijmegen, The Netherlands
e-mail: maurits@mauritskaptein.com

© Springer International Publishing Switzerland 2016
J. Robertson and M. Kaptein (eds.), *Modern Statistical Methods for HCI*,
Human–Computer Interaction Series, DOI 10.1007/978-3-319-26633-6_1

effect exists instead of examining the magnitude and real-world importance of the effect. These latter issues have fuelled arguments by qualitative researchers that HCI work can hardly be examined quantitatively (Cf. Seaman 1999). This however is a lack in our own analysis and reporting of quantitative experiments, rather than a consequence of experiments or other quantitative methods per se.

Colleagues within the community may argue—correctly—that there is more to HCI than quantitative methods. They may make the case that it is an engineering field, focussed on building applications which meet users' needs. Some practitioners might prefer to focus on design and aesthetics, considering their work to be more artistic than scientific. Others chose to focus on qualitative methods since aspects of our field are too complex to meaningfully be captured in quantitative experiments. These are all valid view-points. Our view here is however that quantitative methods currently *do* have an important place in HCI research, and that we should examine whether we as a field are using these methods appropriately. If not, there needs to be a discussion about how we will address this problem. Can we improve our practice? This question is relevant even if quantitative methods are only a part of our practice. And, if so, what is the best approach to doing so? Or should we even give up on statistical inference altogether?

We chose the optimistic position that it is possible to improve practice, and that for the health of our field, we should try to do so. This volume offers practical explanations and examples of techniques which can be used to help us interpret data with clarity, insight and with a wary respect for the strength of our claims. We hope that others within the community will build on these in the future.

1.2   Earlier Commentaries on Statistical Methods in HCI and Beyond

Critiques of methods used in any field have a time and place. Why do we at this place and time raise an issue about the statistical methods in HCI? We believe that HCI is ready for such a discussion for several reasons. First, this same discussion has recently (re-) emerged in neighbouring disciplines such as psychology (Wagenmakers et al. 2011) computer science (Cairns 2007; Gray and Salzman 1998; Seaman 1999), and economics (Ziliak and McCloskey 2008). Second, our contribution to CHI 2012 saw a critical discussion of quantitative methods in the field (Kaptein and Robertson 2012) which was greeted with considerable interest. Our aim here is to follow up on these arguments and in this book make a positive and practical contribution to those who wish to avoid the pitfalls identified which have consistently been identified.

We start by reviewing some of the fiercest critiques of Null Hypothesis Significance Testing (NHST) out there today. In 2008 Ziliak and McCloskey published their book called "The cult of statistical significance: how the p-value is costing us jobs, money, and lives". As is clear from the title the main issue of the book is a consideration of the use of what the authors call *qualitative* tests which decide only between whether or not an effect exists without considering the size or importance of the effects. Further, the "qualitative" test—the NHST—introduces an arbitrary cut-off (often $p < 0.05$) to guide decision making. The authors give a number of examples of (a) statistically significant results that bear no real-world importance, and (b) insignificant results that do bear real-world importance. They argue that a heuristic that errs in both directions can hardly be a reliable guide for our decisions.

While Zilliak and McCloskey's critique of NHST is zealous to an extent that might harm their arguments, they are certainly not alone in their crusade against NHST as the only basis for sense-making of quantitative data. In Psychology, authors such as Wagenmakers et al. (2011) attack the NHST approach primarily for its inability to quantify evidence in favour of the null-hypothesis. These authors point to Bayesian alternatives of the NHST test—see "the fallacy of the transposed conditional" below. Many scholars have picked up on Bayesian alternatives to NHST in psychology (Rouder et al. 2009), cognitive science (Kruschke 2010), bioinformatics (Fox and Dimmic 2006), and economics (Conley et al. 2008). While we believe that often Bayesian methods might improve the quality of statistical analysis, we do not think that Bayesian "equivalents" to NHST should blind fully overtake current NHST methods. You can find out how to conduct Bayesian analysis in Sect. 1.3 of the book.

Ioannidis's (2005) critique of our standard practices of NHST testing is different from that of authors pushing Bayesian methods. His critique focuses more on the asymptotic properties of our tests, and how these seem to be violated by over-testing, and biases in the selection of publications and variables. It is becoming more and more apparent that within the orthodox frameworks that we use regularly to analyse our quantitative data many "researcher degrees of freedom" exist: hence, while scientists hoped to have converged on objective methods, it seems that also our objective methods allow for researcher subjectivity. Ioannidis's (2005) shows convincingly based on simulation that it is very likely that these researcher-degrees of freedom are indeed often used: they are the core driver of the conclusion that "most published research findings are false".

Gelman and David (2009) raises an additional worry that might threaten our scientific findings coined the "significance filter". The worry is not so much that findings are wrong, but more that the effects we identify are overestimated. The idea is simple if we have a treatment for which the effect is "borderline significant" given a specific sample size: some of our studies will show a significant result, and some will not purely by chance. Those that do have a sampling error in the direction of the effect are over-estimates of the effect. The significance filter as such is analogues to regression towards the mean: if we select high (or low) scoring groups out of a sample based on some measure that contains error, it is most likely that the error was upwards (or downwards) for the selected individuals. Hence, one would expect them to "regress towards the mean": the selected high (or low) scoring individuals are likely to score lower (or higher) on a re-test. The significance filter introduces the same problem into our estimates of effect sizes. A related concern is often termed the "file drawer effect" which refers to bias in the literature introduced by researchers (or journals) neglecting to publish experiments with null results (Rosenthal 1979).

It is not just our related disciplines who discuss possible shortcomings of the quantitative methods that we use. Researchers and practitioners within HCI have identified several problems both with the methods used in the field as well as with the reporting of these methods. In 1998 Gray and Salzman (1998) evaluated the validity of the methodological and statistical procedures used in five famous studies comparing Usability Evaluation Methods. Besides many methodological threats to validity they identify a number of issues regarding statistical validity. The authors note that for the five important HCI studies that they examine often sample sizes are too low, and researchers test too many comparisons without controlling for increasing error rates. Surprisingly the authors close their section on statistical validity with the remark that "...practitioners should keep in mind that, if an effect is too unstable for statistics to show a significant difference, then it is too unstable to be relied on as guidance when selecting UEMs" [Usability Evaluation Methods].While we would often concur with such a recommendation it needs to be established first that the power of the experiment was sufficient to warrant a conclusions of non-guidance based on an experiment versus the conclusion to conduct a more elaborate experiment. As we will discuss in more detail below, a failure to detect an effect is not the same as lack of an effect.

Subsequently Cairns (2007) examined the ubiquity of statistical problems in HCI work. The author selects papers from several respected HCI outlets (such as Human Computer Interaction and the ACM transactions on Human Computer Interaction) and examines their use of statistical tests. The author finds that over half of the papers report statistical tests, and all but one make errors. Cairns identifies errors in the writing related the APA norms (American Psychological Association 2009), assumption checking (the assumptions underlying the test are often not checked), over testing (researchers use too many comparisons), and the use of inappropriate tests (using a test in which clearly the probability model does not fit the data generating process). Besides showing the ubiquity of statistical problems in HCI work, the author also questions the value of NHST tests for the field and recommends that HCI should explore other frameworks for doing statistics.

In 2009 Dunlop and Baillie (2009) discussed the value of NHST for mobile HCI. Based on the critiques of NHST in neighboring fields they introduce five core problems of the NHST approach. First, they highlight the drawback of using p-values only for a binary approval stating that "there is nothing magical about 0.05". Next the authors highlight the common confusion between p-values and effect sizes: a low p-value implies a combination of effect size *and* measurement precision and the two are often confused. Thirdly the authors note that statistical tests are often misused (or even abused): distributional properties that underlie reported tests are not actually met (see Chap. 7 for how to test assumptions about the properties of data using [R]). Fourth, the authors criticize the interpretation of non-significant result as an indication of no effect: often a non-significant result cannot be grounds to conclude that the effect indeed does not exist. Finally, the authors highlight that often p-values are interpreted erroneously to indicate the probability of the null hypothesis being true, while this is not the actual meaning of the p value.

We hope the above discussion makes clear that there is an increasing concern about the statistical methods used both in HCI as well as in our neighboring fields. While we believe that there are no "one size fits all" analysis schemes available to perfect our practice, there are many improvements that can be made to our statistical practice that would increase the likelihood that HCI research findings are not false. Below we will first briefly introduce the basic ideas of NHST to provide a common background in front of which we can illustrate the most common statistical problems we encounter as a field.

1.3 Some of the Very Basic Ideas of Our Common "NHST" Method

The "orthodox" (Ziliak and McCloskey 2004; Ziliak 2008) approach to statistics within many scientific fields is to use NHST methods.[1] In the common decision making procedure, the "null hypothesis" is scrutinized and either rejected—leading to accepting the alternative hypothesis—or it is concluded that there is not sufficient evidence to reject the null hypothesis, and subsequently it is accepted. The great advantage of this decision-making procedure is that long-term error rates are known, and therefore can be controlled. Researchers can control for both Type I and Type II errors. *Type I* errors occur when the null hypothesis is rejected when it is actually true and can be controlled by specifying an alpha value (before beginning data collection) that specifies the level of significance under which the null hypothesis will be rejected. *Type II* errors occur when the null hypothesis is accepted when it is actually false: that is, there is an effect that has not been detected. The proportion of times the null is false but was accepted is called *Beta*. The power of an experiment (1-*Beta*) is the probability of detecting an effect given that the effect really exists in the population. If it is sufficiently unlikely that the observed data was generated by a process that is adequately described by the null hypothesis, then the null is rejected and another, alternative, hypothesis is accepted. To summarize: The experimenter specifies a decision criterion alpha in advance. Using the NHST decision procedure, alpha*100 % of the time she will accept the null when there is no effect (Type I error). Beta is the probability that she make a type II error—detecting an effect when the true effect is zero. Statistical power (1-beta) is then the probability of avoiding a Type II error: of detecting a true effect.

Sufficiently unlikely as referred to in the previous paragraph is in most null hypothesis tests defined in terms of a ratio of signal and (sampling) error. To understand the basic idea of this procedure it is useful to consider the one-sample t-test:

$$t = \frac{\bar{x} - \mu_0}{s/\sqrt{n}} \tag{1.1}$$

---

[1]While technically the often applied methods are an—arguably erroneous—hybrid between methods introduced by Neymann-Pearson and Fisher, we focus here on the common practice.

The so-called t value is given by the difference of the sample mean $\bar{x}$ and the (hypothesized) population mean u_0 (often zero in this particular test)—the signal— divided by the sample standard deviation over the square root of the number of subjects—the sampling (or standard) error. Higher t-values indicate that it's less likely that the sample mean (given the standard deviation and the number of observations) would be observed if indeed in the population mean was equal to u_0. Thus high t-values lead to low p—values: *the probability of observing the current data (or more extreme data) given the null hypothesis that the sample mean is indeed equal to the population mean.* When a p-value, the probability of the data given the null hypothesis, is lower than alpha we reject the null.

Low p-values—often those lower than 0.05—would thus drive most researchers to conclude that the null-hypothesis is *not* true, and some alternative hypothesis should be accepted. It is easy to see that high t-values (and thus low p-values) can be obtained through a combination of a large signal (difference between $\bar{x}$ and u_0), and a small sampling error (small s and / or high n) (See also Baguley 2012).

The basic idea underlying the t-test can be extended in many directions. The way we currently test differences in proportions (Chan and Zhang 1999), examine the "significance" of regression coefficients (Paternoster et al. 1998), test the effects of factors in ANOVA analysis (Gelman 2005), and a whole range of other tests all depend on the same principle: There is some quantification of the signal—in the above example the difference between the sample mean and the tested population mean—and some quantification of how certain we can be of the observed signal. Lots of noise, wide distributions, or a small number of observations lead to uncertainty and thus a failure to reject the null hypothesis. In all cases, the cut-off value of p (often 0.05) is arbitrary.

1.4   The Common, and Well-Acknowledged, Problems with Our Current NHST Methods

Now that we share a common understanding of NHST we can discuss the most frequently occurring problems that originate from it. Despite being introduced as only one of the *many* tools of disposal for analyst by William Gosset in 1908 (Student 1908; See also: Box 1987), the NHST test has become one of the only, if not the only, reported outcome of experiments and other quantitative explorations throughout the social sciences. Owing to this narrow focus on NHST, and a lack of understanding of the associated p-value, erroneous conclusions make their way into the literature. Below we describe six common misunderstandings surrounding the use of the NHST test.

1.4.1 Misinterpretations of the P-Value

The NHST approach, fiercely promoted by Fisher in the 1930s (Fisher 1934 and also Pearson et al. 1994), has become the gold standard in many disciplines including quantitative evaluations in HCI. However, the approach is rather counter-intuitive; and subsequently many researchers misinterpret the meaning of the p-value. To illustrate this point Oakes (1986) posed a series of true/false questions regarding the interpretation of p-vales to *seventy* experienced researchers and discovered that *only two* had a sound understanding of the underlying concept of significance.

So what does a p-value actually mean? "...the p-value is the probability of obtaining the observed value of a sample statistic (such as t, F, χ^2) or a more extreme value if the data were generated from a null-hypothesis population and sampled according to the intention of the experimenter" (Oakes 1986, p. 293). Because p-values are based on the idea that probabilities are long run frequencies, they are properties of a collective of events rather than single event. They *do not* give the probability of a hypothesis being true or false for this particular experiment, they only provide a description of the long term Type I error rate for a class of hypothetical experiments—most of which the researcher has not conducted.

1.4.2 The Fallacy of the Transposed Conditional

The erroneous interpretation of the p-value by many researchers brings up the first actual threat to the validity of conclusions that are supported by null-hypothesis testing. Researchers often interpret the p-value to quantify the probability that the null hypothesis is true. Thus, a p-value smaller than 0.05 indicates to large groups of researchers—be it conscious or unconscious—that the probability that the null hypothesis is true (e.g. $\bar{x} = u_0$) is very small.

Under this misinterpretation the p-value would quantify $P(H_0/D)$—the probability of the null hypothesis (H_0) *given* the data collected in the experiment. However, the correct interpretation of the p-value is rather different: it quantifies $P(D/H_0)$—the probability of the data *given that H_0 is true*. Researchers who state that it is very unlikely that the null hypothesis is true based on a low p-value are attributing an incorrect meaning to the p-value.

The difference between $P(H_0/D)$ and $P(D/H_0)$ is not merely a statistical quirk that is unlikely to affect anything in practice. Not at all. It is easy to understand why this misconception is incorrect and hugely important by the following example: consider the probability of being dead after being shot, $P(D = true/S = true)$. Most would estimate this to be very high, say 0.99. However, the mere observation of a dead person does not lead most people to believe that the corpse was shot—after all, there are many possible ways to die which don't involve shooting. $P(S = true/D = true)$ is estimated to be rather small. Luckily, the relationship between $P(D/H_0)$ and $P(H_0/D)$ is well-known and given by Bayes rule (Barnard and Bayes 1958). Thus, if one wishes to estimate $P(H_0/D)$—which we often do—the proper analytical tools are at our disposal. For an accessible introduction to Bayesian analysis, see Chap. 8 and Kruschke (2011b).

1.4.3 A Lack of Power

The use of p-values enables researchers to control Type I errors—or the rejection of H_0 when in fact it is true. However, controlling Type II errors (the failure to reject H_0 when it is false) by estimating the *power* of an experiment appears to be attended to less frequently (Dienes 2008). The power of a statistical test is the long-term probability that a given test *will find an effect assuming that one exists in the population*. Thus, power indicates whether your experimental setup is capable of detecting the effect that you wish to find. The power is a function of sample size, population effect size and the significance criteria (known as the alpha (or p) value, which is set by convention at 0.05).

The standard accepted power within psychology is 0.80 (Cohen 1992) which means that there would $20\%(1 - 0.80)$ chance that the researcher fails to reject the null hypothesis when it is false. Hence, the researcher does not "discover" the effect that in reality does exist. Reviews of the psychology literature reveal that the majority of published studies lack power, resulting in a confusing literature with apparently contradictory results (Maxwell 2004). In studies with low power, getting a null result is not particularly informative: *it does not distinguish between the cases where the null is true and where the experimental set-up did not detect the null.* Chap. 5 introduces power calculations in [R].

1.4.4 Confusion of P-Values and Effect Size Estimates

Besides the often-erroneous interpretation of p-values and low power, the focus on null hypothesis significance testing in HCI has another severe consequence: *we are slowly turning our quantitative science into a qualitative one.* We seem to be more concerned with the mere fact that a finding is statistically significant than with interpreting the actual importance of the effects we are studying. The latter can only be assessed by considering effect sizes and appropriate loss functions. Effect size calculations in [R] are covered in Chap. 5 of this volume.

A p-value smaller than 0.05 does not necessarily imply that the effect is important—it only informs us that the noise was small compared to the signal. Also, a p-value smaller than 0.001— according to some "highly significant" does also not inform us that the effect is more important. Especially for large data sets (which often lead to very powerful tests) low p-values are common but do not inform our search for scientific answers. Only an informed *interpretation* of the numerical estimated effect can tell us whether a "significant" effect is indeed important to us and warrants further research or a theoretical explanation. For example, if there was a significant difference in the time taken to learn two competing versions of a software package, but the size of the effect was only 1.2 s (over a total use time of the software of 2+ years), this would likely not have a very large practical impact.

Perhaps surprisingly, the flip side of the argument also holds: a high p-value does not imply that the effect under study was unimportant. It only means that it was measured with a relatively high sampling error. Compelling examples of this can be found in neighbouring disciplines, and even in the court room: the painkiller Vioxx was in tested in a clinical trial against Naproxen, a general already-on-the-market painkiller. During the trial one person died that was taking Naproxen. For Vioxx however, five people died. The difference *was not statistically significant, $p > 0.05$,* and thus written off as unimportant. The lawsuits against Vioxx in 2005 proved the researchers wrong: The real-life, and regrettably more powerful test, showed that Vioxx severely—although initially not significantly—raised risks of cardiovascular side effects. If statistical significance is neither a sufficient nor a necessary criterion for importance, what good does it do?

Currently the "size-less stare" at p-values does a lot of harm (Ziliak and McCloskey 2008). In some fields, where historically researchers were trained in graphing their data and exploring the numerical values, means, and confidence intervals, this practice seems to be decreasing due to the fixation on p-values (Ziliak and McCloskey 2008). In computing fields it is not clear that effect size reporting was ever common; Dunlop and Baillie have identified lack of effect size reporting in HCI as "dangerous" and in the related field of software engineering experiments, a review of 92 experiments published between 1993 and 2002 shows that only 29 % of the papers reported estimates of effects (Kampenes et al. 2007).

1.4.5 Multiple Comparisons

An important aspect of the orthodox NHST procedure is to control for Type 1 errors, to protect against the possibility of a falsely rejecting the null hypothesis. For each test carried out, the probability of finding an effect where there is actually none (a false alarm) is generally set to be 5 %. However, this picture is complicated when we consider the experiment-wise error rates. Typically, researchers will wish to carry out more than one test on the same data set, and with each further tests carried out, the probability of a false positive result is inflated. In an experimental design with k experimental conditions, the number of possible comparisons is given by the formula:

$$c = k(k - 1) * 1/2 \tag{1.2}$$

The experiment-wise error rate is $1(1 - \alpha)^c$, where α is the per comparison false alarm rate (again, usually set to be 0.05), and the comparisons are assumed to be structurally independent of each other (Kruschke 2011b)

Suppose that there are three experimental conditions, and so three comparison tests are carried out. Although the probably of making a Type 1 error when considering each test in isolation is 5 %, the experiment-wise error rate rises to 14 %. In a more complex design, say with 5 groups, comparisons between each group would inflate the experiment-wise error rates to 40 %—which is considered unacceptably high. A solution to this problem is to use an omnibus test (we will consider ANOVA in the following examples) to find whether there are overall main effects, and then conduct follow up t-tests to establish where the differences lie. *Planned contrasts* test relationships which the research has predicted in advance based on theory or previous results. *Post-hoc tests* are pairwise comparisons which were not specified when the experiment was designed, but which the researcher uses to explore interesting emergent relationships. Running all possible comparisons without correcting for inflated Type I error rates would negate the point of doing an omnibus test in the first place, so it is good practice to control family-wise error rates by applying a correction which uses more stringent values for a result to be considered significant. See Chap. 7 if you would like to know how to correct ANOVA results for multiple comparisons in [R].

An anomaly in NHST practice is that it is acceptable to conduct planned comparisons without correcting for experiment-wise error rates, while post-hoc tests do require it. This relates to the incoherence regarding the experimenter's intention embedded in NHST (Kruschke 2011a). Imagine two researchers who conducted the same experiment, and analysed the same data set but who started out with different opinions about which hypotheses should be tested. They could find different results because Researcher A—who didn't predict the effect at the outset—must use stringent corrections on his post-hoc comparisons, while smug researcher B—who had the foresight to bury his hypotheses in a time capsule along with a copy of a daily newspaper—has the luxury of using less conservative significance values.

1.4.6 Researcher Degrees of Freedom

Simmons et al. recently introduced the concept of "researcher degrees of freedom" to describe the series of decisions which researchers must make when designing, running, analysing and reporting experiments. The result of ambiguity when making such decisions is that researchers often (without intention of deceit) perform multiple alternative statistical analyses and then choose to report the form of analysis which found statistically significant results. The authors show through a cleverly constructed simulation study that "It is unacceptably easy to publish "statistically significant" evidence consistent with *any* hypothesis" (Simmons et al. 2011, p. 1). The authors illustrate this by reporting evidence in support of the hypothesis that listening to the song "When I'm 64" reduces chronological age. The simulation study investigated how the significance of the results changed when different forms of analyses were conducted on a simulated data set randomly drawn from the normal distribution, repeated 15,000 times. The different forms of analysis manipulated common researcher degrees of freedom: selecting dependant variables, setting sample size, the use of covariates and reporting only selected subsets of experimental conditions. If the researcher is flexible about when she stops data collection—a common practice although it is not at all advocated in the NHST literature—and gathers more data after doing a significance test, the false positive rate increases by 50 %. By using covariates, such as the ubiquitous gender factor, the researcher can introduce a false positive rate of 11 %, and by reporting only a subset of the data, a false positive rate of 12.6 % is produced. Finally, if our researcher was too flexible in *all* four of these areas, the false positive rate would be 61 %.

Simmons et al. (2011) recommend a set of ten simple practices which reduce the problem of false positives. Firstly, they recommend that authors should decide in advance on their criteria for when to stop data collection. Given the prevalence of problems of underpowered tests, it would be sensible to use stopping rules based on power analysis. The second guideline of providing at least 20 observations per cell is directly related to power, and reduces the risk of type II errors. According to guidelines 3 and 4, authors would be required to report all the variables collected, and all experimental conditions investigated even if they are not reported in the final analysis in the paper. This would enable readers to judge how selective authors are in reporting their results. Guideline 5 recommends that if observations (such as outliers) are removed, they should report both the results with and without their removal to enable the reader to determine what effect it has. To reduce the occurrence of false positives by the introduction of covariates, guidelines 6 recommends that results should be reported with and without covariates. As changes in authorial practices require monitoring by reviewers, Simmons et al. (2011) propose four related guidelines for reviewers, starting with ensuring that authors follow the first 6 recommendations. Following these guidelines is likely to lead to publications with fewer significant and less perfect seeming results; reviewers are therefore encouraged to be more tolerant of imperfections in results (but less tolerant of imperfections in methodology!). Reviewers are also asked to check that the authors have demonstrated that their results don't depend on arbitrary decisions while conducting the analysis, and that the analytic decisions are consistent across studies reported in the same paper. Lastly, Simmons et al. (2011) invite reviewers to make themselves unpopular by requiring that authors conduct replications of studies where data collection or analysis methods are not compelling.

1.4.7   What Is the Aim of Statistical Analysis?

So, despite our common and ubiquitous use of NHST methods the methods are plagued with errors. Then why are these methods so ubiquitous? Are the problems described above perhaps only theoretical, and would they only have an impact on practice in special borderline cases?

The problems are real, and they plague real studies and conclusions in many fields (see Chap. 14 to see a critical examination of the problems in highly cited HCI papers). To understand however why these methods are ubiquitous in spite of their flaws we need to make the aim of our statistical procedures explicit.

Statistical methods of inference allow us to do the following: given some hypothetical idea about our data generating process, we set out to actually collect data—our sample—and next answer questions about our data generating process. For example, we have a hypothetical description of a fair coin toss where $P(Heads) = p^k(1 - p)^{1-k}$ (where $k = \{0, 1\}$, heads or tails). Next, we observe ten actual tosses (H, H, T, T, H, H, T, H, H, H— our sample). Based on this data we can start answering questions about the relationship between our hypothetical ideas of the data generating process and the actually observed data. We could for example ask: "How likely is the data that we observed given that we postulate the coin to be fair ($p = 0.5$)?" Hence, we assume that the data generating process is $P(Heads) = 0.5^k(1 - 0.5)^{1-k}$ using the Bernoulli distribution. Next, we examine whether our observed data—containing 7 heads instead of the 5 heads which would be most likely given the postulated long term proportion of 0.5—are still sufficiently likely to have originated from the assumed data generating process. This is a standard NHST question.

We use our statistical methods to answer the above question, and we want tests that do so which are easy to compute, easy to understand, and in the end lead to a presentation of our results that will enable us to get our work published. The NHST satisfies all these latter criteria easily: software packages to compute p-values for various experimental design are widely available, we generally believe we understand the p-value (despite (Oakes 1986)), and if we manage to find p-values lower than 0.05 we are also almost guaranteed publication. Hence, the NHST test satisfies all of the secondary requirements that good statistical methods should have.

If we are honest however, the answer to the question "How likely is the data that we observed given that the coin is fair ($p = 0.5$)" is only marginally interesting. What is really interesting, given our above sample, is to answer questions like: "what is the probability that this coin will turn heads if I flip it again?" We do not just want to contrast our collected data to the hypothetical scenario where $p = 0.5$ (the coin is fair), but we would actually like to learn about P(Heads) of the coin itself given the data that we have collected (the quantity $P(H_0|D)$ as described above). We want to estimate p (as used in the formulation of P(Heads), not in p-value), and quantify our uncertainty around this estimate. From such a quantification we can then assess whether (e.g.) this coin would be suitable for usage in a casino or not. Or, whether it is "fair enough" for our application of the coin. Or perhaps whether we are too uncertain to answer any of the above questions and we should obtain a few more tosses before rushing to decisions.

The coin introduced in this section is obviously exemplar for any data generating process. We collect data, and often, using NHST examine only a very limited question: we postulate a very strict and often unrealistic data generating process and next ask ourselves how likely it is that the data originated from this process. The focus on NHST—we believe in part due to its satisfying of the "secondary requirements" of a statistical procedure lead us to not properly examine the broader scientific questions into the actual size of the effect—the true value of p in this case. All too often these questions are left unanswered. Regrettably answering the latter questions does not necessarily satisfy the secondary requirements: they are not always easy to compute, and will require thought to interpret. Furthermore methods that do answer these questions will not necessarily get the work published. Our intention in editing this book is to show readers that recent advances in computational power and freely available packages in [R] give you the opportunity to answer the sorts of research questions which matter. Our authors have also provided examples of how to interpret the results of their analyses to help you understand how the techniques might apply to your own data.

1.5   Broadening the Scope of Statistical Analysis in HCI

We find that on one hand our currently used "toolbox" (see also Chap. 13) for statistical analysis is being increasingly criticized. On the other hand, we see that in statistics, machine learning, and a number of related fields novel methods are being introduced at a steady pace. This book aims to (a) critically evaluate our current practice and support a less rigid, procedural view of statistics in favour of "fair statistical communication" (see Chap. 13), and (b) provides scholars and practitioners with the methods and tools to do so.

References

American Psychological Association (2009) Publication Manual of the American Psychological Association, APA, 6th edn, p. 272

Baguley T (2012) Serious stats: a guide to advanced statistics for the behavioral sciences. Palgrave Macmillan, Basingstoke

Barnard GA, Bayes T (1958) Studies in the history of probability and statistics: IX. In: Thomas Bayes's essay towards solving a problem in the doctrine of chances. Biometrika 45(3/4):293–315

Box JF (1987) Guinness, gosset, fisher, and small samples. Stat Sci 2(1):45–52

Cairns P (2007) HCI... not as it should be: inferential statistics in HCI research. In: Proceedings of HCI 2007. Lancaster, UK, pp 195–201

Chan ISF, Zhang Z (1999) Test-based exact confidence intervals for the difference of two binomial proportions. Biometrics 55(4):1202–1209

Cohen J (1992) Statistical power analysis. In: Current directions in psychological science, pp 98–101

Conley T, Hansen C, Mcculloch R, Rossi P (2008) A semi-parametric Bayesian approach to the instrumental variable problem. J Econom 144(1):276–305

Dienes Z (2008) Understanding psychology as a science: an introduction to scientific and statistical inference, 1st edn. Palgrave Macmillan, Basingstoke, p 150

Dunlop MD, Baillie M(2009) Paper rejected (p> 0.05): an introduction to the debate on appropriateness of null-hypothesis testing. Int J Mob Hum Comput Interact 1(3):86

Fisher RA (1934) Statistical methods for research workers, 5th edn. Oliver and Boyd, Edinburgh

Fox RJ, Dimmic MW (2006) A two-sample Bayesian t-test for microarray data. BMC Bioinform 7:126

Gelman A (2005) Analysis of variance: why it is more important than ever. Ann Stat 33(1):1–31

Gelman A, David W (2009) Of beauty, sex, and power: statistical challenges in estimating small effects. Am Sci 97:310–316

Gray WD, Salzman MC (1998) Damaged merchandise? a review of experiments that compare usability evaluation methods. Hum Comput Interact 13:203–261

Ioannidis's JPA (2005) Why most published research findings are false. In: Jantsch W, Schaffler F (eds.) PLoS Med 2(8), e124

Kampenes V, Dyba T, Hannay J, Sjoberg D (2007) A systematic review of effect size in software engineering experiments. Inform Softw Technol 49(11–12):1073–1086

Kaptein MC, Robertson J (2012) Rethinking statistical methods for HCI. In: Proceedings of the 2011 Annual Conference on Human Factors in Computing Systems, CHI 212. ACM Press, New York, New York, USA, pp 1105–1114

Kruschke JK (2010) What to believe: Bayesian methods for data analysis. Trends Cogn Sci 14(7):293–300

Kruschke JK (2011a) Bayesian assessment of null values via parameter estimation and model comparison. Perspect Psychol Sci 6(3):299–312

Kruschke JK (2011b) Doing bayesian data analysis: a tutorial with R and BUGS. Elsevier, Burlington

Maxwell SE (2004) The persistence of underpowered studies in psychological research: causes, consequences, and remedies. Psychol Methods 9(2):147

Oakes M (1986) Statistical inference: a commentary for the social and behavioural sciences, p. 196. Wiley, New York

Paternoster R, Brame R, Mazerolle P, Piquero A (1998) Using the correct statistical test for the equality of regression coefficients. Criminology 36(4):859–866

Pearson K, Fisher RA, Inman HF (1994) Karl Pearson and R.A. Fisher on statistical tests: a 1935 exchange from nature. Am Stat 48(1):2–11

Rosenthal R (1979) The file drawer problem and tolerance for null results. Psychol Bull 86(3):638

Rouder JN, Speckman PL, Sun D, Morey RD, Iverson G (2009) Bayesian t tests for accepting and rejecting the null hypothesis. Psychon Bull Rev 16(2):225–237

Seaman, C. B. (1999). Qualitative methods in empirical studies of software engineering. IEEE Trans Softw Eng 25(4):557–572

Simmons JP, Nelson LD, Simonsohn U (2011) False-positive psychology: undisclosed flexibility in data collection and analysis allows presenting anything as significant. Psychol Sci 22(11):1359–1366

Student (1908) The probable error of a mean. Biometrika 6:1–25

Wagenmakers E, Wetzels R, Borsboom D, Van der Maas HLJ (2011) Why psychologists must change the way they analyze their data: The case of psi: Comment on Bem. J Pers Soc Psychol 100:426–443

Ziliak S, McCloskey D (2008) The cult of statistical significance: how the standard error costs us jobs, justice and lives. University of Michigan Press, Ann Arbor

Ziliak ST (2008) The Cult of statistical significance: how the standard error costs us jobs, justice, and lives. J Econ Lit 47(2):499–503

Ziliak ST, McCloskey DN (2004) Size matters: the standard error. J Socio-Econ 33(5):527–546

Part I
Getting Started With Data Analysis

Despite the fact that this book came about, partially, as a critique on the current use of null-hypothesis significance testing (NHST) methods in HCI, we do not want to delve directly into technical arguments or alternatives. Rather, we want to stress that many analyses would benefit first and foremost from a strong exploratory effort, of which data visualization is a core component. Before one reports, one needs to understand.

This first part of the book therefore starts with an explanation of the software that is used throughout the book, with the minor exception of the specialist Bayes Factor software introduced in Chap. 9 all chapters use [R]. Second, we will have a look at data visualization: a key to understanding any dataset is the ability to explore it using both descriptive statistics as well as readable and intuitive plots. Finally, we end this part of the book by presenting methods that deal with "missingness" in a collected dataset: if the data you would like to analyze contains missing observations, likely you want to decide on how to deal with those prior to running your actual analysis. Thus, this part provides a starting point for the more elaborate methods discussed in later chapters.

Chapter 2: Getting Started With [R]
Chapter 2, contributed by Ms. L. Ippel, introduces the use of [R] for the analysis of data in HCI. We included this chapter for several reasons: a) one of the editors loves [R] and always uses it for his analysis (yes, we ourselves consider this a fairly bad reason, but still), b) many novel statistical methods appear first in [R], not in proprietary software, and c) pretty much all of the chapter authors use [R] for their examples. Hence, we need, for those with no experience using [R] whatsoever, a brief intro. Ippel was kind enough to provide one.

In her chapter Ippel briefly introduces how to download [R] and get started. The chapter discusses using [R] directly by writing scripts (code), despite the fact that in the past few years a number of "point-and-click" solutions have been created (see also the "Editor suggestions"). However, since all the chapters following this chapter use [R] by directly writing code, we choose this approach also for this introduction chapter. The chapter details how data files can be opened and manipulated, discusses well-known descriptive statistics such as means, variances, correlations, etc., and discusses how a default installation of [R] can be extended by importing new packages: an approach that is adopted in many of the subsequent chapters. If you are well acquainted with [R] you can probably skip this chapter. However, if you find functionalities of [R] (such as data manipulations, the loading of packages, quick descriptives, and quick plots using the [R] core plotting library) in subsequent chapters that are not clear, likely they are explained in here.

Chapter 3: Data Visualization
This chapter of the book introduces the science and art of visualizing data. Data visualizations (plots, graphs, etc.) are useful for two primary reasons: first, they help you, the analyst, understand the data at hand. For this process it is useful to have quick access to meaningful, non-distorting visualizations. Second, data visualizations can be used to formally communicate your results. For this purpose one would like the ability to produce meaningful (and perhaps even fancy looking) figures that communicate clearly.

As mentioned by the authors of this chapter, Dr. J. Young and Dr. J. Wessnitzer, data visualization is a research field in its own right on which many books and articles have been written. Hence, the authors point to several authoritative books in the field for readers interested in the details of this science. However, within the chapter the authors introduce a brief history of data visualization, and its main principles. Second, the authors illustrate how to create a large variety of graphs using the `ggplot2` package in [R]. The chapter introduces a structured grammar of graphics, and highlight the pros and cons of different types of visualizations.

We would like to stress that data visualization is, in part, software dependent. Although the main principles of clear communication using visualizations do not change, the ability of an analyst to quickly produce meaningful figures depends heavily on her experience with the software that is used to create the figures. Within [R], a number of different methods to produce plots exist. Most notably, [R] provides a number of `core` plotting functions (some of which are discussed in Chap. 2), and [R] provides the extension packages `lattice` and `ggplot2`. The latter two packages allow for intricate figures, but the syntax (and code) needed to produce figures using these two packages is quite different. In this chapter the use of `ggplot2` is illustrated, but it has to be noted that many other methods (in [R] or using other software packages) can be used to produce the figures introduced in this chapter. In any case, we would advise any analyst to choose a package that she or he is comfortable with and study it in detail since the ability to visualize quickly can greatly improve the understanding of a dataset.

Chapter 4: Missing Data
In Chap. 4 Dr. T. Baguley and Dr. M. Andrews discuss the often occurring problem of missing data. After running an observational study, or even after running an experiment, we might end up with an incomplete dataset. This can have all kinds of reasons: some users might forget to fill in answers to some items, the technology used to measure user behavior might break, or respondents might be reluctant to fill out some of the questions and consciously omit responses. Whatever the cause, the problem should be dealt with before starting any meaningful analysis.

In this chapter the authors motivate that the "standard" method of dealing with missing data (pretending the user never existed in the first place) severely hampers the subsequent analysis and conclusions. Missing data introduces both a loss of precision, and bias in the estimates, which are not at all relieved by closing ones eyes and pretending the missing data were never there (we are very aware of the fact that this is an odd sentence). The authors also highlight that the cause of the missing data might actually matter a lot: whatever mechanism caused the missing data likely impact how you should deal with the missingness. Through a series of practical examples using the Mango Watch data (or parts thereof) the authors show both the effect that missing data of various origin can have on the subsequent analysis, and suggest remedies.

Dealing with missing data, just like data visualization, is a topic of study in itself. This chapter introduces the main topics (types of missingness, single and multiple imputation, etc.) and provides the reader with a thorough understanding of the underlying issues. However, the chapter certainly does not cover all available methods for dealing with missing data. It does however extensively reference the missing data literature: hence if you are unable to use the presented examples one-on-one for your missing data challenge, we encourage following up on the references in the specific parts: these will quickly guide you to ready to use methods for your application. Please note that there are some parts in this chapter which apply Bayesian techniques. If you are reading the book in the order that it is printed, you may wish to skip these for now until you have read Part 3.

Editor Suggestions

For each of the five parts of this book we (the editors) will try to point readers to additional materials (as far as this is not yet done by the authors themselves) that we ourselves found useful in understanding the topics that are discussed here.

For more on [R] please consider:

- The [R] website is the definite starting point for downloads and documentation: https://www.r-project.org.
- A well-developed and well-supported "point and click" interface to [R], although it definitely supports writing code, is RStudio which can be found here: https://www. rstudio.com/products/RStudio/. Next to the extensive documentation that can be found online, a number of introductory books to [R] exist. For those starting from scratch the book *The art of R programming* by Norman Matloff (2011) might provide a good starting point. Books like *R Cookbook* by Paul Teetor (2011) also start from the beginning, but provide a slightly wider overview of the possibilities of [R]. Tailored more to data analysis and visualization, we can also recommend *R for Everyone: Advanced Analytics and Graphics* by Jared P. Lander (2013).
- For those wishing to really use [R] to its fullest, we definitely recommend *Advanced R* by Hadley Wickham (2014).

For more on data visualization, outside of the books recommended in the chapter itself, please consider:

- For more on ggplot, the package used in Chap. 3, consider *ggplot2: Elegant Graphics for Data Analysis (Use R!)* by Hadley Wickham (2009).

- An alternative plotting package in [R] is `lattice`: see for more info *Lattice: Multivariate Data Visualization with R (Use R!)* by Deepayan Sarkar (2008).

And finally, for more on missing data please consider *Flexible Imputation of Missing Data* by Stef van Buuren (2012). This book covers both the basic theory, as well as a large number of modern data-imputation methods.

Chapter 2
Getting Started with [R]; a Brief Introduction

Lianne Ippel

Abstract In this chapter we provide some basics into [R] that will get you started and provide you with tools to continue the development of your skills in doing analyses in [R].

2.1 Introduction

Many statistical software packages are out there (SPSS, SAS, STATA, Mplus, just to name a few), each of them has its pros and cons. However, they have one common disadvantage: they all come with a (rather expensive) price tag. In contrast, [R] is an open source programming environment and is freely downloadable. Additionally, it allows a researcher to conduct the analyses exactly in the way she wants the analyses done. Data analysis in [R] does require some programming skills, for which we provide a short introduction. For issues beyond this introduction, you will find many of your questions answered with a search in your favorite search engine.

Step one of doing your data cleaning and analysis in [R] is, of course, to get the program on your computer. You can download [R] from https://cran.r-project. org.[1] Choose the version matching your operating system, and you are good to go. For those who desire some point-and-click options in [R], several Integrated Development Environments such as 'R Studio' exist, although we do not go into them here.

A few remarks before you get started and confused: (1) [R] is a case sensitive language, so be careful with how you name your variables, $x1 \neq X1$. (2) Unlike other program languages such as C, which read the entire script at once before executing it, [R] reads one line at a time. [R] will continue reading until it has reached the end of

---

[1]Note that if you use [R] for your reports, do not forget to mention the version of [R] you used, because slightly different results may come from different versions of [R], or the packages you used. we used [R] 3.2.2, 64-bit.

L. Ippel (✉)
Department of Methodology and Statistics, Tilburg University,
Warandelaan 2, 5000 AB Tilburg, The Netherlands
e-mail: g.j.e.ippel@uvt.nl

© Springer International Publishing Switzerland 2016
J. Robertson and M. Kaptein (eds.), *Modern Statistical Methods for HCI*,
Human–Computer Interaction Series, DOI 10.1007/978-3-319-26633-6_2

a command or found something it does not understand, which will produce an error. (3) Errors tell you approximately where it went wrong. However be aware, the fact that [R] did not produce an error does not mean it has done what you intended to do, it just has done exactly what you told it to do. What [R] did and what you wanted to do, are not necessarily the same thing. In fortunate cases, [R] will produce a warning when something did not fully go according to plan. Whether or not to take these warnings seriously is dependent on the warning and what you were aiming at doing. However in unfortunate cases, [R] does not produce an error or a warning, while still not doing what you aimed to do. Therefore always check whether the results make sense. (4) If you want to prevent yourself from doing the exact same command over and over again, you won't use the *console* of [R], but rather use a *script* (File → New script). You run the script either by 'right-click → run', or 'ctrl + r'. Lastly (5) to prevent you from trying to read your code a week after you produced it and being clueless about what you tried to do: insert comments in your code. Doing so is easy: inserting a # will tell [R] to skip this line, giving you the opportunity to write down what the code should do.

The organization of this chapter is as follows. First we discuss the types of data [R] can deal with and how these data are handled in [R]. We mention some useful tools to get some insight in your data. In Sect. 2.2 we detail how you can write your own commands with the use of functions and how to incorporate code written by others. The final section might be the most important section, because it contains the [R] help manual and additional literature.

2.1.1 Data Types

[R] can handle both numerical and character input. The difference between the two is denoted by adding quotation mark(s) in case of characters, for instance:

```
> # an example of a numerical variable:
> x1 <- 10
> x1
 [1] 10
> x1 + x1
 [1] 20
>
> # an example of a string variable:
> x2 <- '10'
> x2
 [1] ''10''
> x2 + x2
 Error in x2 + x2 : non-numeric argument to binary
  operator
```

In the above example, $x1$ is a numerical variable containing a single value, 10, with which you can do calculations. However $x2$ is a string variable because we placed quotation marks around the input, instructing [R] it should treat it as characters, with which you obviously cannot do computations. [R] can do all computations (as long as it concerns numerical values) your simple calculator can do too. Besides the obvious commands $(+, -, *, /, \hat{\ }$, sqrt(), exp()), $**$ can be used interchangeably for $\hat{\ }$. A third data type we want to illustrate is 'boolean', a data type which is either TRUE or FALSE. Although booleans look like characters, you can do computations with them, as TRUE translates to 1 and FALSE to 0. This data type is generated when you use a logical expression, for instance to see if two variables are equal to each other:

```
> # logical expressions
> x1==10 # equal to
 [1] TRUE
> x1 <= 5 # smaller or equal
 [1] FALSE
> x1 > 5  # larger
  [1] TRUE
> x1 != 5 # unequal to
 [1] TRUE
> # an example of computations with booleans
 > (x1 == x1)+1 # TRUE +1 = 2
 [1]  2
```

2.1.2 Storage

Besides different input (number vs. character), the input can be wrapped differently. You can think of these wrappings as different storages: they vary in size and flexibility. Depending on what you want to do with your data, one or the other storage can be more efficient. There are five different storage types: vector, matrix, array, data frame, and list. They all can deal with characters or numbers. In the first example ($x1$ and $x2$) both variables were vectors with only one element. Now we focus on larger vectors:

2.1.2.1 Vectors

We start with a vector, using command c(data):

```
> x3 <- c(1,2, NA)
> x3
 [1] 1  2  NA
```

In the example above, we created a variable $x3$, which is now a vector with three elements, two knowns and one missing.[2] If there is input missing, whether it is non response in your data collection or something else, you can instruct [R] to leave a blank space using NA (Not Available).

The command 'c()' is one of the ways to create a vector. Other common used commands for vectors are:

```
> # a vector containing a sequence, is created using
> # seq(from, to, by ):
> x4 <- seq(from = 1, to = 10, by = 2)
> x4
 [1] 1 3 5 7 9
>
> # note a sequence with interval of 1:
> x5 <- c(1:5)
> x5
 [1] 1  2  3  4  5
>
> # a vector containing series of repeated elements,
> # rep(data, times, each)
> # data = what should be repeated
> # times = number the data are repeated
> # each = number a single element is repeated
> x6 <- rep(c(1:2), times=3, each=2)
> x6
 [1] 1  1  2  2  1  1  2  2  1  1  2  2
```

You can also select separate elements from a vector, as follows.

```
> # select second element of vector x3
> x3[2]
 [1] 2
> # add fourth element to x3
> x3[4] <- 4
> x3
 [1] 1  2  NA  4
> # this also works:
> x3_new <- c(x3, 5)
> x3_new
 [1] 1  2   NA  4  5
```

---

[2]Be aware of how you name you variables, because you do not want to overwrite a command that already exist in [R]. Simply typing in the name you want to use for your object in the console will give insight in whether this name is already in use.

As you can see from the above example, there are often multiple ways which yield the exact same result. For small vectors, different ways of adding data and/or selecting elements do not really make a difference, however once you start working with large data sets (like data frames and lists) it pays to check for the fastest option.

2.1.2.2 Matrix

An extension of a vector is a matrix, which unlike a vector which is unidimensional, has two dimensions: rows and columns.

```
> x7 <- matrix(data = c(1:4), nrow = 2, ncol = 2)
> x7
     [,1] [,2]
[1,]    1    3
[2,]    2    4
```

Basically, what this command does is: you give [R] a vector and instruct [R] to break it down into the number of rows and columns. When the matrix has more cells than the number of elements in the provided vector, [R] will fill up the matrix, starting from the beginning, without error or warning!

```
> x8 <- matrix(data = c(1:3), nrow = 3, ncol = 2)
> x8
     [,1] [,2]
[1,]    1    1
[2,]    2    2
[3,]    3    3
```

So we cannot repeat this too often, check whether [R] did what you wanted to do even, or maybe especially, when no error or warning was produced. One way to do so is check whether the elements are positioned the way you expected. Selecting or adding data from a matrix is very similar to a vector, with the minor difference of having to specify two dimensions. In line with algebraic rules, [R] will take the first input as row number and the second input as column number: [1,1] will select top left element, while [2,1] will select the element on the second row, first column. When you leave the first dimension open, [,1], the entire column is selected or when you leave the second dimension open, [1,], the entire row is selected.

```
> # select element on second row, first column of x7
> x7[2,1]
[1] 2
> # select second row
> x7[2,]
```

```
   [1]  2  4
> # select second column
> x7[,2]
   [1]  3  4
> # add row to x7 using rbind(data, new_row):
> # rbind binds the new row to the data
> x7_new_row <- rbind(x7, c(1,2))
> x7_new_row
        [,1] [,2]
  [1,]   1    3
  [2,]   2    4
  [3,]   1    2
> # add column to x7 using cbind(data, new_column)
> # cbind binds the new column to the data
> x7_new_column <- cbind(x7, c(5,6))
> x7_new_column
        [,1] [,2] [,3]
  [1,]   1    3    5
  [2,]   2    4    6
```

2.1.2.3 Data Frame

A data frame is a special case of a matrix. It also consists of two dimensions, with
the cases stored in the rows and the variables in the columns. The example dataset on
fruit-based smart watch performance provided as supplementary material is a data
frame, which will be used throughout the book to explain multiple analyses. A data
frame is created as follows:

```
> x9 <- data.frame(id=factor(c(1:3)), obs=c(10:12))
> x9
   id obs
 1  1  10
 2  2  11
 3  3  12
```

where the first column (without heading), denotes the row numbers, the second column is a nominal variable of the data frame (in this case labeled 'id'). Nominal
variables can be created using the command 'factor()'. The third column is a numerical variable (labeled 'obs').

Because a data frame is a special case of a matrix, selecting and adding data can
also be done similarly. However, because it is a special case and not exactly the same,
it can also be done differently. The advantage of a data frame is that the columns
have labels, which you can use to select elements or columns or add variables.

```
> # select element on second row, first variable of x9
> x9$id[2]
[1] 2
Levels: 1 2 3
> x9[2,1]
[1] 2
Levels: 1 2 3
> # or select a case with a particular number,
> # convenient when row numbers != id numbers:
> x9[x9$id==2,]
  id obs
2  2  11
> # select variable
> x9$obs
[1] 10 11 12
> # add variable
> x9$new_var <- c(20:22)
> x9
  id obs new_var
1  1  11      20
2  2  12      21
3  3  13      22
```

2.1.2.4 Array

Next we turn to the two larger storages which have a flexible number of dimensions. First an 'array' which is an extension of a matrix, and can have many dimensions. An array with only two dimensions is equivalent to a matrix.

```
> # array(data, dim = c(rows, columns, slices, etc.))
> x10 <- array(data = c(1:4), dim = c(1, 3, 2))
> x10
, , 1

     [,1] [,2] [,3]
[1,]    1    2    3

, , 2

     [,1] [,2] [,3]
[1,]    4    1    2
```

Again we see that [R] fills up the array, starting from the beginning. Variable $x10$ has 1 row (first entry of the dim argument), 3 columns (second entry of the dim argument), and 2 slices (third entry of the dim argument). The only downside of an array is that you have to keep in mind how many dimensions you have and which dimension is which. Of course we could continue and add more dimensions but for the sake of clarity we stop at three dimensions. We skip adding and selecting elements from an array, because it is similar to a matrix.

2.1.2.5 List

The last storage is a 'list', which is different from the other storages in the sense that a list wraps storages. For instance, a list can contain a vector in the first cell, a data frame in the second, an other list in the third and so on. This makes a list very flexible and complicated at the same time. A list can be very convenient as an output of your analyses, storing all results in one place, however selecting one single number from a large list might end up challenging.

```
> # list(cell 1, cell 2, cell 3, etc.)
> x11 <- list(scalar=x1, vector=x3, array=x10, c(1,2))
> x11
 $scalar
 [1] 10

$vector
 [1]  1   2 NA

$array
 , , 1
        [,1] [,2] [,3]
 [1,]     1    2    3
 , , 2
        [,1] [,2] [,3]
 [1,]     4    1    2

[[4]]
[1] 1 2
```

Note that you can label the different cells, but it is not necessary to do so. You label the cells by adding the label before the object you stored in the cell: scalar = $x1$ labels the first cell as *scalar*. As mentioned above, selecting an element from a list is somewhat odd in the sense that adding or selecting an element depends on what you have stored in the list and whether you have labeled the different cells. If you have labeled the cells you can select the cell just like you would select a variable in a data frame, if you did not you select a cell using double squared brackets:

```
> # select second cell from list x11
> x11$vector
 [1]  1  2  NA
> x11[[2]]
 [1]  1  2  NA
```

Selecting an element within a cell then depends on which storage is in the cell, and it would be repetition of the text above to illustrate how each of them work.

2.1.3 Storage Descriptives

As mentioned above, it is very important to inspect the result [R] produced to check whether it actually did what you intended. Sometimes looking at the entire object at once is cumbersome. [R] has some tools that make a first inspection whether your object looks like what you expected:

- class(x, …): x is an arbitrary object. This function tells you which storage type is between the brackets
- str(x, …): x is an arbitrary object. This function tells you whether x contains strings or numbers
- summary(x, …): x is an arbitrary object. This function returns, depending on the kind of object you want the summary from, statistics such as number of cases, averages, standard deviations, etc.
- length(x): gives the length of the object x, usually x is a vector, but it works for other objects as well.
- dim(x): x is anything but a vector. The function gives the dimensions: first number of rows, then number of columns etc.
- nrow(x): x can be a vector, matrix, array or data frame. The function returns the number of rows
- ncol(x): like nrow, however this function returns columns

Note that some function have '…' and others do not; these dots imply that additional arguments could be included in the function.

2.2 Working with [R]

2.2.1 Writing Functions

Now you have some sense of how data looks like in [R], you of course want to do something with these data. The tools to work with are called functions. Without being explicit about it, we already came across many functions. All the commands we have used so far, whether it is to make a vector (c()), or to get some summary about an object (summary()), these are functions integrated in [R] already. You can, and most likely will, write functions yourself as well. Writing functions is done as follows:

```
> test <- function(argument_1, argument_2, ...)
+ {
+     actions
+     return()
+ }
>
> result <- test(argument_1 = X, argument_2 = Y)
```

You define a function (in this case: test) and you provide the function with arguments. A (very simple) example could be

```
> multiplier <- function(input, times)
+ {
+     local_result<- input*times
+     return(local_result)
+ }
>
> global_result <- multiplier(input=5, times=2)
> global_result
 [1] 10
> # note local_result is defined within the function
> # therefore it doesn't exist globally:
> local_result
 Error: object'local_result' not found
```

Note that, although we indent the code, this is not required. Indentation improves readability, but it does not have any other function in [R].

Sometimes you only want your function to perform the action if a certain condition or conditions are satisfied, for instance if the result of the multiplier is zero, you might want to add 1:

```
> multiplier_not_zero<- function(input, times)
+ {
+   local_result<- input*times
+   if(local_result==0)
+   {
+     local_result<- 1
+   }
+   return(local_result)
+ }
> multiplier_not_zero(input = 3, times = 0)
 [1]  1
```

When there are multiple conditions you want to be satisfied before your function should run you can make combinations using the "and" and "or" operators which are written as "&" and "|" respectively. For example:

- | : if($x1 <= 1|x1 >= 15$) { action }: or-statement
- & : if($x1 >= 1&x1 * x1 < 10$) { action }: and-statement

2.2.2   Data: Input and Output

2.2.2.1   Loading Data into [R]

Next, we discuss how you get your data in [R] to handle them. How to get your data into [R] depends on the format in which the data is stored. Most data formats (*.txt, *.RData, *.csv) can be easily included:

```
> # *.txt file: are there variable names: header=T
> # what separates different values? sep=''
> my_dat1 <- read.table('directory/filename.txt',
+ header, sep='')
> # *.RData file
> my_dat2 <- load('directory/filename.RData')
> # *.csv file
> my_dat3 <- read.csv('directory/filename.csv',
+ header, sep='')
```

For files with other extensions, you might need an additional package to load the data, for instance the package 'foreign' or 'Hmisc' for SPSS and SAS.

To prevent yourself from typing in the same directory repeatedly and having very long calls for your data, you can also set (and get) your working directory as follows:

```
> setwd('the/directory/you/want/to/work/in')
> getwd()
  [1] 'the/directory/you/are/working/in'
```

Knowing in which directory you are working saves you an elaborate search in all your files and folders when you saved an [R] object, which can be done as follows:

```
> # *.txt file
> write.table('directory/filename.txt', header,
+ sep='')
> # *.RData file
> save('directory/filename.RData')
> # *.csv file
>  write.csv('directory/filename.csv', header, sep='')
```

2.2.2.2 Simulate Data

When you do not have any data but you do want to practice with [R], or more likely, you want to test a new method it is useful to create data. [R] has plenty functions to generate (random) data. We put random between brackets because [R] will never provide you with fully random data, simply because your computer has a set of rules to create these data and therefore it cannot be completely random. Although this is an interesting topic, the point we want to make is that you can get the exact same 'random' data by fixing the begin point of the algorithm which creates the data using 'set.seed(number)'. For instance, if you want 3 draws from a normal distribution with mean = 10, and standard deviation = 2:

```
> set.seed(64568)
> rnorm(n=3, mean=10, sd=2)
[1] 10.468961  8.574238  9.754691
```

You will see that if you insert this code that you will have the exact same three numbers. Besides generating data using 'rnorm()' you can get other distributional information about the normal distribution using either

- dnorm(x, mean, sd): x is a scalar, the function returns the density of normal distribution at x
- pnorm(x, mean, sd): like above, though this function returns the lower tail probability
- qnorm(x, mean, sd): opposite of the above one: x is the probability and the function returns the quantile belonging to probability x

Similar functions exist for many distributions. Because different distributions require different parameters, the arguments within the function differ, though the idea is similar.

2.2.3 For Loop

One of the tools which is common in many program languages is the for loop. The for loop in [R] is a simple function to go line by line through the data. Because it is a simple function it makes life easy when doing for instance simulations, however it also makes life slow. The for loop in [R] has the downfall that it can be rather slow when working with complex computations in combination with large datasets. In case of complex computations, you might want to look into the plyr package, which has some integrated functions which also perform computations on every line of data, though do it more quickly. For now, let us have a look at the for loop.

The function works as follows:

```
> # for loop example
> # if you want to store the result
> # you have to define the result outside the for loop:
> row_average <- c()
> for(i in 1 : nrow(x7))
+ {
+    row_average[i] <- mean(x7[i,])
+    print(row_average[i])
+ }
 [1]   2
 [1]   3
> row_average
 [1]   2   3
```

First note that you should store the result of the computation performed by the loop in a variable which will not be over-written. Second, objects defined within the for loop are accessible outside the local scope of the for loop. Apart from the fact that this is just a very simply example to illustrate for loops, the same result could have been obtained alternatively by

```
> (row_average <- rowMeans(x7))
 [1]   2   3
> # putting brackets around an assignment
> # tells [R] to print the object
>
> # example of one of plyr functions
> adply(.data=x7, .margins=1, .fun=mean)
   X1 V1
 1  1  2
 2  2  3
```

where the adply function returns a data frame with $X1$ the variable which indicates the row numbers and $V1$ being the averages per row.

2.2.4 Apply Function

An example of a function which is already more efficient but also more advanced than the for loop is the 'apply' function. It is incorporated in the [R] base, so no additional packages are required. The function loops through either arrays or matrix-like objects (as long as it has more than one dimension). The function works as follows:

```
> # example of apply function
> # apply(array, margin, function)
> apply(x10, 1, mean)
[1] 2.166667 # mean of the 2 rows
> apply(x10, 2, sum)
[1] 5 3 5 # sum of each column
> apply(x10, 3, FUN=function(x)
+ {return(x*2)})
      [,1] [,2]
 [1,]    2    8
 [2,]    4    2
 [3,]    6    4
> # per slice the elements are multiplied by 2,
> # column 1 = slice 1, column 2 = slice 2
```

The apply function can deal with many preprogrammed functions. You can also write your own functions. When you get the hang of these functions, you also might want to look of variations of the apply function (among others):

- mapply(function, arguments): multiple argument version of apply,
- lapply(x, function): like apply, but it returns a list as result, of the same length as the array you put in,
- sapply(x, function): an easier function which does the same as lapply,
- tapply(x, margin, function): applies a function to each cell of a ragged array.

2.2.5 Common Used Functions

You do not have to program every single function you can think of yourself, because many of the simple descriptives are already included in [R], for instance:

- mean(x, ...): x is a vector (other storages will be vectorized), the function returns arithmetic mean,
- sd(x, ...): like the previous, returning the standard deviation,
- var(x, ...): like the previous, returning the variance,
- cov(x, ...): x consist of two dimensions, the function returns the covariance,
- corr(x, ...): like the previous, returning the correlation,
- table(x, ...): this function returns a frequency table
- max(x, ...): x is an arbitrary object, the function returns highest value,
- min(x, ...): like the previous, returning the lowest value.

among many more. Fill in your object of interest between the brackets and [R] returns the answer in no time. Besides these numerical descriptives of your data, [R] allows you to inspect your data graphically with different kind of plots:

- plot(x, …): add type='l' such that a line will connect the data points
- lines(x, …): add more lines to your plot
- points(x, …): add more data points to your plot
- hist(x, …): histogram
- boxplot(x, …)
- barplot(x, …)

Even many analyses are ready-to-use in [R], so no additional programming is required to do:

- anova(x, …): x containing the results returned by a model fitting function (e.g., lm or glm). The function can do both model testing as well as model comparisons.
- glm(formula, data, …): to fit generalized linear models
- lm(formula, data, …): to fit linear regression
- princomp(formula, data, …): to do principle component analysis
- t.test(x, …): the function wants at least one vector, additional arguments can be included to test one or two sided etc.

2.2.6 Packages

When you want to do some analysis which is not included in [R] base, you either have to program it yourself or see if others have done it before you (and made it publicly available). If the latter is the case you can include this code as follows:

```
> install.packages('plyr')
```

which will install the plyr package, which we already discussed above. What happens next is a pop-up window to select the server it should download the package from. Select your country (or something close) to complete the installation of the package. In order to use the package you have to attach the package to your working environment as follows:

```
> library(plyr)
```

Each time you open [R] you do have to attach packages again, but you do not have to install them every time. Thus, you do not want to put 'install.packages()' in your script (but in the console), however you do want to include 'library()' in your script so when you run your entire script it will automatically load the packages.

2.2.6.1　Useful Packages

There are a lot of packages available, not all of them of very good quality. Here we shortly list packages that are useful and/or used throughout the book

- digest: allows users to easily compare arbitrary [R] objects by means of hash signatures
- directlabels: adds nice labels to (the more fancy) plots
- foreign: allows you to include data files from other software programs such as SPSS
- GGally: to make a matrix of plots produced by ggplot2
- ggplot2: to make pretty plots
- gridExtra: to arrange multiple grid-based plots on a page
- lattice: to make pretty plots
- lme4: to do multi-level analyses
- MASS: functions and datasets to support Venables and Ripley (2002)
- plyr: for faster for loops
- poLCA: to perform latent structure analysis
- psych: for multivariate analysis and scale construction using factor analysis, principal component analysis, cluster analysis and reliability analysis
- reshape2: to transform data between wide and long formats
- xtable: export tables to LaTeX or HTML

2.3　Mastering [R]

This is of course a very short introduction in [R] which allows you to do the very basics of data analysis and hopefully understand what the authors of the following chapters are doing. There is only one way to truly learn [R], which is hands on. Practice (eventually) makes perfect, so do not be discouraged when you are faced with many errors, warnings or unexpected results. There is an extensive help function in [R]: if you do not know how a function works, you can get information by putting it within the help function or, put one or two question marks before the name of the function.

```
> help(plot)
> ?plot
>??plot
```

One question mark will provide you with the web page with information about the particular function including examples. Two question marks will give you an overview of closely related topics. When these pages do not provided you with the information you need or understand, there is also a large community of [R] users, which have answered many questions at the many forums out there. Do not be afraid to plug your error, warning, or problem in a search engine on the Internet, because you will be amazed about the amount of information, examples and ready-to-use solutions that is out there, whether you have beginner questions or more advanced problems.

2.3.1   Further Reading

Below we listed some readings, which are either focused on introducing and working with [R], or on statistics using [R], both have proven to be useful.

- http://cran.r-project.org/doc/manuals/R-intro.pdf: A users guide to [R] in which the topics covered in this chapter are discussed in more details, including some code to work with
- http://cran.r-project.org/doc/contrib/Torfs+Brauer-Short-R-Intro.pdf: This article has besides what is mentioned in this chapter, an additional overview of some integrated functions
- Discovering statistics using R by Field et al. (2012): This is more a stats book than a [R] manual, but it does what you expect: it explains statistics in [R]
- Bayesian computation in [R] by Albert (2009): Similar story to the above one, though dealing with Bayesian analysis
- Introduction to Applied Bayesian Statistics and Estimation for Social Scientist by Lynch (2007): different angle, similar in content to the above one

References

Albert J (2009) Bayesian computation with R, 2nd edn. Springer
Field A, Miles J, Field Z (2012) Discovering statistics using R. Sage, London
Lynch SM (2007) Introduction to applied Bayesian statistics and estimation for social scientist. Springer
Venables W, Ripley B (2002) Modern applied statistics with S, 4th edn. Springer

Chapter 3
Descriptive Statistics, Graphs, and Visualisation

Joanna Young and Jan Wessnitzer

The greatest value of a picture is when it forces us to notice what we never expected to see.

–John Tukey

Abstract Good exploratory data analysis starts with the ability to describe and plot a data set. Exploratory data analysis has taken flight in recent years and there there is a pressing need to use the right tools to express the data correctly. In this chapter, we introduce basic descriptive statistics, principles of visualisation, and novel plotting methods using the [R] package ggplot2. We illustrate the grammar of graphics of ggplot2 with examples of commonly used graphs.

3.1 Introduction

Our reliance on data has increased considerably in the last decade, as new methods and technologies have emerged to capture, store and process a range of different types of information. These methods are now being integrated into everyday software and products and they have become more accessible. Capturing data and making informed decisions based on the results is fast becoming ubiquitous: at home, smart meters assess how we consume electricity; in business, marketing analytics and business processes are optimised based on data; in government, policies are formed from vast amounts of data; in advertising, products are recommended based on user interactions.

J. Young (✉) · J. Wessnitzer
The Scientific Editing Company Ltd., Edinburgh, UK
e-mail: j.young@scieditco.com
URL: http://www.scieditco.com

J. Wessnitzer
e-mail: jan.wessnitzer@gmail.com

© Springer International Publishing Switzerland 2016   37
J. Robertson and M. Kaptein (eds.), *Modern Statistical Methods for HCI*,
Human–Computer Interaction Series, DOI 10.1007/978-3-319-26633-6_3

Managing this flow of information raises several important challenges and issues: the volume of data we are producing is increasing rapidly and the rate at which we are generating it is still rising; storage solutions need to be cheap and accessible; tools to process and display the data need to be easy to learn and use. Last but not least, the information has to be displayed in a way that is relatively easy to interpret. It is this final aspect that we will focus on in this chapter, introducing the reader to a number of ways to visualise and interpret data using descriptive statistics and graphs. As with other chapters in this book, examples using the free open source software[1] [R] will be used and provided.

3.1.1 Why Do We Visualise Data?

The process of displaying basic but informative quantitative information in a visual format has been in existence for centuries: the *Turin papyrus map*, a detailed drawing displaying topographic and geological information dating from 1150BCE, was created by the ancient Egyptians, and the Romans developed accurate maps such as the *Tabula Peutingeriana*, a map of the Roman road network that dates from the 5th century AD. Fast forward to 18th century Britain and the evolution of statistical graphics was experiencing something of a Cambrian explosion. By the latter half of the century, with the industrial revolution well underway and a rising need to respond to the rapidly changing social and economic conditions, datasets were being generated for economic, medical and geographical purposes.

One of the first individuals to produce notable statistical graphics was William Playfair, who published *The commercial and political atlas* in 1786, a volume which contained over 40 time series plots and is the publication credited with inventing the bar chart. Prior to publication, datasets and information were being recorded and stored in tables that could be referred to later and used to inform decisions. Playfair recognised that the interpretation of financial and economic data in this tabular format was inefficient and information could be easily forgotten, so he invented a new method of information communication: visualisation of data through statistical graphics. Playfair was a pioneer in the then embryonic field of data visualisation and he is credited with inventing the line graph, bar chart and the pie chart, all of which are commonly used today.

The 19th century saw other major contributors to this field. In medicine, John Snow's *On the Mode of Communication of Cholera*, published in 1853, included a graphic showing cases of cholera in a region of London which detailed both quantitative and spatial information. This image elegantly demonstrated how graphics could be used to highlight key pieces of information, in this case it identified the water pump that was the source of the cholera outbreak. The use of statistics to inform medical practitioners and policy makers was taken even further by Florence Nightingale, whose polar area diagrams (also known as rose diagrams) were created

---

[1]http://www.r-project.org/.

to quantitatively show the various causes of death of soldiers in the Crimean War. Her diagrams revealed that the majority of soldiers were not dying from direct war related casualties, but overcrowding and poor sanitation. As a direct result of Nightingale's work, death rates in military hospitals were drastically reduced.

Descriptive statistics did not see many major advances in the early 20th century, but a renaissance began in 1969 with John Tukey's invention of the box plot and the field has expanded rapidly since. The advent of the Internet and the rapid generation of data in so many aspects of daily life now underline a requirement for efficient and accurate ways to visualise and interpret complex information. Human perception is biased towards visual information processing; we do not facilitate communication by presenting people with tables of numbers or randomly organised groups of images, but instead we can use images to demonstrate patterns and relationships in data that would otherwise be difficult to extract. A fairly complete history of statistical graphs and data visualisation can be found in Friendly and Denis (2001).

In the remainder of this chapter, we define exploratory analysis and we explore what makes efficient graphs for communicating the data clearly. The grammar of graphics and the [R] package `ggplot2` will be introduced and example code will be presented.

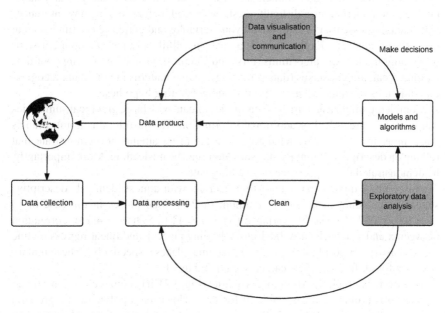

Fig. 3.1 A typical data science process

Table 3.1 Statistical sample properties of Anscombe's quartet

Sample property	Value
Mean $\bar{x}$	9
Variance of x	11
Mean $\bar{y}$	7.50 (to 2 decimal places)
Variance of y	4.122 or 4.127 (to 3 decimal places)
Correlation between x and y	0.816 (to 3 decimal places)
Linear regression line	$y = 3.00 + 0.500x$ (to 2 and 3 decimal places, respectively)

3.2 Descriptive Statistics and Exploratory Data Analysis

A typical data science process is shown in Fig. 3.1 which illustrates that graphs and visualisation have two important roles: *exploration* and *communication*. The ultimate aim of any visualisation is to communicate the data clearly without any bias, distortion or unnecessary information.

For statisticians and non-statisticians alike, determining what analysis and statistical tests to undertake is a difficult question. Indeed, before making any inferences from data, it is essential to examine all your variables and graphing is a fundamental part of your analysis. Exploratory data analysis fulfills a range of important steps in building models and algorithms. First and foremost, visually exploring your data facilitates catching mistakes (data screening), seeing patterns in your data, recognising violations of statistical assumptions, and generating hypotheses.

Complementing basic numeral summaries of data with basic graphical summaries can provide a great deal of additional information. To illustrate this point, Francis Anscombe, in 1973, constructed four datasets in an attempt to demonstrate that relying on descriptive summary statistics alone can be misleading. More importantly, he demonstrated the importance of graphing data.

Anscombe's quartet consists of four datasets with almost identical[2] descriptive statistics, including mean (to a minimum of 2 decimal places in the case of y) ($\bar{x} = 9.0$, $\bar{y} = 7.50$), sample variance ($SD(x) = 11.0$, $SD(y) = 4.12$), correlation between x and y in each case (0.816 to 3 decimal places), and linear regression line in each case (y = 3.00 + 0.500x, to 2 and 3 decimal places respectively). The summary statistics for all four data sets can be seen in Table 3.1.

However, by graphing Anscombe's quartet (Fig. 3.2), it becomes clear that a linear regression is probably a reasonable fit for set 1. However, a polynomial regression fit is more appropriate for set 2. By plotting sets 3 and 4, the effects of outliers on descriptive statistics is clearly demonstrated. In both cases, the fitted regression line is "skewed" by a single outlier. The outliers could be genuine outliers or they could be

---

[2]To at least two decimal places.

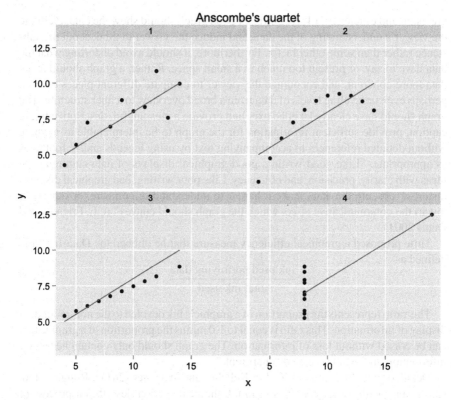

Fig. 3.2 Anscombe's quartet

erroneous data points, e.g., typos during data entry, but they highlight the importance of screening your data visually.

3.3 Principles of Visualisation

Creating effective data visualisations is challenging. A first step is to identify the purpose of your graph, i.e., what question is to be answered, and how can the graph help the reader understand your message? When deciding which type of graph to use further depends on the variables themselves (e.g., discrete versus continuous, univariate versus bivariate, etc.). Next steps often begin by drawing a first graph, then modifying the graph to be clear, non-distorting and well-labeled. A final step would be the dissemination of the graph (e.g., include it in a report or publication).

In his book *The Visual Display of Quantitative Information*, Edward Tufte defines 'graphical displays' and principles for effective graphical display as follows: "Excellence in statistical graphics consists of complex ideas communicated with clarity, precision and efficiency" (Tufte 2001). A good graph should show the data, facilitate the viewer's understanding of the data, and induce the viewer to think about the substance rather than some other factor. Furthermore, it should avoid distorting what the data have to say, or present too much in a small space. Rather, a graph should make data more coherent, and encourage the viewer to compare different pieces of data, perhaps even unraveling levels of data from a broad overview to a finer structure. The graph should have clearly labelled axes and provide a meaningful, descriptive figure caption, provide sufficient information for the graph to be interpretable as a whole without detailed references to accompanying text by using legends and/or footnotes as appropriate. "Like good writing, good graphical displays of data communicate ideas with clarity, precision, and efficiency. Like poor writing, bad graphical displays distort or obscure the data, make it harder to understand or compare, or otherwise thwart the communicative effect which the graph should convey" (c.f., Friendly and Denis 2001).

Tufte proposed a graphical efficiency measure that he dubbed the Data-Ink ratio defined as

$$\frac{\text{ink used portraying data}}{\text{total ink used}} \tag{3.1}$$

This ratio represents the proportion of a graphic's ink devoted to the non-redundant display of information. This ratio is equal to 1.0 minus the proportion of a graphic that can be erased without loss of information. The graph should only contain necessary information and avoid so-called "chart junk".

Detailed guidelines are outlined in Kelleher and Wagener (2011), Rougier et al. (2014) and, with these principles in mind, the next section describes a process of creating graphs.

3.4 ggplot2—A Grammar of Graphics

In his landmark book *The Grammar of Graphics*, Leland Wilkinson describes how graphics can be broken down into abstract concepts (Wilkinson 2005). Wilkinson's grammar tells us that a statistical graphic is a mapping from data to aesthetic attributes of geometric objects and describes the basic elements that make up a graph. This approach of handling elements of a graph separately and building the features up in a series of layers allows for versatility and control, building step by step towards powerful and informative graphs.

The grammar in Wickham's [R] package ggplot2 defines the components of a plot as: a default dataset and set of mappings from variables to aesthetics, one or more layers, with each layer having one geometric object, one statistical transformation, one position adjustment, and optionally, one dataset and set of aesthetic mappings, one scale for each aesthetic mapping used, a coordinate system, and the facet specification (Wickham 2010). These high-level components are quite similar to those of Wilkinson's grammar (Wickham 2010) and will be explained in the remainder of this chapter.

Several [R] graphing packages implement a *grammar of graphics*. Examples include ggplot2, ggvis, ggmap, ggdendro, ggsubplot, etc. Here, we will focus on ggplot2.

3.4.1 ggplot2

ggplot2 is a large, versatile data exploration and visualisation package and a complete introduction is beyond the scope of this chapter. The reader is encouraged to refer to Wickham (2010) for a comprehensive introduction.

To install and load ggplot2, run the following:

```
# install ggplot2 package
install.packages("ggplot2")
# load ggplot2
library(ggplot2)
```

3.4.1.1 Layers

A ggplot graph consists of two necessary components—a ggplot object and at least one layer. For example, in order to create Fig. 3.2a, we first need to define the data vectors and create a dataframe from these vectors. Then, the plot is instantiated by first creating a ggplot object and then layers are added to display the data:

```
# data vectors - Anscombe's first dataset
x1 <- c(10.0,8.0,13.0,9.0,11.0,14.0,6.0,4.0,12.0,7.0,5.0)
y1 <- c(8.04,6.95,7.58,8.81,8.33,9.96,7.24,4.26,10.84,4.82,5.68)

# create dataframe from vectors - ggplot2 requires dataframes
anscombe <- data.frame(x1,y1)

# create the ggplot
p <- ggplot(data=anscombe, aes(x=x1, y=y1)) +
  # add layer with data points
  layer(
    geom="point"
  ) +
  # add layer with regression line
  layer(
    geom="smooth",
    method="lm",
    se=FALSE
  )
```

```
# display the plot
p
```

The plot is instantiated by first creating a `ggplot` object, where `data` specifies the dataframe and `aes` maps the variables to the axes of the plot. Then, layers are added to display the data. The `aes()` defines the "how"—how data is stored and how data is split. Then we add two layers. First, we plot the data points and then we add a layer displaying a linear regression line. The `geom` is the "what"—what the data looks like (point or line in this example). The + operator is used to construct further specifics by appending layers and connecting the "how" (aesthetics) to the "what" (geometric objects).

However, many wrapper functions exist that define layers for commonly used graphical aspects by providing short-hand forms. For example, an alternative but equivalent way of plotting a scatterplot of Anscombe's first data set is:

```
# create the ggplot
p <- ggplot(data=anscombe, aes(x=x1, y=y1)) +
  geom_point() +
  geom_smooth(method=lm, se=FALSE)
# show the graph
p
```

A schematic illustrating the structure of `ggplot2` plots is shown in Fig. 3.3. A layer is defined by an R data frame and its aesthetic properties (`data+aes`), a geometric object to visually represent the data (`geom`), and an optional position adjustment to move overlapping geometric objects out of their way (`position`) and a statistical approach to summarize the rows of that frame (`stat`).

3.4.1.2   Coordinates, Scales, Facets, and Themes

Formatting plots and graphs for publication requires setting coordinates, overriding default perceptual mappings, and fine-tuning parameters of axes and legends. For these reasons, besides layers, a plot also has a coordinate system, scales, a faceting specification (shared among all layers in the plot), and themes.

3.4.1.3   Coordinate System

The coordinate system of a plot (together with the x and y position scale) determines the location of a geom, for example, whether the data is presented in a Cartesian or polar coordinate system.

3.4.1.4   Scales

Scales affect the `data+aes` defined in the layers of a plot. A scale affects the mapping of an attribute of the data into an aesthetic property of a geom (e.g., a geom's position along the y-axis, or a geom's fill color in a color space).

3.4.1.5   Facets

Adding a facet specification to a plot generates the same plot for different subsets of data. It specifies how the data should be split up and how the data should be arranged (e.g., as a grid). Figure 3.2 provides an example of the use of facets.

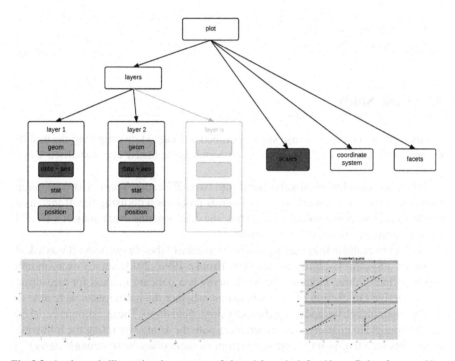

Fig. 3.3 A schematic illustrating the structure of plots. A layer is defined by an R data frame and its aesthetic properties, a geometric object to visually represent that summary, and an optional position adjustment to move overlapping geometric objects out of their way and a statistical approach to summarize the rows of that data frame. Scales affect the data+aes defined in the layers of a plot

3.4.1.6 Themes

`ggplot2` provides a theme function which controls the presentation of non-data elements; for example, text formatting of axis labels, graph titles etc. can be set using `theme()`. A good overview can be found on.[3]

3.4.1.7 Saving Your Work

Saving your work to be included in reports, presentations, etc. is simply done by calling `ggsave()` and specifying a file name. The file format is determined by the file extension provided (c.f., `?ggsave` for details). For more info the reader is referred to the `ggplot2` documentation.[4]

```
# save graph as PNG file
ggsave(file="anscombe1.png")
```

3.5 Case Study

In this section, data from a case study (outlined in Chap. 1) investigating the usability and performance of the *Mango* smart watch is evaluated and visualised using `ggplot2`.

The sales team has been subdivided into two sub-teams, Team A is continuing with solely using computers whereas Team B proceeds with using the *Mango* as a means to receive email notifications. Thus, the data contains every subject's ID and their assignment to one of the two teams.

In order to evaluate the usability and performance of the *Mango*, team B was asked to fill out a System Usability Scale (SUS, Brooke 1996, 2013) survey every month over a period of three months. The SUS survey is a standard method for measuring the subjective satisfaction of the participants, whether the participants were able to achieve their objectives and how efficiently they could do so. The questionnaire asked the salespeople to quantify their experiences with the *Mango* by rating the following statements on a five-point Likert scale (from *strongly disagree* to *strongly agree*):

1. I think that I would like to use this system frequently.
2. I found the system unnecessarily complex.
3. I thought the system was easy to use.
4. I think that I would need the support of a technical person to be able to use this system.
5. I found the various functions in this system were well integrated.

[3]http://docs.ggplot2.org/dev/vignettes/themes.html.
[4]http://docs.ggplot2.org/dev/.

6. I thought there was too much inconsistency in this system.
7. I would imagine that most people would learn to use this system very quickly.
8. I found the system very cumbersome to use.
9. I felt very confident using the system.
10. I needed to learn a lot of things before I could get going with this system.

Finally, the email response times for both teams were measured over three months. Average monthly email response times by members of 2 sales teams (between subjects) over 3 months (within subjects) are available.

The first step in exploratory data analysis is to summarise each variable in the dataset using both numerical and graphical summaries. Identifying the types of variables (e.g., quantitative or categorical) is important as some statistical analyses are only appropriate for specific types of variables. In [R], basic numerical summary statistics can be obtained with summary().

Univariate analysis involves describing the distribution of a single variable, including its central tendency (e.g., the mean, median, and mode) and dispersion (e.g., the range and quantiles of the data-set, and measures of spread such as the variance, standard deviation, range, and interquartile range (IQR)). The shape of the distribution may also be described via indices such as skewness and kurtosis but may also be described visually using probability density functions. Characteristics of a variable's distribution may also be depicted in graphical or tabular format, including histograms and stem-and-leaf displays. In the remainder of this section, we will plot the case study data using many of these graphs. The code for all the examples is available in the online repository which can be found at SPRINGERURL.

Fig. 3.4 Bar chart

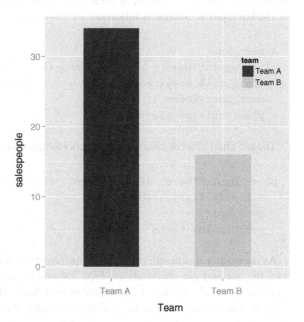

Fig. 3.5 Pie chart

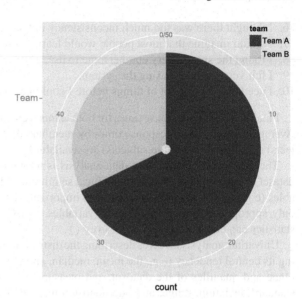

3.5.1 Team Size

The researcher might first consider whether the size of the teams is similar. Figures 3.4 and 3.5 show the team sizes represented using a pie chart and a bar chart respectively. Both figures enable us to answer this readily, but what if we want to ascertain the difference in size? How can we accurately describe such information with graphs?

The bar chart is created as follows:

```
# bar chart
p1 <- ggplot(base,  aes( x=Team , fill = as.factor(Team))) +
  scale_fill_grey(name="team") +
  geom_bar(width=.5) +
  ylab("salespeople")
```

The pie chart is a bar chart in a polar coordinate system:

```
p2 <- ggplot(base, aes(x ="Team", fill = as.factor(Team)) ) +
  scale_fill_grey(name="team") +
  geom_bar() +
  coord_polar(theta ="y")
```

As previously discussed, representing information accurately is important. Consider the bar and pie charts above, Figs. 3.4 and 3.5 respectively, and answer the simple question *does Team A have more or less than twice as many members than Team B?* Put in other words, *does Team A consist of more or less than 66.6% of all salespeople?* Which graph facilitates this information better? This simple information can be extracted more readily from a bar chart. Bar charts indeed facilitate comparisons better than pie charts. Pie charts represent percentage data as pie slices (using angles, sizes, and non-orthogonal lines). Generally speaking, pie charts are not as effective as either bar or error-bar graphs since they do not facilitate comparison of the relative size of similar-sized slices. Furthermore, many small slices become difficult to label and annotate (but this is also true for other types of graphs). Bar charts are considered more appropriate for illustrating quantities, such as totals or percentages for categories or the means of different groups or variables. The x-axis typically shows the categories, groups or variables, the y-axis shows the quantity (frequency, percentage, or a statistic such as a mean).

3.5.2 SUS Scores

The researcher may want to ascertain the usability of the *Mango* by analysing the responses of the salespeople to the SUS survey items. A standard approach for interpreting a SUS survey is described in Lewis and Sauro (2009). In summary, the responses of every user are aggregated into a final score as follows: for positively-worded items (1, 3, 5, 7 and 9), the score contribution is the scale position minus 1. For negatively-worded items (2, 4, 6, 8 and 10), it is 5 minus the scale position. To get the overall SUS score, multiply the sum of the item score contributions by 2.5. Thus, SUS scores range from 0 to 100 in 2.5-point increments. Note, the scores are not percentages! Typically, a score of around 70.0 is considered average (Lewis and Sauro 2009).

After calculating the SUS scores, the researcher may now wish to plot the SUS scores and ascertain whether the scores have changed over the three month period. The following code plots as a bar graph with error bars:

```
p <- ggplot(SUS, aes(x=Time, y=Mean, fill=as.factor(Time)))
p <- p + xlim(0.0, 4.0) +
   geom_bar(stat="identity", width=.5) + # aes(fill = SUS$Time)) +
   geom_errorbar(aes(ymin=Mean-SD, ymax=Mean+SD), width=.3) +
   scale_x_continuous(breaks=c(1.0,2.0,3.0)) +
   scale_fill_grey(name="month") +
   xlab("Time (month)") +
   theme_minimal()
```

Over the three month period, the mean SUS scores have increased as shown in the bar chart in Fig. 3.6. The error bars represent the standard deviations.

The bar chart does not tell us much about the distribution of the data. However, bar charts are commonly used in academic studies but rarely included are scatterplots, box plots, and histograms that allow readers to more critically evaluate continuous data.

Fig. 3.6 SUS scores of
Mango wearers over a 3
month period

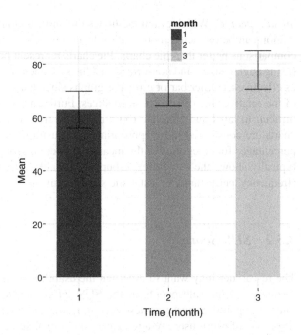

Instead of just showing the means and standard deviations in the bar chart, boxplots show other descriptive statistics, including the median, the first and third quartiles, minimum and maximum values, and thus giving us a better understanding of the spread of the distributions of the SUS scores.

The SUS scores can be compared using boxplots, as shown in Fig. 3.7, as follows:

```
p <- ggplot(SUS_sums, aes(x=Time, y=Score))
p <- p + xlim(0.0, 4.0) +
   geom_boxplot(aes(fill=as.factor(Time))) +
   scale_x_continuous(breaks=c(1.0,2.0,3.0)) +
   scale_fill_grey(name="month") +
   xlab("Time (month)") +
   theme_minimal()
```

The core element of the boxplot is the box whose length/height is the IQR (interquartile range) but whose width is often arbitrary (although some versions use the width to represent the sample size).

A boxplot allows to observe key values, such as the median, the 25th and 75th percentiles, and, any potential outliers and their values (Tukey), or the minimum and maximum values (Spear). The whiskers, in the two most commonly used conventions, extend to the most extreme data point no further than 1.5 * IQR from the edge of the box (Tukey) or to the minimum and the maximum values (Spear) (Krzywinski and

Fig. 3.7 Box plots of SUS
scores

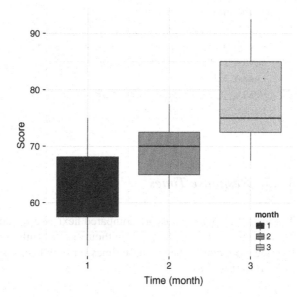

Altman 2014). Furthermore, the boxplot shows how tightly the data is grouped and whether it is symmetrical around the median or skewed.

Many variations of boxplots exist: notched boxplots, violin plots (`geom_violin()`), Tufte's minimal quartile plot (Tufte 2001; Wickham and Stryjewski 2011). Using boxplots in communications should be carefully considered as the general public is often not familiar with this type of graph.

However, the boxplot does not show variation in between the key values that it shows. Another alternative is to show the scores as histograms with overlayed density plots. A histogram looks similar to a bar chart but its horizontal axis is continuous whereas a bar chart may show gaps between bars (as its horizontal axis represents different categories). The histogram facilitates the discovery of the underlying frequency distribution (or shape) of a set of continuous data.

First, the histograms are created:

```
# create histograms of SUS scores over a three-month period
bin_width <- 5
p <- ggplot(SUS_sums, aes(x=Score)) +
  geom_histogram(data=SUS_sums, aes(
    y = ..density.., group=Time),  binwidth=bin_width, alpha = 0.5
  )
```

Then, the layer containing the density plots are added:

```
p <- p + geom_density(data=SUS_sums, aes(
  y = ..density.., group=Time
), alpha = 0.5)
```

Last, the graph is formatted:

```
p <-  p + scale_fill_grey(name="time") +
   scale_color_grey() +
   theme_bw() +
   scale_y_continuous(breaks=c(0.0,0.05,0.1)) +
   facet_grid(Time ~ .)
```

3.5.3 Response Times

The teams' response times are compared next. We would like to convey the teams' performances on a single graph without facets whilst including the factor month. Plotting a boxplot of the response times for both teams, seen in Fig. 3.9, is achieved as follows (Fig. 3.8):

```
p1 <- ggplot(email, aes(x=as.factor(Team), y = responseTime)) +
   geom_jitter() + #coord_cartesian(xlim = c(-100, 10)) +
   geom_boxplot(aes(fill=as.factor(Time))) +
   xlab(" ") +
```

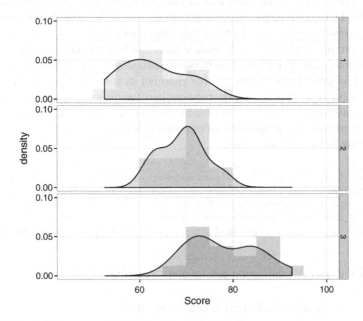

Fig. 3.8 Facetted histograms with density plots of SUS scores

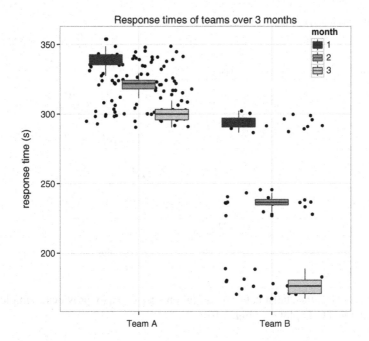

Fig. 3.9 Response times for each team by month

```
ylab("response time (s)") +
ggtitle("Response times of teams over 3 months") +
scale_fill_grey(name="month") +
scale_color_grey() +
theme_bw()
```

Figure 3.9 show that the response times of both teams decrease over a 3-month period. However, it clearly shows that the *Mango* users managed better response times. To complement the boxplots, another layer was added containing the data points using the line geom_jitter().

Looking at the graphs, the researcher may now wish to confirm statistically whether the SUS scores increased significantly or whether the time responses decreased significantly over the 3-month period.

In order to avoid violating any assumptions of NHST statistical tests, it is recommended to test for normality. Many tests (Student's t-test, analysis of variance) require that the data is normally distributed and a common graph to check for normality is a quantile-quantile scatterplot. The so-called Q-Q plot graphs the theoretical quantiles of a normal distribution against the quantiles from a data sample. The points in the Q-Q plot will approximately lie on the line $y = x$ if the two distributions being compared are similar.

Fig. 3.10 Quantile-quantile plot

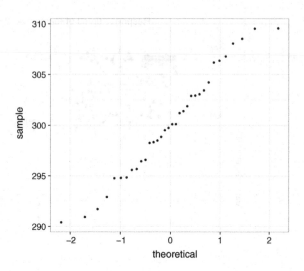

In ggplot2, the statistical transformation stat_qq() provides a simple way of producing a Q-Q plot (see Fig. 3.10):

```
# get email response times of Team A during month 3
S <- email[email$Time==3,]
S <- S[S$Team=="Team A",]

# plot quantile-quantile plot
p <- ggplot(S, aes(sample=S$responseTime)) +
    stat_qq() +
    theme_bw()
```

3.5.4 Model Predictions

The researcher may want to predict the response time for *Mango* users in month 4. Response variables (the variables we want to predict, i.e., the response time) with the use of explanatory variables (i.e., month). Simple regression assumes a linear relationship between the independent variables (or explanatory variables) and the dependent variables (or response variables). Plotting the response times with a linear regression model is achieved as follows:

```
p <- ggplot(email,aes(x=Time,y=responseTime)) +
    geom_point() +
    xlim(0,5) +
```

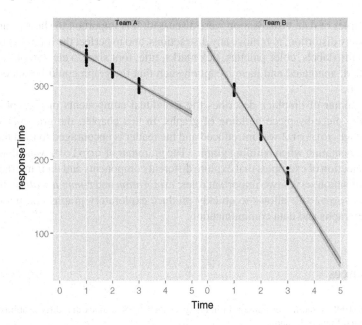

Fig. 3.11 Model predictions

```
stat_smooth(method="lm",fullrange=TRUE,level=0.95) +
facet_grid(~Team)
```

In today's data-intensive world, predictive analysis methods are important in decision-making processes. Such predictive analysis involves searching for meaningful relationships between variables and describing these relationships with the use of statistical models. A model's value is synonymous with the quality of its predictions. In R, the model fit can be summarised as follows (see Fig. 3.11):

```
fit <- lm(responseTime ~ Time, data=email)
summary(fit)
```

3.6 Summary

The goal of data visualisation is two-fold: to explore data and to effectively communicate information. Indeed, key discoveries were enabled through visualisation facilitating the discovery of relationships and patterns, making comparisons or understanding causality. Modern information graphics or infographics are prime examples of presenting complex information clearly.

Principles of data visualisation were discussed. It is important to show your data, to avoid any distortion, to remove any distractions, and to perfect the little (but important) details (labels, color palettes, tick marks, title, font size,...) etc. Graphs should be labelled, annotated and have a caption such that the graph could be understood on its own.

A grammar of graphics describes the individual components of a graphic and allows the piece-by-piece building of graphs. In this chapter, the grammar of the [R] package `ggplot2` was introduced and the reader is encouraged to read through the documentation when building graphs. The grammar of `ggplot2` was illustrated with a selection of examples that explore different components and their interactions.

Visualisation serves two important roles: *exploration* and *communication*. In both use cases, `ggplot2` allows to quickly produce exploratory graphs and iteratively improve graphs and data communication.

References

Brooke J (1996) Usability evaluation in industry, chapter SUS: a quick and dirty usability scale. Taylor and Francis, London

Brooke J (2013) SUS: a perspective. J Usability Stud 8(2):29–40

Friendly M, Denis D (2001) Milestones in the history of thematic cartography, statistical graphics, and data visualization. http://www.datavis.ca/milestones

Kelleher C, Wagener T (2011) Ten guidelines for effective data visualization in scientific publications. Environ Model Softw 26(6):822–827

Krzywinski M, Altman N (2014) Visualizing samples with box plots. Nat Methods 11(2):119–120

Lewis J, Sauro J (2009) The factor structure of the system usability scale. In: Human centered design. Springer, New York, pp 94–103

Rougier N, Droettboom M, Bourne P (2014) Ten simple rules for better figures. PLoS Comput Biol 10(9):e1003833

Tufte E (2001) The visual display of quantitative information, 2nd edn. Graphics Press, New York

Wickham H (2010) A layered grammar of graphics. J Comput Graph Stat 19(1):3–28

Wickham H, Stryjewski L (2011) 40 years of boxplots. Am Statistician

Wilkinson L (2005) The grammar of graphics. Springer, New York

Chapter 4
Handling Missing Data

Thom Baguley and Mark Andrews

Abstract This chapter provides an overview of the topic of missing data. We introduce the main types of missing data that can occur in practice and discuss the practical consequences of each of these types for general data analysis. We then describe general and practical solutions to the problem of missing data, discussing common but flawed approaches as well as more powerful approaches such as *multiple imputation*, which is an approach to dealing with missing data that is suitable for many—although not all—situations. Finally, we consider the topic of missing data as part of statistical inference more generally, and how it can be handled in both maximum likelihood and Bayesian approaches to inference.

4.1 Introduction

Missing data poses a challenge for almost every field of research—and particularly for research that involves data from human participants. Data might be missing for a large number of reasons. These include incomplete responses from participants, bugs in software and equipment failure. Data may also be missing as a deliberate feature of the design of a study (e.g., in a large project where collecting data on all measures is too expensive).

The starting point for dealing with the problem of missing data is to understand why it is a problem. One of the fundamental ideas in statistics is that the accuracy of an estimate is a function of two properties: *precision* and *bias*. Missing data is potentially disastrous for both of these properties. If you lose data you almost inevitably reduce the precision with which you measure what you are interested in. Worse still, more often than not, the processes that cause you to lose data are not completely random and therefore will also introduce bias. In certain applications of

T. Baguley (✉) · M. Andrews
Division of Psychology, Nottingham Trent University,
Nottingham, UK
e-mail: thomas.baguley@ntu.ac.uk

M. Andrews
e-mail: mark.andrews@ntu.ac.uk

© Springer International Publishing Switzerland 2016   57
J. Robertson and M. Kaptein (eds.), *Modern Statistical Methods for HCI*,
Human–Computer Interaction Series, DOI 10.1007/978-3-319-26633-6_4

statistics, bias is negligible (e.g., the usual estimate of the standard deviation as the square root of the unbiased variance estimate has a small bias that is negligible in large samples and usually inconsequential in small samples). Unfortunately, missing data also has the potential to introduce considerable distortions into an analysis—ones that can plausibly alter the magnitude or even direction of effects in some contexts. For many years the seriousness of this problem was not fully appreciated, and thus many common methods of dealing with missing data (including methods that are still widely used) merely hide the problem rather than deal with it.

A key message to take away from this chapter is that there is information in the pattern of missing data of an incomplete data set. The aim of this chapter is to show that a researcher can incorporate this information into his or her analysis, increasing statistical power and reducing the bias that arises when data are discarded or the presence of missing data is ignored.

4.2   Missing Data: Problems and Pitfalls

In order to understand why missing data might be a serious problem, it is helpful to think about the processes that led to an incomplete data set. The following discussion introduces three different scenarios that represent the most common classification of missing data and illustrates the practical consequences of each type by way of examples.

4.2.1   Mechanisms of Misssingness

The best known classification of the mechanisms that lead to missing data was presented by Rubin (1976) (see also Little and Rubin 2002). This described three broad mechanisms of how the data *missingness* (as it is termed in the literature) was generated: The data may be *missing completely at random* (MCAR), *missing at random* (MAR), or *missing not at random* (MNAR). These concepts, and the accompanying concept of *ignorability*, represent profoundly different processes of missing data, each with their own practical consequences and potential solutions. In what follows, we will first introduce these concepts informally before providing a more a formal description.

Missing data are MCAR if the mechanism that leads to the loss of data is "completely random", or completely independent of other variables that are known. Although often implausible in practice, some missing data may indeed be considered random in this way. Examples include equipment malfunction or having to terminate an experiment due to a fire-alarm. MCAR missing can also be part of the design of a study (see, Graham 2009). For example, respondents in a survey may be required only to complete a random subset of all the available items.

Missing data are MAR if the mechanism that leads to missing observations depends only on fully observed variables. The data are thus missing "at random" in the technical sense of being missing randomly conditional on observed variables (see, Schafer and Graham 2002; Graham 2009). MAR is, unlike MCAR, regarded as a plausible account of the mechanisms that produce missing observations in many research contexts. For instance, in intervention studies, participants are measured at regular intervals throughout the study. Participants who are not benefiting from the intervention may be more likely to drop out than participants who are benefiting. Thus, the probability than an outcome is missing may depend on whether they are receiving the intervention or not, which is known. It should be noted that treating missing data of this kind as MCAR would be a mistake. The data from remaining participants in the control group, are now a biased sample, of those that began the study. This is particularly problematic in medical or health interventions where the incomplete data sets might contain unusually healthy participants in the control group but a more representative (but less healthy) treatment group.

The final mechanism to consider is MNAR. Data are missing "not at random" if the mechanism that leads to missing data depends on the values of the missing data. This poses a serious threat to the validity of any analysis based on only the remaining data. In fact, as we will see, if the mechanism that produces missing data is MNAR then it not possible to derive an unbiased analysis of the data without explicitly modelling how the missing data were generated. As an example, missing values would be MNAR if the probability of an individual dropping out of a drug intervention study depended on the effect of the drug on that individual. Similarly, missing data from e-commerce product ratings would be MNAR if ratings were likely to be made only by those who had either an extremely positive or an extremely negative experience (see, Marlin et al. 2011). The distorting effects of MNAR can be ameliorated somewhat by including more observed variables in the analysis and then treating the missing data as MAR conditional on these new variables. For example, in the drug intervention case, we could use each patient's test scores prior to drop out as a measure of the drug effectiveness for that person. Now, the probability of being missing can be conditioned on this fully observed information.

Describing the mechanisms of missingness more formally is essential to fully appreciate the practical consequences of missing data in any analysis, as well to appreciate the potential solutions to these problems. To do so, it is necessary to introduce some notation. Let us assume, for simplicity, that our data set consists of two observable variables x and y for each of n individuals, i.e., $x = x_1 \ldots x_n$, $y = y_1 \ldots y_n$. These could be, for example, the sex and age of n individuals, with $x_i \in \{0, 1\}$ coding whether person i is male ($x_i = 0$) or female ($x_i = 1$) and y_i being that person's age. Our aim could be to model age as function of sex as follows:

$$y_i \sim N(\alpha + \beta x_i, \sigma^2), \quad \text{for } i \in \{1 \ldots n\}. \tag{4.1}$$

Let us also assume that the sexes $x_1 \ldots x_n$ are observed in full, but that ages $y_1 \ldots y_n$ contain some missing values. We now introduce indicator variables $I_1 \ldots I_n$ that indicate which values of y are missing:

$$I_i = \begin{cases} 1, & \text{if } y_i \text{ is missing,} \\ 0, & \text{if } y_i \text{ is observed.} \end{cases} \tag{4.2}$$

If the data are MCAR, a probabilistic model of I might be

$$I_i \sim \text{dbern}(p), \quad \text{for } i \in \{1 \ldots n\}. \tag{4.3}$$

Here, the value of I_i is being treated as equivalent to the outcome of coin toss with bias p and as such is independent of either x or y. This independence of I from the values of x or y is the defining feature of MCAR missingness. If, on the other hand, whether the age of a person is missing depends on whether they are male or female, i.e. with males being more or less likely to report their age, then a model of I might now be

$$I_i \sim \text{dbern}(p_i), \quad \log\left(\frac{p_i}{1 - p_i}\right) = a + bx_i, \quad \text{for } i \in \{1 \ldots n\}. \tag{4.4}$$

Here, the probability $I_i = 1$ now obviously varies as a function of x_i. However, it is still independent of y_i. This is therefore an example of MAR missingness: The value of I_i is conditioned only on fully observed variables. Finally, it could be the case that whether a person's age is missing depends on what their age is. For example, people over a certain age may be less likely to report their age than others. This tendency could also vary by sex. For example, males over a certain age may be more or less likely than females of the same age to report their age. In this case, a model of I might be

$$I_i \sim \text{dbern}(p_i), \quad \log\left(\frac{p_i}{1 - p_i}\right) = a + bx_i + cy_i + dx_iy_i, \quad \text{for } i \in \{1 \ldots n\}. \tag{4.5}$$

Here, we obviously have I_i being dependent on both x_i and y_i, where y_i is itself possibly missing. This scenario, where the probability of a variable being missing depends on the true value of that variable is the definition of MNAR.

The practical consequences of these three types of missing mechanisms is best appreciated when we consider the problem of inference of the parameters of the original data model, i.e. inferring α and β in our example. For simplicity, we will collectively refer to the parameters of the original data model by θ and the parameters of the missing data mechanism (e.g. a, b or a, b, c, d in our MAR and MNAR examples, respectively) by Ω. We will also split the y variable into y^{obs} and y^{mis}, which are the observed and missing values of y, respectively.

In general, the likelihood function of θ and Ω—which encapsulates all the information in the observed data for inferences concerning θ and Ω—is as follows:

$$P(y^{\text{obs}}, I | x, \theta, \Omega) = \int P(y^{\text{obs}}, y^{\text{mis}} | \theta, x) P(I | x, y^{\text{obs}}, y^{\text{mis}}, \Omega) dy^{\text{mis}}. \tag{4.6}$$

By definition, in the case of MCAR, we will always have $P(I|x, y^{obs}, y^{mis}, \Omega) \doteq P(I|\Omega)$. As such, the likelihood function simplifies to

$$P(y^{obs}, I|x, \theta, \Omega) = P(I|\Omega) \int P(y^{obs}, y^{mis}|\theta, x) dy^{mis} \qquad (4.7)$$

Similarly, in the case of MAR, where $P(I|x, y^{obs}, y^{mis}, \Omega) \doteq P(I|x, \Omega)$, the likelihood function simplifies to

$$P(y^{obs}, I|x, \theta, \Omega) = P(I|x, \Omega) \int P(y^{obs}, y^{mis}|\theta, x) dy^{mis} \qquad (4.8)$$

In both these cases, therefore, the likelihood function decouples into the product of two separate functions: The likelihood function for θ and the likelihood function for Ω. As such, in the case of MCAR and MAR, if the primary interest is in inferring θ, the missing data mechanism need not be modelled. In these cases, the missing data mechanism is said to be *ignorable*.

Crucially, however, in the case of MNAR, the likelihood function can not decouple—the likelihood functions of θ and of Ω both depend on y^{mis}. As such, the missing data mechanism is *nonignorable*: It is not possible to infer θ without also having an explicit probabilistic model for the missing data and simultaneously inferring Ω. Clearly, this introduces a considerable, yet unavoidable, increase in complexity to the data analysis.

4.2.2 Comparing Three Missing Data Scenarios

To illustrate the impact of missing data on a data set, consider a simple example based on pilot data for the mango study. This pilot involves 200 sales staff with half randomly allocated to the mango smart watch intervention (mango) and half to a comparison group (no mango) for a 3 month period. The data set comprises three main variables: the group to which each salesperson as allocated (group), their average email response time in minutes (aveRT) and their average daily sales in dollars (sales).

The following R code creates a data frame containing simulated mango pilot data:

```
group <- gl(2, 100, labels=c('no mango','mango'))
set.seed(14)
mango.effect <- c(rep(0.78, 100), rep(1, 100))
aveRT <- round(mango.effect * rnorm(200, 10, 3), 2)
set.seed(19)
sales <- round(rnorm(200, 500, 50), 2) - aveRT*12
mango.pilot <- data.frame(group, aveRT, sales)
```

To understand the impact of missing data on the analysis it is helpful to start with an analysis of the complete data set and then explore what happens when data are removed from the analysis. A good start is to plot the complete data set to get a feel for the pattern of sales in each group. In this case, a bean plot is used to summarise the data in each group, which is particularly useful here because it uses a kernel density estimate to give a feel for the shape of the distribution as well as depicting the mean (the long central black line) and the individual data points (the shorter black lines).

```
install.packages('beanplot')
library(beanplot)
beanplot(sales ~ group, data = mango.pilot,
      col ="lightgray", border = "grey", cutmin = 0,
      xlab='Group',
      ylab='Average daily sales (dollars)', main='(a)'
)
```

It is also helpful to look at the relationship between average response times and sales using a simple scatter plot:

```
with(mango.pilot, plot(sales ~ aveRT, pch=1, xlab=
      'Average response time (minutes)', main='(b)',
      ylab='Average daily sales (dollars)')
)
```

These two plots are reproduced in panel (a) and (b) of Fig. 4.1. The bean plot in panel (a) shows the distribution of sales for each group and suggests—counter to predictions—that sales may be lower for the mango group than the no mango

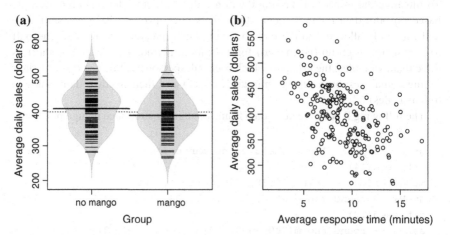

Fig. 4.1 Summary of the complete mango pilot data set. Panel **a** shows a *bean plot* of the sales by group while panel **b** is a *scatter plot* of the relationship between the average daily sales and average email response times

group. In contrast, the scatter plot in panel (b) suggests—as anticipated—that faster response times are associated with higher sales. The main interest focuses on the differences in sales between the groups. This can be tested in several ways, but for present purposes a simple linear regression with sales as the outcome and group as the predictor (equivalent to a t test of the difference in groups) will suffice:

```
complete.mod <- lm(sales ~ group , data= mango.pilot)
summary(complete.mod)
```

This produces the following output:

```
Call:
lm(formula = sales ~ group, data=mango.pilot)

Residuals:
    Min     1Q  Median     3Q     Max
-126.13  -42.62   0.59  38.51  185.97

Coefficients:
             Estimate Std. Error t value Pr(>|t|)
(Intercept)   405.816      5.898  68.810   <2e-16 ***
 groupmango   -18.323      8.341  -2.197   0.0292 *
---
Signif. codes: 0 '***' 0.001 '**' 0.01 '*' 0.05 '.' 0.1 ' ' 1

Residual standard error: 58.98 on 198 degrees of freedom
Multiple R-squared:  0.02379,Adjusted R-squared:  0.01886
F-statistic: 4.826 on 1 and 198 DF,  p-value: 0.02919
```

This supports what the pattern in Fig. 4.1a suggests: the difference in sales between the no mango group and the mango group is statistically significant, $t(198) = 2.20$, $p = 0.029$. The estimate of the difference in sales between groups is around 19 dollars/month, although a Bayesian hypothesis test (see Rouder et al. 2009 and Chaps. 8 and 9 of this book) suggests that the evidence for the advantage of the no mango group is relatively weak:

```
> install.packages('BayesFactor')
> library(BayesFactor)
> ttestBF(formula= sales ~ group, data=mango.pilot)

Bayes factor analysis
--------------
[1] Alt., r=0.707 : 1.448814 0%

Against denominator:
  Null, mu1-mu2 = 0
---
Bayes factor type: BFindepSample, JZS
```

How will these results change as a consequence of missing data? The answer will depend on the mechanism that leads to missingness—specifically whether it is MCAR, MAR or MNAR.

4.2.2.1   Scenario 1: MCAR

To illustrate MCAR, we simply randomly delete certain salespersons using a random number generator. The following code implements this deletion and re-runs the previous analysis without these sales staff:

```
> set.seed(100)
> mango.pilot.mcar <- mango.pilot
> mango.pilot.mcar[,3] <- replace(
+       mango.pilot[,3], round(runif(200, 0, 11) +1) == 5, NA
+ )
> mcar.mod <- lm(sales ~ group, data = mango.pilot.mcar)
> summary(mcar.mod)

Call:
lm(formula = sales ~ group, data = mango.pilot.mcar)

Residuals:
     Min      1Q   Median      3Q      Max
-122.817  -42.717    0.694   40.623  188.494

Coefficients:
             Estimate Std. Error t value Pr(>|t|)
(Intercept)   402.507      6.286  64.034   <2e-16 ***
groupmango    -17.541      8.817  -1.989   0.0482 *
---
Signif. codes:
0 '***' 0.001 '**' 0.01 '*' 0.05 '.' 0.1 ' ' 1

Residual standard error: 59.3 on 179 degrees of freedom
Multiple R-squared:  0.02163,   Adjusted R-squared:  0.01617
F-statistic: 3.958 on 1 and 179 DF,   p-value: 0.04817

> ttestBF(formula= sales ~ group,
+     data = na.omit(mango.pilot.mcar))
Bayes factor analysis
--------------
[1] Alt., r=0.707 : 1.00488 ±0%
```

```
Against denominator:
  Null, mu1-mu2 = 0
---
Bayes factor type: BFindepSample, JZS
```

Re-running the simple linear regression on the incomplete data set (losing 19 cases) produces a similar pattern of results with a lower average sales for the no mango group of around 18 dollars. However, the test of the difference in groups is now only just statistically significant at the 0.05 level; $t(179) = 1.99$, $p = 0.048$. In addition, the Bayes factor—previously providing some weak evidence (BF = 1.4) of a difference in groups—is now equivocal ($BF \approx 1$). The reduced sample size—for a virtually identical size of effect—now suggests that there is no evidence that the groups differ.

4.2.2.2   Scenario 2: MAR

The MAR mechanism can be illustrated by considering what happens if the probability of that data are missing depends on the outcome (*average sales*) and the group they were in. In this scenario a large number of sales staff are discovered to have artificially inflated their sales figures (e.g., booking false sales, double counting or poaching sales from other staff) and their sales data—being fraudulent—are excluded from the study. Notably, the staff in the mango group and staff with lower sales are under more pressure to sell well and this have a higher probability of having their sales figures be excluded. Missingness therefore depends on two variables (group and sales) that are in the analysis and one (average response time) that is in the data set that is known to predict sales and is missing at random with respect to the available data.

The following R code simulates data from the scenario in which sales figures are more likely to be missing for those staff with lower sales and who are in the mango group:

```
set.seed(19)
prob.missing <- (
  pnorm(scale(mango.pilot[2]))) * c(rep(.20,100),
       rep(1,.90,100)
)
set.seed(10)
missing.vals <- rbinom(200,1, prob.missing)

mango.pilot.mar <- mango.pilot
mango.pilot.mar[,3] <- replace(mango.pilot[,3],
    missing.vals ==1, NA)
```

This time, with MAR data, fitting a linear model to predict sales from group shows a very different pattern:

```
> mar.mod <- lm(sales ~ group , data= mango.pilot.mar)
> summary(mar.mod)

Call:
lm(formula = sales ~ group, data = mango.pilot.mar)

Residuals:
     Min       1Q   Median       3Q      Max
-150.461  -47.717    5.739   40.866  157.369

Coefficients:
             Estimate Std. Error t value Pr(>|t|)
(Intercept)   407.617      6.208  65.665   <2e-16 ***
groupmango      8.474     11.549   0.734    0.464
---
Signif. codes:
0 '***' 0.001 '**' 0.01 '*' 0.05 '.' 0.1 ' ' 1

Residual standard error: 60.82 on 133 degrees of freedom
  (65 observations deleted due to missingness)
Multiple R-squared: 0.004031,
Adjusted R-squared: -0.003457
F-statistic: 0.5383 on 1 and 133 DF,  p-value: 0.4644

> ttestBF(formula= sales ~ group,
+        data = na.omit(mango.pilot.mar))

Bayes factor analysis
--------------
[1] Alt., r=0.707 : 0.2562848 ±0.01%

Against denominator:
  Null, mu1-mu2 = 0
---
Bayes factor type: BFindepSample, JZS
```

Whereas the MCAR and complete data scenarios gave similar estimates of the difference in sales, the analysis of data missing at random produces an estimate that is not only different, but in the opposite direction: with the mango group selling on average around 8.5 dollars per month more than the mango group. This difference is not statistically significant at the 0.05 level; $t(133) = 0.73$, $p = 0.464$. In addition, the Bayes factor now favours the null hypothesis of no differences in the groups of a difference in groups ($BF_0 \approx 1/0.26 = 3.9$). Like MCAR, MAR missingness reduces statistical power through loss of data. However, it also introduces bias—whether in terms of estimating size or (as happened here) in estimating the direction of effect. In this instance, the bias further reduces statistical power because the estimate of the difference, while in the wrong direction, is smaller than that in the complete data set. This is far from inevitable, and it is quite possible for missing data to make an effect appear larger and hence provide strong evidence for a spurious effect or for an effect in the wrong direction.

4.2.2.3 Scenario 3: MNAR

The distinction between data missing not at random and data missing at random is a particularly subtle one. As noted earlier, it is a joint property of the data and the analysis. First note that the mango pilot sales data are a function of the average response time of the sales staff (e.g., see Fig. 4.1b). In the third and final scenario a server failure leads to a catastrophic loss of the response time data for the MAR scenario. As the response time variable (aveRT) was not used in the previous MAR analysis this will not change the analysis in any way—and the MNAR analysis suffers from the same problems (loss of statistical power and bias) as the MAR analysis. What has changed is that the missingness now depends on a variable (aveRT) that is unavailable to the analysis. The implications of data being MNAR are reviewed in the following section when solutions for dealing with missing data are considered.

4.3 Missing Data: Potential Solutions

This section explores some (but by no means all) potential solutions to the missing data problem, focusing on one powerful and flexible approach known as *multiple imputation*. Several widely used, but flawed approaches are reviewed before approaches that capitalise on the information available when data are MAR are introduced. The section ends with an extended example of multiple imputation applied to the three missing data scenarios for the mango pilot data described in the previous section.

4.3.1 Popular but Inadequate 'Solutions'

4.3.1.1 Deletion

The simplest approach to handling missing data in analysis is deletion. In *casewise deletion* any observed unit of study (typically a person in HCI research, but it could be an animal, plant or even a group such as an office or school) with a value missing from one or more variables is dropped from the analysis. This is the approach adopted by default in most software and one that many researchers implement without any particular forethought. The approach is so common that it is sometimes not obvious that it is itself a method of handing missing data. In other words, sticking with the status quo—not doing anything about missing values and running the analysis with only complete cases—involves implicitly (or perhaps explicitly) adopting very strong assumptions about the mechanism that generated the incomplete data set.

A closely related approach is *pairwise deletion*. Pairwise deletion is appropriate when the analysis involves considering only pairs of variables at a time (e.g., multiple *t* tests or calculating a correlation matrix). Each pairwise computation then proceeds only using complete pairs. Pairwise deletion is effectively casewise deletion applied within pairs of variables in the data set, but has the advantage that each step of the analysis (e.g., each correlation coefficient) uses as many observations as possible. For example, if each pair of variables in a data set had only a few units with missing values pairwise deletion would ensure minimal loss of power, whereas casewise deletion might lead to the loss of many cases (except in the unlikely situation that the pattern of missing values was the same for all units).

Deletion methods are, as a rule, extremely dangerous. The most optimistic assessment is that the missing data are MCAR and the only impact is loss of statistical power. However, unless the MCAR assumption is highly plausible (perhaps because the cause of the missing data is both known and random) and the proportion of missing cases is very low (perhaps 5 % at most) deletion methods should be avoided wherever possible. In practice, it is far more likely that the mechanism for missingness is MAR or MNAR. If so, casewise or pairwise deletion has the potential to introduce huge levels of bias, levels of bias sufficient to produce widely inaccurate parameter estimates and inferences (e.g., as shown in the MAR example in Sect. 4.2.2.2).

4.3.1.2 From Mean Substitution to Single Imputation

An alternative to simple deletion approaches is to replace the missing data with an estimate of its true value. This is—at least superficially—an attractive approach because, if done properly, it should reduce bias when data are MAR. Yet even if done properly replacing missing data with an accurate estimate of the true value introduces new dangers.

A good place to start is a fairly common strategy known as *mean substitution*. This involves replacing missing values for a given variable with the mean of that variable. This allows the analysis to take place with complete cases and thus appears to avoid any loss of statistical power. The danger of this approach is twofold. First, replacing the missing value with the mean does not remove any bias if the data are MAR or MNAR (though it would not create bias if the missingness mechanism were MCAR). Second, the increase in statistical power from mean substitution is largely spurious (being accompanied by a increase in the Type I error rate). In the unlikely event that the mean was a perfect estimate of the true mean (that including the missing data), mean substitution would create a new type of bias. Because the replacement values are all identical they would be more similar to each other than real data (which are influenced by sampling error). In particular the variances and covariances of the imputed variables would be underestimated and hence the error terms in any subsequent analysis (e.g., the standard errors used to calculate test statistics or confidence intervals) would be too small.

If the previous argument is not sufficiently persuasive, consider extrapolating the mean substitution approach for a participant that failed to turn up for an experiment. If it is reasonable to add the mean of a variable to replace two or three missing values for a case, then it should also be reasonable to so for all values. In other words, the same argument that supports mean substitution for a partially complete case also supports creating entirely new cases based on the properties of the available data.

A more sophisticated approach is to use *conditional mean substitution* (also known as *regression imputation*). With this technique, rather than use the grand mean of each variable, missing data are replaced with a predicted or expected mean value (one that is conditional on other variables in the data set). For example, in a two group experiment one might replace a missing value by the mean of the group rather than the grand mean or a weighted mean of the two groups. Using multiple regression one can extend this approach to more complex studies by predicting missing values from the values of non-missing variables in the data set. Because condition mean substitution can in principle use all the available information to estimate the missing values it has the potential to produce unbiased parameter estimates when the data are MAR. Unfortunately, like mean substitution, it does not account for the variability inherent in sampling real data. It therefore likewise underestimates sources of error in the data, leading to a spurious increase in statistical power.

In order to get both accurate estimates of the missing data (at least when the data are MAR) and accurate estimates of the variances and covariances of the complete data set, it is necessary to find some way of adding error to the replacement values. This added error is needed to capture the many sources of uncertainty that would influence real data (and presumably the missing data if they were available). One option is to estimate the variability in the available data and add an equivalent quantity of random noise to each of the replacement values. This process of estimating a single replacement value and adding an appropriate amount of noise is known as *single imputation*. It is by far the most satisfactory missing data method of those considered so far, but is still far from ideal. It turns out that single imputation is problematic in two ways. First, adding noise to the imputed estimates makes the parameter estimates less accurate than some simpler approaches such as conditional mean substitution. Second, and perhaps surprisingly, it still underestimates the variability in the data. This is because the variance and covariances of a sample are themselves parameter estimates of the true population variances and covariances. So imputation needs to account for a further source of uncertainty on top of the uncertainty in estimating the conditional means of the data. A further step is required—rather than use a single set of imputed data it is better to impute several such sets. This approach is known as *multiple imputation*.

4.3.2 Multiple Imputation

Multiple imputation is attractive as a method for handling missingness because—if done correctly—it minimises any bias or loss of statistical power caused by missing values when the data are MCAR or MAR. Imputing a data set with missing values is nevertheless a very computationally intensive task. Imputing multiple data sets and pooling the results of the subsequent analyses on the imputed data sets also presents a number of challenges (Graham et al. 2007). Fortunately, recent advances in computing power reduce the difficulty of implementing imputation considerably (except for the very largest data sets). Software to impute data and pool results is now also readily available (e.g., R presently offers several add-on packages for multiple imputation).

The initial step in imputation is to decide on an imputation model. This involves deciding what variables will be used to predict the values of the missing data. Where possible it makes sense to use all the available variables—adopting what is termed an inclusive imputation strategy (Collins et al. 2001). As with any regression model an imputation may also benefit from transforming variables (e.g., if they are heavily skewed) or the inclusion of interaction terms. The main limit on the inclusive approach is that it can become cumbersome (e.g., if many transformed variables or hundreds of interaction terms are added). A sensible approach is to explore the data set and use knowledge of the context to include the most important potential predictors. Auxiliary variables—variables that are in the data set but not included in the analysis play an important role in imputation. This is because the MNAR versus MAR distinction depends on whether all variables that predict missingness are in the imputation model. If these variables are not in the imputation model then a data set that is potentially MAR is MNAR in practice. Including additional predictors makes it more likely that the MAR mechanism describes the processes that generate missing data and more likely that the bias from MNAR is ameliorated.

After an imputation model is decided on, the next step is to determine on the number of imputations that are required. Early work on multiple imputation—when imputing a single data set required considerable programming expertise, computing resources and time—suggested that "excellent" results could be obtained with only 3–5 data sets (Little and Smith 1987; Graham et al. 2007). Little and Smith (1987) showed that m (the number of imputed data sets) required to get sufficiently accurate results from multiple imputation depends on the fraction of missing information (γ) in the analysis. In simple situations, this is merely the proportion of missing cases, but may be lower if the pattern of missing data is highly correlated with values of other variables in the data set. More recently, Graham et al. (2007) have shown that statistical power to detect small effects also suffers when m is low—and this loss of power also depends on the fraction of missing information. Thus Graham (2009) has argued that m should be much higher—say 40 or greater if the fraction of missing information is 50 % or more.

For more specific guidance it is helpful to return to Rubin (1987). This work reveals that standard errors based on m imputed data set are expected to be larger than when making perfect use of available information by a factor of:

$$\sqrt{1 + \gamma/m} \tag{4.9}$$

From a theoretical perspective this equation indicates that imputation is perfectly efficient only when $\gamma = 0$ or when $m = \infty$. With $m = 3$ and $\gamma = 0.5$ (50 % of information missing) the standard errors of a subsequent analysis are likely to be $\approx 8\%$ larger than they would be with infinite imputations. Plugging in the 40 imputations recommended by Graham (2009) reduces the expected degree to which standard errors are inflated to $\approx 0.6\,\%$. Thus even with 40 imputations statistical power to detect very small effects might be compromised.

A popular recent approach to implementing multiple imputation is to use chained equations. Technical details of the chained equation approach is beyond the scope of this chapter, though a brief summary can be found in Azur et al. (2011) and more technical background in Buuren and Groothuis-Oudshoorn (2011). The chained equation is implemented in a number of software packages including the R packages mi (Su et al. 2011) and mice (Buuren and Groothuis-Oudshoorn 2011). Using such software, imputing the missing data for one or more data sets is relatively straightforward. Having obtained the imputed data, the final steps are to run the intended analysis on each data set in turn, before pooling the results from each analysis. Pooling the results minimises bias in parameter estimates and in the variances and covariances, hence providing more accurate inferences.

4.3.3 Pooling Imputations Using Rubin's Equations

The equations in Rubin (1987) for pooling results from analyses on multiply imputed data sets rely on a few basic statistical principles. They can be explained very simply using a regression model in which a single outcome is predicted from one or more predictors. As random noise is added to the imputed data it is independent across the imputed data sets and standard procedures for average independent observations be applied. Thus, if b_j represents a parameter estimate (e.g., slope or intercept) of the jth imputed data set then $\bar{b}$ (the pooled estimate of the m data sets) is their arithmetic mean:

$$\bar{b} = \frac{\sum_{j=1}^{m} b_j}{m} \tag{4.10}$$

The same logic can be applied to taking the mean of the sampling variance (the square of the standard error $\hat{\sigma}_{b_j}$) of each estimate:

$$\hat{\sigma}_{\bar{b}}^2 = \frac{\sum_{j=1}^{m} \hat{\sigma}_{b_j}^2}{m} \tag{4.11}$$

As noted earlier, the quantity $\hat{\sigma}_{\bar{b}}^2$ underestimates the true standard error (because it ignores between-imputation variation). This can be corrected by combining the within-imputation sampling variance with $\hat{\tau}_{\bar{b}}^2$ (the between-imputation sampling variance):

$$\hat{\sigma}_{MI}^2 = \hat{\sigma}_{\bar{b}}^2 + \left(1 + \frac{1}{m}\right) \hat{\tau}_{\bar{b}}^2 \tag{4.12}$$

The between-imputation sampling variance can be calculated from the squared deviations of each estimate from the mean estimate using the standard inferential formula for a variance:

$$\hat{\tau}_{\bar{b}}^2 = \frac{\sum_{j=1}^{m} \left(b_j - \bar{b} \right)^2}{m - 1} \tag{4.13}$$

Inferences can then be obtained from these pooled estimates and sampling variances with relative ease. For example, the t statistic for the coefficient of a linear regression model has the form $\bar{b}/\hat{\sigma}_{MI}^2$ with υ degrees of freedom where:

$$\upsilon = (m - 1)\left(1 + \frac{m\hat{\sigma}_{\bar{b}}^2}{(m + 1)\,\hat{\tau}_{\bar{b}}^2} \right)^2 \tag{4.14}$$

Although the calculations are not too difficult to work out by hand, they are fiddly. Fortunately, modern imputation software will often include the facility to pool results as well as impute data sets. The principles can also be extended to more complex models without too much trouble.

4.3.4   Multiple Imputation in Practice

How easy is it to carry out multiple imputation in practice? This extended example will return to the three missing data scenarios considered earlier for the mango pilot data. All three analyses will use a simple imputation model with one auxiliary variable and default settings in the R package mice. A more complete introduction to the package is provided by Buuren and Groothuis-Oudshoorn (2011).

4.3.4.1   Scenario 1: Multiple Imputation When Data Are MCAR

The primary attraction of multiple imputation when data are MCAR is that it may mitigate the loss of power associated with deleting cases. A further advantage is that the imputed data sets have no missing cells and this can be convenient for certain types of analysis such as analysis of variance where imbalance or unequal cell sizes is an annoyance (e.g., requiring corrections or specialist software). In scenario 1, sales staff were randomly excluded from the analysis. For the purposes of the imputation model, we will assume that only the sales data for those staff were excluded.

Imputing the missing data requires first installing and loading the mice package:

```
install.packges('mice')
library(mice)
```

It is now possible to use the mice() function to impute the missing data using a data frame or matrix as input. The default behaviour of the function is to use all other columns as predictors to impute values in any column with missing variables. For the mango pilot data, it will therefore use both *group* and *aveRT* to impute *sales* (the only variable with missing values).

This call to the mice() function will impute $m = 50$ data sets and assigns the output to a multiply imputed data set (mids) object that other functions in the package will recognize:

```
m.imputations <- 50
mp.imputed.mcar <- mice(
    mango.pilot.mcar, m = m.imputations
)
```

Analysis of the multiply imputed data sets is easy within mice() because there is a version of the lm() function that recognises a mids object and the output of this linear modelling function can then be called by the pool() function:

```
mp.imputed.fit.mcar <- with(
    mp.imputed.mcar, lm(sales ~ group)
)
summary(pool(mp.imputed.fit.mcar))
```

The output of the pooling procedure provides estimates of the coefficients of the regression predicting sales from group, inferential statistics for that regression and the fraction of missing information for each coefficient. Note because the example has not fixed the random number seed, you will obtain slightly different results from those shown here:

```
> summary(pool(mp.imputed.fit.mcar))

                    est          se           t         df
(Intercept) 403.85138   6.470882   62.410562  154.5548
group2      -18.70523    8.751914   -2.137273  178.6332
                  Pr(>|t|)        lo 95       hi 95  nmis
(Intercept) 0.00000000  391.06860  416.634169    NA
group2      0.03393599  -35.97567   -1.434786    NA
                  fmi         lambda
(Intercept) 0.16150225  0.15072151
group2      0.08168361  0.07145926
```

The fraction of missing information because it can guide us on what value of m might be appropriate. Here the fraction of missing information for difference in sales between groups is just over 8 %, so our initial value of $m = 50$ should be sufficient. Indeed, plugging these values into Eq. (4.1) suggests standard errors less than 0.1 % higher than for infinite m. For practical purposes it usually best to start with small values of m (e.g., 5 or 10) when setting up an imputation model, pooling the results and checking the output in R. Once the model is running correctly it is easy to increase

m to some suitably large value (e.g., 50 or more) based on the fraction of missing information and the stability of the output when imputation is repeated.

The output from the multiple imputation of the MCAR data estimates the difference in sales as 18.6 dollars (in favour of the no mango group), $t(178.6) = 2.14$, $p = 0.034$. As anticipated (given that data are missing at random and the fraction of missing information so low) this is close to the pattern of results for the complete data set. Although the BayesFactor ttestBF() function can not take input from the mids object that contains the imputed data, it is possible to obtain a Bayes factor directly from the summary data using other functions in that package. This approach is not as user-friendly (because it outputs the BF on a log scale) but the following R code illustrates how to extract the Bayes factor and place in on the appropriate scale. It also makes sense to adjust the effective sample size per group based on the degrees of freedom of the imputed data sets (rather than n from the complete data).

```
> ess <- (178.6332+2)/2
> exp(ttest.tstat(t=2.137273, n1=ess, n2=ess,
+    rscale = 0.707)[[1]])

[1] 1.329816
```

The imputed data therefore provide evidence—albeit very weak evidence ($BF \approx 1.3$)—suggesting that the mango group have lower sales than the no mango group.

4.3.4.2 Scenario 2: Multiple Imputation When Data Are MAR

In scenario 2 the sales data were more likely to be missing for low values of *sales* (and hence low *aveRT*) or for staff in the mango group. Thus the data are MAR with respect to an imputation model that includes these predictors. The following R code imputes $m = 50$ data sets using this imputation model and pools the results.

```
m.imputations <- 50
mp.imputed.mar <- mice(mango.pilot.mar, m = m.imputations)
mp.imputed.fit.mar <- with(
    mp.imputed.mar,  lm(sales ~ group)
)
summary(pool(mp.imputed.fit.mar))
```

The fraction of missing data is much higher here (around 40%) and the results are not that stable if repeated. For this reason it is worth imputing a much larger number of data sets. Using Eq. (4.1) suggests $m = 400$ will be more than adequate. Re-running the imputation produces the following output:

```
> m.imputations <- 400
> mp.imputed.mar <- mice(mango.pilot.mar, m = m.imputations)
> mp.imputed.fit.mar <- with(mp.imputed.mar,
+    lm(sales ~ group))
> summary(pool(mp.imputed.fit.mar))

                   est         se          t           df
(Intercept) 406.83327    6.130983 66.356944    190.0955
group2      -17.73112   10.397180 -1.705378    127.7734
                 Pr(>|t|)        lo 95       hi 95   nmis
(Intercept)   0.00000000   394.73977   418.926766     NA
group2        0.09055389   -38.30407     2.841823     NA
                      fmi       lambda
(Intercept)   0.03990903   0.02986074
group2        0.33564553   0.32532734

> ess <- (127.7734 +2)/2
> exp(ttest.tstat(t=1.705378, n1=ess, n2=ess,
+    rscale = 0.707)[[1]]

[1] 0.6988488
```

The output from the multiple imputation of the MAR data estimates the difference in sales as 17.7 dollars in favour of the no mango group, $t(127.8) = 1.71$, $p = 0.091$. This effect much closer to the estimate for the complete analysis (and in the same direction) than for the original analysis of complete cases in the MAR scenario. The t statistic is also closer to the original, and while the Bayes factor still favours the null hypothesis of no difference, it does so only weakly ($BF_0 \approx 1/0.70 = 1.4$).

4.3.4.3 Scenario 3: Multiple Imputation When Data Are MNAR

For an MAR analysis using multiple imputation to become MNAR in practice, requires only that the imputation model excludes one or more variables crucial to the prediction of missingness. In scenario 3, we considered what would happen if the *aveRT* auxiliary variable is no longer available. The following R code creates a data frame without the *aveRT* variable:

```
mango.pilot.mnar <- subset(
    mango.pilot.mar, select=c(group, sales)
)
```

What happens if the imputation is repeated with this potentially crucial variable missing?

```
> m.imputations <- 500
> mp.imputed.mnar <- mice(mango.pilot.mnar, m = m.imputations)
> mp.imputed.fit.mnar <- with(mp.imputed.mnar,
```

```
+       lm(sales ~ group))
> summary(pool(mp.imputed.fit.mnar))

                    est         se           t         df
(Intercept) 408.01109   5.978136 68.2505505 188.8420
group2         9.35603 10.685188  0.8756075 114.0281
                    Pr(>|t|)      lo 95       hi 95 nmis
(Intercept) 0.0000000 396.21858 419.80359     NA
group2      0.3830842 -11.81119  30.52325     NA
                    fmi      lambda
(Intercept) 0.04623743 0.03618947
group2      0.40693440 0.39662274

> ess <- (114.0281 +2)/2
> exp(ttest.tstat(t= 0.8756075, n1=ess, n2=ess,
+       rscale = 0.707)[[1]])
[1] 0.2787383
```

There is now insufficient information in the imputation model to predict the missing values and the data are—in effect—MNAR. The results here closely match those for the analysis of incomplete data in the MAR or MCAR scenarios. The estimate of the difference in sales is 9.3 dollars higher for the mango group with $t(114.0) = 0.88$, $p = 0.38$ and the Bayes factor is more strongly in favour of the null hypothesis than for the MAR analysis ($BF_0 \approx 1/0.28 = 3.6$).

4.3.4.4   Comparing Results Across the Three Missing Data Scenarios

At this point it is worth reviewing the patterns of results across the three scenarios with and without imputation. Table 4.1 shows the estimate of the difference in groups ($\hat{\mu}_1 - \hat{\mu}_2$), the standard error of this difference (SE), and a selection of inferential statistics (t, p and BF) for each analysis:

Table 4.1 Comparing the results for three missing data scenarios (MCAR, MAR and MNAR) with and without multiple imputation

	Without imputation					With multiple imputation				
	$\hat{\mu}_1 - \hat{\mu}_2$	SE	t	p	BF	$\hat{\mu}_1 - \hat{\mu}_2$	SE	t	p	BF
Complete data	−18.3	8.34	−2.19	0.029	1.45	−18.3	8.34	−2.19	0.029	1.45
Scenario 1: MCAR	−17.5	8.82	−1.99	0.048	1.00	−18.7	8.75	−2.13	0.034	1.33
Scenario 2: MAR	8.5	11.55	0.73	0.464	0.26	−17.7	10.40	−1.71	0.091	0.70
Scenario 3: MNAR	8.5	11.55	0.73	0.464	0.26	9.35	10.69	0.88	0.383	0.28

Without imputation only the MCAR data set (which has only a small fraction of information missing) produces results similar to that of the analysis of the complete data. Even so, there is some loss of statistical power. The standard error is larger and consequently both the frequentist t test and the Bayesian t test provide results less supportive of the alternative hypothesis (that the sales between the mango and no mango conditions differ). While the MCAR analysis produced relatively unbiased parameter estimates, both the MAR (and hence MNAR results) are biased both in terms of the estimate of the effect and its standard error. The estimate of the difference in groups is lower in magnitude and in the wrong direction, while the standard errors are substantially inflated. The frequentist t is no longer even close to statistical significance, while the Bayes factor now weakly favours the null hypothesis. The key message here is that bias and loss of power inherent in any analysis where the MCAR assumption is not tenable will have a negative impact for any method that merely drops incomplete cases.

With imputation things are much better. The MCAR analysis is again similar to that for the complete data (and indeed parameter estimates and inferences are slightly improved). The most dramatic change, however, is for the MAR scenario where the parameter estimate is very close to (and in the same direction as) the analysis with no missing values. Nevertheless, although the bias is reduced, there is still some loss of statistical power (albeit much less than would happen if incomplete cases were dropped from the analysis). Only in the case of the MNAR scenario does multiple imputation have little impact. Here there is simply not enough information in the set of variables used for imputing the missing values. It is therefore always wise to retain (and perhaps invest resources in collecting) data that might predict missingness. This is especially true if dropout is likely (e.g., in longitudinal research, surveys or long experiments). Even if a variable is not likely to be useful in your intended analysis it may be vital for imputation.

4.4 Maximum Likelihood and Bayesian in Approaches to Missing Data

Missing data present no real conceptual difficulty for either maximum likelihood or Bayesian approaches[1] to model inference. As will be explained, missing data simply necessitate more elaborate probabilistic models of the data, with the original models being extended to include latent variables, or possibly to also include an additional probabilistic model of the missing data mechanism. Practically speaking, of course, these extensions may be far from trivial, and even in the best case scenarios may

---

[1] **Editor note:** In this section the authors discuss Bayesian methods. These have not yet been covered in the previous chapters. The basic ideas behind Bayesian inference are introduced in Chap. 8. We recommend those readers who are totally unaware of Bayesian methods to read Chap. 8 before proceeding.

still require considerable extra modelling effort. In this section, we provide a general overview of these issues.

The starting point for both maximum likelihood estimation and Bayesian inference is the likelihood function. As described in Sect. 4.2.1, the likelihood function of the parameters of our data model, denoted generically by θ, and the parameters of the missing data mechanism, denoted generally by Ω, is generally given by[2]

$$P(y^{\text{obs}}, I|x, \theta, \Omega) = \int P(y^{\text{obs}}, y^{\text{mis}}|\theta, x)P(I|x, y^{\text{obs}}, y^{\text{mis}}, \Omega)dy^{\text{mis}}. \quad (4.15)$$

Maximum likelihood estimation of θ and Ω aims to find

$$\hat{\theta}, \hat{\Omega} = \underset{\{\theta, \Omega\}}{\text{argmax}} \ P(y^{\text{obs}}, I|x, \theta, \Omega), \quad (4.16)$$

while Bayesian inference aims to infer the posterior distribution

$$P(\theta, \Omega|y^{\text{obs}}, I, x) \propto P(y^{\text{obs}}, I|x, \theta, \Omega)P(\theta, \Omega), \quad (4.17)$$

with $P(\theta, \Omega)$ being some suitably chosen prior model for θ and Ω. In the case of MCAR and MAR, however, $P(y^{\text{obs}}, I|x, \theta, \Omega)$ decouples into the product of two independent likelihood functions, one for θ and one for Ω. As such, when attention is primarily focused on inferring θ, as is usually the case, the missing data mechanism is *ignorable* and need not be modelled explicitly in order to infer θ. In this case, maximum likelihood estimation aims to find

$$\hat{\theta} = \underset{\{\theta\}}{\text{argmax}} \ P(y^{\text{obs}}, |x, \theta), \quad (4.18)$$

while Bayesian inference aims to infer the posterior distribution

$$P(\theta, |y^{\text{obs}}, x) \propto P(y^{\text{obs}}, |x, \theta)P(\theta), \quad (4.19)$$

where, in both cases, the likelihood function is now

$$P(y^{\text{obs}}, |x, \theta) = \int P(y^{\text{obs}}, y^{\text{mis}}|\theta, x)dy^{\text{mis}}. \quad (4.20)$$

---

[2]Continuing with the notation introduced in Sect. 4.2.1, here we will denote the fully observed variables in our data by x, the partially observed variables by $y = y^{\text{obs}}, y^{\text{obs}}$, and we will index the missing variables in y by the I. We can also assume that any or all of x, y and I may be multivariate arrays.

4.4.1   Maximum Likelihood Estimation in Ignorable Models Using Expectation-Maximization

Even in the case of ignorable models, the problem of inferring θ is complicated by the fact that the likelihood function involves the integration over the missing values, and maximizing this function with respect to θ is often intractable. A general numerical algorithm that has been routinely applied to problems of this nature—i.e., maximum likelihood estimation in the presence of unobserved variables—is the Expectation-Maximization (EM) algorithm, first introduced in Dempster et al. (1977).

To understand EM, note that maximum likelihood estimation can always be written as

$$\hat{\theta} = \underset{\theta}{\operatorname{argmax}} \log\, P(y^{\mathrm{obs}}, |\theta, x), \qquad (4.21)$$

given that the log is a monotonic function. The objective of the EM algorithm is to provide a functional $\mathscr{F}(q, \theta)$ that bounds Eq. (4.21), and iteratively maximizes this bound with respect to both q and θ. This bound is defined as

$$\log P(y^{\mathrm{obs}}, |\theta, x) = \log \int P(y^{\mathrm{obs}}, y^{\mathrm{mis}}|\theta, x)\, dy^{\mathrm{mis}}, \qquad (4.22)$$

$$\geq \int q(y^{\mathrm{mis}}) \log \left(\frac{P y^{\mathrm{obs}}, y^{\mathrm{mis}}|\theta, x}{q(y^{\mathrm{mis}})} \right) dy^{\mathrm{mis}}, \qquad (4.23)$$

$$= \mathscr{F}(q, \theta), \qquad (4.24)$$

where $q(y^{\mathrm{mis}})$ is an arbitrary probability distribution over y^{mis}. We optimize $\mathscr{F}(q, \theta)$ with respect to both q and θ. This proceeds iteratively, first by holding θ constant and optimizing $\mathscr{F}(q, \theta)$ with respect to q, and then by holding q constant at its optimized value from the previous step and optimizing $\mathscr{F}(q, \theta)$ with respect to θ. In other words, having chosen an arbitrary initial parameter setting θ^0, for $t \geq 0$, we recursively perform the following two steps:

$$q^t = \underset{q}{\operatorname{argmax}}\, \mathscr{F}(q, \theta^t), \quad \text{(E-step)} \qquad (4.25)$$

$$\theta^{t+1} = \underset{\theta}{\operatorname{argmax}}\, \mathscr{F}(q^t, \theta), \quad \text{(M-step)}. \qquad (4.26)$$

It can be readily verified that the E-step is maximized by setting the function q equal to $P(y^{\mathrm{mis}}|y^{\mathrm{obs}}, \theta^t, x)$, which is the probability of y^{mis} conditioned on the observed data and estimate of θ. The subsequent M-step then maximizes the expectation

$$\int p(y^{\mathrm{mis}}|y^{\mathrm{obs}}, \theta^t, x) \log P(y^{\mathrm{obs}}, y^{\mathrm{mis}}|\theta, x)\, dy^{\mathrm{mis}}, \qquad (4.27)$$

with respect to θ. In many commonly used probabilistic models, both the E-step and M-step have simple analytical solutions, with the M-step often being practically identical to maximum likelihood estimation in the corresponding model with no missing data.

It should be emphasized that as an ascent algorithm, EM is an approximate maximum likelihood estimation method that can only be guaranteed to reach *local* maxima of the likelihood function. Nonetheless, for MCAR and MAR problems, EM provides a general means for (approximate) model inference, and one that explicitly integrates over the uncertainty introduced by the missing data. It is also useful to consider the EM algorithm for missing data in a more intuitive manner: We inititially guess the model's parameters, then predict the values of the missing data, then use these predictions to form a complete model of the data from which to infer the model's parameters, and so on. This procedure resembles the process of missing data imputation, followed by model inference, but does so in a iterative manner. This iterative procedure also provides a direct link to the Markov chain Monte Carlo (MCMC) methods used in Bayesian inference.

4.4.2 Bayesian Inference with Missing Data

For ignorable models, as mentioned above, Bayesian inference of the model's parameters involves the calculation of the posterior distribution:

$$P(\theta, |y^{\text{obs}}, x) \propto \int P(y^{\text{obs}}, y^{\text{mis}}|\theta, x)dy^{\text{mis}}P(\theta). \tag{4.28}$$

Even in cases of complete data, the posterior distribution rarely has a closed form, and here, the presence of y^{mis} almost inevitably entails that MCMC methods are required to draw samples from $P(\theta, |y^{\text{obs}}, x)$. One widely used MCMC method is the Gibbs sampler, first described by Geman and Geman (1984). In a Gibbs sampler, we initially assign values to all unobserved variables. In the case of the models we are considering here, the unobserved variables include the missing data variables y^{mis} and the model parameters θ. We then draw a sample from the distribution over each unobserved variable conditional on the assigned values of other variables. This sample is then assigned as the new value of that variable, and the process continues iteratively.

For example, if we index our missing data variables as $y_1^{\text{mis}}, y_2^{\text{mis}} \ldots y_k^{\text{mis}} \ldots y_K^{\text{mis}}$, and index the parameters as $\theta_1, \theta_2 \ldots \theta_s \ldots \theta_S$, the Gibbs sampler proceeds by initially assigning the variables random values. Then, for each y_k^{mis}, we sample from

$$P(y_k^{\text{mis}}|y_1^{\text{mis}}, y_2^{\text{mis}} \ldots y_{k-1}^{\text{mis}}, y_{k+1}^{\text{mis}} \ldots y_K^{\text{mis}}, \theta, x, y^{\text{obs}}) \tag{4.29}$$

and assign the sampled value as the new value of y_k^{mis}. Likewise, for each θ_s, we sample from

$$P(\theta_s|\theta_1, \theta_2 \ldots \theta_{s-1}, \theta_{s+1} \ldots \theta_S, y^{\text{mis}}, x, y^{\text{obs}}). \tag{4.30}$$

By proceeding as follows, we are guaranteed to converge to drawing sample from the joint posterior

$$P(\theta, y^{\text{mis}} | y^{\text{obs}}, x),\tag{4.31}$$

with, for example, the θ samples being effectively drawn from the marginal posterior

$$P(\theta | y^{\text{obs}}, x) = \int P(\theta, y^{\text{mis}} | y^{\text{obs}}, x)\, dy^{\text{mis}}.\tag{4.32}$$

The Gibbs sampler also applies without any conceptual modification to inference in the case of nonignorable models. In this case, we extend the sampler to include inference of the parameters Ω of the missing data mechanism. Now inference concerning Ω are conditioned on all other variables, including I. The remaining unobserved variables y^{mis} and θ are themselves then conditioned on Ω and I. Apart from extending the model to include new variables, the nature of the MCMC sampling is identical.

4.5 Conclusion

Missing data is an almost ubiquitous phenomenon in practice and one that can have catastrophic consequences on the precision and validity of data analysis. Despite this, it is often not treated adequately in practice. For example, Peugh and Enders (2004) estimate that up to 96 % of research in social science employs casewise or pairwise deletion strategies when dealing with missing data, despite the fact that these methods are likely to increase the bias and decrease the precision of most analyses. This chapter has reviewed the main types of missing data, and described some practical and effective solutions for dealing with general missing data problems.

In conclusion, understanding how missing data arise is always the first step to ameliorating its negative consequences. This is particularly the case when the probability that a variable's value is missing depends on the actual value of the variable. In these situations, so called *nonignorable* missingness, it is necessary to explicitly model the missing data mechanism in order to properly estimate a model of the data. However, developing and inferring a model of the mechanism of missingness, while simultaneously inferring the original data model, can readily be handled as a standard example of general Bayesian probabilistic modeling. Given that Bayesian methods have achieved dramatic growth in recent years, it is arguable that this Bayesian approach to missing data will become more common in practice. In addition, Bayesian approaches to the problem of missing data such as Mohan et al. (2013) may also lead to theoretical guarantees for the accuracy of statistical estimates made on the basis of missing data, the validity of the assumptions made about the missingness mechanism and whether those assumptions are empirically testable.

References

Azur MJ, Stuart EA, Frangakis C, Leaf PJ (2011) Multiple imputation by chained equations: what is it and how does it work? Int J Methods Psychiatr Res 20(1):40–49

Buuren S, Groothuis-Oudshoorn K (2011) mice: Multivariate imputation by chained equations in r. J Stat Softw 45(3)

Collins LM, Schafer JL, Kam C-M (2001) A comparison of inclusive and restrictive strategies in modern missing data procedures. Psychol Methods 6(4):330

Dempster MM, Laird NM, Jain DB (1977) Maximum likelihood from incomplete data via the em algorithm. J R Stat Soc 1–38

Geman S, Geman D (1984) Stochastic relaxation, Gibbs distributions and the Bayesian restoration of images. IEEE Trans Pattern Anal Machine Intel 6:721–741

Graham JW (2009) Missing data analysis: making it work in the real world. Annu Rev Psychol 60:549–576

Graham JW, Olchowski AE, Gilreath TD (2007) How many imputations are really needed? Some practical clarifications of multiple imputation theory. Prev Sci 8(3):206–213

Little RJ, Rubin DB (2002) Statistical analysis with missing data. Wiley, New York

Little RJ, Smith PJ (1987) Editing and imputation for quantitative survey data. J Amer Stat Assoc 82(397):58–68

Marlin BM, Zemel RS, Roweis ST, Slaney M (2011) Recommender systems, missing data and statistical model estimation. In: IJCAI proceedings-international joint conference on artificial intelligence, vol 22, pp 2686–2691

Mohan K, Pearl J, Tian J (2013) Graphical models for inference with missing data. In: Burges C, Bottou L, Welling M, Ghahramani Z, Weinberger K (eds) Advances in neural information processing systems, vol 26. Curran Associates, Inc., pp 1277–1285

Peugh JL, Enders CK (2004) Missing data in educational research: a review of reporting practices and suggestions for improvement. Rev Educ Res 74(4):525–556

Rouder JN, Speckman PL, Sun D, Morey RD, Iverson G (2009) Bayesian t tests for accepting and rejecting the null hypothesis. Psychon Bull Rev 16(2):225–237

Rubin DB (1976) Inference and missing data. Biometrika 63(3):581–592

Rubin DB (1987) Multiple imputation for nonresponse in surveys. Wiley, New York

Schafer JL, Graham JW (2002) Missing data: our view of the state of the art. Psychol Methods 7(2):147

Su Y-S, Yajima M, Gelman AE, Hill J (2011) Multiple imputation with diagnostics (mi) in r: opening windows into the black box. J Stat Softw 45(2):1–31

Part II
Classical Null Hypothesis Significance Testing Done Properly

Null hypothesis significance tests (NHST) comprise the core of most statistical analysis in HCI (and broader, the social sciences). Obviously, they deserve a place in this book. Despite the criticisms of the widespread, often procedural, use of NHST, this part aims to both nuance their use, and offer options that go beyond the standard use of NHST methods.

However, as this is not an introductory book on NHST, we assume the reader to be familiar with the main ideas. However, for those who are not, we very briefly introduce the core concept behind these tests before introducing the three chapters in this part.

NHST in very, very, brief

Here we present a very brief statement of what NHST methods do. Before we do so we want to make explicit that the idea here is based on the common, everyday, use of the procedure rather than on the ideas of Neyman & Pearson or Fisher who all, although with conflicting approaches, provided input for the current practice.

Suppose we are investigating whether a coin is fair or not. Hence, we throw the coin a number of times (let's say n) times. So, we now have data $D = \{H, T, T, \ldots, T\}$ containing a list of our heads and tails that is n elements long. Subsequently we define the null hypothesis to test: $H_0 : p = \frac{1}{2}$. Thus, we are stating that we are expecting the probability of heads p to be $\frac{1}{2}$. Our alternative hypothesis will be that this is not the case $H_A : p \neq 0$.

Now, given some model that we assumed generated the data, for example that the observed sequence of heads and tails are realizations of an independent $Bernoulli(p)$ random variable, we can compute the probability of our specific dataset (or something more "extreme") D given that the null hypothesis is true: $P(D|H_0)$. For example, if our sequence is ten tosses long, and we observe only heads, then this is quite unlikely given that the true data generating process is a "fair coin" (that is $D \sim Bernoulli(\frac{1}{2})$). Thus, $P(D|H_0)$ will be small.

The p-value which is then often used to draw a conclusion regarding the hypothesis is $P(D|H_0)$: hence, it is the probability of observing the data D (or more extreme values), given that the null hypothesis holds. If the $p - value$ is too small (often $< .05$), then we "reject" the null-hypothesis and accept that H_A is supported by the data.

Much can be said about the reasoning above, and much has been said about it (see the Editor suggestions). One could argue for example that $P(D|H_0)$ is not very interesting; what we really want is $P(H_0|D)$. This is something we will cover in Part 3 of this book. However, in this part we are broadly concerned with methods that focus on $P(D|H_0)$. Instead of introducing NHST as a mechanical procedure we have tried to encourage authors to discuss NHST in more detail, and focus also on the pitfalls of the standard methods.

Chapter 5: Effect Sizes and Power

Chapter 5 by Dr. K. Yatani briefly introduces NHST methods, and extensively discusses measures of effect size to summarize experiments. The chapter gives readers a feel for the robustness of NHST test for violations of certain assumptions of the test, and, by using simulated data, allows the reader to develop an intuition that goes beyond the procedural use of NHST test. The chapter advocates the use of effect size measure over p-values. Finally, the chapter also discusses power analysis; if one embraces the frequentist NHST framework, then power analysis should be an integral part of the analysis.

Chapter 6: Repeated Measures and Time Series

In the next chapter of this part Dr. D. Fry, Dr. K. Wazny, and Dr. N. Anderson discuss the analysis of repeated measure data or time series data using frequentist methods and NHST. Repeated measures designs often occur within HCI, but are not extensively treated in social science methodology text books: hence, we are very pleased to include a separate chapter on the topic. The authors demonstrate the use of [R] to conduct repeated measure ANONAs and discuss extensively how these can be interpreted.

The authors also introduce the topic of event-history analysis: an analysis aimed at understanding when an event will occur. This latter analysis is not common in HCI, but applicable to many HCI problems (e.g., when will a user install a new piece of software for the first time? Or, when does a user stop using her smart-watch?). Admittedly, the topic of event-history analysis is broad, and it is covered in several fields in the social sciences under different headings; hence, the current chapter only provides an introduction. In the editor suggestions we recommend a number of sources that are not already referenced in the chapter itself to give readers easy access into the topic.

Chapter 7: Nonparametric Tests

The last chapter in this part by Dr. J. Wobbrock and Dr. M. Kay discuss nonparametric statistics and their use in HCI. Often, methodology textbooks that introduce NHST methods focus on parametric tests. However, the field of nonparametric testing is very mature, and, due to the increases in computing power in recent years, many nonparametric test can be computed exactly.

In HCI we often encounter data for which nonparametric tests might be more appropriate than parametric tests. The authors explain in detail which assumptions should be checked before conducting parametric tests, and thus motivate when nonparametric tests should be considered. After discussing the assumptions the authors demonstrate the use of [R] to conduct nonparametric tests on a large number of examples, each time comparing the parametric and nonparametric "versions" of the test. The chapter contains a large number of references, and we recommend the interested reader to follow up on these. We think you will find the clear presentation the nonparametric versions of their more familiar parametric counterparts a useful reference.

Editors' Suggestions
Here are some more pointers, not referenced in the contributed chapters, that we ourselves found useful in understanding the topics that are discussed in this part.

- For a general discussion on controversies in statistics we wholeheartedly recommend the paper *Controversies in the Foundations of Statistics* by Bradley Efron published in The American Mathematical Monthly way back in 1978.
- For a (fierce) discussion of the use of NHST methods in the social sciences, we refer the reader to *The Cult of Statistical Significance: How the Standard Error Costs Us Jobs, Justice, and Lives* by Stephen Ziliak and Deirdre McCloskey (2008).
- In his book *Understanding The New Statistics: Effect Sizes, Confidence Intervals, and Meta-Analysis* Geoff Cumming (2011) provides a thorough overview of the effect sizes.
- The book *Event History Modeling: A Guide for Social Scientists* by Janet Box-Steffensmeier (2004) provides more detail on event-history analysis, geared specifically for the social sciences. The book *Event History Modeling: A Guide for Social Scientists* by Goran Bostrom (2012) details how to use [R] for advanced event history models.

Chapter 5
Effect Sizes and Power Analysis in HCI

Koji Yatani

Abstract Null hypothesis significance testing (NHST) is a common statistical analysis method in HCI. But its usage and interpretation are often misunderstood. In particular, NHST does not offer the magnitude of differences observed, which is more desirable to determine the effect of comparative studies than the p value. Effect sizes and power analysis can mitigate over-reliance on the p value, and offer researchers better informed preparation and interpretation on experiments. Many research fields now require authors to include effect sizes in NHST results, and this trend is expected to be more and more common. In this chapter, I first discuss common misunderstandings of NHST and p value, and how effect sizes can complement them. I then present methods for calculating effect sizes with examples. I also describe another closely related topic, power analysis. Power analysis can be useful for appropriately designing experiments though it is not frequently used in HCI. I present power analysis methods and discuss how they should and should not be used.

5.1 Introduction

Before diving into the main topic in this chapter, let's imagine a quick experiment. Imagine you are running a comparative user study, measuring task completion time with two systems. Each participant is exposed to both systems; that is, systems are a within-subject factor. Then, suppose that you have run ten participants. We prepare fictional data by using the `random` function:

```
> set.seed(123)
> a <- rnorm(10, 10, 2)
> set.seed(456)
> b <- rnorm(10, 11, 2)
```

The code above creates data of two arrays, a and b, representing measured performance time with the two systems; one with the mean of 10 and standard deviation

K. Yatani (✉)
University of Tokyo, Tokyo, Japan
e-mail: koji@iis-lab.org

© Springer International Publishing Switzerland 2016
J. Robertson and M. Kaptein (eds.), *Modern Statistical Methods for HCI*,
Human–Computer Interaction Series, DOI 10.1007/978-3-319-26633-6_5

of 2, and the other with the mean of 11 and the same standard deviation. Now, let's run a paired t-test.

```
> t.test(a, b, paired=T)
```

Then, we get the following result:

```
Paired t-test
data: a and b
t = -1.0795, df = 9, p-value = 0.3084
alternative hypothesis:
true difference in means is not equal to 0
95 percent confidence interval:
 -2.7410162 0.9700802
sample estimates:
mean of the differences
-0.885468
```

The test shows that we do not have a significant result. But what if you were able to run 100 participants instead of 10? Let's do it.

```
> set.seed(123)
> a <- rnorm(100, 10, 2)
> set.seed(456)
> b <- rnorm(100, 11, 2)
> t.test(a, b, paired=T)
Paired t-test
data: a and b
t = -3.915, df = 99, p-value = 0.0001662
alternative hypothesis:
true difference in means is not equal to 0
95 percent confidence interval:
 -1.5977429 -0.5229327
sample estimates:
mean of the differences
-1.060338
```

Voila, now we have a significant result! We do not do any suspicious data manipulation nor modify the statistical method. We simply increase the sample size from 10 to 100 to obtain statistically significant results. What we should understand with this example is that a very simple "trick" of increasing the sample size would give us significant results.

How can we estimate the actual magnitude of the difference in a way that is not affected by the sample size? The absolute value of the difference would not be a universal metric we can apply for different experiments. Intuitively, we want to measure "how much overlap" there is between the two distributions. The effect size, one of the main topics in this chapter, does this job for us.

Let's take a look at how the effect size behaves compared to the p value. With ten participants, the estimated effect size (Cohen's d, which is a commonly used measure) is 0.34 with the 95 % confidence interval (CI) of $[-0.31, 0.97]$ while the p value is 0.31. With 100 participants, it becomes 0.39 (95 % CI: $[0.18, 0.59]$) whereas the p value goes down to 0.0001, giving us a significant result. If we further increase the sample size to 1000, the effect size gets close to 0.40 with a confidence interval of $[0.33, 0.46]$, and the p value becomes extremely small. This example clearly illustrates that the p value can provide inconsistent results depending on the number of samples whereas our estimation of the effect size is consistent (i.e., note that the three estimated Cohen's d are roughly similar and 0.40 is always within confidence intervals). This is one of the advantages that the effect size has; it is much more robust to the sample size than the p value. And as we increase the sample size, the confidence interval of the effect size becomes smaller. This indicates that if we have more samples, we can better estimate the magnitude of the difference, (i.e., the effect), which is in line with what we learned in an introductory statistics class.

In some research disciplines, it is now a de-facto requirement that all statistical results include the report of effect sizes (and even their confidence intervals). This trend became more visible recently in the field of HCI, and it is good time to review it in depth. This chapter first reviews issues in the p value, and explains the notion of effect sizes. We then look into how to calculate effect sizes for well-known null hypothesis significance testing (e.g., t-tests and ANOVA) with examples. This chapter also covers power analysis briefly as a related topic to effect sizes, and concludes with discussions on what the HCI research community should make effort on to improve our reports of statistical results.

5.2 Myths of the p Value

Null hypothesis significance testing (NHST) is one of the most common statistical methods used in the field of HCI. Several reasons contribute to this. Many tools support them (e.g., R, IBM SPSS, SAS, and even Microsoft Excel). Results we get from NHST are very simple to understand; we mainly look for whether the p value is above or below 0.05. NHST is proven to be a useful tool to test potential differences among groups, but we need to be careful about how to use them and interpret results. In particular, many people misunderstand what the p value means and write wrong arguments with incorrectly-interpreted results. Chapters 12 and 13 discuss common misunderstandings of the p value and the effect of sample sizes which could potentially be abused. In addition to them, we review three myths people may believe in order to understand potential danger of over-reliance on the p value. This section is inspired by Field's (2005) discussions about effect sizes.

5.2.1 Myth 1: Threshold of the P Value

You probably already know that if $p < 0.05$, you can argue that there is a significant effect. Some people often report that there is a marginal significant difference if $p < 0.1$. But where did these thresholds (0.05 and 0.1) come from? These thresholds are basically from Fisher's publication back in 1925 (Fisher 1925). In his book, he discussed details of different statistical testing methods around $p = 0.05$. He described his justifications on choosing $p = 0.05$ as follows:

> The value for which P = 0. 05, or 1 in 20, is 1.96 or nearly 2; it is convenient to take this point as a limit in judging whether a deviation is to be considered significant or not. Deviations exceeding twice the standard deviation are thus formally regarded as significant. Using this criterion, we should be led to follow up a negative result only once in 22 trials, even if the statistics are the only guide available. Small effects would still escape notice if the data were insufficiently numerous to bring them out, but no lowering of the standard of significance would meet this difficulty. (Fisher 1925)

This has greatly influenced researchers in psychology. Researchers in other fields also followed them, but we have no theoretical reason for choosing $p = 0.05$. For example, we do not know why $p = 0.04$ is significant and $p = 0.06$ needs to be non-significant. Even in a more extreme example, we do not know why $p = 0.0499$ is significant and $p = 0.0501$ is not. If they have the equal sample sizes, the size of effects is almost the same, but why do we have completely opposite results? These thresholds are surely useful criteria for discussions, but we should not blindly believe this dichotomy. To have the whole picture of results, we need information besides the p value and significance flag.

5.2.2 Myth 2: Magnitude of the Effect

Another common misunderstanding is that the p value indicates the magnitude of an effect. For example, someone might say that the effect with $p = 0.001$ is larger than with $p = 0.01$. This is not true. The p value has nothing to do with the magnitude of an effect. The p value is merely the conditional probability of the occurrence of the data you observed given the null hypothesis. It does not give us any information of how large the effect is, and we need another metric.

5.2.3 Myth 3: "Significant" is "Important"

Even if you have a significant result, it is "significant" only in the context of statistics. It does not necessarily mean that the difference you have is meaningful or important in a practical setting. Imagine that you are reviewing a very typical interaction technique paper. It compares two techniques: one is what the authors developed, and the other is a conventional technique. Suppose that the performance time of some tasks was improved with a new interaction technique by 1% with the standard deviation of 0.1%. In this case, their NHST would show a significant difference. So should you automatically accept that paper because it shows significant improvements backed up with well-known statistical testing methods? No—it is probably too early to decide the fate of the paper. 1% improvement may be a difference between 10 and 9.9 s. Would this 100 ms. be really important? Maybe so for fighter pilots, but we definitely need more contextual information to assess the magnitude of this improvement.

Now you are reviewing another paper. In this paper, the performance time was improved with a new technique by 15%, but the standard deviation was also as large as 15%. The results would not show a significant difference because the standard deviation is too large. So would your conclusion be that the new technique is useless? I would say not. 15% improvement in average (e.g., 10 vs. 8.5 s) could have an impact on user experience. There may have been some factors that caused such variances. For example, some participants might have been able to use experience from other interactive systems (e.g., heavy smartphone users might be able to adapt to new touch interaction more quickly than others). Other researchers might come up with an even better technique which can remove that variance while maintaining faster performance. Thus, the developed technique may be important enough to be shared even though the present paper could not find a significant difference. Assuming the paper is of high quality in other aspects, I think that it should be accepted (though I would ask the authors to explain why the standard deviation was so large and how their technique could be improved to make it smaller). Thus, we should not overrate statistically-significant results and underrate non-statistically-significant results. All results should be interpreted in a larger context.

5.2.4 Summary

The discussions about these myths around the p value may be discouraging to some of you. But if you can use correctly, it is no doubt that NHST is a great tool to analyze your data as long as you:

- Understand the meaning of the p value correctly
- Use the term "significant" appropriately
- Define a null hypothesis that can occur with your data, and
- Seek dichotomous answers (i.e., "yes" or "no").

5.3 Effect Size

An effect size is the metric that indicates the magnitude of the effect attributed to the factor of interest. The effect size is not subject to the sample size, unlike the p

value. Thus, the effect size can complement the information that the p value offers us. Fortunately, calculations of effect sizes are easy to perform in most cases, and R already has powerful libraries for it. Reporting the effect size does not take up much space in your paper. So, we should start the practice of reporting the effect size now, and raise discussions.

However, we should also note that the effect size you can calculate from data is a point estimate. Thus, this estimate should have an error range. This error range is called a confidence interval, which probably you are already familiar with in NHST. Unlike means, confidence intervals for effect sizes can be asymmetric. This means that the estimated effect size may not be the exact average of the lower bound and upper bound of the confidence interval. For example, you can encounter cases where your estimated effect size is 0.5, and the confidence interval is [0.1, 0.7].

5.3.1 Interpretation of Effect Sizes

It is common to interpret effect sizes by comparison to thresholds that are considered "small","medium", and "large". Table 5.1 summarize these values. This chapter explains how to calculate each effect size in the following sections.

However, **we should use this table with care**. These are the values agreed in other research fields, but they may not be appropriate for HCI. I have seen many cases where the estimated effect size is much larger than "Large" values in this table. The HCI community must continue discussions and achieve consensus on what researchers should consider "small", "medium", and "large". But we can still use this table as a guide.

My favorite way to use effect sizes is to look at their confidence intervals and see whether it includes the zero or not (Nakagawa and Cuthill 2007). The zero effect size means that there is no effect by the factor. Simply speaking, if the confidence interval includes zero, we cannot be sure that an effect exists (even though its estimated size is large). Table 5.2 summarizes possible implications given an effect size and its confidence interval.

Table 5.1 Effect sizes commonly used for null hypothesis significance testing and their values considered small, medium, and large effect sizes. This table was created based on existing literature (Cohen 1998; Field 2009; Mizumoto and Takeuchi 2008)

Statistical methods	Effect size	Small	Medium	Large
t-test	Cohen's d	0.2	0.5	0.8
ANOVA	η^2 and η_p^2	0.01	0.06	0.14
Non-parametric tests	R	0.1	0.3	0.5
Correlation	R	0.1	0.3	0.5

Table 5.2 Implications with eight possible combinations of effect sizes (ES) and confidence intervals (CI)

CI includes 0	ES absolute value	CI range	Implication
No	Small	Small	The effect apparently exists, but the effect is small
	Small	Large	(This is unlikely to happen)
	Large	Small	The effect apparently exists, and we are sure that the effect is large
	Large	Large	The effect apparently exists and may be large, but we are not sure about its actual size
Yes	Small	Small	We are sure that the effect is small, but not sure whether the effect really exists
	Small	Large	We are not sure whether the effect exists. We thus need more data
	Large	Small	(This is unlikely to happen)
	Large	Large	We are not sure whether the effect exists. We thus need more data

In this chapter, I provide ways to calculate the confidence interval for some of the effect sizes. Even in other fields, reporting confidence intervals of effect sizes is not common yet (at least as of February 2015 when I wrote this chapter). However, as I described in Table 5.2, confidence intervals of effect sizes can be very informative. Although there are many journal articles, textbooks and online tutorials, methods for calculating the confidence interval of an effect size are not well summarized. I hope that this would serve as a useful guide for HCI researchers to better report effect sizes.

In the following subsections, I look into how to calculate effect sizes of common NHST. I also provide small examples and codes so that you can also execute them yourself. The code is not complicated at all, so even if you are not confident at coding, you should be able to understand. You also see some formulae, but you do not have to remember all of them as R libraries can do the job for you.

5.3.2   Paired t-Test

The t-tests is the most basic parametric testing method. I am sure that most of you have used it. A common effect size used for paired t-tests is Cohen's d. Its definition is as follows:

$$d = \frac{\mu_1 - \mu_2}{SD_{diff}},$$

where μ_1 and μ_2 represent the mean in each group, and SD_{diff} is the standard deviation of the difference between the two groups. To have a large d, a large effect size, the mean difference has to be large or the standard deviation has to be small. This fits well to our intuition. If the difference of the means between two groups is large, we want to say that the effect is large. Even if it is small, when its variance is small, the difference between the two groups is apparent. So we want to consider this case as showing a large effect too. This d does not depend on the sample size because we can transform d as follows (n is the sample size and x_1, x_2 represent data points in each group).

$$d = \frac{\frac{1}{n}\Sigma x_1 - \frac{1}{n}\Sigma x_2}{\sqrt{\Sigma \frac{((x_1 - x_2) - (\mu_1 - \mu_2))^2}{n^2}}} = \frac{\Sigma(x_1 - x_2)}{\sqrt{\Sigma((x_1 - x_2) - (\mu_1 - \mu_2))^2}}$$

Thus, this metric also has the desired characteristics of independence of the sample size.

Fortunately, we have a library to calculate this (and its confidence interval), so you do not have to remember this formula. We will now look at how to calculate Cohen's d with a simple example. Suppose you have conducted a comparative study with two techniques in a within-subject design. In the following, the variables *group* and *value* represent the experimental conditions and participants' performance.

```
> value <- c(1,1,2,3,3,1,2,4,1,2,6,5,2,3,5,2,2,3,4,4)
> group <- c(0,0,0,0,0,0,0,0,0,0,1,1,1,1,1,1,1,1,1,1)
> data <- data.frame(group, value)
> by(data $value, data$group, summary)
  data$group: 0
   Min.  1st Qu.  Median   Mean  3rd Qu.   Max.
   1.00    1.00    2.00    2.00    2.75    4.00
--------------------------------------------------------
  data$group: 1
   Min.  1st Qu.  Median   Mean  3rd Qu.   Max.
   2.00    2.25    3.50    3.60    4.75    6.00
```

This fictional dataset looks like it will have a significant result. Let's run a paired t-test to confirm.

```
> t.test(data[data["group"]==0,2],
>   data[data['group']==1,2], paired=T)
Paired t-test
data:
data[data["group"] == 0, 2] and
data[data["group"] == 1, 2]
t = -2.588, df = 9, p-value = 0.02931
alternative hypothesis:
true difference in means is not equal to 0
95 percent confidence interval:
 -2.9985588 -0.2014412
sample estimates:
mean of the differences
 -1.6
```

Yes, we have a significant difference. Now, we will calculate the effect size. $\mu_1 - \mu_2$ is already in this result view, which is in the last line (-1.6). For SD_{diff}, we can calculate as follows:

```
> sd(data[data$group=="0",2] -
+ data[data$group=="1",2])
1.95505
```

We then use the MBESS library [MBESS]. You need to install it before using. Please refer to other [R] manuals on how to do it).

```
> library(MBESS)
> ci.sm(Mean=1.6, SD=1.95505, N=10, conf.level=0.95)
[1]"The 0.95 confidence limits for the standardized mean are
given as:"
$Lower.Conf.Limit.Standardized.Mean
[1] 0.07897955
$Standardized.Mean
[1] 0.8183934
$Upper.Conf.Limit.Standardized.Mean
[1] 1.52514
```

Thus, the effect size is 0.82 with the 95 % confidence interval of [0.08, 1.53]. Note that 0.8183934 = 1.6/1.95505. We now use Table 5.2. The CI does not include the zero, the absolute value of the effect size is large. And the range of CI is large. Thus, according to Table 5.2, we have some grounds to believe there is a positive effect. But the actual effect can be much smaller (or larger) than the estimate we have here.

5.3.3 Unpaired t-Test

We also use Cohen's d for unpaired t-tests, but the calculation is a little different:

$$d = \frac{\mu_1 - \mu_2}{\sqrt{\frac{(n_1 - 1)\sigma_1^2 + (n_2 - 1)\sigma_2^2}{n_1 + n_2 - 2}}}$$

where μ_i, σ_i, n_i are the mean, standard deviation, and sample size of the group i, respectively. Similar to what we saw in the paired t-test, this metric is not dependent to the sample size. We use the same fictional data again to calculate the effect size.

```
> value <- c(1,1,2,3,3,1,2,4,1,2,6,5,2,3,5,2,2,3,4,4)
> group <- c(0,0,0,0,0,0,0,0,0,0,1,1,1,1,1,1,1,1,1,1)
> data <- data.frame(group, value)
> t.test(data[data["group"]==0,2],
+    data[data['group']==1,2], var.equal=T)
Two Sample t-test
data:
data[data["group"] == 0, 2] and
data[data["group"] == 1, 2]
t = -2.8483, df = 18, p-value = 0.01067
alternative hypothesis:
true difference in means is not equal to 0
95 percent confidence interval:
 -2.7801789 -0.4198211
sample estimates:
mean of x mean of y
      2.0       3.6
```

This time, we run an unpaired t-test, and still have a significant result. What we need for calculating the effect size this time is the t value, which is 2.8483. With the ci.smd function in the MBESS library, we can calculate the Cohen's d as follows:

```
> library(MBESS)
> ci.smd(ncp=2.8483, n.1=10, n.2=10, conf.level=0.95)
$Lower.Conf.Limit.smd
[1] 0.2903809
$smd
[1] 1.273798
$Upper.Conf.Limit.smd
[1] 2.228362
```

Therefore, we have an estimated effect size of 1.27 with 95 % CI = [0.29, 2.23]. This would appear to be a large effect but with a fairly large confidence interval so we require more data for further investigation.

5.3.4 ANOVA

ANOVA (Analysis of variance) is also used in HCI very often. There are a couple of effect sizes which can be used in ANOVA tests. But eta-squared (η^2) and partial eta-squared (η_p^2) are probably the most common, and this section mainly explains them.

The intuition of eta-squared is a ratio of the variance which can be explained by a particular factor over the total variance observed. If a factor has a large effect, it causes measurable differences in your observation. With ANOVA, suppose that you have found that the factor is contributing to generating half of these observed differences (i.e., variances). In this case, the eta-squared is 0.5.

$$\eta^2 = \frac{SS_{factor}}{SS_{total}}$$

where SS_{factor} and SS_{total} represent the sum of square for the factor and all factors (including errors). When the number of factors is large, eta-squared may underestimate the magnitude of the effect as SS_{total} tends to be much larger SS_{effect} than . To mitigate this issue, we have partial eta-squared defined as follows:

$$\eta_p^2 = \frac{SS_{factor}}{SS_{factor} + SS_{error}}$$

The partial eta-squared compares the variance attributed to the factor against the error (i.e., the residual of the total variance after we remove ones by factors). However, this partial eta-squared may overrate the size of the effect (you will see this later). It is important to clarify which you use in your paper.

5.4   One-Way ANOVA

Let's take a look at how we can calculate the effect size when we perform an ANOVA test. Suppose that we are comparing three user groups, each of which consists of eight people. We also have a value for each person which represents some kinds of performance.

```
> Group <- rep(c("A", "B", "C"), each=8)
> Value <- c(1, 2, 4, 1, 1, 2, 2, 3, 3, 4, 4,
+       2, 3, 4, 4, 3, 4, 5, 3, 5, 5, 3, 4, 6)
> data <- data.frame(Group, Value)
```

We perform an ANOVA test (not repeated-measure) with this data.

```
> aov <- aov(Value ~ Group, data)
> summary(aov)
            Df   Sum Sq   Mean Sq   F value    Pr(>F)
Group        2    22.75     11.38      12.1   0.00032 ***
Residuals   21    19.75      0.94
---
Signif. codes:
0 '***' 0.001 '**' 0.01 '*' 0.05 '.' 0.1
```

We find that the Group factor is significant. From this result, we also know that SS_{factor} is 22.75 and SS_{error} is 19.75. As we only have one factor, the total variance SS_{total} is the sum of SS_{factor} and SS_{error}, which is 42.50. We thus can calculate the eta-squared:

$$\eta^2 = \frac{SS_{factor}}{SS_{total}} = \frac{22.75}{42.50} = 0.54$$

Please also note that the partial eta-squared is the same as this eta-squared this time. This is always true for one-way ANOVA by definition. We also calculate the confidence interval of the eta-squared with the MBESS library with the F value and two degrees of freedom:

```
> library(MBESS)
> ci.R2(F.value=12.1, df.1=2, df.2=21,
+       conf.level=.95, Random.Predictor=F)
$Lower.Conf.Limit.R2
[1] 0.1752996
$Prob.Less.Lower
[1] 0.025
$Upper.Conf.Limit.R2
[1] 0.6870796
$Prob.Greater.Upper
[1] 0.025
```

What we need to look for in this result is Lower.Conf.Limit.R2 and Upper.Conf.Limit.R2. Thus, the 95 % confidence interval is [0.18, 0.69]. This suggests that there is a large effect, and that we might want to gather more data to increase our confidence.

5.5   One-Way Repeated-Measure ANOVA

How about if we run a repeated-measure ANOVA test? Let's take a look with the same example.

```
> Group <- rep(c("A", "B", "C"), each=8)
> Value <- c(1, 2, 4, 1, 1, 2, 2, 3, 3, 4, 4, 2, 3,
+       4, 4, 3, 4, 5, 3, 5, 5, 3, 4, 6)
> Participant <- rep(c(1:8),3)
> data <- data.frame(Group, Value, Participant)
> aov <- aov(Value ~ Group +
+       Error(factor(Participant)/ Group), data)
> summary(aov)
Error: factor(Participant)
            Df   Sum Sq   Mean Sq   F value   Pr(>F)
Residuals    7    5.167    0.7381
Error: factor(Participant):Group
            Df   Sum Sq   Mean Sq   F value   Pr(>F)
Group        2    22.75    11.375    10.92     0.00139 **
Residuals   14    14.58    1.042
---
Signif. codes:
0 '***' 0.001 '**' 0.01 '*' 0.05 '.' 0.1
```

Again, we have a significant result but several numbers have been changed. The F value is 10.92. SS_{error} becomes 14.58 while SS_{factor} stays as 22.75. We also have a new "error" for Participant. Its sum of square is 5.17. Thus the eta-squared is:

$$\eta^2 = \frac{SS_{factor}}{SS_{total}} = \frac{22.75}{22.75 + 14.58 + 5.17} = 0.54$$

This is the same value as we had in the previous example. But if we calculate the partial eta-squared, we have:

$$\eta_p^2 = \frac{SS_{factor}}{SS_{factor} + SS_{error}} = \frac{22.75}{22.75 + 14.58} = 0.61$$

This is because we have removed effects of participants' individual differences. The residual of 5.167 means the variance that can be explained as individual differences. You may also notice that $14.58 + 5.17 = 19.75$. This is how repeated-measure ANOVA considers individual differences.

We now calculate the confidence interval of the estimated effect sizes. The procedure is almost the same as one-way ANOVA. We start with the confidence interval for the partial eta-squared. As Group is now a within-subject factor, we have to change Random.Predictor to true.

```
> library(MBESS)
> ci.R2(F.value=10.92, df.1=2, df.2=14,
+        conf.level=.95, Random.Predictor=T)
$Lower.Conf.Limit.R2
[1] 0.1647956
$Prob.Less.Lower
[1] 0.025
$Upper.Conf.Limit.R2
[1] 0.8174432
$Prob.Greater.Upper
[1] 0.025
```

Thus, the estimated effect size is $\eta_p^2 = 0.61$ with 95 % CI = [0.16, 0.82]. Next, we calculate the confidence interval for the eta-squared. Unfortunately, we cannot directly use the F value we see in the ANOVA test result because it is calculated with the residual (error) of each factor. As we calculated the eta-squared, we need to take all errors into account. To do this, we re-calculate the F value:

$$\frac{SS_{factor}/df_{factor}}{SS_{total\_error}/df_{error}} = \frac{22.75/(3-1)}{(14.58+5.17)/((3-1)\times(8-1))} = 0.86$$

```
> ci.R2(F.value=8.06, df.1=2, df.2=14,
+      conf.level=.95, Random.Predictor=T)
$Lower.Conf.Limit.R2
[1] 0.08764731
$Prob.Less.Lower
[1] 0.025
$Upper.Conf.Limit.R2
[1] 0.7755121
$Prob.Greater.Upper
[1] 0.025
```

Thus, $\eta^2 = 0.54$ with 95 % CI = [0.09, 0.78]. With either the eta-squared or partial eta-squared, the confidence interval do not include the zero. Thus, it is likely that we have a large effect according to Table 5.1.

5.6 Two-Way ANOVA

The basic idea of calculating effect sizes in two-way ANOVA is the same as one-way ANOVA. Let's take a look with an example. Suppose that we want to compare user performance differences among two types of devices (a tablet and mobile phone) and three kinds of interaction techniques for text entry (a gesture-based method, pen-based method, and the QWERTY keyboard). Both factors are within-subject, and we have eight participants in total.

```
> Participant <- factor(rep(c(1:8), 6))
> Device <- factor(c(rep("Tablet",24),
+      rep("Mobile",24)))
> Technique <- factor(rep(c(rep("Gesture",8),
+      rep("Pen",8),
rep("QWERTY",8)), 2))
> Time <- c(1.2,1.4,1.8,2.0,1.1,1.5,1.5,1.7,
+ 2.1,2.5,2.2,2.2,2.9,2.3,2.3,2.6,
+ 3.5,3.4,3.3,3.2,2.9,2.8,3.8,3.4,
+ 2.4,1.8,2.5,2.1,2.2,1.9,1.7,2.3,
+ 2.8,3.1,3.2,4.0,2.9,3.6,3.2,3.7,
+ 4.5,4.8,4.7,4.1,4.1,4.2,4.6,4.9)
> data <- data.frame(
+      Device, Technique, Participant, Time)
```

We now run a two-way ANOVA test with the ez library. Please refer to its manual ([R] ezANOVA manual) for more details on how to use the library.

```
> library(ez)
> options(contrasts=c("contr.sum", "contr.poly"))
> ezANOVA(data=data, dv=.(Time), wid=.(Participant),
+     within=.(Technique, Device), type=3, detailed=T)
  $ANOVA
  Effect         DFn   DFd    SSn    SSd       F    p p<.05
1 (Intercept)     1     7  390.4   0.81    3368    1.1e-10 *
2 Technique       2    14   34.2   1.76     135    6.8e-10 *
3 Device          1     7    9.8    0.2     273    7.2e-07 *
4 Tech:Dev        2    14    0.7    1.5     3.4    6.0e-02
  $'Mauchly's Test for Sphericity'
  Effect                        W                  p p<.05
2 Technique          0.7849017          0.4835549
4 Technique:Device   0.4815467          0.1116645
  $'Sphericity Corrections'
  Effect         GGe                  p[GG] p[GG]<.05
2 Technique    0.8229787    1.831468e-08 *
4 Tech:Dev     0.6585649    8.883789e-02
```

There is much information in the result view. First, we need to check if our dataset violates the sphericity assumption (see Chap. 6 for more on sphericity). Under the section of "Mauchly's Test for Sphericity", a main effect factor Technique and the interaction term Technique:Device do not show significant results. Thus, we do not need any correction and use direct interpretation of the ANOVA result. Now, we move to the section of "ANOVA". Technique is significant ($F_{2,14} = 135.8$, $p < 0.001$), and also is Device ($F_{1,7} = 273.8, p < 0.001$), but the interaction term is not ($F_{2,14} = 3.44, p = 0.06$).

Let's calculate the effect size. For the eta-squared of Technique, the denominator is all the sum of square for all factors (except the intercept term) and all errors (including the one associated with the intercept). Thus,

$$\eta^2 = \frac{SS_{Tech}}{SS_{total}} = \frac{34.24}{34.24 + 9.81 + 0.75 + 0.81 + 1.76 + 0.25 + 1.53} = 0.70$$

If we calculate the partial eta-squared instead, the denominator only includes the sum of square associated with the factor of interest. That is,

$$\eta_p^2 = \frac{SS_{Tech}}{SS_{Tech} + SS_{Tech\_error}} = \frac{34.24}{34.24 + 1.76} = 0.95$$

Unlike one-way ANOVA, the values of these two effect sizes are different. Either of them is generally acceptable in publications, but we should know that the partial eta-squared may overestimate the magnitude of the effect.

We then calculate the confidence intervals of our eta-squared and partial eta-squared. We start with calculating the confidence interval for the partial eta-squared. Similar to the case of one-way ANOVA, we need the F value and two degrees of freedom. *Technique* is a within-subject factor, so we set `Random.Predictor` to true (if the factor is between-subject, you need to set it to false):

```
> library(MBESS)
> ci.R2(F.value=135.8, df.1=2, df.2=14,
+       conf.level=.95, Random.Predictor=T)
$Lower.Conf.Limit.R2
[1] 0.8452752
$Prob.Less.Lower
[1] 0.025
$Upper.Conf.Limit.R2
[1] 0.9797964
$Prob.Greater.Upper
[1] 0.025
```

Thus, $\eta_p^2 = 0.95$ with 95 % CI = [0.85, 0.98].

Next, we calculate the confidence interval for the eta-squared. We re-calculate the F value by doing:

$$\frac{SS_{Tech}/df_{Tech}}{SS_{total\_error}/df_{error}} = \frac{34.24/(3-1)}{(0.81 + 1.76 + 0.25 + 1.53+)/((3-1)*(8-1))}$$
$$= 55.1.$$

Here, the denominator is the mean of square for errors, which is the division of the total sum of square for errors by their degree of freedom. The numerator is the mean of square for Technique. Our new F value is 55.1, and we use the ci.R2 function with this:

```
> ci.R2(F.value=55.1, df.1=2, df.2=14,
+       conf.level=.95, Random.Predictor=T)
$Lower.Conf.Limit.R2
[1] 0.6693722
$Prob.Less.Lower
[1] 0.025
$Upper.Conf.Limit.R2
[1] 0.9525595
$Prob.Greater.Upper
[1] 0.025
```

Thus, we have $\eta^2 = 0.70$ with 95 % CI = [0.67, 0.95]. By Table 5.1, this is a rather large effect with fairly small confidence interval.

In case your ANOVA results require corrections (e.g., Greenhouse-Geisser or Huynh-Feldt correction, see Chap. 6), you need to use corrected degrees of freedom to calculate the confidence interval. The example above does not require any correction, but suppose that we decide to do it. According to the result view, Greenhouse-Geisser's is 0.8229787. Thus,

```
> ci.R2(F.value=135.8, df.1=2*0.82, df.2=14*0.82,
+     conf.level=.95, Random.Predictor=T)
$Lower.Conf.Limit.R2
[1] 0.8269647
$Prob.Less.Lower
[1] 0.025
$Upper.Conf.Limit.R2
[1] 0.9819841
$Prob.Greater.Upper
[1] 0.025
```

Note that the confidence interval becomes slight wider this time, which means that the estimation gets a little conservative due to the correction.

5.7 Non-parametric Tests

Effect sizes for non-parametric tests have not been used as often as parametric tests even in other fields. This is probably why t-tests and ANOVA suffice in most cases (i.e., these tests are well robust to violations of assumptions and we also have well-known correction methods). However, non-parametric tests are rather common in HCI, and it is still good to discuss their effect size as well. For more on non-parametric tests, see Chap. 7 of this book.

According to the book written by Field (2009), r is a metric we can use as an effect size for non-parametric tests, defined as:

$$r = \frac{Z}{\sqrt{N}}$$

where Z is the z value we can obtain from non-parametric tests and N is the total number of samples.

Let's take a look at an example of Wilcoxon tests. This is a non-parametric equivalence to a paired t-test. Suppose that we have some results from a 7-Likert scale question:

We then perform an Wilcoxon test with a function in the `coin` library ([R] `coin` manual).

```
> GroupA <- c(1,3,2,4,3,2,1,1,3,2)
> GroupB <- c(3,5,6,4,2,4,7,6,3,5)
> library(coin)
> wilcoxsign_test(GroupA ~ GroupB, distribution="exact")
Exact Wilcoxon-Signed-Rank Test (zeros handled a la Pratt)
data: y by x (neg, pos) stratified by block
Z = -2.366, p-value = 0.01562
    alternative hypothesis: true mu is not equal to 0
```

We thus have a significant result. And the effect size is:

$$r = \frac{Z}{\sqrt{N}} = \frac{2.366}{\sqrt{20}} = 0.53$$

If you ran a Friedman test, you calculate the effect size for pairwise comparison. Unfortunately, we do not have an agreed method to calculate the confidence interval of r. New metrics whose confidence intervals can be calculated have been proposed (Newcombe 2012), and the HCI community should continue to review what would be most appropriate in the context of our research and revising our statistical testing practices.

5.8   Pearson's Correlation

To calculate the confidence interval of the correlation r, we need to obtain z-score by doing the Fisher transformation. We add or subtract the standard error with the factor of 1.96 as we do for normal null hypothesis significance testing. But because of transformation, the standard error is approximately $\frac{1}{\sqrt{n-3}}$. And we then transform back to the space of r. In summary, we have to calculate:

$$\tanh\left(\tanh^{-1}r \pm \frac{1.96}{\sqrt{n-3}}\right)$$

In reality, we do not have to do this; fortunately, the function to calculate the Pearson's correlation also shows its confidence interval. Let's take a look with an example. Suppose you have 10 samples:

```
> x <- c(10,14,12,20,15,13,18,11,10,11)
> y <- c(22,21,25,35,28,29,31,19,17,24)
```

We then calculate the correlation with the cor.test function.

```
> cor.test(x,y,method="pearson")
          Pearson's product-moment correlation
data: x and y
t = 4.7377, df = 8, p-value = 0.001468
alternative hypothesis:
true correlation is not equal to 0
95 percent confidence interval:
 0.4984860 0.9660124
sample estimates:
       cor
0.8586245
```

The results already shows that the confidence interval is [0.50, 0.97], so by Table 5.1 we can be reasonably confident that the effect is large.

5.9   Power Analysis

We have seen effect sizes and how to calculate them. I hope you now have a clearer understanding how effect sizes could be useful to interpret statistical testing results. With the notion of effect sizes, we can perform another analysis, called power analysis. This is not frequently used in HCI research (see Chap. 14), but it can be a useful tool for some of the readers. Before talking about the details of power analysis, we need to understand two types of errors we may have in the decision with statistical testing results.

5.9.1   Type I Error and Type II Error

NHST can tell you how likely randomly-sampled data would be like your data or even more extreme than it given that the null hypothesis is true (e.g., there is no difference in the mean across the comparison groups). As a standard threshold, we use 0.05, and we call this alpha (α). This means that if randomly sampled data can be like your data at lower than a 5 % chance, you reject the null hypothesis (and claim that you observe a difference). Thus, if your p value is lower than the alpha, we say that you have a significant result.

If a difference does not exist but we reject the null hypothesis, this is an error. We call this a Type I error or false positive. As you have seen in various NHSTs, your p value will never be zero (which can be extremely small though). As your p value directly means the probability of this Type I error, there is a very slight chance that your conclusion is wrong even if the p value is very small.

There is another kind of errors we may have in NHSTs as illustrated in Table 5.3. Another possible error is that we fail to reject the null hypothesis although the null hypothesis is in fact false. In other words, we conclude that we do not have a difference although there is a difference. This is called a Type II error or false negative. Its probability is represented as beta (β).$1 - \beta$ represents the probability to have true negative, and it is called power. Power analysis is a way to determine how likely it is that we have a Type II error.

To summarize in a bit more mathematical notation, $\alpha = p$ (Reject H0 | H0 is true). H0 is the null hypothesis. And $p = p$ (Data | H0 is true). If p is smaller than α, we call the result significant. $\beta = p$ (fail to reject H0 | H0 is false), and power = p (reject H0 | H0 is false) = $1 - \beta$.

5.9.2 Conducting Power Analysis

There are four pieces of information used in power analysis.

- Sample size,
- Effect size of the underlying population (not the estimated value),
- Alpha, and
- Beta or Power.

We need three of the above information to estimate the other by power analysis. For example, we can estimate a sample size we would need given the effect size, alpha and power. We can also estimate how likely we have a false negative given the sample size, effect size (note that it is the one for the underlying population, not the one you calculate from your data) and alpha. Based on what you estimate, power analysis often has different names.

- **A priori power analysis**: Estimating the sample size given the effect size, alpha and power,
- **Sensitivity analysis**: Estimating the effect size given the sample size, alpha and power,
- **Criterion analysis**: Estimating the alpha given the sample size, effect size, and power, and
- **Post hoc power analysis**: Estimating the power given the sample size, effect size, alpha.

Table 5.3 Type I and Type II errors

	Rejecting the null hypothesis	Not rejecting the null hypothesis
The null hypothesis is true	**Type I error** (false positive)	True negative
The null hypothesis is false	True positive	**Type II error** (false negative)

In this chapter, we first explain how to perform a priori power analysis because the sample size estimation is often key to determine an experimental design. We then demonstrate post hoc power analysis with Mango Watch data. Other analyses can be performed with the same functions; the only difference is to change arguments. For example, if you want to run a sensitivity analysis, you feed the sample size, alpha and power instead of the effect size, alpha and power (a priori power analysis).

5.9.3 Sample Size Estimation

Let's take a look at an example with *t-test*s. Suppose that we have two groups to compare and we do a within-subject design (so we are using a t paired test). We want to have a difference with $\alpha = 0.05$. It is a little hard to set a proper effect size, but let's say 0.5 (regarded as a middle-size effect, see Table 5.1). The power is also tricky to determine. Here, we shall accept 20 % false negative in cases where the null hypothesis fails to be rejected. So, we set the power to be 0.8. To perform power analysis, we can use the pwr library ([R] pwr manual).

```
> library(pwr)
> pwr.t.test(power=0.8, d=0.5,
+     sig.level=0.05, type="paired")
     Paired t-test power calculation
              n = 33.36713
              d = 0.5
      sig.level = 0.05
          power = 0.8
    alternative = two.sided
NOTE: n is number of *pairs*
```

Thus, we would need 33 samples to meet the criteria we specified. What if we design this experiment as between-subject? It turns out that we would have to increase the sample size for each group to around 64:

```
> pwr.t.test(power=0.8, d=0.5, sig.level=0.05)
     Two-sample t-test power calculation
              n = 63.76561
              d = 0.5
      sig.level = 0.05
          power = 0.8
    alternative = two.sided
NOTE: n is number in *each* group
```

The pwr library also has the function for unbalanced sample sizes. Suppose that we are considering the same between-subject experiment, but this time we are only able to have 50 samples for one group due to some constraints. So our question is

how many samples we would need for the other group. We can do this with the
`pwr.t2n.test` function:

```
> pwr.t2n.test(d=0.5, power=0.8, sig.level=0.05,
+     n1=50)
          t-test power calculation
              n1 = 50
              n2 = 87.70891
               d = 0.5
       sig.level = 0.05
           power = 0.8
     alternative = two.sided
```

Therefore, we would need about 88 samples. You may encounter a following error
with the `pwr.t2n.test` function:

```
> pwr.t2n.test(d=0.5, power=0.8, sig.level=0.05, n1=20)
Error in uniroot(function(n2) eval(p.body) - power,
                 c(2 + 1e-10, 1e+07)) :
f() values at end points not of opposite sign
```

This means that your sample size for one group is too small. Thus the sample size
for the other is infinitely large, and the function was not able to complete a calculation.
So if you see this error, you definitely need more samples in both groups.

For an ANOVA test, we can use the `pwr.anova.test()` function. The parameters are similar except that k for the number of groups to compare, and f for the
effect size called Cohen's f. It can be converted from an eta-squared:

$$f - \sqrt{\frac{\eta^2}{1 - \eta^2}}$$

Suppose that we have three groups to compare, and we hypothesize that the effect
size of the underlying populations is medium. So we assume that it would be 0.06,
which is a plausible choice from Table 5.1. We also set the power to be 0.8. With all
of these, the sample size we would need to have is:

```
> pwr.anova.test(k=3, f=sqrt(0.06/(1-0.06)),
                 sig.level=0.05, power=0.8)
Balanced one-way analysis of variance power calculation
              k = 3
              n = 51.32635
              f = 0.2526456
      sig.level = 0.05
          power = 0.8
NOTE: n is number in each group
```

Thus, we would need 51 samples for each group. If you plan to do a repeated-measure ANOVA test, it is generally the case that you would need a little fewer samples, but this result would still serve as a good sample size estimate.

Similarly, you can perform power analysis on correlation and χ^2 tests with `pwr.r.test` and `pwr.chisq.test`, respectively. The pwr library does not include any function for non-parametric tests. You can use the function matching with equivalent parametric tests (e.g., paired *t-tests* for Wilcoxon tests), and use the results as a guide. You would likely need larger sample sizes than what the results show as non-parametric tests does not assume normality.

5.9.4   Retrospective Power Analysis (Caution: Not Recommended)

Retrospective power analysis is another analysis we should learn. It means that we are trying to estimate the power (or the observed power) based on the observed effect size. This looks similar to post hoc power analysis, but the difference is in the effect size: retrospective power analysis uses the observed power, and post hoc power analysis uses the true effect size of the underlying populations determined in a priori manner. This retrospective power analysis is often considered to be useful to determine if there is really no difference between the groups we are comparing.

However, retrospective power analysis is regarded as inappropriate for determining that differences between the groups do not exist. Many researchers have suggested avoiding this type of analysis. A more detailed discussion is available in Hoenig and Heisey's paper (Hoenig and Heisey 2001), but here is a quick summary of why retrospective power analysis is not appropriate: First, power analysis assumes the effect size of the underlying population. It is known that the estimated effect size (i.e., the one you calculate from the given data) is not generally a good approximation of the true effect size (the one we want to use for power analysis). Analysis with the estimated effect size would just generate results with low reliability.

Second, when you want to claim that there is no difference, you want your p value to be high (so it is unlikely that you say there is a difference although there is not) and your power to be also high (so it is unlikely that you say there is not a difference although there is). However, the p value and the observed power (the power calculated based on the estimated effect size) are somewhat correlated to each other; when the p value becomes large, the power tends to become low.

Unfortunately, there is a misunderstanding on the power analysis, and this retrospective power analysis is often seen in academic publications. When you see it, please interpret it with caution.

5.10 Conclusion

In this chapter, we discuss effect sizes and power analysis. Bruce Thompson cited the words of Roger Kirk to emphasize the importance of effect sizes in his article (Thompson 2007):

> It is evident that the current practice of focusing exclusively on a dichotomous reject–nonreject decision strategy of null hypothesis testing can actually **impede scientific progress** ... In fact, focusing on p values and rejecting null hypotheses actually **distracts us from our real goals**: deciding whether data support our scientific hypotheses and are practically significant. The focus of research should be on our scientific hypotheses, what data tell us about the magnitude of effects, the practical significance of effects, and the steady accumulation of knowledge. (Kirk 2003)

This applies to HCI research. It is very important to interpret statistical results in a broader context. We should pose more critical questions to these results: how large should the effect size be to interest us? What are implications of differences in a realistic setting? What contributions still remain that should the community share even if results are not statistically significant? Even effect sizes are not a panacea. The surface of statistical results would never give us the entire picture of phenomena. It is the responsibility of the researchers'—both authors and readers—to interpret results and discuss them in a fair manner.

References

[R] coin mamual. http://cran.r-project.org/web/packages/coin/coin.pdf
[R] ezANOVA manual. http://cran.r-project.org/web/packages/ez/ez.pdf
[R] MBESS manual. http://cran.r-project.org/web/packages/MBESS/MBESS.pdf
[R] pwr manual. http://cran.r-project.org/web/packages/pwr/pwr.pdf
Cohen J (1998) Statistical power analysis for the behavioral sciences, 2nd edn. Academic Press, New York
Field A (2005) Statistical hell: effect sizes. http://www.statisticshell.com/docs/effectsizes.pdf
Field A (2009) Discovering statistics using SPSS, 3rd edn. Sage Publications
Fisher RA (1925) Statistical methods for research workers. Oliver and Boyd
Hoenig JN, Heisey DM (2001) The abuse of power: the pervasive fallacy of power calculations for data analysis. Am Stat 55:19–24
Kirk RE (2003) The importance of effect magnitude. In: Davis SF (ed) Handbook of research methods in experimental psychology. Oxford, pp 83–105
Mizumoto A, Takeuchi O (2008) Basics and considerations for reporting effect sizes in research papers. English Language Education Society 31:57–66. (written in Japanese)
Nakagawa S, Cuthill IC (2007) Effect size, confidence interval and statistical significance: a practical guide for biologists. Biol Rev 82(4):591–605
Newcombe RG (2012) Confidence intervals for proportions and related measures of effect size. CRC Press, Boca Raton
Thompson B (2007) Effect sizes, confidence intervals, and confidence intervals for effect sizes. Psychol Schools 44(5):423–432

Chapter 6
Using R for Repeated and Time-Series Observations

Deborah Fry, Kerri Wazny and Niall Anderson

Abstract This chapter explores calculating two types of analyses that are often used for repeated measures designs: within-subjects Analysis of Variance (ANOVA) and Event History Analysis. Within-subjects ANOVA is used when members of a particular sample are exposed to several different conditions or experiments and the measurement of the dependent variable is repeated in each condition, thus inducing correlation between the set of dependent variable measurements for each individual. Event history analysis, by contrast, helps researchers to determine the probability that an event occurs at a particular time interval, making it useful for research questions that want to know how long it takes before the event of interest happens. Both of these analyses have particular relevance for the field of human-computer interaction and this chapter will explore how to use **R** for these two types of analyses using the Mango watch example.

6.1 Repeated Measures and Time Series in HCI

Many studies focused on human-computer interaction are interested in evaluating software by manipulating experiments or interactions with the same participants over time and measuring changes in the variables of interest. Thus, the term repeated measures is used to describe participants who engage in all conditions of an experiment or provide data at multiple time points. For example, it may be interesting to measure changes over time to student's learning on a particular Massive Open Online Course (MOOC) if there are different curriculum or pedagogical changes, or

D. Fry (✉)
Moray House School of Education, University of Edinburgh, Edinburgh, UK
e-mail: Debi.fry@ed.ac.uk

K. Wazny
Centre for Global Health Research, Usher Institute of Population Health Sciences
and Informatics, University of Edinburgh, Edinburgh, UK

N. Anderson
Centre for Population Health Sciences, Usher Institute of Population Health Sciences
and Informatics, University of Edinburgh, Edinburgh, UK

© Springer International Publishing Switzerland 2016   111
J. Robertson and M. Kaptein (eds.), *Modern Statistical Methods for HCI*,
Human–Computer Interaction Series, DOI 10.1007/978-3-319-26633-6_6

you could explore changes in user satisfaction with software as they become more familiar with it over several sessions. As the observations made within each subject must be correlated, analysis of these types of studies requires inferential approaches that will allow for the presence of repeated measures. This chapter will highlight two frequently used approaches: the within-subjects Analysis of Variance (ANOVA) and Event History Analysis.

6.2 An Introduction to Within-Subjects Analysis of Variance (ANOVA)

Repeated measures ANOVA, similar to other ANOVA methods, tests the equality of the means of a continuous outcome/dependent variable across a number of experimental groups. Repeated measures ANOVA is used when members of a particular sample are exposed to several different conditions or experiments and the measurement of the dependent variable is repeated in each condition, thus inducing correlation between the set of dependent variable measurements for each individual. This doesn't necessarily mean that every question asked or factor tested needs to be the same across every condition—as long as some are the same, then repeated measures methods should be used.

The difference between a repeated measures ANOVA design and a multivariate design for longitudinal data is that in the repeated measures design, each trial (or time point) represents the measurement of the same characteristic under a different condition. Using our example, a repeated measures ANOVA test can be used to compare the effectiveness of the Mango Watch at months one, two and three. The measurement is the effectiveness of the watch (as measured through productivity and sales), and the condition that changes is the month. A repeated measures ANOVA test, by contrast, should not be used to compare the types of watches worn by the sales team, the price of the watches, etc., as these do not represent different conditions, but different (independent) qualities.

Repeated measures ANOVA is useful in many circumstances. Firstly, it is used for repeated measures designs such as pretest-posttest designs, within-subjects experiments matched designs or multiple measures. Secondly, when a sample is difficult to recruit, repeated measures may be more a more cost effective way to run a trial because each respondent is measured under all conditions. Thirdly, some research questions are more suited to repeated measures designs such as those that look at changes within participants or that use time as a key variable. Finally, repeated measures can be used when respondents have been matched according to a specific characteristic and that characteristic is then used to group respondents. For example, consider choosing a group of students who have different experiences with using online technology for learning and grouping them into pairs having similar technology exposure backgrounds. One respondent from each pair can then be exposed to a different condition (say, two different introductory sessions of a Massive Open Online

Course or MOOC) and afterwards the entire sample is measured again. When sample members are matched, measurements across conditions are treated like repeated measures in a repeated measures ANOVA design. Lastly, within-subjects designs may have more power to detect significance than between-subjects designs. In essence, each participant is also his or her own control group (or there is a related other that serves as a control). This is useful because it can help eliminate variance due specifically to individual differences making the error term used in this technique more precise.

6.2.1 Assumptions of Within-Subjects ANOVA

There are several assumptions underpinning the within-subjects ANOVA design. The first is that the inferential method for within-subjects ANOVA relies on the assumption that the rate of change for all participants is constant. This is most appropriate for experimental designs where the repeated measures are conditions or measurements in the experiment that respondents participate in rather than time points where behaviour is observed, as is the case with more traditional longitudinal data.

Other ANOVA procedures (the between-subjects tests) assume different conditions are independent (i.e., not from the same people over time). This is also an underlying assumption of the *F-test* which is used to examine the null hypothesis of equality of group means. Since repeated measures are by definition obtained from the same participants (or whatever the objects/subjects of the experiment are), the independence assumption is violated which means that variables taken under different experimental conditions are still likely to be related because they are from the same participants. This proves problematic for the accuracy of the F-statistic and leads to a separate assumption for the within-subjects ANOVA of *sphericity*.

6.2.2 Sphericity

Sphericity means that we assume the relationship between pairs of experimental conditions is similar with approximately equal variances between them. In other words, the differences between all possible pairs of groups of the experiment are no more dependent than any other two pairs. If sphericity is violated, then variance calculations may be distorted leading to an inflated F-test statistic (and potential loss of power). Sphericity presents difficulties as well with *post-hoc* comparisons. Post hoc analyses involve looking for patterns or relationships between subgroups of the data (usually by comparing pairs of group means) that were not thought of before data was collected.[1] These tests are done after (or post hoc) the main analyses

---

[1] Chap. 14 discusses the problems resulting from uncorrected multiple comparisons in HCI, while Chap. 13 advises designing experiments in such a way as to avoid unplanned comparisons.

and are usually carried out to understand the patterns across groups that have driven statistically significant findings in the initial ANOVA. To compensate for the multiple comparisons, these tests use stronger criteria for significance to control for *Type 1 errors*, often known as 'false positives' or incorrectly rejecting a true null hypothesis (no difference between the means). In other words, multiple comparisons can lead to an increased likelihood of apparently significant findings where none exist. When sphericity is violated, the Bonferroni post-hoc method may be more robust than other methods for control of the Type 1 error rate (Field et al. 2012). When sphericity is not violated, other post-hoc measures such as *Tukey's Wholly Significant Difference (WSD)* test can be used.

Since sphericity is an assumption of the dependence and equality of variances between treatment conditions, at least three conditions or experiments (or points of data collection) are needed for sphericity to occur and with each additional repeated measures factor, the risk for violating sphericity increases. *Mauchly's test,* which tests the hypothesis that the variances of the differences between the conditions are equal, is therefore used to assess levels of sphericity. If Mauchly's test is significant ($p < 0.05$) then we would conclude that there are significant differences between the variance of differences in conditions and sphericity may not be present in the data.

6.2.3   Correcting for Sphericity

There are two different tests that can be used to correct for sphericity if it is present in the data developed by Greenhouse and Geisser (1959) and Huynh and Feldt (1976) with tests that match the names of the authors that developed them. Academics recommend that when estimates of sphericity are greater than 75 the *Huynh-Feldt correction* should be used but when they are less than 75 or unknown then the *Greenhouse-Geisser correction* can be used (Girden 1992; Field et al. 2012). Since sphericity affects the F-statistic, another option is to use a test that does not rely on the F distribution. One option is to use a multivariate test statistic because they do not make assumptions about sphericity.

6.3   Conceptual Model for Within-Subjects ANOVA

The conceptual model for the Within-Subjects ANOVA is presented in Fig. 6.1. Here we can see the total variability is made up of the within participant variability which is influenced by the effect of the condition plus random error. It shows that the same respondents participate in each condition on the same factors.

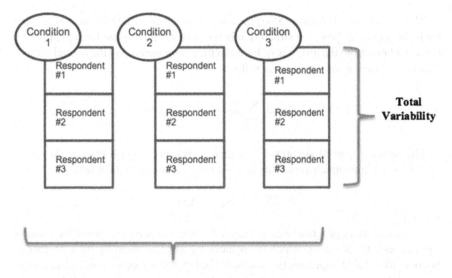

Within Participant Variability = Effect of condition + Error (variation between respondents not explained by the condition)

Fig. 6.1 Conceptual model for within-subjects ANOVA

6.4   Statistical Inference for Within-Subjects ANOVA

We can also present this same concept statistically. To calculate a repeated measures
ANOVA, the total sum of squares, within-participant sum of squares, model sum of
squares, residual sum of squares and mean squares need to be calculated in order to
calculate the F-ratio. Their equations are:

Total sum of squares (SS_T)

$$SS_T = (N - 1)s_{grand}^2$$

where N is the total number of values used in the calculation and $s^2{}_{grand}$ is the grand
variance. This quantity represents the total variability in the dependent variable in a
form that will allow us to partition it into components representing different facets
of the structure of the model, as well as the variability due to residual error (in the
sense of variability unexplained by the model structure).

The within-participant sum of squares (SS_W) identifies the variability across the
repeated measurements for each individual, summing each quantity to give a model
total:

$$SS_W = (n_1 - 1)s_{person\ 1}^2 + (n_2 - 1)s_{person\ 2}^2 + \cdots (n_n - 1)s_{person\ n}^2$$

where n_i represents the number of measurements for the i-th person.

The model sum of squares (SS_M) measures how much variability we can account for by introducing the group structure inherent in the ANOVA model, which is why it is calculated from the differences between the group means and the overall (grand) mean of the dependent variable, as follows:

$$SS_M = \sum_{n=1}^{k} n_k (\bar{x}_k - \bar{x}_{grand})^2$$

The residual sum of squares (SS_R) then represents the converse of the above quantity—i.e. how much variability has not been captured by the model:

$$SS_R = SS_W - SS_M$$

To make further progress with formal inference, we need to convert the sums of squares back to variances, which we achieve by dividing them by their degrees of freedom (df). The df represent the number of independent pieces of information used to calculate the relevant quantity: for example

$$df_R = df_W - df_M$$

where df_M would be the number of groups minus 1 and df_W the number of individuals participating in the study.

To calculate the mean squares (MS_M and MS_R), you use the following equations:

$$MS_M = \frac{SS_M}{df_M}$$

$$MS_R = \frac{SS_R}{df_R}$$

Finally, to calculate the F-ratio:

$$F = \frac{MS_M}{MS_R}$$

A successful model will capture a large proportion of the total variability, which will be identified by the F statistic increasing in size, driven by relatively larger values of MS_M in comparison to MS_R.

Like an independent ANOVA, the F-value is compared against a critical value based on its degrees of freedom (Field et al. 2012).

6.5   Calculating Within-Subjects ANOVA Using R

First we will need to install several packages (see also Chap. 2) and load them using the following functions:

```
> library (pastecs)
> library (ggplot2)
> library (ez)
> library (nlme)
> library (multcomp)
```

Using the Mango watch data (please also see Chap. 2 for how to load the data), we will want to first explore the data utilising descriptive statistics and also to check for sphericity. We want to explore whether usability scores for the Mango watch were different during different months. We will pick one of the usability questions. In our case, we have picked SuS10, which is "I needed to learn a lot of things before I could get going with this system." We would expect that the users would be less likely to agree with this over time as they get used to the watch.

Firstly, we need to ensure we have changed Time to a factor. We do this by inputting:

```
> scale$Time <- factor(scale$Time)
```

We want to ensure that the data appear normal, so we will explore the data using descriptive statistics, separately for each time point. To do this, we input:

```
> by(scale$SUS10, scale$Time, stat.desc)
```

We will see the following table:

Table 6.1 Descriptive statistics for question 10 on the SUS scale

scale$Time: 1

nbr.val	nbr.null	nbr.na	min	max	range	sum
86.0000000	0.0000000	0.0000000	1.0000000	6.0000000	5.0000000	255.0000000
median	mean	SE.mean	CI.mean.0.95	var	std.dev	coef.var
3.0000000	2.9651163	0.1038884	0.2065579	0.9281806	0.9634213	0.3249186

scale$Time: 2

nbr.val	nbr.null	nbr.na	min	max	range	sum
86.0000000	0.0000000	0.0000000	1.0000000	6.0000000	5.0000000	289.0000000
median	mean	SE.mean	CI.mean.0.95	var	std.dev	coef.var
3.0000000	3.3604651	0.1132927	0.2252562	1.1038304	1.0506333	0.3126452

scale$Time: 3

nbr.val	nbr.null	nbr.na	min	max	range	sum
86.0000000	0.0000000	0.0000000	1.0000000	6.0000000	5.0000000	314.0000000
median	mean	SE.mean	CI.mean.0.95	var	std.dev	coef.var
4.0000000	3.6511628	0.1094289	0.2175739	1.0298222	1.0148015	0.2779393

This table displays descriptive statistics such as the minimum and maximum values, along with the mean, median, standard errors and standard deviations for SUS10. You'll notice that at Time 1, 2 and 3, the maximum value is 6. As the SUS Usability Scale is a scale of 1–5, we know that scores of 6 are errors. As such, we must make a decision of how to deal with these scores. When this happens in your research, you must use your judgment to decide how to handle impossible entries. Another, real-life, example of an impossible entry would be an age of 100 in a study of children up to 10 years of age. Sometimes, it is easy to see that the entry is a typo and to see what the entry is meant to be, like in the case of the age of 100—it is likely a 10-year old child. It is always good practice to re-check the original data collection forms, if possible. If the incorrect data is impossible to decipher or if you cannot say with certainty it is a typo, it is better to exclude it from the analysis. These decisions need to be made on a case-by-case basis. In our case, we will assume that the entries with value 6 are typos and were intended to take the value 5. Thus, we will need to change all values of 6 to 5 in order to proceed with our analysis. To do this, we input the following:

```
> scale$SUS10[scale$SUS10>5]<-5
```

Because the questions in the usability scale alternate from being a positive question to a negative one, we need to convert them to being measured on the same scale. We do this by subtracting user-responses of even-numbered SUS questions from five and odd-numbered SUS questions from one. We end up with a scale of 0–4, with four being the most positive response and zero being the most negative. Since we have chosen SUS10, which is an even numbered question, we will need to subtract user-responses from 5. We will create another variable in order to do this (Table 6.1):

```
> scale$SUS10a<-5-scale$SUS10
```

Now we can explore this new variable with some descriptive statistics:

```
> by(scale$SUS10a, scale$Time, stat.desc)
```

The results are presented in Table 6.2:

Table 6.2 Descriptive statistics of the transformed question 10 on the SUS scale

```
scale$Time: 1
      nbr.val      nbr.null       nbr.na          min          max        range          sum       median
   86.0000000     3.0000000    0.0000000    0.0000000    4.0000000    4.0000000  176.0000000    2.0000000
         mean       SE.mean  CI.mean.0.95          var      std.dev     coef.var
    2.0465116     0.1004872    0.1997954    0.8683995    0.9318795    0.4553502
-----------------------------------------------------------------------------------
scale$Time: 2
      nbr.val      nbr.null       nbr.na          min          max        range          sum       median
   86.0000000    11.0000000    0.0000000    0.0000000    4.0000000    4.0000000  143.0000000    2.0000000
         mean       SE.mean  CI.mean.0.95          var      std.dev     coef.var
    1.6627907     0.1079728    0.2146789    1.0025992    1.0012987    0.6021797
-----------------------------------------------------------------------------------
scale$Time: 3
      nbr.val      nbr.null       nbr.na          min          max        range          sum       median
   86.0000000    17.0000000    0.0000000    0.0000000    4.0000000    4.0000000  118.0000000    1.0000000
         mean       SE.mean  CI.mean.0.95          var      std.dev     coef.var
    1.3720930     0.1046740    0.2081199    0.9422709    0.9707064    0.7074640
```

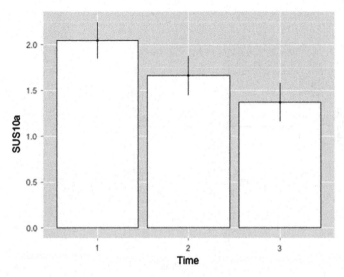

Fig. 6.2   Bar chart with error bars for transformed SUS question 10

Again, we can see descriptive statistics such as the mean, median, minimum, maximum, standard deviation and standard error. We can check that this time, the values fall into the range of what we would expect.

We can also use graphs to explore the data. Using the following script in the ggplot2 package gives us a bar graph with error bars as displayed in Fig. 6.2.

```
> SuSgraph<- ggplot(scale, aes(Time,SUS10a))
> SuSgraph + stat_summary(
+    fun.y=mean,geom="bar",fill="White",
+    colour="Black")+stat_summary(
+    fun.data=mean_cl_normal,geom="pointrange"
+    )
```

If we then input

```
> SuSgraph + geom_boxplot()
```

we will get the boxplot displayed in Fig. 6.3.

Contrary to our intuition, both the graph (Fig. 6.2) and the boxplot (Fig. 6.3) confirm visually that users found the Mango watch more difficult to use as time went on, since 4 is a more positive response and 0 is a more negative one. We can see that users were more likely to give a positive response at Time 1 and less likely to have a positive response at Time 2 and 3 (Figs. 6.2 and 6.3).

The ezANOVA package will let us quickly see whether there are significant differences in usability scores across months one, two and three. This package is useful

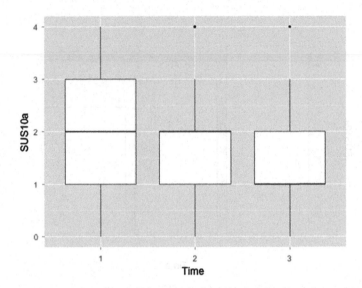

Fig. 6.3 Boxplot overview of the SUS question 10 (transformed) data

```
$ANOVA
        Effect DFn DFd       SSn       SSd         F              p p<.05        ges
1 (Intercept)   1  85 740.18992  77.47674 812.06489 2.899608e-45      * 0.7558220
2        Time   2 170  19.68217 161.65116  10.34935 5.735892e-05      * 0.0760487

$`Mauchly's Test for Sphericity`
  Effect       W        p p<.05
2   Time 0.997653 0.9060218

$`Sphericity Corrections`
  Effect       GGe       p[GG] p[GG]<.05       HFe       p[HF] p[HF]<.05
2   Time 0.9976584 5.828956e-05         * 1.021613 5.735892e-05         *
```

Fig. 6.4 ezANOVA output

to give us a snapshot of whether there are differences and if so, we can move onto a more in-depth analysis using the `nlme` package. To run `ezANOVA`, we enter:

```
> scale$ID <- factor(scale$ID); # Converts ID to a factor, as required by package
>
> ezscale <- ezANOVA(
+   data=scale,dv=.(SUS10a),wid=.(ID),
+   within=.(Time),detailed= TRUE,type=3
+   )
> ezscale
```

Figure 6.4 shows the output that is created using the above command.

As we can see in Fig. 6.4, there is a significant difference across months one, two and three. `ezANOVA` does not show us which months are causing the differences. This will need to be explored in the `nlme` package. We can also see that the requirement of sphericity has been met through Mauchly's test, as the p-value is non-significant.

We will want to set contrasts so that we can see where the differences between groups lie. In order to do this, we'll create dummy variables. The model calculated by *ezANOVA* above uses a standard approach to constructing (or parameterising, to use the statistical jargon) ANOVA models, in that 2 parameters are used to represent the effects at the 3 different time points. Time point 1 is regarded as a reference or baseline value (arbitrarily—one of the other points could play this role as an alternative) and then the first parameter estimates the difference between time points 1 and 2, and the second parameter estimates the difference between time points 1 and 3. In thinking about which months might differ from the others in our case, it could make sense that the steepest learning curve for the Mango watch would occur in Month 1. So, we might prefer to compare Month 1 with Months 2 and 3 taken together and then also to compare Month 2 and Month 3. Or, in this case, we can see that there is the biggest difference graphically between the first month and the second and third. So, we will separate the first month. Therefore, we would like to replace the original two parameters in the model discussed above with 2 *contrasts* representing the new effects of interest, so that we can have the model make these comparisons explicitly.

It is worth noting at this point that there is no obligation to carry out this step in your analysis. However, if you find that there are significant differences in your model and you think the differences are due to comparisons between groups that the regression itself is not able to explore, it may be worth setting up contrasts in order to explore this hypothesis.

When beginning to set up contrasts, you must first think of which groups it would make sense to compare. As previously mentioned, in our case, there seems to be a large difference between the first month and months two and three when exploring the data graphically. Therefore, we want to compare Month 1 with Months 2 and 3 (as a group) before comparing Month 2 with Month 3. Unfortunately, you cannot create an unlimited number of contrasts (and therefore cannot compare everything). The maximum total number of contrasts that can uniquely be estimated is the number of variables minus 1. Once a variable is used independently in a contrast, it cannot be used in the contrast again. So, since we've already used month 1 in comparison to months 2 and 3 together, month 1 cannot be used again in a contrast. Finally, you need to create a weight table using positive and negative integers for your contrasts and the weights should add up to 0. See Table 6.3 for a visual example of a weight table.

Table 6.3 Contrasts table for dummy variables

Month	Contrast 1	Contrast 2
1	2	0
2	−1	1
3	−1	−1
Total	0	0

Contrast 1 works because we assign the same weight to Times 2 and 3, but we ensure that these weights have opposite sign to the weight for Time 1, which must therefore equal 2 to cancel out the other two weights—in spirit we are therefore setting up the subtraction *Time 1—(Time 2 + Time 3)*. Contrast 2 is easier to understand—the 0 weight knocks out Time 1, then directly compares Time 2 against Time 3.

Once we've created our table, we enter the following code to set up the contrasts within **R**:

```
> EarlyvsLate<-c(2,-1,-1)

> TwovsThree<-c(0,1,-1)

> contrasts(scale$Time)<-cbind(EarlyvsLate,
TwovsThree)
```

We then set-up our model using the nlme package using the commands below. The output is presented in Fig. 6.5.

```
> newscale<-lme(SUS10a~Time, random=~1|ID/Time,
data=scale, method="ML")

> baseline<-lme(SUS10a~1,random=~1|ID/Time,
data=scale, method="ML")

> anova(baseline,newscale)

> summary(newscale)
```

The ANOVA table indicates that the Time effect is extremely significant ($p < 0.0001$), as we would expect. The lme() fit indicates that this is substantially due to the difference between month 1 and the two later measurement times, but that the second and third times are perhaps less different (although with a marginal p-value). You will notice that this model shows our contrasts with their names.

If we still want to explore further, we can carry out post-hoc analyses. These analyses will display all the individual comparisons, which will let us see whether there is a difference between month 1 and month 3.

We enter the following into **R**:

```
> postHocs<-glht(newscale,linfct=mcp(Time = "Tukey"))

> summary(postHocs)

> confint(postHocs)
```

```
> anova(baseline,newscale)
          Model df    AIC      BIC     logLik   Test  L.Ratio p-value
baseline      1  4 740.9811 755.1929 -366.4905
newscale      2  6 724.5743 745.8921 -356.2872 1 vs 2 20.40675  <.0001
> summary(newscale)
Linear mixed-effects model fit by maximum likelihood
 Data: scale
       AIC      BIC     logLik
  724.5743 745.8921 -356.2872

Random effects:
 Formula: ~1 | ID
         (Intercept)
StdDev: 0.0001582073

 Formula: ~1 | Time %in% ID
         (Intercept)    Residual
StdDev:    0.9626984 0.008001545

Fixed effects: SUS10a ~ Time
                   Value  Std.Error  DF   t-value p-value
(Intercept)     1.6937984 0.06028860 170 28.094838  0.0000
TimeEarlyvsLate 0.1763566 0.04263048 170  4.136867  0.0001
TimeTwovsThree  0.1453488 0.07383815 170  1.968479  0.0506
 Correlation:
                (Intr) TmErlL
TimeEarlyvsLate 0
TimeTwovsThree  0       0

Standardized Within-Group Residuals:
        Min            Q1           Med            Q3           Max
-0.0176675980 -0.0057218926 -0.0004015363  0.0054207404  0.0226868019

Number of Observations: 258
Number of Groups:
          ID Time %in% ID
          86          258
```

Fig. 6.5 Output of the anova() and summary() functions using the nlme package for the analysis of SUS10 (transformed)

where 'glht' in the **R** code above refers to 'general linear hypothesis' and provides comparisons for parametric models, including generalized linear models, linear mixed effects models, and survival models. Figure 6.6 presents the **R** output.

Simultaneous Tests for General Linear Hypotheses

Multiple Comparisons of Means: Tukey Contrasts

Fit: lme.formula(fixed = SUS10a ~ Time, data = scale, random = ~1 |
    ID/Time, method = "ML")

Linear Hypotheses:
          Estimate Std. Error z value Pr(>|z|)
2 - 1 == 0 -0.3837   0.1468 -2.614   0.0242 *
3 - 1 == 0 -0.6744   0.1468 -4.594   <0.001 ***
3 - 2 == 0 -0.2907   0.1468 -1.980   0.1171

Signif. codes: 0 '***' 0.001 '**' 0.01 '*' 0.05 '.' 0.1 ' ' 1
(Adjusted p values reported -- single-step method)

> confint(postHocs)

Simultaneous Confidence Intervals

Multiple Comparisons of Means: Tukey Contrasts

Fit: lme.formula(fixed = SUS10a ~ Time, data = scale, random = ~1 |
    ID/Time, method = "ML")

Quantile = 2.3437
95% family-wise confidence level

Linear Hypotheses:
          Estimate lwr   upr
2 - 1 == 0 -0.38372 -0.72781 -0.03963
3 - 1 == 0 -0.67442 -1.01851 -0.33033
3 - 2 == 0 -0.29070 -0.63479 0.05340

Fig. 6.6 Output of the glht package, calculating all pairwise comparisons (by both hypothesis tests and confidence intervals) between time points using Tukey's method, for the transformed SUS10 data

6.6 Interpreting and Presenting the Within-Subjects ANOVA Findings

As we can see, there is a significant difference across months one, two and three, although with relatively little difference between months two and three. Mauchly's test indicated that the assumption of sphericity had been met ($p = 0.906$), therefore the degrees of freedom did not need to be corrected. The results show that the learning usability of the Mango watch (as measured by the answer to SUS10 question) was significantly affected by month of use with a significant reduction in usability apparent between months one and three ($p = 0.001$). Further tests need to be conducted to determine if this decrease in usability of the Mango Watch is hampering productivity of the sales executive team, which was the purpose of introducing the watch in the first instance.

6.7 An Introduction to Event History Analysis

Event history analysis helps researchers to determine the probability that an event occurs at a particular time interval, making it useful for research questions that want to know how long it takes before the event of interest happens. *Event History Analysis* is also called *survival analysis* in the biomedical disciplines, where the event of interest is often onset of disease or death from illness; *duration modelling* in econometrics, where the event of interest could be specific policies or major political or economic events; *reliability analysis* in engineering, where the event of interest could be a particular function of a design feature; and *event history analysis* within many of the social sciences, where the event of interest can range from political revolutions to language acquisition to children becoming adopted. Within the human-computer interaction field, which is very interdisciplinary, it may be referred to under any of these terms. Within this chapter, we will refer to it as Event History Analysis.

There is terminology related to Event History Analysis that may be new to readers who have never used this technique before. The first is that the analyses are primarily concerned with *events* (which are sometimes referred to as *failures* even if it's not a negative event) and the time of occurrence to such an event. Table 6.4 gives an example of the types of 'events' that are commonly measured in the human-computer interaction field and what terminology is used in these examples.

The event history is measured in time and time can be measured in different units such as seconds, days, weeks, months, years, or even decades. The duration of time it takes before the event of interest occurs is called *survival time* (or duration time, episode time, waiting time, exposure time or risk period). There may be instances when you do not know the exact time that the event occurred but just that it occurred within a particular interval (such as a year), this is called *discrete-time*. Whether time to event is measured precisely on a continuous scale or whether a discrete-time model is used, both model the risk of the event occurring at time (t).

Table 6.4 Examples of event history analysis in the human-computer interaction field

Start	Event history	Event (and terminology)
Modelling various online subcommunities on the level of participation in threaded discussions in three separate MOOCs	Various measurements across time	Student drop-out in MOOCs (Yang et al. 2014)
Utilising a visual analytic system with cancer patients to explore integrative genomics data in order to put patients into subgroups to provide better care		Death of cancer patients in subgroups (Ding et al. 2014)
Exploring the use of satellite technology (through distance education networks and a primary school network in one state) on access to education in India		Events (such as number of new entrants, number of patents, R&D projects funded, etc.) are matched to an analytical framework of events contributing to system functions (Iyer 2014)
Elderly tremor patients using touchscreen technologies with and without swabbing (an input method for touchscreen systems based on motions)		Error rate using touchscreen technology (Mertens et al. 2012)

Additionally, the dependent or outcome variable is called the *hazard rate*, which examines the conditional probability that an event occurs at a time (t). The independent (or input) variables that can influence this can either be *fixed* (do not change across time) such as a respondent's race, ethnicity or place of birth or these variables can be *time-varying* (they do change across time) such as age, educational attainment and training, attitudes, etc.

Event History Analysis is based on regression models but with different likelihood estimates than ordinary least squares (OLS) models. Likelihood functions are needed for fitting parameters or making other kinds of inferences with the data. Due to the element of repeated measures over time leading to an event, and with the likelihood of some missing data, the Event History Analysis takes into account censored data.

6.7.1 Censoring

Censoring occurs when there is only partial information about the time to event outcome measurement for a study participant, and this "missing" data may occur in the survival analysis in a number of different ways. *Right censoring* occurs when a subject leaves the study before an event occurs, or the study ends before the event has occurred. So in our example, if someone had left the Mango watch company before month three, these participants would be censored with respect to relevant time to event outcome measurements. *Left Censoring* is where the event of interest (or loss to follow-up) has occurred before enrolment into the study (this is more rare).

6.8 Statistical Model for Event History Analysis

In the following section, we will be using the Kaplan Meier product limit estimate, the log-rank test and Cox's Proportional Hazards Model for survival.

The Kaplan Meier product limit estimate is a step function that estimates the probability of surviving to time k, and is calculated as

$$p_k = p_{k-1} \times \frac{r_k - f_k}{r_k}$$

where p is the probability of surviving for k days, r_k is the number of individuals alive before time k and f_k deaths occur at time k.

To calculate the confidence interval around the Kaplan-Meier curve, the following formula is used

$$SE(p_k) = p_k \sqrt{\sum_{j=1}^{k} \left[\frac{f_j}{r_j(r_j - f_j)} \right]}$$

For the log-rank test, we use the expected and observed events (or deaths) at each time point at which there is an event, forming a 2×2 table of events and non-events by group. The expected numbers of deaths are calculated in the usual way for a 2×2 table, and then we calculate the total number of observed events (O1) and non-events (O2) and expected events (E1) and non-events (E2) across all of the contingency tables for the data set. We can then test the null hypothesis that the distributions of events are identical between the two groups using a chi-squared test with 1 degree of freedom based on the following test statistic.

$$\chi^2 = \frac{(O_1 - E_1)^2}{E_1} + \frac{(O_2 - E_2)^2}{E_2}$$

The Cox Model is defined in terms of the hazard function, h(t), which represents the instantaneous risk of an event at time t, assuming the absence of an event prior to time t. If we have several covariates of interest, say X_1 to X_p, the proportional hazards model says that the hazard function, h(t), is given by

$$h(t) = h_0(t) \exp (b_1 X_1 + b_2 X_2 + \cdots + b_p X_p).$$

Here $h_0(t)$, the baseline (or underlying) hazard function, corresponds to the hazard function when all of the covariates take the value zero. The function $h_0(t)$, together with the regression coefficients b_1 to b_p, are all estimated from the data.

Under the model, the hazard function for any individual is thus assumed to be a multiple of the underlying hazard ratio, and the ratio of the hazard functions for any two individuals will be constant for all values of t (since t is not involved in the exp() term on the right-hand side of the equation above). For example, in our case, we have Group A and Group B. This structure can be represented by a single covariate that has a value of 0 for Group A and 1 Group B, so that then the hazard functions for individuals in groups A and B (assuming no other covariates are of interest) will be:

$$h_A(t) = h_0(t) \exp(0) = h_0(t),$$
$$h_B(t) = h_0(t) \exp(b)$$

and then the hazard ratio of an individual in group B relative to an individual in group A will be

$$h_B(t)/h_A(t) = \{h_0(t) \exp(b)\} / h_0(t) = \exp(b)$$

which is a constant value, independent of t. This gives rise to the term "proportional hazards" in the name of the model, and this forms a key underlying assumption when we come to fit Cox models to data.

6.9   Calculating Event History Analysis Using R

In order to calculate survival analysis, we will need to load the survival library:

```
> library(survival)
```

We will be asking if there is a difference in time to respond to emails during month three between Mango watch users and non-Mango watch users. In this case, not having responded to an email is synonymous with not having died in a classic survival analysis—the event, which is usually death is now responding to an email.

Because we will be looking solely at month 3 of the email data, our first step will be to create a new data frame restricted to that time frame. We will do this by:

```
> email3<-subset(email,Time==3)
```

Now, our new data frame is called 'email3.' We also need to create a status column for those who have responded versus those who have not responded. Fortunately for us, this company is amazing, everyone responds to their emails and nobody quit their job and ran away with the new Mango watch. So, we can create this column by:

```
> email3$status<-rep("Responded",dim(email3)[1])
```

Here, the "dim(email3)" part of the code is saying to write "Responded" by the dimensions of the email3 data frame. But, if your world isn't as perfect as ours, you will need to manually code the Status column for each participant. This is easiest to do if your participants are organized so that the first X amount have responded and the last Y amount have not. For example, if there are 200 participants and the first 150 have responded but the last 50 have not, you could use the following to add the status column:

```
> email3$status<-c(rep(
```

```
+    "Responded",150),rep("No Response",50))
```

We found that the email data weren't amenable for the full analyses that we wanted to demonstrate, so we also created another data frame called "email3swap." In the real world, not everyone will stay at a company or answer an email. So, we've added some censoring to make the data more realistic. Please switch to this data frame for the remaining analyses.

After attaching our new data frame (thus ensuring that we can refer to individual variables without the data.frame$variable.name full-length reference),

```
> attach(email3swap)
```

we can examine the survival object that will be used as the outcome variable in further survival modelling functions:

```
> Surv(responseTime,status=="Responded")
```

In this object, censored observations are marked with a + sign, so that the Surv() object is a composite one consisting of both the survival time and the censoring flag.

Now, we'll create Kaplan-Meier plots to graphically view the survival curves for Mango watch users and non-Mango watch users for time to email response. First, we'll create a survfit object. In our case, we will get information from this because we do not have considerable censoring; however, there will be instances where non-censored events will not even make up half the total events, making a median inestimable. The resulting plot is presented in Fig. 6.7.

Fig. 6.7 The Kaplan-Meier
plot for response time in
Teams A and *B*

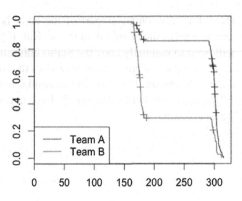

```
> surv.byTeam<-survfit(Surv(

+     responseTime,status=="Responded")~Team)

> Surv.byTeam; # For descriptive statistics


Call: survfit(formula = Surv(responseTime, status =="Responded") ~
  Team)


          records n.max n.start events median 0.95LCL 0.95UCL
Team=Team A     109   109     109     99    301     299     302
Team=Team B      91    91      91     84    177     176     179

> plot(surv.byTeam,conf.int=F,col=c("black","red"))

> legend("bottomleft",

+     c("Team A","Team B"),

+     col=c("black","red"),lty=1)
```

In this Kaplan-Meier plot, the black line represents Team A and the red, Team B.
Each 'tick' on the graph represents an episode of censoring. In a typical 'survival'
plot, this would represent someone either dropping out of the study or dying. However
in our case, this is more likely due to someone quitting, deleting the email prior to
responding, the Mango watch breaking or some explanation other than answering the
email. If censoring were to have occurred disproportionately on one side or the other,
that could be a sign of bias in your study. Our survival curve has very few downward
"steps"; however, normally survival curves have many small drops which indicate
events (i.e. deaths, or in our case, responses to an email). In this study, the majority
of the respondents in Team A seemed to have responded at the 160–180 second mark
or just after 300 s before the experiment closed whereas team B, who received the

```
Call:
survdiff(formula = Surv(responseTime, status == "Responded") ~
    Team)

                N Observed Expected (O-E)^2/E (O-E)^2/V
Team=Team A 109       99    136.2     10.2      42.1
Team=Team B  91       84     46.8     29.6      42.1

Chisq= 42.1  on 1 degrees of freedom, p= 8.56e-11
```

Fig. 6.8 Output of the log rank test for response time

Mango watch, responded slightly earlier. In either case, customers got a fairly fast response time, and we might wonder whether shaving a couple of minutes off an email response time really has enough of an impact on sales to merit the cost of the Mangos (see Chap. 14 for more discussion of effect size and real world significance).

We can use a log rank test to explore whether the two survival curves are identical. To do this, we input:

```
> survdiff(Surv(responseTime,

+    status==''Responded'')~Team).
```

which produces the output presented in Fig. 6.8.

We can now try to fit a Cox Proportional Hazards model. To do this, we enter the following (result displayed in Fig. 6.9):

```
> team.ph<-coxph(

+        Surv(responseTime,status==''Responded'')~Team)

> summary(team.ph)
```

We will also check the assumption of proportional hazards using the following formula (results presented in Fig. 6.10):

```
> cox.zph(team.ph)

> plot(cox.zph(team.ph))
```

The function calculates a correlation (rho) between the residuals and the Kaplan-Meier estimate of survival at each time, which takes the value -0.318, suggesting that the "hazard" of a response is decreasing over time. The Chi-squared test (of the null

```
Call:
coxph(formula = Surv(responseTime, status == "Responded") ~ Team)

   n= 200, number of events= 183

              coef exp(coef) se(coef)     z Pr(>|z|)
TeamTeam B 0.9689    2.6350   0.1543 6.28 3.39e-10 ***
---
Signif. codes:  0 '***' 0.001 '**' 0.01 '*' 0.05 '.' 0.1 ' ' 1

           exp(coef) exp(-coef) lower .95 upper .95
TeamTeam B     2.635     0.3795     1.947     3.565

Concordance= 0.653  (se = 0.02 )
Rsquare= 0.171    (max possible= 1 )
Likelihood ratio test= 37.52  on 1 df,    p=9.052e-10
Wald test              = 39.44  on 1 df,    p=3.386e-10
Score (logrank) test = 42.13  on 1 df,    p=8.558e-11
```

Fig. 6.9 Output of the Cox proportional hazards model for response time in terms of Team

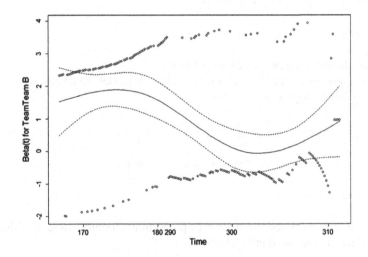

Fig. 6.10 Checking the proportional hazard assumption for the response time Cox model

hypothesis that this change is equal to 0) is extremely significant, so the proportional hazards assumption is not satisfied—it appears that the relative likelihood of a Team B member responding compared to a Team A member reduces over time, rather than being constant as the Cox model assumes.

6.10 Interpreting and Presenting the Event History Analysis Findings

In this study, the majority of the respondents in Team A responded at the 160–180 second mark or just after 300 s before the experiment closed whereas team B, who received the Mango watch, responded slightly earlier with few people quitting, deleting the email prior to responding or other events such as the Mango watch breaking. The differences between these two groups are significant suggesting that the conditional probability of responding to an email in month three is higher among Mango watch users. However, there is some evidence that this effect decreases over time, and therefore we would not want to place any weight on the hazard ratio of 2.6 (95 % CI: 1.95, 3.56) that we obtain from the Cox model—the group difference appears to be reducing noticeably at the longer response times, which prevents a single numerical measure like a hazard ratio capturing the behaviour exhibited by the data.

Unlike other measures, event history analysis shows the differences over time and the amount of time duration before one or more events happen. This can be incredibly helpful for figuring out optimal time points for interventions or the amount of time needed before a particular outcomes is seen.

Please note: All analyses were done on a Mac using OS 10.10.5 and in **R** Studio using version 0.98.1102. Very small numerical differences may be expected when using different operating systems or versions of **R** or **R** Studio or when using different versions of the packages used for the analyses.

References

Ding H, Wang C, Huang K, Machiraju R (2014) iGPSe: a visual analytic system for integrative genomic based cancer patient stratification. BMC Bioinformatics 15(203):1–13

Field AP, Miles J, Field Z (2012) Discovering statistics using R. Sage, London

Girden ER (1992) ANOVA: repeated measures. Sage university papers series on quantitative applications in the social sciences, vol 84. Sage, Thousand Oaks, CA

Greenhouse SW, Geisser S (1959) On methods in the analysis of profile data. Psychometrika 24:95–112

Huynh H, Feldt LS (1976) Estimation of the box correction for degrees of freedom from sample data in randomized block and split=plot designs. J Educ Stat 1:69–82

Iyer CG (2014) Harnassing satellite technology for education development: case studies from India. Innov Dev 4:129–143

Mertens A, Hurtmanns J, Wacharamanotham C, Kronenburger M, Borchers J, Schlick CM (2012) Swabbing: touchscreen-based input technique for people with hand tremor. Work 41:2405–2411

Yang D, Wen M, Kumar A, Xing EP, Rose CP (2014) Towards an integration of text and graph clustering methods as a lens for studying social interaction in MOOCs. Int Rev Res Open Distance Learn 15:215–234

Chapter 7
Nonparametric Statistics in Human–Computer Interaction

Jacob O. Wobbrock and Matthew Kay

Abstract Data not suitable for classic parametric statistical analyses arise frequently in human–computer interaction studies. Various nonparametric statistical procedures are appropriate and advantageous when used properly. This chapter organizes and illustrates multiple nonparametric procedures, contrasting them with their parametric counterparts. Guidance is given for when to use nonparametric analyses and how to interpret and report their results.

7.1 Introduction

The field of human–computer interaction (HCI) is diverse in many ways. Its researchers and practitioners come from all over the academic spectrum, from social sciences like psychology, sociology, and anthropology, technical endeavors like computer science, information science, and electrical engineering, and design disciplines like product design, graphic design, interaction design, and architecture. With such a wide range of backgrounds, methods, and phenomena of interest, it is no wonder that almost any kind of data may arise as part of a study in HCI.

Whether we are examining people's interactions with existing technology or evaluating new technologies that we invent, it is common to find that our data is not amenable to conventional parametric analyses. Such analyses, most commonly the familiar analysis of variance (ANOVA), are based on assumptions often violated by data arising from HCI studies. Different "nonparametric" analyses are needed to properly draw conclusions from such data.

J.O. Wobbrock (✉)
The Information School, University of Washington, Seattle, WA 98195-2840, USA
e-mail: wobbrock@uw.edu

M. Kay
Department of Computer Science and Engineering, University of Washington, Seattle,
WA 98195-2350, USA
e-mail: mjskay@uw.edu

© Springer International Publishing Switzerland 2016   135
J. Robertson and M. Kaptein (eds.), *Modern Statistical Methods for HCI*,
Human–Computer Interaction Series, DOI 10.1007/978-3-319-26633-6_7

This chapter reviews nonparametric analyses, many of which are commonly found in HCI studies, and others that are more recently emerging but could be of value to HCI researchers and practitioners. For historical context, this chapter endeavors to cite the original articles where the analyses first appeared. But before plunging into the analyses themselves, let us first understand when to use nonparametric analyses.

7.2   When to Use Nonparametric Analyses

As Chap. 3 described, every data set should be explored with descriptive statistics and visual plots to ascertain the shape of its distribution. Preparing to analyze data with nonparametric procedures is no different. A lot can be learned by examining the shape of data to see whether it appears to conform to a normal distribution, also known as a Gaussian distribution or "bell curve." The concept behind most nonparametric analyses is that they do not assume a normal distribution and effectively destroy the distribution inherent in a data set by operating on ranks, rather than on the original data points themselves. Ranks destroy the intervals between values, so ascending data points like 1, 5, 125 and 1, 3, 5 both become ranks 1, 2, 3.

Certain types of measures in HCI tend to fall normally while others almost never do. Common non-normal data distributions that arise frequently in HCI studies are:

- Preference tallies, such as from studies of competing technologies
- Completion times, which may be skewed and long-tailed
- Error rates, which may have numerous zeroes amidst other values
- Ordinal scales, such as responses on Likert-type scales
- Rare events, such as recognition errors from an accurate gesture recognizer

The above examples are just some of the types of data that arise in HCI and may warrant nonparametric analyses.

7.2.1   Assumptions of Analysis of Variance (ANOVA)

The familiar analysis of variance procedure, or ANOVA, is often more powerful than analogous nonparametric procedures for the same data. The oft-used t-test and F-test are two examples. Such tests are therefore generally preferred to their nonparametric cousins. But t-tests and F-tests cannot always be used when data violates one or more of three underlying assumptions required by such analyses. HCI researchers and practitioners seeking to use ANOVA procedures should first ensure that their data conforms to the three assumptions. When violations occur, nonparametric procedures may be preferred.

The three underlying assumptions of ANOVA, and how to test for them, are:

1. *Independence.* Responses must be distinct measurements independent from one another, except as correlated in a within-subjects design. Put another way, the

value of one measure should not determine the value of any other measure. *How to test?* The independence assumption is not tested mathematically but is verified by an experiment design that ensures this assumption is met.
2. *Normality.* Residuals are the differences between model predictions and observed measures. The normality assumption requires that residuals are normally distributed. In practice, the normality assumption can be regarded as referring to the distribution of the response within each group under consideration. Mild deviations from normality often do not pose serious threats to drawing valid statistical conclusions, particularly when sample sizes are large. However, in the presence of substantial deviations from normality, especially with small sample sizes as are common in HCI, nonparametric procedures ought to be used. *How to test?* A histogram of the residuals or the data itself can often reveal obvious deviations from normality, such as data that conforms to log-normal, Poisson, or exponential data distributions. More formal tests of normality can be conducted, such as the Shapiro-Wilk test (Shapiro and Wilk 1965) or the Kolmogorov-Smirnov test (Kolmogorov 1933; Massey 1951; Smirnov 1939). R code for executing these tests is provided elsewhere in this chapter. A good review of these and other goodness-of-fit tests can be found in the literature (D'Agostino 1986).
3. *Equal variances.* The equal variances assumption is more formally known as the assumption of "homogeneity of variance" or "homoscedasticity." It requires that the variance, or equivalently the standard deviation, among different experimental groups should be about the same. *How to test?* A histogram of the data from each group being compared can reveal whether some groups have different variances than others. More formally, Levene's test can be used (Levene 1960). If homoscedasticity is violated, a Welch ANOVA or White-corrected ANOVA can be used (Welch 1951; White 1980), which do not have the equal variances assumption. An alternative is to use a nonparametric analysis, such as those covered in this chapter.

7.2.2 Table of Analogous Parametric and Nonparametric Tests

Many HCI researchers and practitioners are more familiar with parametric tests than nonparametric tests. It can be helpful to see how the two types of tests relate. By understanding the relation among parametric tests and their nonparametric equivalents, researchers and practitioners can more confidently choose which nonparametric test is right for their data.

This chapter is far from a comprehensive treatment of nonparametric statistics. There are myriad nonparametric tests that might benefit researchers and practitioners in HCI. This chapter focuses on the most common, widely available, and versatile nonparametric tests. For a complete approach to nonparametric statistics, the reader is directed to comprehensive treatments on the subject (Higgins 2004; Lehmann 2006).

Table 7.1 Parametric tests and their nonparametric cousins

Samples			Parametric test	Nonparametric test
1			• One-sample t-test	• One-sample chi-square test • Binomial test • Multinomial test
≥1				• N-sample chi-square test • G-test • Fisher's exact test
Factors	Levels	Between- or within-subjects	Parametric test	Nonparametric test
1	2	B	• Independent-samples t-test	• Median test • Mann-Whitney U test
1	≥2	B	• One-way ANOVA	• Kruskal-Wallis test
1	2	W	• Paired-samples t-test	• Sign test • Wilcoxon signed-rank test
1	≥2	W	• One-way repeated measures ANOVA	• Friedman test

≥1	≥2	B	• N-way ANOVA	• Aligned rank transform
				• Generalized linear models[†]
				  –Multinomial logistic
				  –Ordinal logistic
				  –Poisson
				  –Gamma

≥1	≥2	W	• N-way repeated measures ANOVA	• Aligned rank transform • Generalized linear mixed models[†] • Generalized estimating equations

[†]Generalized linear models and generalized linear mixed models may be considered parametric analyses but the distributions on which they operate may be non-normal

Table 7.1 categorizes the tests covered in this chapter based on the number of "factors" and their "levels." Factors are the independent variables manipulated in an experiment, such as *Device* when comparing mice to a trackballs. They may also be covariates, like *Sex*, which are not manipulated but are still of interest for their possible effect on dependent variables, or responses. Factors can be "between-subjects" or "within-subjects," owing to whether each participant is assigned only one level of the factor or more than one. Levels are the number of values any given factor can assume. For example, *Device*, above, has two levels (mouse, trackball), as does *Sex* (male, female). Note that *Device* could be a within-subjects factor if every participant utilized both devices. *Sex*, on the other hand, is generally considered only a between-subjects factor.

Besides factors and levels, another distinguishing feature of certain tests is whether they are "exact tests." Exact tests do not rely on approximations or asymptotic properties of the sampling distribution to derive p-values. Rather, they calculate their p-values directly and exactly. HCI studies often have small sample sizes, which can cause problems for asymptotic tests, and exact tests are then preferred. The Chi-Square test is a popular asymptotic test. It may underestimate p-values at less than 1000 samples, increasing the chance of falsely rejecting null hypotheses. Exact tests are currently under-utilized in HCI, largely due to conventions established before advances in computing made exact tests widely practicable. Where possible, we provide R code for running exact tests in this chapter.

Having established the criteria that are used to inform whether to use parametric or nonparametric analyses, we now turn to the analyses themselves. In each case, an (inappropriate) parametric analysis is conducted prior to any nonparametric analyses for comparisons. These parametric analyses are flagged with a $\oslash$ symbol to indicate caution. For continuity, the storyline about the sales teams using the new Mango smartwatches is used.

7.3 Tests of Proportions

Often in HCI studies, researchers and practitioners elicit responses from participants or users, count those responses, and then wish to draw conclusions from those counts. Responses of these kinds tend to be categorical in nature. For example, in a survey respondents may be asked to express a preference for one of a variety of technologies, like web browsers. Some number of respondents may choose Microsoft Internet Explorer, while others may choose Google Chrome, while still others may choose Mozilla Firefox or Apple Safari. One-sample tests of proportions can reveal whether responses differ significantly from chance or from known probabilities—in this case, perhaps the global market share percentage of each browser.

Going further, we may wish to know how respondents' browser preferences differ by country. We now would use a two-sample test of proportions. Known probabilities may now need to be adjusted by the market share of each browser in each country.

A three-sample test would allow us to determine whether sex plays a role. A four-sample test might include respondents' income bracket. And so on... In short, tests of proportions tell us whether observed proportions differ from chance or from otherwise hypothesized probabilities.

7.3.1 One-Sample Tests of Proportions

Let us introduce our scenario for our one-sample tests. At one point prior to the companywide adoption of Mango smartwatches, 75 sales representatives were recruited for a pilot study in which each Mango smartwatch was outfitted with one of two email applications, A-mail or B-mail. After 3 weeks, the watches were updated to remove the first mail program and install the second. Another 3 weeks passed. At the end of 6 weeks, each sales representative had used both A-mail and B-mail. The representatives were then asked for their preference. As the data file `prefs1AB.csv` shows, A-mail was preferred by 46 sales representatives and B-mail was preferred by 29 representatives. The question is whether there was a significant preference for one email application over the other.

As stated above, for comparisons we briefly report an (inappropriate) parametric test prior to the preferred nonparametric tests.

⊘ *One-sample t-test.* The one-sample t-test is a simple parametric test that assumes the population response is normal (Student 1908). For our example, we can assume that if respondents showed no overall preference, $75/2 = 37.5$ respondents would vote for each email application. In other words, no overall preference would mean a 50 % chance of preferring one or the other applications. In our data, we have $46/75 = 61.3\%$ of respondents preferring A-mail, and $29/75 = 38.7\%$ preferring B-mail. Is this a statistically significant difference?

The R code for performing a one-sample t-test on `prefs1AB.csv` is:

```
> prefs1AB = read.csv("chapter7/prefs1AB.csv")
> t.test(prefs1AB$email_preference == "A-mail", mu=0.5)

        One Sample t-test

data: prefs1AB$email_preference == "A-mail"
t = 2.002, df = 74, p-value = 0.04895
alternative hypothesis: true mean is not equal to 0.5
95 percent confidence interval:
 0.5005335 0.7261332
sample estimates:
mean of x
0.6133333
```

The p-value is 0.049, which is less than the critical value of $\alpha = 0.05$, meaning the 46 votes for A-mail do represent a statistically significant preference for A-mail over B-mail. The test result is reported as $t(74) = 2.00$, $p < 0.05$.

One-sample Chi-Square test. The most common way to test proportions is using a one-sample Chi-Square test (Pearson 1900), which is a nonparametric alternative to the one-sample t-test. Unlike the t-test, the Chi-Square test does not require that the data be sampled from a normal distribution. However, it is an asymptotic test, not an exact test, so for small sample sizes it must be used with caution. The premise behind the test is the same as before, where we compare observed proportions to chance, i.e., to 50/50.

The R code for performing a one-sample Chi-Square test on `prefs1AB.csv` is:

```
# assuming prefs1AB.csv is already loaded
# chisq.test expects frequency tables as input: here we
# create a cross tabulation (hence xtabs) of the number of
# responses for each level of email_preference
> email_preferences = xtabs( ~ email_preference, data=prefs1AB)
> email_preferences
email_preference
A-mail B-mail
   46     29
> chisq.test(email_preferences)

    Chi-squared test for given probabilities

data: email_preferences
X-squared = 3.8533, df = 1, p-value = 0.04965
```

The truncated p-value is 0.049, again indicating that the 46 votes for A-mail represent a statistically significant preference over B-mail. The test result is reported as $\chi^2(1, N = 75) = 3.85$, $p < 0.05$, where 1 is the value of df above.

Binomial test. The binomial test is a nonparametric test used to compare two categories against expected probabilities, often called the probability of "success" or "failure." Unlike the Chi-Square test, which relies on approximations, the binomial test is an exact test. A common use of the binomial test is to see whether responses in two categories are equally likely to occur, such as testing whether a coin is fair from a series of tosses. We can use the binomial test to see whether the probability of someone preferring one of the email programs is significantly different from chance (i.e., 50 %).

The R code for performing a binomial test on prefs1AB.csv is:

```
# assuming prefs1AB.csv is already loaded
> email_preferences = xtabs( ~ email_preference, data=prefs1AB)
> binom.test(email_preferences)

    Exact binomial test

data:  email_preferences
number of successes = 46, number of trials = 75,
p-value = 0.06395
alternative hypothesis: true probability of success is not
equal to 0.5
95 percent confidence interval:
 0.4937958 0.7236319
sample estimates:
probability of success
           0.6133333
```

The p-value is 0.064, greater than the critical value of $\alpha = 0.05$, meaning we fail to reject the null hypothesis that the two categories are equally probable. In this case, the one-sample Chi-Square test underestimated the *p*-value: we rejected the null hypothesis when using the asymptotic Chi-Square test and failed to reject when using the exact binomial test. Since modern computers allow us to easily run an exact test in this case, we should prefer the exact result to the Chi-Square result. The test result is reported as a binomial test of $N = 75$ responses, a 50/50 hypothesized response probability, and a *p*-value of 0.0640.

Multinomial test. What if there are more than two response categories? The binomial test cannot be used. In such cases, the nonparametric multinomial test is appropriate. Like the binomial test, the multinomial test is an exact test, and should be preferred to the Chi-Square test.

Suppose the original study had compared three email programs instead of two. Preferences were elicited from the 75 sales representatives. The data in `prefs1ABC.csv` indicates that 35 respondents preferred A-mail, 22 preferred B-mail, and 18 preferred C-mail. The question is whether these counts differ significantly from chance, i.e., a third of respondents in each category. The code for performing a multinomial test on `prefs1ABC.csv` is:

```
> library(XNomial)
> prefs1ABC = read.csv("chapter7/prefs1ABC.csv")
> email_preferences = xtabs(~ email_preference, data=prefs1ABC)
> xmulti(email_preferences, c(1/3, 1/3, 1/3), statName="Prob")

P value (Prob) = 0.04748
```

The *p*-value is 0.047, indicating that we should reject the null hypothesis that each email program is preferred equally. The test result is reported as a multinomial test of $N = 75$ responses, equal chance hypothesized response probability (i.e., a 1/3 chance of each email application being preferred), and a *p*-value less than 0.05.

The one-sample Chi-Square test we utilized above can also accommodate more than two response categories like the multinomial test. The following R code runs a one-sample Chi-Square test on `prefs1ABC.csv`:

```
# assuming prefs1ABC.csv is already loaded
> email_preferences = xtabs(~ email_preference, data=prefs1ABC)
> chisq.test(email_preferences)

        Chi-squared test for given probabilities

data:  email_preferences
X-squared = 6.32, df = 2, p-value = 0.04243
```

The *p*-value is 0.042. According to this Chi-Square test, there is a statistically significant difference between the observed preferences and chance. Observing the preference counts, we surmise a significant preference for A-mail over the other two mail programs. Note that the Chi-Square test underestimates the p-value compared to the exact multinomial test. The multinomial test should be preferred where computationally feasible, typically for sample sizes of less than 1000.

7.3.2 N-Sample Tests of Proportions

Regardless of how many response categories there are, if only one dimension of data is considered, a multinomial test or a one-sample Chi-Square test is an option. But what if we wish to categorize responses along more than one dimension? Consider the question of whether preferences for the Mango email applications—A-mail, B-mail, or C-mail—were different in Sales Team X versus Sales Team Y. One dimension lies along the sales teams, with two possible categories. A second dimension lies along the email applications, with three possible categories. Thus, we have a 2×3 contingency table, also known as a "crosstabulation" or "crosstabs".

Data appearing in `prefs2ABC.csv` contains 75 responses from each of two sales teams. Its 2×3 contingency table is shown in Table 7.2.

The question is whether the email application preferences of the two sales teams differ significantly.

N-Sample Chi-Square test. We have thus far been generating 1×2 and 1×3 contingency tables using the `xtabs` command. This command can generate crosstabs with an arbitrary number of dimensions, making N-Sample Chi-Square tests a simple extension of the procedures we have already employed above.

The R code for running a two-sample Chi-Square test of proportions is:

```
> prefs2ABC = read.csv("chapter7/prefs2ABC.csv")
# we specify multiple factors in the xtabs formula to get
# crosstabs of higher dimensions.
> email_preferences = xtabs( ~ email_preference + team,
                             data=prefs2ABC)
> chisq.test(email_preferences)
    Pearson's Chi-squared test
data: email_preferences
X-squared = 6.4919, df = 2, p-value = 0.03893
```

Table 7.2 A 2×3 contingency table of email application preferences by 75 members each of Sales Team X and Sales Team Y

		Email application preference			
		A-mail	B-mail	C-mail	Total
Sales team	X	35	22	18	75
	Y	21	35	19	75
	Total	56	57	37	**150**

The p-value is 0.039, indicating a significant difference in email application preferences between the two sales teams. The test result is reported as $\chi^2(2, N = 150) = 6.49$, $p < 0.05$.

Other N-sample tests. Here we highlight two alternative tests of proportions that use a similar syntax as chisq.test. One test that is gaining popularity is the *G*-test (Sokal and Rohlf 1981), which, although an asymptotic test, is considered more accurate than the Chi-Square test, which employs approximations where the *G*-test directly computes likelihood ratios. The test is conducted in R using the G.test function in the RVAideMemoire package.

Another popular test is Fisher's exact test (Fisher 1922), which is an exact test used primarily on 2×2 contingency tables but is capable of being extended to general $r \times c$ tables provided sufficient computational resources (Mehta and Patel 1983). The test is conducted in R using the fisher.test function, and is natively capable of handling general $r \times c$ contingency tables.

7.4 Single Factor Tests

In the previous section, we discussed tests for data that counted respondents—and more precisely, their preferences—as measures of interest. In the rest of this chapter, we consider the results of experimental designs in which people are assigned treatments and the measures of interest involve the behavior or attributes of those people under those treatments. We first consider single-factor tests. Before doing so, however, we introduce statistical tests for the assumptions of ANOVA, which may be used to determine whether nonparametric tests are warranted in the first place.

7.4.1 Testing ANOVA Assumptions

Recall from the outset of this chapter that the three assumptions of ANOVA are independence, normality, and equal variances. Here we examine these assumptions for the salesXY.csv data file, which arises from the following scenario. Let us assume members of one company sales team, Sales Team X, were given Mango smartwatches over a three-month period. During the same period, members of another company sales team, Sales Team Y, were not given the smartwatches so as to serve as a control group. Each representative's sales were measured during the three-month period and multiplied by four to reflect estimated annualized sales. Thus, we have a single between-subjects factor, *Team*, and a continuous measure for each participant, annualized sales, in dollars.

The first assumption is independence. Do the measures arise independent of one another? Assuming the salespeople work independently and that there are many more sales opportunities than sales representatives, and thus one salesperson's gain is not inherently another salesperson's loss, we can trust that the independence assumption is met.

The second assumption is normality. Before conducting formal tests of normality, let us visually examine the distribution of data with a histogram, one for each sales team (Fig. 7.1).

The histograms are clearly non-normal in their appearance. As with most measures of income, the annualized sales data conforms to an exponential distribution. This hunch can be formally tested with goodness-of-fit tests. We briefly review two popular goodness-of-fit tests here. We recommend Shapiro-Wilk for testing normality; the Kolmogorov-Smirnov test can be used to test the goodness-of-fit of non-normal distributions. For more on goodness-of-fit tests, the reader is directed elsewhere (D'Agostino 1986).

Shapiro-Wilk test. The Shapiro-Wilk test considers whether data from a sample originated from a normal distribution (Shapiro and Wilk 1965). It has been shown to have the best power of the three tests considered here (Razali and Wah 2011).

The R code for conducting a Shapiro-Wilk test on each team in `salesXY.csv` is:

```
> salesXY = read.csv("chapter7/salesXY.csv")
> shapiro.test(salesXY[salesXY$team == "X",]$sales)
    Shapiro-Wilk normality test
data: salesXY[salesXY$team == "X", ]$sales
W = 0.8368, p-value = 1.238e-07
> shapiro.test(salesXY[salesXY$team == "Y",]$sales)
    Shapiro-Wilk normality test
data: salesXY[salesXY$team == "Y", ]$sales
W = 0.791, p-value = 6.013e-09
```

The p-value for both teams is $p < 0.0001$, indicating a statistically significant difference between the distribution of their annualized sales and a normal distribution.

Fig. 7.1 The distribution of annualized sales for each sales team. Team X had Mango smartwatches. Team Y did not yet have the Mango smartwatches. Histograms can be generated using the hist function, as in hist(salesXY [salesXY$team =="X",]$sales)

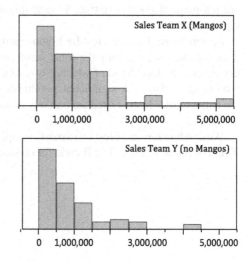

Kolmogorov-Smirnov test. The Kolmogorov-Smirnov test considers how a data
sample compares to a given probability distribution (Kolmogorov 1933; Massey
1951; Smirnov 1939). It calculates the distance between the empirical distribution
function of a sample and the cumulative distribution function of the given probability
distribution. Thus, the Kolmogorov-Smirnov test can be used to test against non-
normal distributions.

The R code for executing the Kolmogorov-Smirnov test is:

```
# assuming salesXY.csv is already loaded
> lillie.test(salesXY[salesXY$team == "X",]$sales)

    Lilliefors (Kolmogorov-Smirnov) normality test

data:   salesXY[salesXY$team == "X", ]$sales
D = 0.1445, p-value = 0.0005212
> lillie.test(salesXY[salesXY$team == "Y",]$sales)

    Lilliefors (Kolmogorov-Smirnov) normality test

data:   salesXY[salesXY$team == "Y", ]$sales
D = 0.1791, p-value = 2.904e-06
```

The p-values for the teams are $p < 0.001$ and $p < 0.0001$, again indicating statistically significant departures from normality. Thus, from visual inspection and
from both formal goodness-of-fit tests, we conclude the data violates the normality
assumption of ANOVA.

The third assumption of ANOVA is equal variances. The standard deviation
of annualized sales for Sales Team X is $1,169,590.80. For Sales Team Y, it is
$904,175.91. Of course, with highly non-normal distributions, standard deviations
are not particularly descriptive. So how might we formally test the assumption of
equal variances?

Levene's test. Levene's test for homogeneity of variance, or homoscedasticity, is
a formal method for testing the equal variances assumption (Levene 1960). The test
determines the likelihood of whether two data samples are drawn from populations
with equal variance. A significant p-value below the $\alpha = 0.05$ level indicates that
the data samples being tested are unlikely to have come from populations with equal
variances.

We conduct Levene's test on two data samples, the annualized sales of Sales Team
X and of Sales Team Y. The R code for conducting Levene's test is:

```
# assuming salesXY.csv is already loaded
> library(car)
> leveneTest(sales ~ team, data=salesXY)
Levene's Test for Homogeneity of Variance (center = median)
       Df   F value    Pr(>F)
group   1    2.9567   0.08761  .
       148
---
Signif. codes:
0 '***' 0.001 '**' 0.01 '*' 0.05 '.' 0.1 ' ' 1
```

The p-value is 0.088, above the $\alpha = 0.05$ threshold for declaring that the equal variances assumption has been violated. Even still, with a trend-level result such as this one, we ought to be wary of utilizing parametric tests. The result of Levene's test is reported as $F(1,148) = 2.96$, $p = 0.088$.

We have heretofore demonstrated that the data in salesXY.csv is not suitable to analyse via parametric ANOVA. Nonparametric tests are therefore warranted. Let us now turn to those tests.

7.4.2 Single-Factor Between-Subjects Tests

We continue with our scenario comparing the annualized sales of two sales teams, Sales Team X wearing Mango smartwatches and Sales Team Y without such watches. As above, for comparisons we briefly report an (inappropriate) parametric test prior to the preferred nonparametric options.

⊘ *Independent-samples t-test.* The independent-samples t-test is a parametric test for one-factor two-level between-subjects designs (Student 1908). Due to the violation of normality, the test is inappropriate for the data in salesXY.csv. Nevertheless, the R code for executing such an analysis is shown below. Note that by default, R uses the Welch t-test (Welch 1951), which does not require equal variances, having been formulated for this purpose.

```
# assuming salesXY.csv is already loaded
> t.test(sales ~ team, data=salesXY)
    Welch Two Sample t-test
data: sales by team
t = 2.2293, df = 139.173, p-value = 0.02739
alternative hypothesis: true difference in means is not
equal to 0
95 percent confidence interval:
  43049.83 718064.85
sample estimates:
mean in group X mean in group Y
      1250090.3         869532.9
```

The p-value is 0.027, which indicates that the annualized sales of the two teams are significantly different. Specifically, the sales of Sales Team X are higher than those of Sales Team Y, suggesting that the Mango smartwatches are having a positive effect. The test result is reported as $t(139.2) = 2.23$, $p < 0.05$.

Median test. A more appropriate test is the nonparametric median test (Brown and Mood 1948, 1951). The median test considers whether the medians from the populations from which two data samples are drawn are the same. A simple test, the median test counts each data point as above or below the median in the combined sample. Traditionally, then a Chi-Square test—although we can also use an exact test—is used to see whether the counts of data points from each sample differ. The median test is the preferred choice if any data points are extreme outliers.

The R code for conducting a median test is:

```
# assuming salesXY.csv is already loaded
# the distribution="exact" parameter specifies the exact
# version of this test, and can be dropped if an
# asymptotic test is needed (e.g., if this code
# takes too long to execute).
> library(coin)
> median_test(sales ~ team, data=salesXY, distribution="exact")
      Exact Median Test
data: sales by team (X, Y)
Z = -3.0923, p-value = 0.003157
alternative hypothesis: true mu is not equal to 0
```

The p-value is 0.003, indicating a significant difference in sales between the teams. The test result is reported as an exact median test $Z = -3.09$, $p < 0.01$.

Mann-Whitney U test. Like the median test, the nonparametric Mann-Whitney U test[1] operates on one-factor two-level between-subjects designs (Mann and Whitney 1947). It is more common in the field of HCI than the median test and usually more powerful. The test converts data to ranks and is generally more powerful than the parametric t-test for non-normal data.

The R code for conducting the test is:

```
# assuming salesXY.csv is already loaded
> library(coin)
> wilcox_test(sales ~ team, data=salesXY, distribution="exact")
      Exact Wilcoxon Mann-Whitney Rank Sum Test
data: sales by team (X, Y)
Z = 2.2346, p-value = 0.02521
alternative hypothesis: true mu is not equal to 0
```

---

[1] The Mann-Whitney U test has multiple and sometimes confusing names. It is also known as the Wilcoxon-Mann-Whitney test, the Mann-Whitney-Wilcoxon test, and the Wilcoxon rank-sum test. None of these should be confused with the Wilcoxon signed-rank test, which is for one-factor two-level *within*-subjects designs.

Fig. 7.2 The distribution of annualized sales for Sales Team Z

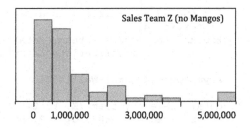

The p-value is 0.025, similar to that of the independent-samples t-test. The test result is reported as an exact Mann-Whitney $Z = 2.23$, $p < 0.05$.

The Mann-Whitney U test is a good option for analyzing one-factor two-level between-subjects designs. But what if we have one factor with more than two levels? For example, let us consider 75 additional sales representatives, this time from Sales Team Z, added to the study. Like Sales Team Y, Sales Team Z was not given Mango watches at this time. The distribution of the team's annualized sales is shown in Fig. 7.2.

We now have a one-factor three-level between-subjects design. The factor is *Team* and the levels are X, Y, and Z. We will use `salesXYZ.csv`, which extends the data table to include the data from Sales Team Z.

⊘ *One-way ANOVA.* The popular parametric analysis for one factor with more than two levels is a one-way ANOVA (Fisher 1921, 1925). As with the t-test above, this analysis is inappropriate for these data due to the violation of the normality assumption.

The R code for conducting a one-way ANOVA is:

```
> salesXYZ = read.csv("chapter7/salesXYZ.csv")
> summary(aov(sales ~ team, data=salesXYZ))
              Df    Sum Sq    Mean Sq   F value   Pr(>F)
team           2   5.438e+12  2.719e+12   2.345   0.0982 .
Residuals    222   2.574e+14  1.159e+12
---
Signif. codes:  0 '***' 0.001 '**' 0.01 '*' 0.05 '.' 0.1 ' ' 1
```

The p-value is 0.098, which is not statistically significant at the $\alpha = 0.05$ level. The test result is reported as F(2,222) = 2.35, $p = 0.098$.

Kruskal-Wallis test. The nonparametric Kruskal-Wallis test extends the Mann-Whitney U test to one factor with more than two levels (Kruskal and Wallis 1952). Like the Mann-Whitney U test, the Kruskal-Wallis test operates on ranks. It is a more appropriate test to conduct on salesXYZ.csv than a one-way ANOVA.

The R code for executing a Kruskal-Wallis test is:

```
# assuming salesXYZ.csv is already loaded
library(coin)
kruskal_test(sales ~ team, data=salesXYZ,
             distribution="asymptotic")

Asymptotic Kruskal-Wallis Test

data:  sales by team (X, Y, Z)
chi-squared = 5.1486, df = 2, p-value = 0.07621
```

The p-value is 0.076, indicating no significant differences among groups. The test result is reported as a Kruskal-Wallis test $\chi^2(2, N = 225) = 5.15, p = 0.076$.

Many studies in HCI utilize designs in which multiple responses are received from each participant. We now turn to nonparametric tests for one-factor within-subjects designs.

7.4.3 Single-Factor Within-Subjects Tests

In an effort to collect more data per participant, and generally to increase the power of statistical tests on that data, many HCI researchers and practitioners prefer to utilize within-subjects factors rather than between-subjects factors. Within-subjects factors expose participants to more than one of their levels, for example, by having each sales representative not use *and* use a Mango smartwatch over different time periods. Such was the case for Sales Team Y, which initially was not given the Mango smartwatches to serve as a control for Sales Team X. After three months, Sales Team Y was given the watches, thereby enabling within-subjects comparisons for Sales Team Y.

The data in salesYY.csv contains the same pre-Mango sales data for Sales Team Y as shown in Fig. 7.1. It also contains post-Mango sales data for each representative, shown in Fig. 7.3. Thus, we have a single within-subjects factor, *Watch*, and a continuous measure for each participant: their annualized sales, in dollars.

As before, we begin with an (inappropriate) parametric test for comparisons.

Fig. 7.3 The distribution of annualized sales for Sales Team Y after the adoption of the Mango smartwatches

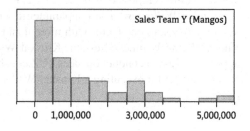

⊘ **Paired-samples t-test.** A paired-samples t-test is a parametric within-subjects test when two measures are taken from each participant (Student 1908). Due to the violation of normality, the test is inappropriate for the data in `salesYY.csv`. Nevertheless, the R code for executing such an analysis is:

```
> salesYY = read.csv("chapter7/salesYY.csv")
> library(reshape2) #for dcast
# for a paired t-test we must use a wide-format table. Most
# functions in R do not require a wide-format table, but the
# dcast function offers a quick way to translate long-format
# into wide-format when we do need it. This creates "pre"
# and "post" columns containing pre- and post-watch sales.
> salesYY_wide = dcast(salesYY, subject ~ watch,
                       value.var="sales")
> t.test(salesYY_wide$pre, salesYY_wide$post, paired=TRUE)
    Paired t-test
data: salesYY_wide$pre and salesYY_wide$post
t = -2.4309, df = 74, p-value = 0.01748
alternative hypothesis: true difference in means is
not equal to 0
95 percent confidence interval:
 -732056.10  -72552.05
sample estimates:
mean of the differences
          -402304.1
```

The p-value is 0.017, which indicates that after the adoption of the Mango smart-watches, the annualized sales of Sales Team Y were different. The t-test result is reported as $t(74) = -2.43$, $p < 0.05$. By examining the means and distributions, we can see that the sales went up, from a median of about \$580,000 before the watches to about \$870,000 after the watches:

```
# generate summary statistics for the sales, split
# into groups according to the levels of watch
> ddply(salesYY, ~ watch, function(data) summary(data$sales))
   watch    Min.   1st Qu.   Median    Mean  3rd Qu.     Max.
1   post   10000    342500   870300 1272000  1911000  5000000
2    pre   10000    239800   580300  869500  1091000  4351000
```

Sign test. The sign test is a nonparametric alternative to the paired-samples t-test (Dixon and Mood 1946; Stewart 1941). It is analogous to the median test but for paired data rather than unpaired data. The test is particularly useful when paired values do not have scalar magnitudes but simply a greater-than or less-than relationship, even coded as just 1 or 0.

The intuition behind the sign test is if the paired samples are not significantly different, then subtracting one value from its paired value should result in a positive number (vs. a negative number) about 50% of the time. A binomial test is then used to test for significant departures from an equal number of positive versus negative differences.

The R code for conducting a sign test on salesYY.csv is:

```
# assuming salesYY_wide was constructed as above
# We can conduct a sign test simply by cross-tablulating the
# number of times post-watch sales are greater than pre-watch.
> post_sales_greater = xtabs( ~ post > pre, data=salesYY_wide)
> binom.test(post_sales_greater)

    Exact binomial test

data:   post_sales_greater
number of successes = 31, number of trials = 75, p-value =
0.1654
alternative hypothesis: true probability of success is not
equal to 0.5
95 percent confidence interval:
 0.3007536 0.5329729
sample estimates:
probability of success
               0.4133333
```

The p-value is 0.165, indicating that the Mango smartwatches did not statistically significantly affect the probability an individual team member's annualized sales increased on Sales Team Y. The test result is reported as a sign test of $N = 75$ paired observations and $p = 0.165$.

Recognizing the relative statistical weakness of the sign test, Wilcoxon developed a more powerful test, the signed-rank test, which considers not just direction of paired differences but their magnitude as well.

Wilcoxon signed-rank test. The Wilcoxon signed-rank test, not to be confused with the Wilcoxon rank-sum test (see Footnote 1), is a powerful and widely used nonparametric test for one within-subjects factor with two levels (Wilcoxon 1945). In HCI studies, the test is often used when individual participants try each of two alternatives, say input devices or webpage designs, and the best alternative is to be determined. Like many nonparametric tests, it operates on ranks rather than on raw observations.

The R code for executing a Wilcoxon signed-rank test is:

```
# assuming salesYY.csv is already loaded
> library(coin)
# here we specify the response variable (sales), the within-
# subjects variable (watch), and the variable identifying each
# subject (subject).
> wilcoxsign_test(sales ~ watch | subject, data=salesYY,
                  dist="exact")

    Exact Wilcoxon-Signed-Rank Test

data:  y by x (neg, pos)
     stratified by block
Z = -2.2178, p-value = 0.02615
alternative hypothesis: true mu is not equal to 0
```

The p-value is 0.026, indicating a statistically significant difference in annualized sales for Sales Team Y pre- and post-adoption of the Mango smartwatches. The test result is reported as an exact Wilcoxon $Z = -2.22$, $p < 0.05$. We note that whereas the sign test did not find a statistically significant difference, the Wilcoxon signed-rank test did, confirming the greater power of this test and a reason for its preference.

The Wilcoxon signed-rank test is powerful but limited in an important way: it can only compare two levels of a single factor. What if there are more than two levels to be compared at once? Let us imagine that the company, pleased with the increase in annualized sales due to the Mango smartwatches, decided to have Sales Team Y conduct a third three-month experiment in which sales representatives would wear *two* Mango smartwatches, one on each wrist. (Perhaps in the hope that if one smartwatch is good, two might be better!)

The distribution of annualized sales is shown in Fig. 7.4.

The data for two watches represented above are captured in `salesYY2.csv`. They are accompanied by the data for Sales Team Y for no watch (Fig. 7.1) and one watch (Fig. 7.3). We therefore have one factor, *Watch*, now with three levels: none, one watch, and two watches.

As above, we begin with an (inappropriate) parametric test for comparisons.

⊘ *One-way repeated measures ANOVA.* The parametric repeated measures ANOVA can be used when multiple measures are taken from the same participant. It

Fig. 7.4 The distribution of annualized sales for Sales Team Y when each sales representative wore two Mango smartwatches, one on each wrist

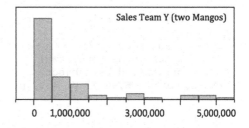

is important to use a corrected test such as a Greenhouse-Geisser correction (Greenhouse and Geisser 1959) in the event that sphericity is violated. Sphericity is a property of the data related to the covariance among experimental groups that can be tested with Mauchly's test of sphericity (Mauchly 1940). When sphericity is not violated, an uncorrected test can be used.

The R code for conducting Mauchly's test of sphericity and the ensuing repeated measures ANOVA is:

```
> salesYY2 = read.csv("chapter7/salesYY2.csv")
> library(ez)
# here we specify the dependent variable (sales), within-
# subjects variables (watch), and the variable that
# identifies subjects (subject).
> m = ezANOVA(dv=sales, within=watch,wid=subject,data=salesYY2)
# we then check the model for violations of sphericity
> m$Mauchly
  Effect              W              p p<.05
2  watch    0.9518013    0.1647936
# and given no violations, examine the uncorrected ANOVA. If
# violations were found, we would instead look at m$Sphericity.
> m$ANOVA
  Effect   DFn   DFd         F          p p<.05          ges
2  watch     2   148  2.973636   0.05418002       0.02593512
```

Mauchly's test of sphericity gives $W = 0.952$, $p = 0.165$, indicating that sphericity is not violated and that an uncorrected test can be used. The repeated measures ANOVA gives F(2,148) = 2.97, $p = 0.054$, falling just shy of statistical significance. Of course, given the violations of normality, we know this result to be specious. A nonparametric test should be used instead.

Friedman test. The nonparametric Friedman test is a rank-based test for a single within-subjects factor of any number of levels (Friedman 1937). The test is particularly useful in HCI studies where participants work with more than two variations of a user interface. For our example, we will use it to compare the annualized sales of Sales Team Y when its representatives wore zero, one, and two Mango smartwatches.

The R code for initiating a Friedman test on salesYY2.csv is:

```
# assuming salesYY2.csv is already loaded
> library(coin)
> friedman_test(sales ~ watch | subject, data=salesYY2)

        Asymptotic Friedman Test

data:    sales by
         watch (none, one, two)
         stratified by subject
chi-squared = 6.9067, df = 2, p-value = 0.03164
```

Table 7.3 Pairwise comparisons of annualized sales among the three levels of *Watch* using Holm's sequential Bonferroni procedure

	No watch	One watch	Two watches		
Median Sales	$580,320.00	$870,290.00	$337,919.00		
Comparison	Wilcoxon W		p-value	Holm's α	Significant?
One watch versus two watches	457.0		0.0153	$\alpha/3 = 0.0167$	Yes
No watch versus one watch	420.0		0.0262	$\alpha/2 = 0.0250$	No
No watch versus two watches	190.0		0.3189	$\alpha/1 = 0.0500$	No

The p-value is 0.032, indicating a statistically significant difference in annualized sales among the levels of *Watch*. The test result is reported as $\chi^2(2, N = 75) = 6.91$, $p < 0.05$.

With three levels of *Watch*, we may wish to know which pairwise comparisons are significant. Three pairwise comparisons may be conducted, but we must be careful to apply a correction to avoid inflating the Type I error rate—the possibility of false positives. A correction such as Holm's sequential Bonferroni procedure can avoid inflating the Type I error rate (Holm 1979).[2] We conduct the pairwise comparisons using Wilcoxon signed-rank tests, the results of which are shown in Table 7.3.

We can conduct all pairwise comparisons in R and use the p.adjust function to apply Holm's sequential Bonferroni procedure follows:

```
# assuming salesYY2.csv is already loaded
> library(plyr)
# get all pairwise combinations of levels of the watch factor,
# equivalent to combn(levels(salesYY2$watch),2,simplify=FALSE).
comparisons = list(c("none", "one"), c("none", "two"),
c("one", "two"))
# run wilcoxon signed-ranks on each pair of levels, collecting
# the test statistic and the p-value into a single table.
> post_hoc_tests = ldply(comparisons, function(watch_levels){
    wt = wilcoxsign_test(sales ~ factor(watch) | subject,
        data=salesYY2[salesYY2$watch %in% watch_levels,],
        dist="exact")
    data.frame(comparison = paste(watch_levels,collapse=" - "),
        z = statistic(wt), pvalue = pvalue(wt)
    )
})
```

---

[2] Holm's sequential Bonferroni procedure for three pairwise comparisons uses a significance threshold of $\alpha = 0.05/3$ for the lowest p-value, $\alpha = 0.05/2$ for the second lowest p-value, and $\alpha = 0.05/1$ for the highest p-value. Should a p-value compared in that ascending order fail to be statistically significant, the procedure halts and any subsequent comparisons are regarded as statistically non-significant.

```
# derive adjusted p-values using Holm's sequential Bonferroni
# procedure
> post_hoc_tests$adjusted_pvalue =
                 p.adjust(post_hoc_tests$pvalue, method="holm")
> post_hoc_tests
    comparison          z           pvalue       adjusted_pvalue
1  none - one     2.217834       0.02615427          0.05230854
2  none - two    -1.003306       0.31893448          0.31893448
3   one - two    -2.413214       0.01532255          0.04596764
```

Corrected pairwise comparisons show that one Mango smartwatch produced different sales than two Mango smartwatches. Looking at median sales, it is clear that two smartwatches *hindered* sales compared to one smartwatch. Perhaps information overload had a deleterious effect on sales representatives' productivity!

We have thus far considered nonparametric tests of proportions and nonparametric single-factor tests with two or more levels. Our final consideration in this chapter is nonparametric multifactor tests—those used when more than one factor is being tested in the same experimental design.

7.4.4 Multifactor Tests

Modern experiments in HCI often involve more than one factor. Multifactor experimental designs examine more than one factor simultaneously. Each factor may have two or more levels. Chief among statistical concerns are tests for "interactions," wherein levels of one factor interact with levels of another factor to differentially affect responses. For example, perhaps one Mango smartwatch email application creates higher sales for Sales Team X, while a different email application creates higher sales for Sales Team Y. This situation would result in a statistically significant *Team × Application* interaction.

Nonparametric statistical methods for multifactor designs can be quite complex and are a topic of active statistical research (Sawilowsky 1990). This chapter offers a pragmatic but cursory review of four techniques: the Aligned Rank Transform, Generalized Linear Models, Generalized Linear Mixed Models, and Generalized Estimating Equations. For full treatments, the reader is directed to books on nonparametric statistics (Higgins 2004; Lehmann 2006).

7.4.5 ⊘ N-Way Analysis of Variance

As above, we begin with an (inappropriate) parametric analysis for comparisons. Let us reuse the data from Sales Team Y with zero, one, and two Mango smartwatches, but now embellished with the city in which each sales representative operated: Babol,

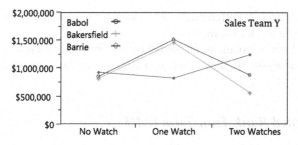

Fig. 7.5 Annualized sales for Sales Team Y by *Watch* and by *City*. A significant *Watch* × *City* interaction is suggested by this graph. A similar graph can be generated by the R code with(salesYY2city, interaction.plot(watch,city, sales))

Bakersfield, or Barrie. Thus, *City* is a three-level between-subjects factor, as each sales representative worked only in one city. As before, *Watch* is a three-level within-subjects factor. We therefore have a two-factor mixed design. These data are shown in salesYY2city.csv.

The R code for executing a two-way factorial ANOVA with one within-subjects factor, *Watch*, and one between-subjects factor, *City*, is:

```
> salesYY2city = read.csv("chapter7/salesYY2city.csv")
> library(ez)
> m = ezANOVA(dv=sales, between=city, within=watch,
              wid=subject, data=salesYY2city)
> m$Mauchly
        Effect         W          p p<.05
3        watch 0.9619982 0.2527474
4 city:watch 0.9619982 0.2527474
> m$ANOVA
        Effect DFn DFd         F          p p<.05        ges
2         city   2  72 0.2622249 0.77006952       0.00255353
3        watch   2 144 3.1014944 0.04800009     * 0.02717733
4 city:watch   4 144 2.5909015 0.03915842     * 0.04459346
```

Although *City* alone was not a statistically significant main effect, there was a significant *Watch* × *City* interaction as indicated by *p*-value of 0.039, meaning each level of *Watch* resulted in different annualized sales depending on the city in which the sales representative worked. Although a formal analysis would use pairwise comparisons to draw conclusions, for our purposes we simply eyeball the graph shown in Fig. 7.5. The graph suggests that although sales in all three cities were similar without a Mango smartwatch, with one watch, sales in Babol and Bakersfield improved, but not in Barrie. But with two Mango smartwatches, sales in Barrie improved, but were worse in Babol and Bakersfield. (Perhaps the Barrie salespeople were all ambidextrous!) Differential results like these are what cause the statistically significant *Watch × City* interaction.

Given the known violations of normality, the above parametric ANOVA is an inappropriate analysis. We now turn to multifactor nonparametric procedures.

7.4.6 *Aligned Rank Transform (ART)*

Rank transforms have been utilized extensively in nonparametric procedures (Conover and Iman 1981). However, ANOVAs applied to rank transforms are known to drastically inflate Type I error rates for interaction effects (the chance of declaring a significant interaction effect when there is not one), and therefore are not suitable as multifactor analyses (Higgins and Tashtoush 1994; Mansouri 1999b; Salter and Fawcett 1993).

One rank-based procedure that avoids this problem is called the *Aligned Rank Transform (ART)*. The nonparametric ART procedure originated in the 1980s (Fawcett and Salter 1984; Salter and Fawcett 1985) and has been a subject of attention ever since (Higgins et al. 1990; Higgins and Tashtoush 1994; Mansouri 1999a; Mansouri et al. 2004; Richter 1999; Salter and Fawcett 1993). Before ranking, the ART procedure "aligns" the data separately for each effect by subtracting estimates of all effects other than the effect of interest from each response (Hodges and Lehmann 1962). The idea is to "strip out" any effects except one from the data. The aligned data is then ranked and a factorial ANOVA is performed with the aligned ranks as the response. Importantly, only the effect for which the responses were aligned is examined in the effects table; others are ignored. Thus, a separate aligning-ranking-ANOVA process is conducted for every effect of interest, whether a main effect or interaction. As aligning and ranking for every effect is tedious, tools have been developed to automate the process (Wobbrock et al. 2011).

The authors of this chapter have created an R package for performing the ART procedure called `ARTool`, based on a prior tool for Microsoft Windows of the same name (Wobbrock et al. 2011). The package performs the aligning-and-ranking process and automates running an ANOVA for each main effect and interaction.[3] Using this package, the ART procedure is run on the data in `salesYY2city.csv` using the following code:

---

[3] Rather than using traditional repeated measures ANOVAs, `ARTool` uses mixed-effects analyses of variance, explained below in the section on Generalized Linear Mixed Models.

```
# assuming salesYY2city.csv is already loaded
> library(ARTool)
> m = art(sales ~ watch * city + (1|subject),data=salesYY2city)
> anova(m)
Aligned Rank Transform Anova Table (Type III tests)

Response: art(sales)

                F   Df     Df.res      Pr(>F)
watch      4.3132    2        144     0.01516 *
city       0.0165    2         72     0.98361
watch:city 2.0173    4        144     0.09510 .
---
Signif. codes: 0'***' 0.001'**' 0.01'*' 0.05 '.' 0.1'' 1
```

As with the parametric two-way ANOVA above, we have a statistically significant effect of *Watch* on annualized sales F(2,144) = 4.31, $p < 0.05$. Also as above, *City* alone did not exhibit a statistically significant effect. However, unlike above, the *Watch* × *City* interaction is not statistically significant here but only a trend. This result is to be trusted over the parametric result, given the evident violation of normality.

The ART procedure can facilitate post hoc comparisons, provided levels are compared within the aligned-and-ranked effects from which they came (Mansouri et al. 2004). We can conduct pairwise comparisons for all levels of the *Watch* factor using the following R code:

```
# assuming m is the result of the call to art() above
> library(lsmeans)
> lsmeans(artlm(m, "watch"), pairwise ~ watch)
$lsmeans
watch   lsmean        SE  df   lower.CL   upper.CL
none  108.5600  7.359735 216   94.05391   123.0661
one   130.0133  7.359735 216  115.50724   144.5194
two   100.4267  7.359735 216   85.92057   114.9328

Results are averaged over the levels of: city
Confidence level used: 0.95

$contrasts
 contrast      estimate        SE  df t.ratio   p.value
 none - one  -21.453333  10.40824 144  -2.061    0.1017
 none - two    8.133333  10.40824 144   0.781    0.7150
 one  - two   29.586667  10.40824 144   2.843    0.0141

Results are averaged over the levels of: city
P value adjustment: tukey method for a family of 3 means
```

The lsmeans procedure reports p-values corrected for multiple comparisons using Tukey's method (Kramer 1956; Tukey 1949, 1953). As for the post hoc tests conducted above, we find the only significant difference is between one and two watches, reported as $t(144) = 2.84$, $p < 0.05$.

7.4.7 Generalized Linear Models (GLM)

The classic ANOVA we have been utilizing in this chapter can be mathematically formulated by what is called the General Linear Model (LM).[4] This model describes a family of analyses where the dependent variables are a linear combination of independent variables[5] plus normally-distributed errors. However, when the assumption of normality is not met, the General*ized* Linear Model (GLM) can utilize non-normal response distributions (Nelder and Wedderburn 1972). GLMs are specified with a distribution and a link function, which describe how factors relate to responses. The LM is subsumed by the GLM when the distribution is "normal" and the link function is "identity." Many distribution-link function combinations are possible. Here we review four common uses of the GLM for data arising in HCI studies. It is important to note that such models are suitable only for between-subjects factors. For within-subjects factors, we must add random effects to the models, as described in the next subsection.

Multinomial logistic regression. Multinomial logistic regression, also referred to as nominal logistic regression, is used for categorical (nominal) responses[6] (Nelder and Wedderburn 1972). In this respect, it can be used on data also suited to N-sample Chi-Square tests of proportions. Recall the contingency data in Table 7.2, contained in prefs2ABC.csv. We can use multinomial logistic regression with *Team* as a two-level factor and *Preference* as a response to discover whether there were statistically significant differences in preference between sales teams.

In terms of the GLM, multinomial logistic regression uses a "multinomial" distribution and "logit" link function. The R code for executing such an analysis is:

---

[4] General Linear Models are often called "linear models" and may be abbreviated "LM." These should not be confused with General*ized* Linear Models, which may be abbreviated "GLM." However, some texts use "GLM" for linear models and "GZLM" for generalized models. Readers should take care when encountering this family of abbreviations.

[5] While not covered in this chapter, LMs and GLMs also offer the ability to use continuous independent variables, not just categorical independent variables (see Chap. 11).

[6] Multinomial logistic regression—when used with dichotomous responses such as Yes/No, True/False, Success/Fail, Agree/Disagree, or 1/0—is called "binomial regression." The GLM for binomial regression uses a "binomial" distribution and "logit" link function. It can be conducted using the glm function in much the same way as Poisson regression explained below, except with the parameter family=binomial.

```
> prefs2ABC = read.csv("chapter7/prefs2ABC.csv")
> library(nnet) #for multinom
> library(car) #for Anova
> m = multinom(email_preference ~ team, data=prefs2ABC)
> Anova(m)
Analysis of Deviance Table (Type II tests)

Response: email_preference

        LR Chisq   Df   Pr(>Chisq)
team    6.5556     2        0.03771 *
---
Signif. codes: 0 '***' 0.001 '**' 0.01 '*' 0.05 '.' 0.1 ' ' 1
```

The p-value is 0.038, indicating a significant difference in preference. The test result is reported as a multinomial logistic regression $\chi^2(2, N = 150) = 6.56$, $p < 0.05$.

Multinomial logistic regression is useful for multifactor analyses as well. The file `prefs2ABCsex.csv` has the same preferences data now embellished with the sex of each sales representative. Thus, we have *Team* with two levels (Sales Team X or Y) and *Sex* with two levels (male or female).

The R code for executing multinomial logistic regression on `prefs2ABC sex.csv` is:

```
> prefs2ABCsex = read.csv("chapter7/prefs2ABCsex.csv")
> library(nnet) #for multinom
> library(car) #for Anova
# set contrasts for each factor to be sum-to-zero contrasts.
# this is necessary for the Type III Anova we will use.
> contrasts(prefs2ABCsex$team) <- "contr.sum"
> contrasts(prefs2ABCsex$sex) <- "contr.sum"
> m = multinom(email_preference ~ team * sex,data=prefs2ABCsex)
# We use a Type III Anova since it simplifies interpreting
# significant main effects in the presence of interactions.
> Anova(m, type=3)
Analysis of Deviance Table (Type III tests)

Response: email_preference

            LR Chisq   Df   Pr(>Chisq)
team        6.4923     2        0.03892 *
sex         0.1029     2        0.94985
team:sex    0.5136     2        0.77354
---
Signif. codes: 0 '***' 0.001 '**' 0.01 '*' 0.05 '.' 0.1 ' ' 1
```

As with our contingency table analysis, here there was a statistically significant effect of *Team* on email application preference ($\chi^2(2, N = 150) = 6.49, p < 0.05$). However, as one would expect, there was no statistically significant effect of *Sex* or significant *Team* × *Sex* interaction.

Ordinal logistic regression. Ordinal logistic regression, also called ordered logit, proportional odds logistic regression, or the cumulative link model, is analogous to multinomial logistic regression but for ordered responses rather than unordered categories (McCullagh 1980). Such responses occur frequently in HCI studies that utilize Likert scales, e.g., with subjective responses ranging from "strongly disagree" to "strongly agree." Ordinal logistic regression is an extension of multinomial logistic regression to ordered response categories.

Let us assume that each sales representative was asked to indicate how much they liked the email application they most preferred. On a 1–7 scale with end-points "strongly disagree" to "strongly agree," they rated their agreement with the statement, "I love my preferred Mango smartwatch email application." The data in prefs2ABClove.csv reflects their responses.

The R code for running ordinal logistic regression on prefs2ABClove.csv is:

```
> prefs2ABClove = read.csv("chapter7/prefs2ABClove.csv")
> library(MASS)
> library(car)
> contrasts(prefs2ABClove$team) <- "contr.sum"
> contrasts(prefs2ABClove$sex) <- "contr.sum"
# transform numeric variable into an ordinal variable
> prefs2ABClove$love = ordered(prefs2ABClove$love)
> m = polr(love ~ team * sex, data=prefs2ABClove)
> Anova(m, type=3)
Analysis of Deviance Table (Type III tests)

Response: love

              LR Chisq    Df      Pr(>Chisq)
team           0.0149      1         0.9029
sex           29.5134      1       5.553e-08 ***
team:sex       0.0285      1         0.8659
---
Signif. codes: 0 '***' 0.001 '**' 0.01 '*' 0.05 '.' 0.1 ' ' 1
```

There was no significant effect of *Team* on how much sales representatives love their preferred Mango email application. There was also no *Team* × *Sex* interaction. But there was a significant effect of *Sex*, reported as ordinal logistic $\chi^2(1, N = 150) = 29.51, p < 0.0001$. The average 1–7 Likert rating for males was 4.45; for females it was 5.70. Perhaps the female sales representatives were a more positive bunch!

Poisson regression. Poisson regression is used for nonnegative integers that represent count data (Nelder and Wedderburn 1972; Bortkiewicz 1898). A common use of Poisson regression in HCI is for counts of rare events. For example, accurate gesture recognizers or automatic spelling correction systems that produce relatively few errors from every 100 attempts may lend themselves to Poisson regression.[7]

For our scenario, let us pretend that the Mango smartwatch email applications tracked and counted the number of customers to whom each sales representative failed to respond within 48 hours. Since sales representatives are trained to respond quickly to customers, such occurrences should be relatively rare. The file `prefs2ABClate.csv` contains the email application preferences data embellished with the number of late responses for that sales representative during the three-month study. Now, the preferred email application is treated not as a response but as an independent variable potentially influencing the new response. Thus, we have a 2 × 2 × 3 three-factor design with *Team* (X, Y), *Sex* (M, F), and *Preference* (A-mail, B-mail, C-mail).

In the GLM, Poisson regression uses a "Poisson" distribution and "log" link function, specified by the `family` argument to the `glm` function. It is executed in R with the following:

```
> prefs2ABClate = read.csv("chapter7/prefs2ABClate.csv")
> contrasts(prefs$ABClate$team) <- "contr.sum"
> contrasts(prefs2ABClate$sex) <- "contr.sum"
> contrasts(prefs2ABClate$email_preference) <- "contr.sum"
> m = glm(late_responses ~ team * sex * email_preference,
          data=prefs2ABClate, family=quasipoisson)
> Anova(m, type=3)
Analysis of Deviance Table (Type III tests)

Response: late_responses

                             LR Chisq   Df    Pr(>Chisq)
team                          20.8684    1    4.919e-06  ***
sex                            1.2934    1       0.25541
email_preference              3.3016    2       0.19190
team:sex                      2.0317    1       0.15405
team:email_preference         0.1471    2       0.92907
sex:email_preference          5.2803    2       0.07135  .
team:sex:email_preference     4.1328    2       0.12664
---
Signif. codes: 0 '***' 0.001 '**' 0.01 '*' 0.05 '.' 0.1 ' ' 1
```

---

[7] Given data with a large number of zeroes, it is prudent to consider an extension to Poisson regression called "`zero-inflated`" Poisson regression. This model incorporates binomial regression to predict the probability of a zero alongside Poisson regression to model counts. See the `zeroinfl` function in the `pscl` package.

There was a significant effect of *Team* on number of late responses, reported as a Poisson regression $\chi^2(1, N = 150) = 20.87$, $p < 0.0001$.

```
> ddply(prefs2ABClate, ~ team, function(data)
        summary(data$late_responses))
  team Min. 1st Qu.  Median      Mean 3rd Qu. Max.
1    X    0       0       1     1.080       2    4
2    Y    0       1       2     2.307       3    8
```

The average number of late responses for Sales Team X was 1.08; for Sales Team Y, which did not have the Mango smartwatch yet, it was 2.31. We can also extract the estimated ratio of rates of late responses between the two teams:

```
> library(multcomp)  #for glht
> library(lsmeans)   #for lsm
> team_effect = confint(glht(m, lsm(pairwise ~ team)))

    Simultaneous Confidence Intervals

Fit: glm(formula = late_responses ~ team * sex *
email_preference, family = quasipoisson, data = prefs2ABClate)
Quantile = 1.96
95% family-wise confidence level


Linear Hypotheses:

            Estimate     lwr      upr
X - Y == 0   -0.6594  -0.9465  -0.3723

# effects in a Poisson model are on a log scale (because of the
# log link), so we often exponentiate them to interpret them.
> exp(team_effect$confint)
        Estimate       lwr       upr
X - Y  0.5171661 0.3880856 0.6891797
attr(,"conf.level")
[1]  0.95
attr(,"calpha")
[1]  1.959964
```

Thus, we should expect members of Team X to have about 0.517 times the rate of late responses as Team Y (95 % confidence interval: [0.388, 0.689]).

Gamma regression. For data conforming to a Gamma distribution, a GLM can be fitted with a "log" link function.[8] A Gamma distribution applies to skewed, continuous data with a theoretical minimum, often zero. It is defined by two parameters, "shape" and "scale." The inverse of the scale parameter is called the "rate." The exponential distribution is a special case of Gamma distribution where the shape parameter equals one.

The data contained in `salesXY.csv` and graphed in Fig. 7.1 can be modeled by a Gamma distribution. That data has now been embellished with the sex of each salesperson in `salesXYsex.csv`. The question now is how *Team* and *Sex* may have affected annualized sales.

The R code for executing a GLM with a Gamma distribution and log link function is:

```
> salesXYsex = read.csv("chapter7/salesXYsex.csv")
> contrasts(salesXYsex$team) <- "contr.sum"
> contrasts(salesXYsex$sex) <- "contr.sum"
> m = glm(sales ~ team * sex, data=salesXYsex,
          family=Gamma(link="log"))
> Anova(m, type=3)
Analysis of Deviance Table (Type III tests)

Response: sales

          LR Chisq    Df    Pr(>Chisq)
team       5.1408      1      0.02337  *
sex        1.9128      1      0.16666
team:sex   0.1767      1      0.67420
---
Signif. codes: 0 '***' 0.001 '**' 0.01 '*' 0.05 '.' 0.1 ' ' 1
```

The results indicate that there was a statistically significant effect of *Team* on annualized sales ($\chi^2(1, N = 150) = 5.14$, $p < 0.05$). The same conclusion was reached with the Mann-Whitney U test, whose p-value of 0.025 was similar. It does not appear that *Sex* or *Team* $\times$ *Sex* had any effect on annualized sales.

7.4.8 Generalized Linear Mixed Models (GLMM)

The GLMs reviewed in the last section are powerful models but with a major limitation—they are unable to handle within-subjects factors because they cannot

---

[8]Although the canonical link function for the Gamma distribution is actually the "inverse" function, the "log" function is often used because the inverse function can be difficult to estimate due to discontinuity at zero. The two functions provide similar results.

account for correlations among measures of the same participant. This restriction limits their utility in HCI studies in which the same participants are measured repeatedly in one session or over time.

The Generalized Linear Mixed Model (GLMM) is an extended model that allows for within-subjects factors (Gilmour et al. 1985; Stiratelli et al. 1984). A "mixed-effects model" refers to the combination of both "fixed" and "random" effects. Thus far in this chapter, we have only considered fixed effects, which are those whose levels are purposefully and specifically chosen as treatments. By contrast, random effects have levels whose values are not themselves of interest, but that represent a random sample from a larger population about which we wish to generalize. In HCI studies with repeated measures, the random effects are almost always the human participants in the experiment. By modeling *Subject* as a random effect, the correlation among measures taken from the same participant can be accounted for.

In other respects, GLMMs are similar to the GLMs reviewed above. Distributions and link functions can be specified for non-normal data.

Let us again consider the annualized sales for Sales Team Y with no Mango smartwatch, one Mango smartwatch, and two Mango smartwatches in salesYY2city. csv. (See Fig. 7.5.)

The R code for executing a factorial GLMM with a Gamma distribution, log link function, and *Subject* as a random effect[9] is:

```
> salesYY2city = read.csv("chapter7/salesYY2city.csv")
> library(lme4)        #for glmer
> library(car)         #for Anova
> contrasts(salesYY2city$city) <- "contr.sum"
> contrasts(salesYY2city$watch) <- "contr.sum"
# here (1|subject) indicates a random intercept
# dependent on subject.
> m = glmer(sales ~ city * watch + (1|subject),
            data=salesYY2city, family=Gamma(link="log"))
> Anova(m, type=3)
Analysis of Deviance Table (Type III Wald chisquare tests)

Response: sales

                Chisq  Df  Pr(>Chisq)
(Intercept) 37079.7322  1    < 2e-16 ***
city            1.0191   2    0.60077
watch           5.4790   2    0.06460 .
city:watch     10.9741   4    0.02686 *
---
Signif. codes:  0 '***' 0.001 '**' 0.01 '*' 0.05 '.' 0.1 ' ' 1
```

---

[9] This model uses an intercept-only random effect. There are other types of random effects such as slopes-and-intercept random effects that are described in Chap. 11.

The results show a statistically significant *Watch* × *City* interaction ($\chi^2(4, N = 225) = 10.97$, $p < 0.05$) and a nonsignificant main effect of *Watch* ($\chi^2(2, N = 225) = 5.48$, $p = 0.065$). These results differ somewhat from those of the Aligned Rank Transform, which showed a statistically significant main effect of *Watch* (F(2,144) = 4.31, $p < 0.05$) and a nonsignificant *Watch* × *City* interaction (F(4,144) = 2.02, $p = 0.095$). In neither analysis was *City* statistically significant. The discrepancies in these results indicate the degree to which statistical conclusions may vary depending on the analyses used.

7.4.9 Generalized Estimating Equations (GEE)

When the relationship among factors and responses is not known or there is no discernable structure, a Generalized Estimating Equation (GEE) can be used (Liang and Zeger 1986; Zeger et al. 1988). Unlike GLMMs, GEEs are less sensitive to covariance structure specification and can handle unknown correlation among outcomes. Responses may be continuous, nominal, or ordinal. Statistical inference is commonly performed with the Wald test (Wald 1943).

The R code for using a GEE with a Gamma distribution and log link function on `salesYY2city.csv` is:

```
> salesYY2city = read.csv("chapter7/salesYY2city.csv")
> library(geepack)
# geeglm requires data sorted by grouping variable, so we sort
# by subject (so that all rows for a given subject are
# contiguous).
> salesYY2city = salesYY2city[order(salesYY2city$subject),]
> m = geeglm(sales ~ city * watch, id=subject,
             data=salesYY2city, family=Gamma(link="log"))
> anova(m)
Analysis of 'Wald statistic' Table
Model: Gamma, link: log
Response: sales
Terms added sequentially (first to last)

            Df      X2     P(>|Chi|)

city         2     0.46      0.795
watch        2     7.94      0.019 *
city:watch   4    12.03      0.017 *
---
Signif. codes:
0 '***' 0.001 '**' 0.01 '*' 0.05 '.' 0.1 ' ' 1
```

The results show a statistically significant *Watch* main effect ($\chi^2(2, N = 225) = 7.94$, $p < 0.05$) and *Watch* × *City* interaction ($\chi^2(4, N = 225) = 12.03$, $p < 0.05$).

However, geeglm does not support Type-III ANOVAs,[10] and as a result, our interpretation of these tests is slightly different: The significant effect of *Watch* can be interpreted as a significant effect only outside the presence of a significant *Watch* × *City* interaction, which this model contains. Therefore, we ignore the significant *Watch* main effect and focus any further analysis on the interaction. As above, *City* is statistically nonsignificant.

7.5 Summary

The field of human-computer interaction is a field devoted both to invention and to science. Its researchers and practitioners often transition fluidly from inventing new interactive technologies to scientifically evaluating the behavior of people with interactive technologies. The ability to correctly draw conclusions about this behavior is therefore of paramount importance in focusing the efforts of these professionals. Although not all studies in HCI require statistical inference, those that do must utilize it correctly or risk missing actual benefits or proclaiming phantom ones.

With the wide variety of data collected in HCI studies, nonparametric statistics are rife with opportunity for broad application. Such statistics may be understood best by their relationship to more familiar, but often inapplicable, parametric statistics. This chapter has provided an overview of nonparametric statistics useful in HCI at an exciting time when the appreciation of their utility is growing in the field.

References

Anderson TW, Darling DA (1952) Asymptotic theory of certain "goodness of fit" criteria based on stochastic processes. Ann Math Stat 23(2):193–212

Anderson TW, Darling DA (1954) A test of goodness of fit. J Am Stat Assoc 49(268):765–769

Brown GW, Mood AM (1948) Homogeneity of several samples. Am Stat 2(3):22

Brown GW, Mood AM (1951) On median tests for linear hypotheses. In: Proceedings of the second Berkeley symposium on mathematical statistics and probability, Berkeley, California. University of California Press, Berkeley, California, pp 159–166

Conover WJ, Iman RL (1981) Rank transformations as a bridge between parametric and nonparametric statistics. Am Stat 35(3):124–129

D'Agostino RB (1986) Tests for the normal distribution. In: D'Agostino RB, Stephens MA (eds) Goodness-of-fit techniques. Marcel Dekker, New York, pp 367–420

Dixon WJ, Mood AM (1946) The statistical sign test. J Am Stat Assoc 41(236):557–566

Fawcett RF, Salter KC (1984) A Monte Carlo study of the F test and three tests based on ranks of treatment effects in randomized block designs. Commun Stat Simul Comput 13(2):213–225

---

[10] The ANOVA type indicates how the sums-of-squares are computed. In general, Type III ANOVAs are preferred because they can support conclusions about main effects in the presence of significant interactions. For Type I and Type II ANOVAs, significant main effects cannot safely be interpreted in the presence of significant interactions.

Fisher RA (1921) On the "probable error" of a coefficient of correlation deduced from a small sample. Metron 1(4):3–32

Fisher RA (1922) On the interpretation of χ^2 from contingency tables, and the calculation of P. J R Stat Soc 85(1):87–94

Fisher RA (1925) Statistical methods for research workers. Oliver and Boyd, Edinburgh

Friedman M (1937) The use of ranks to avoid the assumption of normality implicit in the analysis of variance. J Am Stat Assoc 32(200):675–701

Gilmour AR, Anderson RD, Rae AL (1985) The analysis of binomial data by a generalized linear mixed model. Biometrika 72(3):593–599

Greenhouse SW, Geisser S (1959) On methods in the analysis of profile data. Psychometrika 24(2):95–112

Higgins JJ, Blair RC, Tashtoush S (1990) The aligned rank transform procedure. In: Proceedings of the conference on applied statistics in agriculture. Kansas State University, Manhattan, Kansas, pp 185–195

Higgins JJ, Tashtoush S (1994) An aligned rank transform test for interaction. Nonlinear World 1(2):201–211

Higgins JJ (2004) Introduction to modern nonparametric statistics. Duxbury Press, Pacific Grove

Hodges JL, Lehmann EL (1962) Rank methods for combination of independent experiments in the analysis of variance. Ann Math Stat 33(2):482–497

Holm S (1979) A simple sequentially rejective multiple test procedure. Scand J Stat 6(2):65–70

Kolmogorov A (1933) Sulla determinazione empirica di una legge di distributione. Giornale dell'Istituto Italiano degli Attuari 4:83–91

Kramer CY (1956) Extension of multiple range tests to group means with unequal numbers of replications. Biometrics 12(3):307–310

Kruskal WH, Wallis WA (1952) Use of ranks in one-criterion variance analysis. J Amer Stat Assoc 47(260):583–621

Lehmann EL (2006) Nonparametrics: statistical methods based on ranks. Springer, New York

Levene H (1960) Robust tests for equality of variances. In: Olkin I, Ghurye SG, Hoeffding H, Madow WG, Mann HB (eds) Contributions to probability and statistics. Stanford University Press, Palo Alto, pp 278–292

Liang K-Y, Zeger SL (1986) Longitudinal data analysis using generalized linear models. Biometrika 73(1):13–22

Mann HB, Whitney DR (1947) On a test of whether one of two random variables is stochastically larger than the other. Ann Math Stat 18(1):50–60

Mansouri H (1999a) Aligned rank transform tests in linear models. J Stat Plann Inference 79(1):141–155

Mansouri H (1999b) Multifactor analysis of variance based on the aligned rank transform technique. Comput Stat Data Anal 29(2):177–189

Mansouri H, Paige RL, Surles JG (2004) Aligned rank transform techniques for analysis of variance and multiple comparisons. Commun Stat Theory Methods 33(9):2217–2232

Massey FJ (1951) The Kolmogorov-Smirnov test for goodness of fit. J Am Stat Assoc 46(253):68–78

Mauchly JW (1940) Significance test for sphericity of a normal n-variate distribution. Ann Math Stat 11(2):204–209

McCullagh P (1980) Regression models for ordinal data. J R Stat Soc Ser B 42(2):109–142

Mehta CR, Patel NR (1983) A network algorithm for performing Fisher's exact test in r × c contingency tables. J Am Stat Assoc 78(382):427–434

Nelder JA, Wedderburn RWM (1972) Generalized linear models. J R Stat Soc Ser A 135(3):370–384

Pearson K (1900) On the criterion that a given system of deviations from the probable in the case of a correlated system of variables is such that it can be reasonably supposed to have arisen from random sampling. Philos Mag Ser 5 50(302):157–175

Razali NM, Wah YB (2011) Power comparisons of Shapiro-Wilk, Kolmogorov-Smirnov, Lilliefors and Anderson-Darling tests. J Stat Model Anal 2(1):21–33

Richter SJ (1999) Nearly exact tests in factorial experiments using the aligned rank transform. J Appl Stat 26(2):203–217

Salter KC, Fawcett RF (1985) A robust and powerful rank test of treatment effects in balanced incomplete block designs. Commun Stat Simul Comput 14(4):807–828

Salter KC, Fawcett RF (1993) The ART test of interaction: a robust and powerful rank test of interaction in factorial models. Commun Stat Simul Comput 22(1):137–153

Sawilowsky SS (1990) Nonparametric tests of interaction in experimental design. Rev Educ Res 60(1):91–126

Shapiro SS, Wilk MB (1965) An analysis of variance test for normality (complete samples). Biometrika 52(3, 4):591–611

Smirnov H (1939) Sur les écarts de la courbe de distribution empirique. Recueil Mathématique (Matematiceskii Sbornik) 6:3–26

Sokal RR, Rohlf FJ (1981) Biometry: the principles and practice of statistics in biological research. W. H. Freeman, Oxford

Stewart WM (1941) A note on the power of the sign test. Ann Math Stat 12(2):236–239

Stiratelli R, Laird N, Ware JH (1984) Random-effects models for serial observations with binary response. Biometrics 40(4):961–971

Student (1908) The probable error of a mean. Biometrika 6(1):1–25

Tukey JW (1949) Comparing individual means in the analysis of variance. Biometrics 5(2):99–114

Tukey JW (1953) The problem of multiple comparisons. Princeton University, Princeton

von Bortkiewicz L (1898) Das Gesetz der kleinen Zahlen (The law of small numbers). Druck und Verlag von B.G. Teubner, Leipzig

Wald A (1943) Tests of statistical hypotheses concerning several parameters when the number of observations is large. Trans Amer Math Soc 54(3):426–482

Welch BL (1951) On the comparison of several mean values: an alternative approach. Biometrika 38(3/4):330–336

White H (1980) A heteroskedasticity-consistent covariance matrix estimator and a direct test for heteroskedasticity. Econometrica 48(4):817–838

Wilcoxon F (1945) Individual comparisons by ranking methods. Biomet Bull 1(6):80–83

Wobbrock JO, Findlater L, Gergle D, Higgins JJ (2011) The Aligned Rank Transform for nonparametric factorial analyses using only ANOVA procedures. In: Proceedings of the ACM conference on human factors in computing systems (CHI '11), Vancouver, British Columbia, 7–12 May 2011. ACM Press, New York, pp 143–146

Zeger SL, Liang K-Y, Albert PS (1988) Models for longitudinal data: a generalized estimating equation approach. Biometrics 44(4):1049–1060

Part III
Bayesian Inference

The previous part of this book, while introducing topics that are not often focused on in methodology textbooks, still discussed "classical" significance testing. This can be typified by a "frequentist" approach to statistical inference. To a frequentist (and in layman's terms) probabilities are considered long-run frequencies. As such, there is an interest in the long-run frequency of the data D given the hypothesis H_0. Hence, the frequentist aims to answer the hypothetical question: "If I would do this experiment again and again, and H_0 is indeed true, how would my data be distributed over these repeated experiments?" Hence, the frequentist treats the hypothesis *fixed* and given, and the data as *random*.

The Bayesian has a different view: for a Bayesian the data are fixed and given, and he is interested in the "degree of belief" regarding the hypothesis. This degree of belief in the hypothesis is considered *random*, and is informed by the information that is present in the fixed data. Hence, while the frequentist is interested in $P(D|H_0)$, the Bayesian is interested in $P(H_0|D)$. Now, these two quantities might coincide, but this is not generally the case.

Computing the transposed conditional (thus going from $P(D|H_0)$ to $P(H_0|D)$) is often relatively easy, and its computation is well known and undisputed by Frequentists and Bayesians alike: $P(\theta|D) = \dfrac{P(D|\theta)P(\theta)}{P(D)}$

However, the frequency of use of the above equation and the impact of the prior $P(\theta)$ remain disputed.

We believe the Bayesian view provides an extremely useful addition to the (mostly frequentist) methods that are part of the typical HCI methods curriculum. Hence, we have invited two authors to contribute on this topic.

Chapters 8 and 9 of this book introduce Bayesian inference and highlight the possibilities of Bayesian testing for HCI. As was stated in the earlier introduction part, but it is particularly true for this part, the chapters can only be seen as good introductions to their respective topics: Bayesian analysis is a field in its own right.

Chapter 8: Bayesian Inference
In Chap. 7 Dr. M. Tsiderdekis introduces Bayesian inference in general, and provides several examples of the use of [R] to quantify $P(\theta|D)$. The chapter starts with an introduction to Bayesian reasoning, and a didactical example. We hope that this introduces the basic ideas sufficiently to the reader to, at least, read the remainder of

the material with heightened interest. Next, several analyses using Bayesian methods are presented. For each example the code to produce the analysis as well as an elaborate discussion of the interpretation of the results is included.

Chapter 9: Bayesian Testing of Constrained Hypothesis

Chapter 8 illustrates clearly how, by adopting a Bayesian approach, relevant research questions that cannot be tested using a frequentist framework can be solved. Dr. J. Mulder introduces the use of the Bayes Factors (a Bayesian model comparison "tool") to test (order) constrained hypotheses.

Tests of constrained hypotheses are extremely useful in HCI: we often do not merely have the hypothesis that there is no difference between our experimental groups (the standard frequentist null-hypothesis), but rather we have a theory describing how the groups should be ordered. The Bayes Factor allows researchers to directly quantify the evidence in favor of specific orderings, compared to others, that is provided by the data.

Contrary to the other chapters in the book, this chapter uses a specialized software package called BIEMS to conduct the presented analysis. The chapter points readers to the location where the software can be downloaded for free.

Editor suggestions

There is much much more to the Bayesian approach than can be included in this part. Hence, we strongly encourage readers to further deepen their understanding of this topic by consulting the following classical works in this area:

- Also referenced in Chapter 7, but still worth recommending separately is the book *Bayesian Data Analysis* by Andrew Gelman and John B. Carlin (2013). It provides an extensive overview of the theory and its use in practice.
- The book *Bayesian Methods* by Jeff Gill (2007) is also recommended as a starting point.
- Taking a computer science / AI approach, the authoritative book *Pattern Recognition and Machine Learning* by Christopher Bishop (2007) focuses heavily on applied Bayesian Methods.

Chapter 8
Bayesian Inference

Michail Tsikerdekis

Abstract Bayesian inference has a long standing history in the world of statistics and this chapter aims to serve as an introduction to anyone who has not been formally introduced to the topic before. First, Bayesian inference is introduced using a simple and analytical example. Then, computational methods are introduced. Examples are provided with common HCI problems such as comparing two group rates based on a binary variable, numeric variable, as well as building a regression model.

8.1 Introduction

Dennis V. Lindley, arguably one of the leading advocates of Bayesian statistics has said that "Inside every non Bayesian there is a Bayesian struggling to get out" (Jaynes 2003). To someone that has never heard of Bayesian statistics, this statement could sound a bit condescending. It could be interpreted as an attack towards "classical" statistics taught in most colleges as the main introductory statistics course. Such an attack is not without precedence. A "war" between Bayesians and Frequentists (a term often reserved for non-Bayesians), has been ongoing for the majority of the 20th century. Ronald A. Fisher, one of the leading contributors to frequentist statistics has referred to Bayesian statistics as "fallacious rubbish" (Aldrich 2008). Others have followed in his example and a campaign to devalue Bayesian statistics has been going strong ever since. Yet, Bayesian statistics are still strong and often used in many scientific fields especially Computer Science. This is of no surprise since Alan Turing, seen by many as the father of Computer Science, has used Bayesian logic in his infamous Enigma machine meant to decipher German encrypted messages (McGrayne 2011). Since then, Bayesian logic has been utilized in various problems such as artificial intelligence, machine learning, pattern recognition and even email spam classification. Why utilize Bayesian statistics to solve such problems? Looking back at Lindley's statement one may find the answer. Doing Bayesian statistics is in

M. Tsikerdekis (✉)
School of Information Science, University of Kentucky,
Lexington, KY, USA
e-mail: tsikerdekis@uky.edu

© Springer International Publishing Switzerland 2016
J. Robertson and M. Kaptein (eds.), *Modern Statistical Methods for HCI*,
Human–Computer Interaction Series, DOI 10.1007/978-3-319-26633-6_8

many ways how we intuitively perceive the world as humans; having a prior belief about a statement, looking at the evidence and adjusting our prior belief based on the evidence.

Human-Computer Interaction (HCI) has largely been a field of frequentism when it comes to quantitative research. This can in part be attributed to the lack of proper introductory curriculum for Bayesian statistics in HCI but also a lack of software that can accompany research. Just a few decades ago the computing power was simply non-existent for the complex models and calculations that are required to conduct Bayesian inference (Robert and Casella 2011). Fast-forward a few decades and today Bayesian statistics are not only popular in a number of scientific fields but one can claim that they are not any more difficult to use than frequentist statistics. Bayesian inference is arguably more powerful and more informative due to its robustness for comparing hypotheses including the null hypothesis as well as making use of more information that is available to a researcher through the use of priors (Wagenmakers et al. 2008). This chapter serves as an introduction to Bayesian inference by presenting examples of typical HCI problems and Bayesian solutions to them.

8.2 Introduction to Bayes' Theorem

We will consider a computer science adaptation of the popular sunrise problem (Chung and AitSahlia 2003) in order to understand how Bayesian inference works. Imagine a child receiving their first technology device (e.g., computer, laptop, tablet, etc.) and turning it on for the first time. After spending some time using the device, the child turns it off and goes to sleep. What would the probability be that the device will turn on again when the child wakes up? Frequentist solutions may just assign 100% probability to the event that the device will turn on or may express that if the device fails it would be a 1:1 odds for that event to happen. The difficulty of frequentist statistics for this particular problem is that they are not equipped to provide answers for statements requiring an expression of probabilities from an observer's perspective. They work well for cases such as survey research, where a phenomenon is standardized and repeatable, but, they fail when it comes to answering questions when an infinite number of repetitions (even hypothetical) may not be possible.

This introduces the first major difference between Bayesian inference and frequentist statistics. In the latter, the data (D) are random while the rate that the device turns on (θ) is an unknown yet it is a fixed value. In Bayesian inference, we are concerned with the present without involving hypothetical multiple future attempts. The data (D) are fixed, objective and known while the rate that the device will turn on (θ) is unknown and random. As pointed out by Jackman (2009), this does not mean that the rate θ (the rate the device turns on) keeps changing but rather that our belief about it changes as we observe the digital device turning on each time. Hence, while a frequentist sees the probability of a device turning on as a characteristic of the device, a Bayesian sees the probability of a device turning on as a degree of one's belief given the observations. While both incorporate uncertainty, the frequentist approach fails in some problems since uncertainty is defined as a measurement error of finding the characteristic of a device. In contrast, a Bayesian's uncertainty is expressed in weaker probabilities that represent a belief due to limited data at hand or data that comes in conflict with prior beliefs.

This perspective gives a Bayesian statistician the power to assign probabilities to statements or beliefs. In our case that would be assigning probabilities to the rate θ. We can say that there are two different outcomes for the child's digital device: $\theta = 0$ the device does not turn on, and, $\theta = 1$ the device turns on. Or better yet, we may stipulate that the possibilities of the rate θ should be expressed in terms of a likelihood scale. We can say that the possibilities (or possible values) for our parameter θ will represent that a device will: Not Turn On, Not Very Probable to Turn On, Not Probable to Turn On, Probable to Turn On, Very Probable to Turn On, Turn On. Having six possibilities for our θ and assuming a range between 0 to 1, we can give θ six different numeric possibilities that correspond to our likelihood scale. So, θ is denoted by $\{0, 0.2, 0.4, 0.6, 0.8, 1\}$.

Before we see any data (D) and even begin evaluating a problem, we have certain preconceptions or *prior* beliefs. These are prior probabilities ($p(\theta)$) that are assigned to each possible value (or outcome) for θ and should always sum to 1. For those fancying formal expressions that would be:

$$\sum_{i=0}^{n} p(\theta_i) = 1 \qquad (8.1)$$

where n is all the discrete possible values for theta based on our made up likelihood scale.

If we believe prior to seeing any data that digital devices usually turn on, we can assign more weight on the $\theta = 1$ which corresponds to the *will turn on* belief in our likelihood scale and gradually decrease our assigned probabilities. Our *probability mass* for our prior beliefs for $p(\theta)$ will be 0.1, 0.15, 0.15, 0.20, 0.20, 0.4. Such a prior is considered to be a *subjective* prior. However, one can also decide that there is no apriori knowledge before one observes the data (D) and assign uniform probabilities to the prior $p(\theta)$ such as 0.2, 0.2, 0.2, 0.2, 0.2, 0.2. This is often called an *objective* prior since all possible outcomes for θ have equal probabilities ($p(\theta)$). However, even the uniform prior is not the least informative prior which can be selected[1] but it is considered sufficiently uninformative for many problems. Figure 8.1 shows the probability mass for the two examples of priors.

For our example we will assume that a friend informed the child that devices usually turn on and it is rare that they would not turn on. The child has a prior knowledge on the likelihood that a device will turn on, therefore we assume a prior belief that the device is likely to turn on. In R this will look like:

---

[1]Priors with higher variance can be considered less informative in this setting.

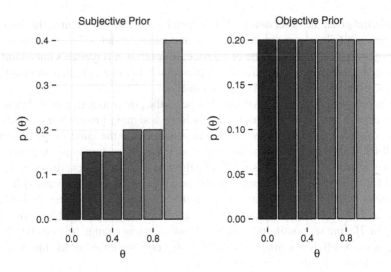

Fig. 8.1 Probability mass for prior beliefs. Left figure shows an subjective prior while right figure shows an objective prior

```
> Theta = c(0,0.2,0.4,0.6,0.8,1)
> pTheta = c(0.1,0.15,0.15,0.20,0.20,0.4)
```

After declaring our prior beliefs, the next step involves processing the data D that the child has observed. This is usually expressed as the *Likelihood* or $p(D|\theta)$ which translates as the probability of the Data (D) given each θ. In our example, a device can turn on and turn off. Since this is a binary problem, we can define that the device can turn on as θ and device not turning on as $1 - \theta$. Given that the possible outcomes for θ belong to the range of decimals between 0 and 1, you can think of the outcome *turning on* (θ) and outcome *not turning on* ($1 - \theta$) as "polar" opposites. To avoid any confusion, the possible outcomes $\{\theta, 1 - \theta\}$ which are derived from our data, are different from our arbitrarily defined possible values for $\theta = \{0, 0.2, 0.4, 0.6, 0.8, 1\}$. For example, we could represent θ in a three point scale such as $\theta = \{1, 2, 3\}$ and perceive the values as a discrete scale that means *Not Likely*, *Neutral* and *Likely*.

The likelihood ($p(D|\theta)$) is calculated using the binary data outcomes and observations (successes and failures) regarding these outcomes for each possible value θ. This is formally defined as:

$$\underbrace{p(D|\theta)}_{\text{likelihood}} = \underbrace{\theta^s}_{\text{succeses}} \underbrace{(1 - \theta)^f}_{\text{failures}} \tag{8.2}$$

Fig. 8.2 Probability mass
for likelihood $p(D|\theta)$

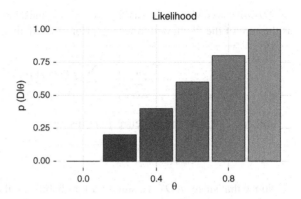

where s represents the numbers of times where the digital device turned on and
f represents the number of times where the digital device failed to turn on.[2] In R we
can write this using the following code:

```
> Data = c(1)
> s = sum( Data == 1 )
> f = sum( Data == 0 )
> pDataGivenTheta = Theta^s * (1-Theta)^f
```

This will result in $p(D|\theta)$ with probabilities for each possible θ: 0.0, 0.2, 0.4, 0.6,
0.8, 1.0 which are also shown in Fig. 8.2. Since we had just one success in turning on
the device the biggest probability for our θ likelihood scale is placed in $\theta = 1$ with
gradually decreasing probabilities on the rest possible values for θ. Notice that $\theta = 0$
that represents the *will not turn on* case has virtually a zero probability of occurring.

Of course, Bayesian inference is all about the transformation of our prior beliefs
($p(\theta)$) to a posterior belief ($p(\theta|D)$) having seen the data through the likelihood
($p(D|\theta)$). The posterior is basically our set of probabilities for θ after we have seen
the data. To achieve this we use a mathematical formula called *Bayes' Rule*. It was
conceptualized by Reverend Thomas Bayes in 1740s and later was given a formal
mathematical form and scientific application by Pierre Simon Laplace. It is formally
defined as (Kruschke 2010):

$$p(\theta|D) = \underbrace{p(D|\theta)}_{} \underbrace{p(\theta)}_{} / \underbrace{p(D)}_{} \qquad (8.3)$$
$$\underset{\text{posterior}}{} \quad \underset{\text{likelihood}}{} \underset{\text{prior}}{} \quad \underset{\text{evidence}}{}$$

In other words, having a prior belief, $p(\theta)$, times the likelihood, $p(D|\theta)$, divided
by the evidence, $p(D)$, we can obtain a posterior belief conditional on the data

---

[2]A more formal version of the likelihood would be $p(\{y_1, ..., y_n\}|\theta) = \prod_i \theta^{y_i}(1 - \theta)^{(1-y_i)}$, where
the set $D = \{y_1, ..., y_n\}$ represents the outcome for the sequence of attempts to turn on the device
(Kruschke 2013).

$p(\theta|D)$. In cases where θ has a discrete set of values, the evidence can be calculated as the sum of the likelihood times the prior or formally defined as:

$$\underbrace{p(D)}_{\text{evidence}} = \sum_{i=1}^{n} \underbrace{p(D|\theta_i)}_{\text{likelihood}} \underbrace{p(\theta_i)}_{\text{prior}} \tag{8.4}$$

In R, we calculate the evidence $p(D)$ using:

```
> pData = sum( pDataGivenTheta * pTheta )
```

Notice that since $p(D)$ is a sum of all probabilities, the result is a number (in our example $p(D) = 0.77$) and not a probability mass like we had in the case of $p(\theta)$ and $p(D|\theta)$.

Having calculated all the necessary components we can finally calculate our posterior probabilities based on our data using:

```
> pThetaGivenData = pDataGivenTheta * pTheta / pData
```

The posterior probabilities for $p(\theta|D)$ are 0.00, 0.04, 0.08, 0.16, 0.21, 0.52. This is also shown in Fig. 8.3. Due to our prior belief favoring the the possible values for θ where a device will most likely turn on, and, the fact that the data through the likelihood also favored the case where a device turned on, our posterior belief is elevated higher towards the possibility that a device will turn on.

The answer provided by Bayesian inference may appear to be terminal but this is not the case. Just like in real life, we hold a belief and we update it as new evidence (or data) comes in. This process can be iterative with today's posterior belief becoming tomorrow's prior.

The child may accept her current beliefs about the device turning on. After ten days she can use those same beliefs as a new prior and calculate the new posterior but this time having observed ten successful times where the device turned on.

Fig. 8.3 Probability mass for posterior $p(\theta|D)$

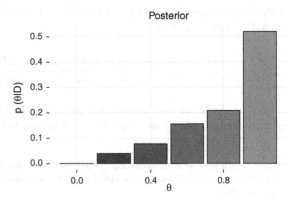

Fig. 8.4 Overview of prior, likelihood, and posterior

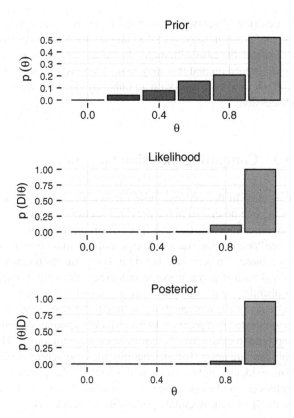

This transformation of beliefs is shown in Fig. 8.4 and it is the core concept behind Bayesian inference. Repeated times of following this process and having continuous success in turning the device on will place even more weight in $\theta = 1$ for the posterior $p(\theta|D)$, however, this will never become 100%. There is always uncertainty and this unknown property of probability is included in Bayesian inference.

The example in this section has been using a discrete θ for instructional purposes. In practice, a continuous θ should be used instead. The exact mathematical approach for solving this problem would require a prior $(p(\theta))$ that would be a continuous probability distribution and not discrete. There is also a need for a likelihood function $(p(D|\theta))$ that when combined with the prior, produces a posterior probability distribution of the same form with the prior. The prior of this form is often called a conjugate prior. This binary problem is mathematically solved using a Beta distribution prior and a Binomial likelihood.[3] The computational approach for this problem

---

[3]In the Beta/Binomial approach, the prior is defined using the Beta distribution's probability density function (PDF). The simplified form of Beta's PDF (for this type of problem), is $p(\theta|\alpha, \beta) \propto \theta^{\alpha-1}(1-\theta)^{\beta-1}$. Assuming that the friend told the child that he/she has seen these devices turn on ten times ($\alpha = 10$) and fail to turn on two times ($\beta = 2$), our prior would be: $p(\theta|\alpha = 10, \beta = 2) \propto \theta^{10-1}(1-\theta)^{2-1}$. The likelihood function is based on the Bernoulli distribution

is described later on in this chapter. An alternative mathematical approach for this type of problem is the use of a Gamma prior and a Poisson likelihood (Lynch 2007).

As it is the case with many digital devices, at some point in the future the device will not turn on and that may make us question our belief in induction, positivism, and, our ability to deal with an unhappy child. However, this is a matter for another discussion.

8.3 Computing Bayesian Statistics

It is easy to demonstrate how Bayesian statistics work in a simple problem such as the one described in the previous section, however, nowadays we do not conduct Bayesian inference by hand. The issue is one of complexity as problems are defined in more "detail." For example, the probability mass for our posterior may be determined by a more complex likelihood ($p(D|\theta)$) function that involves more outcomes for θ. Additionally, the possible outcome values for θ may not be discrete (e.g., the probability scale metaphor that we have used in our previous example) but can be instead continuous involving a range of values (e.g., a range from 0 to 1 with all possible decimal points in between). For example, studying user reaction times when replying to emails would require such a continuous θ. The posterior probabilities in this case are not called a probability mass but a *probability density* (Kruschke 2010). The evidence $p(D)$ which is the sum of the likelihood times the prior for all θ values cannot be calculated as such since there could be an infinite number of values with all of their decimals possibilities. Hence, we calculate instead the integral of the likelihood times the prior for all θ values which in layman's terms produces an approximation of what the sum would be if we could calculate it. Such complex problems require a different approach to the analytical approach that we have used in the previous section.

Monte Carlo Markov Chain algorithms are used as a tool in order to solve complex problems since they can approximate model parameters such as the parameter θ in our previous example (Gilks 2005). They use random walks (switching between different values of all parameters in a model) based on a model of probabilities derived from our observed data to approximate the point where a probability mass (or probability density) for parameters is reaching a state of "equilibrium." The random walk creates a sequence which is called a *chain* (also known as Markov chain) and the length of a chain (called the *sample*) is important for accurately determining the value of a

---

(Footnote 3 continued)
with 1 successes and 0 failures expressed as $p(D|\theta) \propto \theta^1(1-\theta)^0$. Using Bayes' Rule we can combine the likelihood and prior to produce the posterior distribution: $p(\theta|D) \propto p(D|\theta)p(\theta) = \theta^{10-1}(1-\theta)^{2-1}\theta^1(1-\theta)^0 = \theta^{10}(1-\theta)^1$. The posterior density is a beta density that we can easily interpret if we calculate its α and β parameters: $\alpha = 10 + 1$ and $\beta = 1 + 1$. As such the mean for θ is $M = \alpha/(\alpha + \beta) = 11/(11 + 2) = 0.846$ or the child's beliefs that the device will turn on is focused at 84.6%. The standard deviation is $SD = \sqrt{\frac{\alpha\beta}{(\alpha+\beta)^2(\alpha+\beta+1)}} \approx 0.0093$. The probability interval with a 95% probability will be $0.846 \pm 1.96 \times 0.0093$ which places the child's belief in the device turning on between 82.7% and 86.4%.

parameter. Each step in a chain is considered to be "memoryless." In essence, each step transitions between various states for a state space and the probability distribution for every step is only dependent on the previous step. Theoretically, an infinite sample would create the most accurate result but in practical terms we usually obtain a large enough sample (Plummer et al. 2006).

Figure 8.5 demonstrates how the algorithm works step by step to approximate the probability "equilibrium." The top two plots demonstrate a small sample. Our sample

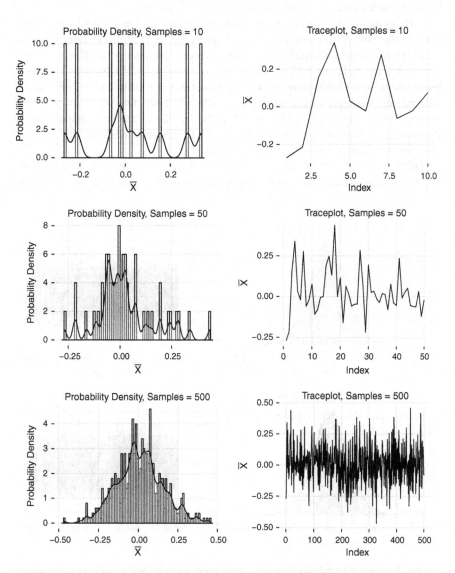

Fig. 8.5 Example of Probability Density plot and Trace plot of MCMC with varying samples for $\bar{X}$ parameter

is just 10 which creates 10 steps in our chain (also called an *interval*). The algorithm walks randomly between values but still within the constraints of observed data. The *traceplot* demonstrates this walk and chain. The index represents each step of the walk while the y-axis shows the sampled value for that step. If we summarize these ten values we can create a probability *density plot* for our parameter $\bar{X}$. It is evident that a sample of 10 is not large enough to obtain an accurate estimate. However, as we increase the sample (seen in the rest of the plots in Fig. 8.5) we slowly achieve higher accuracy and approximate our probability "equilibrium."

Early in the sample, chains often appear to be random. They can take a while to get into the "sweet" spot of a parameter's probabilities. For this reason, we often decide to ignore the early parts of a chain and retain the latter parts. This is called a *burnin*. For example, we may decide to retrieve a sample of 15,000 steps but have a burnin of the first 15,000 steps. Figure 8.6 demonstrates a sample of 15,000 without a burnin and a sample with a burnin of 15,000. The lower two plots basically start from the 15,000th step and end at 30,000th. Notice that for the first sample without the burnin, the chain moves slightly downward. Chains that take longer to converge are often referred to as *slow-mixing* (Lynch 2007).

The process of random walking utilized by MCMC algorithms can lead to chains that look different each time. Using multiple chains and aggregating the results into

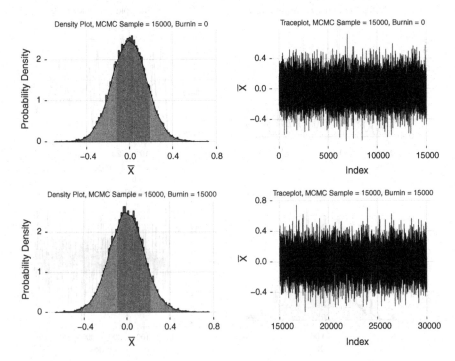

Fig. 8.6 Example of Probability Density plot and Trace plot of MCMC with the same sample size but different burnin for $\bar{X}$ parameter

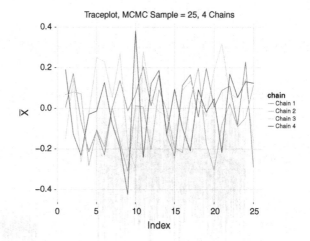

Fig. 8.7 Example of Trace plot with the same sample size with 4 chains for $\bar{X}$ parameter

one ensemble can create a more accurate estimate. Figure 8.7 demonstrates 4 different chains for a small MCMC sample.

An MCMC sample with a large interval and many chains can be a computationally intensive task especially depending on the number of parameters we wish to retain in order to construct their probability density distribution. In order to make this process more memory efficient for computational systems the idea of *thinning* was invented. Thinning retains only every nth element in a chain therefore reducing the size of the sample in memory (Albert 2009).

While we know that MCMC algorithms can produce a desired probability distribution for a parameter, we can never be sure how long it will take for a chain to converge to that distribution. We may set an interval of 100,000 and a chain may still not converge. For this reason, we use tests of *convergence* (Rossi et al. 2005). There are several tests to verify an MCMC sample's convergence. We can test for convergence visually or using algorithms that test for it.

Visual inspection for convergence can be done by viewing traceplots for chains and their *mixing*. If a chain takes longer to move through the whole parameter space then it will take longer to converge. Good mixing appears as a trace that tends to be stable within the values of the parameter (or parameter space). Figure 8.8 provides an example of a sample that converges and one that does not.

The *Gelman and Rubin shrink factor* is another way to verify that the convergence (Gelman and Rubin 1992). The measure uses within-chain and between-chain variance to produce a value of how well the model is converging over time. If the shrink factor is close to 1 then our model has converged while values beyond 1.2 are indicative of a model that may have not converged and requires a longer chain. However, there may be an occasion where one may receive a value that is smaller than 1.2 by chance. Hence, plotting the statistic over time is considered to be a more accurate approach. Figure 8.9 shows two *Gelman plots* for two parameters. The shrink factor appears to reach 1 and hover around it after approximately the 2,000th step in the

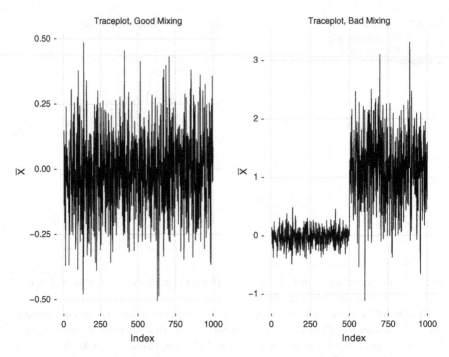

Fig. 8.8 Example of Trace plot that converges and one that does not for $\bar{X}$ parameter

sample. This is the point where the model started to converge. In this case, a 3,000 interval for our MCMC sample would be sufficient.

The *Geweke diagnostic* is another popular measure for detecting convergence (Cowles and Carlin 1996). The diagnostic tests for convergence on a per chain basis. The test retrieves samples from the chain of two non-overlapping samples (by default the first 10 % and the last 50 % of a chain) and conducts a test of equality of means. If convergence has occurred the means should be virtually the same. The result is a Z-score where scores below 1.98 indicate convergence and greater than 1.98 indicate statistically significant difference for the samples derived from a chain using a significance level 0.05 (5 % probability that we are wrong over repeated samples). One can also produce a plot over time for the statistic which is demonstrated in Fig. 8.10. In this case, we can notice that parameter muX is having trouble converging. Some of the points are beyond the threshold lines that mark the ± 1.98 limit. One also has to take into account whether an MCMC chain had a burnin which would affect convergence diagnostic.

Finally, there other diagnostics that can verify convergence for MCMC algorithms such as measuring autocorrelation lag, Raferty and Lewis diagnostic, and, Heidelberg and Welch diagnostic Cowles and Carlin 1996.

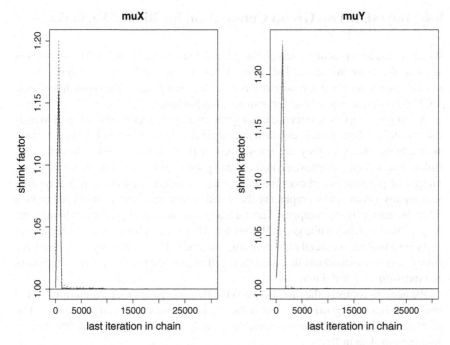

Fig. 8.9 Example of Gelman and Rubin shrink factor plot for two parameters

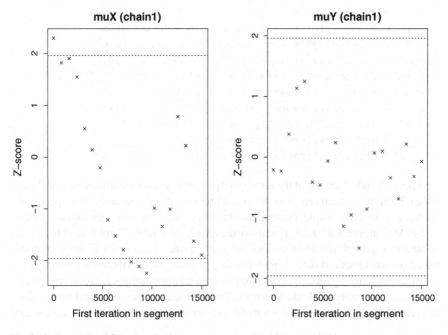

Fig. 8.10 Example of Geweke plot for two parameters based on one chain

8.4   Bayesian Two Group Comparison for Binary Variables

We can consider a practical example in order to demonstrate how MCMC algorithms assist in Bayesian inference. The example below can also be solved using a mathematical approach with a combination of a Beta prior and a Bernoulli likelihood. MCMC is used in this section for instructional purposes.

A company wishes to improve employees email practices by investing in Mango smart watches. The employees use mainly their desktop computers but need to carry their tablets whenever they are away from their workspace. Tablets however are bulkier and so many employees prefer to carry their personal cell phones with them. The use of personal cell phones for work-related matters is a security risk according to company policy and so replacing them with smart watches is considered to be a safer alternative by the company. The company conducts an experiment where group A gets smart watches while group B does not. They receive back answers on whether users have utilized their cell phones during the study. The results were measured in a binary scale for individuals that used their cell phones during the period of the study and individuals that did not.

We need to compare the rates between the two groups in order to determine if the smart watches are a good choice for reducing the likelihood for cell phone use.[4] The problem involves a dichotomous variable (exactly a yes or no question). We start by defining our data in R:

```
> source("generate.R")
> email$usedcellphone = 0 #generating random data
> email$usedcellphone[email$team == 0] = sample(c(0,1),
+ nrow(email[email$team == 0,]),2,prob=c(.80,.20))
> email$usedcellphone[email$team == 1] = sample(c(0,1),
+ nrow(email[email$team == 1,]),2,prob=c(.20,.80))
> s1 = sum(email$usedcellphone[email$team == 0])
> s2 = sum(email$usedcellphone[email$team == 1])
> n1 = nrow(email[email$team == 0,])
> n2 = nrow(email[email$team == 1,])
```

where $s1$ and $s2$ represent the number of people who end up using their cellphones for each group respectively, and, $n1$ and $n2$ represent the total number of people on each group. In our example, the total number of people varies between the two groups.

MCMC algorithms work based on the process of model building. The aim is to structure probability distributions for our parameters in order to simulate them based on our observed data. Understanding probability distributions beforehand is essential for building models. For example, normal distributions are reserved usually for numeric variables and take as parameters the mean of a variable and the standard deviation. In the case of binary variables, beta distributions are more appropriate

---

[4]An alternative approach to solving the problem would be to use Bayesian Probit Regression Jackman 2009.

Fig. 8.11 Example Beta distributions based on different α and β

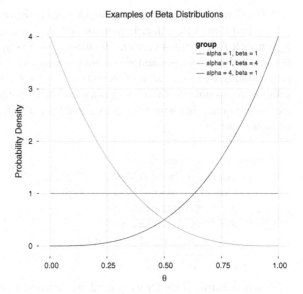

because they are continuous, bound between 0 and 1 and take two parameters α and β, which define the slope of the distribution. Figure 8.11 shows examples of beta distributions for a θ parameter. In our previous example with the digital device, we decided that θ values will represent a likelihood scale. In this problem, we can decide that θ values will denote the likelihood of cell phone use with 1 representing an absolute probability for using a cell phone while 0 representing no probability of using a cell phone. As such, α and β become representations of using and not using a cell phone for our beta distribution.

Just like our digital device problem turning on and off, we can define a parameter denoting cell phone use for each group, $\theta 1$ for group 1 and $\theta 2$ for group 2. These rates will also need to be assigned priors based on our prior belief. In this case, we decide that we do not have prior knowledge on what the outcome may be for our experiment and we define equal prior "results":

```
> s1prior = 1
> f1prior = 1
> s2prior = 1
> f2prior = 1
```

where $s1prior$ and $s2prior$ are the prior rates of people that use cell phones for the two groups and $f1prior$ and $f2prior$ are the prior rates for people that do not use cell phones for each group respectively. In this case the values for all variables are 1 but they could have been any number as long as high and low values are equal so that we can produce a uniform set of prior probabilities (see Fig. 8.11 first example).

MCMC modelling in R is represented by a set of distributions and their parameters (e.g., α and β for a Beta distribution) as well as functions. All of these are enclosed within an R function that contains the model. Models unlike programming code do not have to be written sequentially as they are not executed as such. Additionally, in programming we often declare functions as y = x + z where y is the unknown while x and z are variables with known values. In MCMC models, we could also declare the same function but with x and y as variables with a known value and z being the unknown variable.

```
> jags.bin <- function() {
+       theta1 ~ dbeta(s1prior,f1prior)
+       theta2 ~ dbeta(s2prior,f2prior)
+       s1 ~ dbin(theta1,n1)
+       s2 ~ dbin(theta2,n2)
+       delta <- theta1 - theta2
+ }
```

Our two distributions for $\theta 1$ and $\theta 2$ are declared within the JAGS model. JAGS stands for Just Another Gibbs Sampler and it is a program for analyzing Bayesian models using MCMC sampling. We first supply parameters and their assigned prior beliefs (which are uniform in this case) to our model. We also need to define the likelihood. Binomial distribution is our choice for this problem which is a discrete distribution using parameters as the probability rate (probability of using a cell phone) and the total number of sequences. From a programming perspective this may appear a bit peculiar, however, models do not have to operate sequentially or have functions and distributions being sequentially defined. As long as all variables, distributions and parameters are all accounted for, the model will produce results. In this case, $s1$, $s2$, $n1$, $n2$ are known discrete variables and $\theta 1$ and $\theta 2$ are unknown albeit with priors defined. Finally, we can also calculate the difference between $\theta 1$ and $\theta 2$ called δ (in the R code defined as delta).

After setting up our model we can proceed by setting the parameters for MCMC using the command *jag.model* and then utilize *coda.samples* to generate posterior samples based on the parameters of interest. The process simulates all variables for our model however the sampled chains that are returned are only those that interest us. These are declared as a list.

```
> n.simu <- 50000
> n.burnin <- n.simu/2
> par <- c("theta1","theta2","delta","deltaprior",
+       "theta1prior","theta2prior")
> D <- list(s1 = s1, s2 = s2, n1 = n1, n2 = n2,
+       s1prior = s1prior, s2prior = s2prior,
+       f1prior = f1prior, f2prior = f2prior)
> m.jags <- jags.model("jags.txt", data = D,
```

```
+       n.adapt = n.burnin, quiet = TRUE, n.chains = 4)
> s <- coda.samples(m.jags, par,
+       n.iter = n.simu - n.burnin, quiet = TRUE)
```

The object produced by *coda.samples* contains all the variables requested using the list *par*. The object can be converted to a data frame containing all chains for easier post-processing. The downside to this approach is that the data frame can be quite large unless thinning is applied. Using the data frame we can then obtain the mean value of the posterior sample for $\theta 1$, $\theta 2$, and δ.

```
> df = as.data.frame(as.matrix( s ))
> mean(df$theta1)
[1] 0.2335576
> mean(df$theta2)
[1] 0.7144396
> mean(df$delta)
[1] -0.480882
```

In this case, we can see that group B has a higher cell phone use rate than group A. The difference δ is almost half (0.481) for our values of θ that range between 0 and 1. Just like traditional confidence intervals in frequentist statistics we can also calculate 95 % probability intervals. The commonly used probability interval for Bayesian statistics is called *High Density Interval* (HDI) included in R's *BEST* package.

```
> c(hdi(df$theta1,.95)[1],hdi(df$theta1,.95)[2])
     lower      upper
0.0930076 0.3841601
> c(hdi(df$theta2,.95)[1],hdi(df$theta2,.95)[2])
     lower      upper
0.4879375 0.9260797
> c(hdi(df$delta,.95)[1],hdi(df$delta,.95)[2])
      lower      upper
-0.7445349 -0.2098999
```

We can observe that the probability interval for the difference is quite broad which is likely a result of a small sample. However, we can still be confident based on the results that group B exhibited higher cell phone use. In other words, the implementation of devices in group A had a substantial improvement in reducing cell phone use and therefore improving security in compliance with what the company wanted to achieve. But, how about hypothesis testing?

Bayesian inference also provides paths to perform hypothesis testing. A popular formula is *Bayes Factor* which allows us to test the odds ratio between two hypotheses (e.g., $H0$: $\delta = 0$ and $H1$: $\delta \neq 0$). This is covered in Chap. 9 of this book. An alternative to the Bayes Factor is provided by Kruschke (2010), which is similar to equivalence testing used in biomedical sciences. One can define a *Region of Practical Equivalence* (ROPE) around a point of non-difference between rates and determine on whether a practical difference exists between two rates. In our case, we could suggest that for the point of equivalence ($\delta = 0$) we define a ROPE in a ±0.20. The definition is dependent on the context and experimental design. For example, in our binary problem of cell phone use, we may assume that if the difference between two groups is less than 0.2 then we may decide that the smart watches are not a worthwhile investment. Different companies may be willing to invest on the smart watches with differences as low as 0.1. After a ROPE is defined, we identify whether we can accept the hypothesis of $\delta = 0$ or whether our 95 % HDI falls within the ROPE or falls completely outside the ROPE. As our sample size grows, 95 % HDI tends to accumulate more around the mean of the posterior sample and as such probability around the posterior mean value increases.

To calculate the percentage of our posterior sample that falls within the ROPE we need to determine if any of the sample values fall within our ROPE.

```
> ROPE = c(-0.2,0.2)
> (pcInROPE =   sum( df$delta > ROPE[1] & df$delta <
+ ROPE[2] ) / length( df$delta ) )
[1] 0.02984
```

Determining the amount of HDI that falls within the ROPE requires us to calculate what is the 95 % of our posterior sample for δ and then use a similar approach to determine what amount falls within the ROPE. The code for this is provided in the supplementary materials of the book.

For this particular example, 2.984 % of our posterior sample falls within the ROPE, while 0 % of our HDI falls within the ROPE. We can therefore reject the null hypothesis and accept that there is a substantial difference between groups.

Similar to our previous example, the advantage of using Bayesian inference to determine the improvement of processes due to the implementation of a product or user interface is that we can relaunch an experiment for future device implementations. The second experiment can then utilize the posterior results from the first experiment as priors.

8.5   Bayesian Two Group Comparison for Numeric Variables

In HCI, we often want to evaluate the difference for a numeric variable between two groups. In our smart watch example, we have measured the email response times between group A that had the smart watch and group B that did not have the smart watch.

The process of obtaining posterior samples for each group and hypothesis testing is similar to testing binary rates. The main difference involves establishing a model that can reflect the nature of the numeric variable.

In this case, distributions of numeric variables are usually normal. A normal distribution is a continuous probability distribution that accumulates around a single point and gradually dissipates (see Fig. 8.6). Comparing two rates between normal distributions is establishing the difference between their two means. Hence, our likelihood portion for our model will include a loop between our data for each group using a normal distribution.

```
> jags.bin <- function() {
+     for (i in 1:n1) {
+         group1[i] ~ dnorm(muX, tauX)
+     }
+     for (i in 1:n2) {
+         group2[i] ~ dnorm(muY, tauY)
+     }
+     muX ~ dnorm(0, 0.001)
+     muY ~ dnorm(0, 0.001)
+     sigmaX ~ dunif(0, 1000)
+     sigmaY ~ dunif(0, 1000)
+     tauX <- 1 / (sigmaX * sigmaX)
+     tauY <- 1 / (sigmaY * sigmaY)
+     delta <- muY - muX
+ }
```

Notice that in this case the known part is the list of values for *group1* and *group2* that are indexed by i within the loop. The means, μ_X and μ_Y (in the code typed as muX and muY), as well as the standard deviations, τ_X and τ_Y (in the code typed as tauX and tauY), are the unknown components. Normal distributions in JAGS use standard deviations using τ and not σ which is more common in statistics. We need to take this into account when modeling.

Since the means μ_X and μ_Y are our rates of interest (just like θ previously), we need to represent them in the form of a probability distribution not a single point estimate. As such we can set their priors in a form of a normal distribution. We also set the standard deviations, τ_X and τ_Y, derived from σ_X and σ_Y (in the code typed as sigmaX and sigmaY) in a form of a uniform distribution where all probabilities are the same for all possible values.

Finally, we add to the model any final calculated variables such as the difference between the means, δ (in the code typed as delta).

By declaring the model using JAGS, we can obtain posterior samples and determine the means for the two groups. These can be obtained as a point estimate (e.g.,

Fig. 8.12 Probability
distributions between Group
A and Group B for the smart
watch experiment

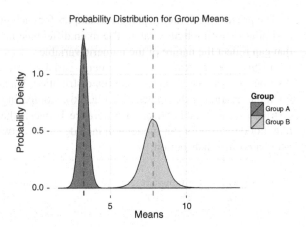

based on the mean of posterior sample) or as a posterior probability distributions for the two groups which can be plotted. These are shown on Fig. 8.12.

It is evident that the implementation of smart watches for group A had a dramatic effect in reducing email response time. Notice that the two probability distributions do not overlap and that we are more certain about a point estimate for group A.

We can further calculate the point estimate based on the mean for the posterior samples of the two means, their 95 % HDI, and further use the posterior sample for δ to determine based on a ROPE whether to reject or accept the null hypothesis.

The results for this particular experiment suggest that there is a considerable difference between group A ($M = 3.222$, 95 % HDI [2.597, 3.822]) and group B ($M = 7.835$, 95 % HDI [6.372, 9.239]) since the 95 % HDI for δ falls outside the ROPE of ± 0.2. The mean difference is 4.6 minutes which can have a considerable effect on productivity. Just like before, whether smart watches are a worthwhile investment depends on the company and the threshold used as a ROPE. For example, in our case the managers have decided on using a really small ROPE, which is a 0.2 minutes difference. On the other hand, if managers were to decide that an investment was worth it only if email response time was beyond three minutes then the ROPE would have to be set to 3. Even for this case, the HDI falls outside the ROPE so the smart watches are a good investment. An alternative model to the one offered in this chapter for a Bayesian t-test can be found by Lee and Wagenmakers (2014).

8.6 Bayesian Regression with Numeric Predicted Variable

Aside from determining how an experimental design may influence the outcome of email response time, we can also attempt to determine information such as how technical efficacy of people may affect email response time. We can start by generating an artificially correlated variable for illustrative purposes.

```
> source("generate.r")
> email$technicalEfficacy = email$responseTime *
+     runif(length(email$responseTime), 0.0, 5.0)
```

Regression models that involve numeric predictors are implemented using the regular regression formula ($y = b_0 + b_1 * x$) with a slight modification:

```
> jags.bin <- function() {
+     for(i in 1:N) {
+         y[i] ~ dnorm(f[i], tau)
+         f[i] <- b0 + b1 * x[i]
+     }
+
+     # Priors
+     tau <- 1/pow(sigma,2)
+     sigma ~ dunif(0, 1000)
+     b0 ~ dnorm(0, 0.001)
+     b1 ~ dnorm(0, 0.001)
+
+     # R-squared calculation
+     y.mean <- mean(y[])
+     for (i in 1:N) {
+         ss.res.temp[i] <- y[i] - f[i]
+         ss.res[i] <- pow(ss.res.temp[i], 2)
+         ss.reg.temp[i] <- f[i] - y.mean
+         ss.reg[i] <- pow(ss.reg.temp[i], 2)
+         ss.tot.temp[i] <- y[i] - y.mean
+         ss.tot[i] <- pow(ss.tot.temp[i], 2)
+     }
+     r.squared <- (sum(ss.reg[])) / (sum(ss.tot[]))
+ }
```

In this case, the known variables are y (representing response time), x (representing technical efficacy) and N which is the total number of cases that are used for our loop. Our modeled variable is f which forms the typical regression formula with b_0 being the intercept and b_1 the coefficient for our predictor variable.

Priors are defined in our model for τ, σ, b_0 and b_1. The priors in this case are objective since there is no prior knowledge for these variables. Priors for the coefficients have a mean of 0 and a small standard deviation while sigma is a uniform distribution, which is a distribution with equal probability for all outcomes.

Using the coefficients b_0 and b_1, we can obtain all relevant data for our regression model similar to a frequentist linear regression. We can also implement within the model other calculated statistics. An important measure for regression is calculating R^2 (the amount of explained variance by our model) and in Bayesian regression we

Fig. 8.13 Probability distribution for R^2 when modeling email response time and technical efficacy. *Red dotted line* indicates the mean for the posterior sample. The more narrower the curve around a single point, the more likely the R^2 is around that single point. Narrower curves also produce tighter HDIs for R^2 which increases are certainty for the accounted variance of a model around a specific point

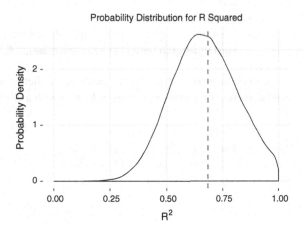

can obtain a probability distribution for it. In this example, the implementation of R^2 uses the exact same formula used in frequentist regression.

We can then obtain our posterior samples the same way we did before using *JAGS* and *coda.samples*. Figure 8.13 demonstrates the probability distribution for R^2 which indicates a substantial amount of accounted variance.

We can further obtain point estimates for our coefficients as well as their 95 % HDIs.

```
> mean(df$b0)
[1] 2.230924
> c(hdi(df$b0,.95)[1],hdi(df$b0,.95)[2])
   lower    upper
1.463655 3.008316
> mean(df$b1)
[1] 0.1877244
> c(hdi(df$b1,.95)[1],hdi(df$b1,.95)[2])
   lower    upper
0.1433942 0.2326414
> mean(df$r.squared)
[1] 0.6821717
> c(hdi(df$r.squared,.95)[1],hdi(df$r.squared,.95)[2])
   lower    upper
0.3720231 1.0010375
```

Notice that the upper bounds for the R^2 95 % HDI exceed 1 which is the otherwise analytical upper limit. However, since in Bayesian statistics we simulate calculated variables, these could go beyond the limits for metrics such as R^2. It is a consequence caused by the "noise" created by our simulation. As the sample size increases this behavior will dissipate and R^2 will be bounded between 0 and 1 as it is expected to be.

The accounted variance (R^2) informs us that technical efficacy is an important factor that affects email response time. The coefficient for technical efficacy $(b1)$ has a mean of 0.18 according to its posterior probability distribution. The arbitrary scale for technical efficacy used in this example varies between 0 and 51 with lowest scores representing higher efficacy. Assuming that email response time is measured in minutes, this translates to about a minute of slower response time for every five-point increase (less technical expertise) in the technical efficacy scale. The result suggests that training individuals to have better technical skills will result in a substantial increase in email response time. On the other hand, if the email response time was measured in seconds, the increase in response time may have been negligible even though our model will still suggest a large accounted variance between technical efficacy and email response time.

8.7 Do Not Reinvent the Wheel

The examples demonstrated in this chapter are not meant to cover a complete view of Bayesian inference but rather serve as an introduction. At this point, it may seem that Bayesian inference may involve a lot of work for HCI professionals, however, this is not the case. Bayesian statistics were prevented from appearing in mainstream curriculum due to the computational inefficiency that existed for MCMC algorithms over the past decades. This fact has also restricted many to develop software for Bayesian statistics that requires the same effort comparable to building a traditional t-test or linear regression model. At the moment, software for Bayesian statistics is not as flexible for building complex models and *JAGS* or similar modeling software is necessary. However, many methods frequently used by HCI professionals such as a variety of regression models as well as various statistical tests (e.g., t-test) are available. For example, the package *BEST* in R Kruschke (based on 2013) provides a way for testing two group means. Also, packages such as *Zelig* Imai et al. 2008 include an ensemble of many Bayesian methods such as Bayesian Logistic Regression, Multinomial Logistic Regression, Linear Regression and Ordered Probit Regression. As a brief example, the regression model that we tested previously can be built using Zelig with just two lines of code.

```
> z.out <- zelig(output ~ predictor,
+     model ="normal.bayes", data=df,
+     mcmc = n.simu - n.burnin, burnin = n.burnin)
> summary(z.out)

Call: zelig(formula = output ~ predictor,
      model = "normal.bayes", data = df,
```

```
       mcmc = n.simu - n.burnin, burnin = n.burnin)

Iterations = 25001:50000
Thinning interval = 1
Number of chains = 1
Sample size per chain = 25000

  Mean, standard deviation, and quantiles
    for marginal posterior distributions.

                Mean      SD    2.5%     50%    97.5%
(Intercept)   2.2323  0.3848  1.4725  2.2316  2.9955
predictor     0.1876  0.0223  0.1440  0.1875  0.2316
sigma2        2.7399  0.6624  1.7388  2.6451  4.3284
```

Research papers in HCI as well as other fields have utilized Bayesian analysis as the main analytical method or as a supplementary method Tsikerdekis 2013; Triantafyllopoulos and Pikoulas 2002; Muchnik et al. 2013; Volf et al. 2014; Trusov et al. 2010. When utilizing Bayesian methods the degree of introduction can vary. Some authors choose to provide a bit more background information on the methods used while others prefer to publish the result and refer readers to textbooks for more information on the methods. The same degree of variance can be found in the use of probability distribution charts. At times, authors choose to display point estimates even though Bayesian analyses offer probability distributions for the parameters of interest. The language can also vary when it comes to reporting results. For example, consideration should be given when one needs to report MCMC sample, burnin, thinning and additional measures that may be essential for replicating the same results or approximating them.

Bayesian inference has arrived and it is not just easier to perform but much more powerful compared to frequentist statistics Wagenmakers et al. 2008. It adds more diversity to HCI research and thus produces more intuitive results that can be directly interpreted based on current and past knowledge. It is time for all of us to listen to our inner Bayesian that is struggling to get out!

References

Albert J (2009) Bayesian Computation with R. Number 3 in Use R! Springer, New York

Aldrich J (2008) R.A. Fisher on Bayes and Bayes Theorem. Bayesian Anal 3(1):161–170

Chung KL, AitSahlia F (2003) Elementary probability theory: with stochastic processes and an introduction to mathematical finance. Springer Undergraduate Texts in Mathematics and Technology, Springer

Cowles MK, Carlin BP (1996) Markov Chain Monte Carlo convergence diagnostics: a comparative review. J Am Stat Assoc 91(434):883–904

Gelman A, Rubin DB (1992) Inference from iterative simulation using multiple sequences. Stat Sci 7(4):457–472

Gilks WR (2005) Markov chain monte carlo. In: Encyclopedia of biostatistics. Wiley

Imai K, King G, Lau O (2008) Toward a common framework for statistical analysis and development. J Comput Graph Stat 17(4):892–913

Jackman S (2009) Bayesian analysis for the social sciences. Wiley, Hoboken, NJ

Jaynes ET (2003) Probability theory: the logic of science. Cambridge University Press, Cambridge

Kruschke JK (2010) Doing bayesian data analysis: a tutorial with R and BUGS, vol 1 (Academic Press)

Kruschke JK (2013) Bayesian estimation supersedes the t test. J Exp Psychol: Gen 142(2):573–603

Lee MD, Wagenmakers EJ (2014) Bayesian cognitive modeling: a practical course. Cambridge University Press, Cambridge

Lynch SM (2007) Introduction to applied bayesian statistics and estimation for social scientists. Springer

McGrayne SB (2011) The theory that would not die: how Bayes' rule cracked the enigma code, hunted down russian submarines, and emerged triumphant from two centuries of controversy. Yale University Press

Muchnik L, Aral S, Taylor SJ (2013) Social influence bias: a randomized experiment. Science 341(6146):647–651

Plummer M, Best N, Cowles K, Vines K (2006) CODA: convergence diagnosis and output analysis for MCMC. R News 6(1):7–11

Robert C, Casella G (2011) A short history of Markov Chain Monte Carlo: subjective recollections from incomplete data. Stat Sci 26(1):102–115

Rossi PE, Allenby GM, McCulloch R (2005) Bayesian statistics and marketing. Wiley

Triantafyllopoulos K, Pikoulas J (2002) Multivariate Bayesian regression applied to the problem of network security. J Forecast 21(8):579–594

Trusov M, Bodapati AV, Bucklin RE (2010) Determining influential users. J Mark Res, XL VII:643–658

Tsikerdekis M (2013) Dynamic voting interface in social media: Does it affect individual votes? In: Boas PvE, Groen FCA, Italiano GF, Nawrocki J, Sack H (eds) SOFSEM 2013: theory and practice of computer science, Springer, pp 552–563

Volf P, Jakubuv J, Koranda L, Sislak D, Pechoucek M, Mereu S, Hilburn B, Nguyen DN (2014) Validation of an air-traffic controller behavioral model for fast time simulation. In: 2014 Integrated communications, navigation and surveillance conference (ICNS), conference proceedings, IEEE. pp T1–1–T1–9

Wagenmakers E-J, Lee MD, Lodewyckx T, Iverson G (2008) Bayesian versus frequentist inference. In: Hoijtink H, Klugkist I, Boelen PA (eds) Bayesian evaluation of informative hypotheses in psychology. Springer, New York, pp 181–207

Chapter 9
Bayesian Testing of Constrained Hypotheses

Joris Mulder

Abstract Statistical hypothesis testing plays a central role in applied research to determine whether theories or expectations are supported by the data or not. Such expectations are often formulated using order constraints. For example an executive board may expect that sales representatives who wear a smart watch will respond faster to their emails than sales representatives who don't wear a smart watch. In addition it may be expected that this difference becomes more pronounced over time because representatives need to learn how to use the smart watch effectively. By translating these expectations into statistical hypotheses with equality and/or order constraints we can determine whether the expectations receive evidence from the data. In this chapter we show how a Bayesian statistical approach can effectively be used for this purpose. This Bayesian approach is more flexible than the traditional p-value test in the sense that multiple hypotheses with equality as well as order constraints can be tested against each other in a direct manner. The methodology can straightforwardly be used by practitioners using the freely downloadable software package BIEMS. An application in a human-computer interaction is used for illustration.

9.1 Introduction

In many applications people have expectations or theories regarding a certain phenomenon which they want to test based on the observed data. In medical research for example we want to know whether a new drug treatment works better than a placebo treatment; in sociology want to know whether people with low socio-economic status have less access to health care than people with high socio-economic status; and in marketing we want to know whether sales representatives who wear a smart watch respond faster to their emails and sell more products than sales representatives who don't wear a smart watch. In order to answer such questions we need empirical data

J. Mulder (✉)
Department of Methodology and Statistics, Tilburg University,
Tilburg, The Netherlands
e-mail: j.mulder3@tilburguniversity.edu

© Springer International Publishing Switzerland 2016
J. Robertson and M. Kaptein (eds.), *Modern Statistical Methods for HCI*,
Human–Computer Interaction Series, DOI 10.1007/978-3-319-26633-6_9

to determine whether our expectations are supported or not. This can be done by first translating our expectations to statistical hypotheses and then use a statistical testing criterion to determine which hypothesis receives most support from the data. In this chapter we discuss how the Bayes factor, a relatively new criterion for hypothesis testing, can effectively be used for this purpose.

9.1.1 Multiple Hypothesis Testing in HCI

For the purpose of this book we consider a human-computer interaction (HCI) application where the interest is in the effect of smart watches on the response times of sales representatives to their email. In this application we use hypothetical data containing the response times of the representatives in two sales teams: representatives in team B received a smart watch, referred to as the 'Mango', which allowed them to check their email at all time, and representatives in team A did not receive a smart watch. For this application we are interested in testing the effects between the two teams as well as testing time effects across the three months. We consider competing hypotheses with different relationships between the response time means: μ_{A1}, μ_{A2}, μ_{A3}, μ_{B1}, μ_{B2}, and μ_{B3}, where μ_{A1} denotes the mean response time of team A in the 1st month, for example.

In the first hypothesis a positive team effect is expected, i.e., team B responds faster to emails than team A on average, as well as a positive time effect, i.e., representatives respond faster to their email over consecutive months. Note that the direction of the effect is formulated in terms of the speed of a response. So a positive effect implies a faster response and thus a smaller response time. The motivation of the positive team effect is that having email on ones wrist causes faster response times. The motivation of the positive time effect is that sales representatives in both teams become more efficient in responding to their emails over time. This expectation can be translated to the 'all positive effects hypothesis' H_1 with the following combination of order constraints between the mean response times:

$$H_1 : \begin{cases} \mu_{A1} > \mu_{A2} > \mu_{A3} \\ \vee \qquad \vee \qquad \vee \\ \mu_{B1} > \mu_{B2} > \mu_{B3}. \end{cases} \tag{9.1}$$

In the second hypothesis we assume that there is only a positive time effect for team B and no time effect for team A. The motivation is that for team A nothing changes over time and therefore no time effect is expected. For Team B on the other hand a learning effect is expected because the representatives need to learn how to use the Mango effectively. This 'only positive time effect for Mango users hypothesis' H_2 can be written as a combination of equality and order constraints on the means,

$$H_2 : \begin{cases} \mu_{A1} = \mu_{A2} = \mu_{A3} \\ \vee \qquad \vee \qquad \vee \\ \mu_{B1} > \mu_{B2} > \mu_{B3}. \end{cases} \tag{9.2}$$

In the third hypothesis no time effect is expected for both teams and a positive team effect is expected. The motivation is that no learning effect is expected over time. The 'positive team effect, no time effect hypothesis' H_3 can be formulated as

$$H_3 : \begin{cases} \mu_{A1} = \mu_{A2} = \mu_{A3} \\ \vee \qquad \vee \qquad \vee \\ \mu_{B1} = \mu_{B2} = \mu_{B3}, \end{cases} \qquad (9.3)$$

The fourth hypothesis is based on the idea that wearing a smart watch has no effect on the response times in addition to smart phones which are already used by all representatives in both teams. A positive time effect is expected on the other hand because past results have shown that representatives tend to challenge themselves more and more every month to communicate with customers more efficiently. The 'positive time effect, no team effect hypothesis' H_4 can be formulated as

$$H_4 : \begin{cases} \mu_{A1} > \mu_{A2} > \mu_{A3} \\ \| \qquad \| \qquad \| \\ \mu_{B1} > \mu_{B2} > \mu_{B3}, \end{cases} \qquad (9.4)$$

The fifth hypothesis corresponds to the classical null hypothesis that neither a team effect nor a time effect is expected. The 'no effects' H_5 with only equality constraints between the means can be written as

$$H_5 : \begin{cases} \mu_{A1} = \mu_{A2} = \mu_{A3} \\ \| \qquad \| \qquad \| \\ \mu_{B1} = \mu_{B2} = \mu_{B3}, \end{cases} \qquad (9.5)$$

Finally the sixth hypothesis assumes that none of the above hypotheses are true. This 'complement hypothesis' H_6 can be written as

$$H_6 : ``H_1, \ldots, H_5 \text{ not true}". \qquad (9.6)$$

Thus the testing problem comes down to determining which hypothesis of H_1 to H_6 receives most evidence from the observed data. The difficulty of this test lies in the fact that the hypotheses of interest contain equality constraints as well as order constraints. In addition, we consider a multiple hypothesis test instead of testing a single hypothesis against one other hypothesis.

9.1.2 Limitations of Classical Methods

The most commonly used technique for testing statistical hypotheses is the classical p-value. A p-value quantifies how close the observed data are from a null hypothesis if it would be true. Thus, a small value indicates that the null hypothesis may be false. Typically we reject the null hypothesis if the p-value is smaller than some prespecified significance level. Although most users only use the p-value for testing a null hypothesis with only equality constraints (i.e., H_5 given above) against the classical alternative H_A : "at least one pair of means is unequal", there are two types of p-value tests available for hypotheses with order constraints. First, p-value tests are available for testing a null hypothesis with only equality constraints against an alternative with only order constraints. So a p-value can be computed of the 'no effects hypothesis' H_5 against the 'all positive effects hypothesis' H_1. Second, p-values can be used for testing a null hypothesis with only order constraints against an unconstrained alternative. For example, a p-value test is available for testing H_1 against its complement. Classical references on this methodology are Barlow et al. (1972), Robertson et al. (1988), and Silvapulle and Sen (2004). The multiple hypothesis testing problem given above however does not fall in either one of these two categories. For example, a p-value is not available for testing the 'positive team effect, no time effect hypothesis' H_3, with equality as well as order constraints, against the 'positive time effect, no team effect hypothesis' H_4, also with equality as well as order constraints. Furthermore, we are interested in testing all six hypotheses simultaneously. Classical p-value tests however are designed for testing one specific null hypothesis against one other hypothesis. Finally it is important to note that p-values can only be used to determine if a null hypothesis is false; p-values cannot be used to quantify evidence in favor of a null hypothesis.

Because of the limitations of this methodology, testing complex hypotheses with equality and/or order constraints between the parameters of interest are often performed using post-hoc tests. The general idea is that we first perform an omnibus test of a null hypothesis (i.e., H_5 in the above test) against its complement H_A that at least one pair of means is unequal using a prespecified significance level α (typically 0.05). Subsequently, if there is enough evidence to reject H_0 (i.e., $p < \alpha$), we perform post-hoc tests between every pair of means in order to find out how the parameters are related to each other. This approach suffers from several problems however.

The omnibus test has two possible outcomes. First, we may observe a p-value that is larger than the significance level which implies that there is not evidence in the data to reject the null hypothesis. In this scenario we end up in a state of ignorance because there is not enough evidence in the data to reject the null hypothesis but we also cannot claim there is support for the null hypothesis. Again note that a p-value can only be used to falsify the null hypothesis, not to quantify evidence for the null (Wagenmakers 2007).

Second we may observe a p-value that is smaller then the significance level which implies that there is enough evidence in the data to reject the null hypothesis that all means are equal. In this case we need to perform post-hoc tests to determine which pair of means is unequal. In the above example where we compare six different means, there are 15 different pairs of means and thus we need to perform 15 post-hoc tests in total, namely, $H_0 : \mu_{A1} = \mu_{A2}$ versus $H_A : \mu_{A1} \neq \mu_{A2}$, $H_0 : \mu_{A1} = \mu_{B1}$ versus $H_A : \mu_{A1} \neq \mu_{B1}$, ..., until $H_0 : \mu_{B2} = \mu_{B3}$ versus $H_A : \mu_{B2} \neq \mu_{B3}$. Performing 15 different hypothesis tests based on the 15 p-values is very problematic.

If we do not correct for the fact that we performed 15 different hypothesis significance tests, we will get a huge inflation of the type I error probability of incorrectly rejecting a null hypothesis. If we would correct for performing that many tests (e.g., using Bonferroni by dividing the significance level α by 15) the tests are very conservative. Consequently there is a large chance that we end up not rejecting any null hypothesis even though some effects are present (van de Schoot et al. 2011). Another problem with post-hoc tests is that we may end up with conflicting conclusions, e.g., there is not enough evidence to reject $H_0 : \mu_{A1} = \mu_{A2}$ or $H_0 : \mu_{A1} = \mu_{A3}$ but there is enough evidence to reject $H_0 : \mu_{A2} = \mu_{A3}$. This suggests that $\mu_{A1} = \mu_{A2}$ and $\mu_{A1} = \mu_{A3}$ while $\mu_{A2} \neq \mu_{A2}$ which is problematic to interpret. For this reason, the omnibus test in combination with the post-hoc tests is not recommended for the multiple hypothesis test discussed in Sect. 9.1.1.

Another class of criteria that can be used for hypothesis testing (and model comparison) is the class of information criteria. Akaike's information criterion (AIC) (Akaike 1973), the Bayesian (or Schwarz') information criterion (BIC) (Schwarz 1978), and the deviance information criterion (DIC) (Spiegelhalter et al. 2002) are popular examples. These methods are useful when more than two hypotheses (or models) have been formulated. The basic idea is that each hypothesis is evaluated based on its fit to the data and based on the complexity of the statistical model underlying each hypothesis. The complexity of a hypothesis is quantified through the number of free parameters. For example the null hypothesis $H_0 : \mu_{A1} = \mu_{A2}$ has one parameter less than the alternative hypothesis $H_A : \mu_{A1} \neq \mu_{A2}$. And therefore, when the estimates for μ_{A1} and μ_{A2} are equal for a given data set, this suggests that both hypotheses H_0 and H_A fit the data equally well, and therefore an information criterion will result in preferring H_0 because it is the least complex hypothesis. When a hypothesis contains order constraints however the number of free parameters is ill-defined. For example how many free parameters does $H_1 : \mu_{A1} < \mu_{A2}$ contain in relation to $H_A : \mu_{A1} \neq \mu_{A2}$? Another potential issue with information criteria is that the scale of information criteria is difficult to interpret. For example when three competing hypotheses result in AIC values of 1202, 1200, and 1209, respectively, we learn that the second hypothesis is the best because it has the smallest AIC value. The AIC values however do not tell us *how much* better the second hypothesis is in comparison to the first or third hypothesis. For this reason, we do not know anything about the certainty of our conclusions when selecting the second hypothesis for the data at hand.

9.1.3 Bayes Factors for Multiple Hypothesis Testing

The issues discussed above are avoided when using the Bayes factor, a Bayesian criterion for hypothesis testing and model selection originally developed by Jeffreys (1961). As will be shown the Bayes factor can be used for testing multiple hypotheses with equality and/or order constraints in a direct manner. Furthermore, Bayes factors can be translated to the posterior probability of each hypothesis to be true after observing the data. These posterior probabilities give a clear answer how much evidence there is in the data given the hypotheses under consideration.

For a thorough overview of the use of Bayes factors for testing scientific theories, see a classic reference such as Kass and Raftery (1995). For more information about Bayes factor tests in the context of hypotheses with order constraints we refer the interested reader to Klugkist et al. (2005) in the context of ANOVA models, Kato and Hoijtink (2006) for linear mixed models, Mulder et al. (2009) for repeated measures models, Braeken et al. (2015) for regression models, van de Schoot et al. (2012) and Gu et al. (2014) for structural equation models, Mulder (In Press) for testing order constraints in correlation matrices, or Hoijtink (2011) for an overview or various methods on this topic.

9.1.4   Outline

The chapter is organized as follows. Section 9.2 starts with an introduction to Bayesian estimation of the HCI application discussed in the introduction. In Sect. 9.3 Bayesian hypothesis testing is discussed using the Bayes factor. Section 9.4 discusses a Bayesian test for a simple example using BIEMS (Bayesian inequality and equality constrained model selection, Mulder et al. 2012), a freely downloadable statistical software package that can be used for Bayesian hypothesis testing. Section 9.5 discusses the evaluation of the constrained hypotheses in the HCI application discussed in Sect. 9.1.1. Finally, Sect. 9.6 ends with a short discussion.

9.2   Bayesian Estimation in the HCI Application

Before going into detail about Bayesian hypothesis testing in the HCI application we discuss some basics about Bayesian estimation for readers who are not familiar with this topic. As will be seen the Bayesian approach can result in the same conclusions as the classical approach using maximum likelihood when no prior knowledge is available. When prior knowledge is available on the other hand, the Bayesian approach allows one to combine this with the information in the data in a natural way via Bayes' theorem. For an introduction to Bayesian data analysis we refer the interested reader to Chap. 8 of this book, Lynch (2007), or Gelman et al. (2004).

9.2.1   The Multivariate Normal Model

In the first stage of a Bayesian data analysis a statistical model must be formulated that captures the dependency structure and the nature of the data. In the HCI application discussed in the introduction we can assume that the average monthly response times are independent across the two groups. Furthermore, the average monthly response times of each representative over the three months are assumed to be dependent. For example, an executive who is relatively fast (slow) in the first month is likely to be fast (slow) in the second month. For this illustration, we will also assume that the monthly average response times of the representatives are normally distributed. Note that slight violations of the normality assumption is not problematic due to large sample theory (e.g., see Gelman et al. 2004). Finally, we assume unequal means over time and between teams and equal error covariance matrices for both teams. Thus the following multivariate analysis of variance (MANOVA) model is used for these data

$$\mathbf{y}_{A,i_A} = N(\boldsymbol{\mu}_A, \boldsymbol{\Sigma}) \text{ and } \mathbf{y}_{B,i_B} = N(\boldsymbol{\mu}_B, \boldsymbol{\Sigma}), \qquad (9.7)$$

where $\mathbf{y}_{A,i_A}$ and $\mathbf{y}_{B,i_B}$ are vectors of length 3 with the measurements of the i_Ath representative in team A and the i_Bth representative in team B, for $i_A = 1, \ldots, n_A$, and $i_B = 1, \ldots, n_B$, $\boldsymbol{\mu}_A = (\mu_{A1}, \mu_{A2}, \mu_{A3})'$ and $\boldsymbol{\mu}_B = (\mu_{B1}, \mu_{B2}, \mu_{B3})'$ contain the measurement means in month 1, 2, and 3, for team A and team B, respectively, and $\boldsymbol{\Sigma}$ denotes the common positive definite error covariance matrix. In these data team A consisted of $n_A = 114$ representatives and team B consisted of $n_B = 86$ representatives.

9.2.2   The Prior: A Formalization of Prior Beliefs

After the model is specified a *prior distribution* (or simply *prior*) needs to be chosen for the unknown model parameters, $\boldsymbol{\mu}_A$, $\boldsymbol{\mu}_B$, and $\boldsymbol{\Sigma}$. The prior is denoted by $p(\boldsymbol{\mu}_A, \boldsymbol{\mu}_B, \boldsymbol{\Sigma})$. The prior reflects the information we have about the model parameters before observing the data. Depending on the amount of prior information that is available we can specify a *noninformative* prior, a *weakly informative* prior (which contains very little information relative to the information in the data), or an *informative* prior. A commonly used noninformative prior is the improper Jeffreys prior which is given by $p^J(\boldsymbol{\mu}_A, \boldsymbol{\mu}_B, \boldsymbol{\Sigma}) \propto |\boldsymbol{\Sigma}|^{-\frac{P+1}{2}}$, where $P = 3$ is the number of dependent measurements. Note that the Jeffreys' prior for $\boldsymbol{\mu}_A$ and $\boldsymbol{\mu}_B$ is flat and therefore every value for these model parameters is equally likely a priori. For this reason we can state that the Jeffreys prior reflects prior ignorance.[1]

On the other hand, prior information may be available about the mean response times, for example, based on past results or personal experience. When prior information is available about the response times, an informative prior can be specified. For example the company may expect that the response times will be close to the response times in the previous months which were approximately equal to, say, 350

---

[1]Note that the Jeffreys prior is not a proper probability distribution (it is improper). This implies that it does not integrate to 1. Improper priors can be used in Bayesian estimation when there is enough information in the data to obtain a proper posterior. In this application this is the case when $n_A + n_B \geq 5$ (i.e., $P = 3$ plus the number of groups/teams), and $n_A, n_B \geq 2$.

s. If the executive board is uncertain about the response times in the following months a weakly informative prior can be specified with mean 350 and a standard deviation of 100. This implies that the board has 95 % prior beliefs that the monthly response times lies between 154 and 546. This prior can be qualified as 'weakly informative' because essentially all board members (even very optimistic or pessimistic board members) are confident that the monthly response times of the sales representatives will fall in this region. This weakly informative prior (with index WI) can be written as $p^{WI}(\mu_A) = N(3501_3, 100^2 I_3)$ and $p^{WI}(\mu_B) = N(3501_3, 100^2 I_3)$, where 1_3 is a vector of length 3 with ones and I_3 is the identity matrix of length 3.

It may also be the case that the board is confident that the mean response times are very close to the response time means of previous months. This more informative prior state can be translated to an informative prior with means of 350 and smaller standard deviations of, say, 10. This implies that the board expects that they have 95 % prior belief that the true response time means lie between 330 and 370. This informative prior (with index I) can be written as $p^I(\mu_A) = N(3501_3, 10^2 I_3)$ and $p^I(\mu_B) = N(3501_3, 10^2 I_3)$.

Specifying an informative prior for the covariance matrix Σ is often more difficult because the error (co)variances are more difficult to interpret than the means. For this reason we set the noninformative Jeffreys prior for Σ in the weakly informative prior as well as in the informative prior for the means. In sum, the noninformative Jeffreys' prior, the weakly informative prior, and the informative prior are then given by

$$p^J(\mu_A, \mu_B, \Sigma) \propto |\Sigma|^{-2}$$
$$p^{WI}(\mu_A, \mu_B, \Sigma) = N_{\mu_A}(3501_3, 10^2 I_3) \times N_{\mu_B}(3501_3, 10^2 I_3) \times |\Sigma|^{-2} \quad (9.8)$$
$$p^I(\mu_A, \mu_B, \Sigma) = N_{\mu_A}(3501_3, 100^2 I_3) \times N_{\mu_B}(3501_3, 100^2 I_3) \times |\Sigma|^{-2},$$

respectively.

Finally note that we could also have specified different priors for the mean response times of team A and team B. This would be reasonable if the board is confident that the means across teams will be different a priori. We choose to set equal priors for all means however to reflect prior ignorance regarding the differences between the means.

9.2.3   The Posterior: Our Belief After Observing the Data

The data are contained in the $(n_A + n_B) \times 3$ data matrix Y where the first n_A rows of Y contain the average response times of the sales representatives in team A over the three months and the remaining n_B rows contain the response times of the sales representatives in team B over the three months. The information in the data about the model parameters is reflected in the likelihood function, denoted by $p(Y|\mu_A, \mu_B, \Sigma)$. The likelihood quantifies how likely the observations are given the unknown model parameters.

In a Bayesian data analysis our prior knowledge, reflected in the prior distribution, is updated with the information in the data, reflected in the likelihood function, using Bayes' theorem:

$$p(\boldsymbol{\mu}_A, \boldsymbol{\mu}_B, \boldsymbol{\Sigma}|\mathbf{Y}) = \frac{p(\mathbf{Y}|\boldsymbol{\mu}_A, \boldsymbol{\mu}_B, \boldsymbol{\Sigma})p(\boldsymbol{\mu}_A, \boldsymbol{\mu}_B, \boldsymbol{\Sigma})}{p(\mathbf{Y})}, \tag{9.9}$$

where $p(\boldsymbol{\mu}_A, \boldsymbol{\mu}_B, \boldsymbol{\Sigma}|\mathbf{Y})$ denotes the posterior distribution of the model parameters and $p(\mathbf{Y})$ denotes the marginal likelihood of the data under the model. The posterior distribution reflects the information we have about the model parameters after observing the data. The marginal likelihood plays an important role in Bayesian hypothesis testing as will be shown in the next section. In Bayesian estimation, the marginal likelihood only serves as a normalizing constant in (9.9) because it does not depend on the unknown parameters. For this reason, Bayes' theorem is sometimes written in the simpler form,

$$p(\boldsymbol{\mu}_A, \boldsymbol{\mu}_B, \boldsymbol{\Sigma}|\mathbf{Y}) \propto p(\mathbf{Y}|\boldsymbol{\mu}_A, \boldsymbol{\mu}_B, \boldsymbol{\Sigma})p(\boldsymbol{\mu}_A, \boldsymbol{\mu}_B, \boldsymbol{\Sigma}), \tag{9.10}$$

which reads as "posterior is proportional to likelihood times prior".

The posterior can be used to get useful statistics, such as Bayesian point estimates or Bayesian credibility intervals (the Bayesian equivalence to classical confidence intervals) for the unknown parameters. A relatively easy and flexible way to obtain such statistics is by drawing a sample of sufficient size, say, 1,000,000 draws, of the unknown parameters $(\boldsymbol{\mu}_A, \boldsymbol{\mu}_B, \boldsymbol{\Sigma})$ from the posterior in (9.10). This can be done using a Gibbs sampler. The general idea of a Gibbs sampler is to sequentially sample each parameter, $\boldsymbol{\mu}_A$, $\boldsymbol{\mu}_B$, and $\boldsymbol{\Sigma}$, separately, given the other parameters using the conditional posterior distributions of the model parameters. The Gibbs sampler for this model is given in detail in Appendix 1.

Thus, based on a sample of say $S = 1,000,000$ draws we can compute the posterior mean of each parameter. For example, the posterior mean of, μ_{A1}, can then be obtained by taking the arithmetic mean of the respective posterior draws, i.e., $\bar{\mu}_{A1} \approx \frac{1}{S} \sum_{s=1}^{S} \mu_{A1}^{(s)}$, where $\mu_{A1}^{(s)}$ denotes the sth posterior draw of μ_{A1}. Furthermore, a 95 %-credibility interval for μ_{A1} can be obtained by ordering the posterior draws and discard the lowest 2.5 % and the largest 2.5 %. The posterior can also be used to compute other interesting statistics for which no classical equivalences are available. For example we could determine the posterior probability that the mean response time of team A in the first month is larger than the mean response time of team B in the first month. This can be estimated as the proportion of posterior draws that are in agreement with this constraint, i.e., $\Pr(\mu_{A1} > \mu_{B1}|\mathbf{Y}) \approx \frac{1}{S} \sum_{s=1}^{S} I(\mu_{A1}^{(s)} > \mu_{B1}^{(s)})$, where $I(\cdot)$ is the indicator function which is equal to 1 is the constraints hold and 0 otherwise.

Table 9.1 Maximum likelihood (ML) estimates of the response time means for 6 mean parameters, and the numerical estimates of the posterior means and 95 %-credibility intervals using different priors

		μ_{A1}	μ_{A2}	μ_{A3}	μ_{B1}	μ_{B2}	μ_{B3}
ML estimates		251.5	349.7	347.1	332.2	307.1	280.8
Jeffreys' prior	Post. means	351.5	349.7	347.1	332.2	307.1	280.8
	UB	355.1	353.5	351.0	336.4	311.4	285.4
	LB	347.9	346.0	343.2	328.0	302.9	276.3
Weakly infor-mative prior	Post. means	351.5	349.7	347.1	332.2	307.2	280.9
	UB	355.1	353.5	351.0	336.4	311.4	285.4
	LB	347.9	346.0	343.2	328.0	302.9	276.3
Informative prior	Post. means	351.4	349.7	347.3	332.7	309.0	284.2
	UB	355.0	353.4	351.1	336.8	313.3	288.8
	LB	347.9	346.1	344.4	328.6	304.7	279.8

9.2.4 HCI Data Example

Hypothetical data were generated consisting of $n_A = 114$ representatives in team A and $n_B = 86$ representatives in team B with true model parameters of $\mu_A = (350, 350, 350)'$, $\mu_B = (330, 310, 280)'$, and $\Sigma = 400\mathbf{I}_3$, where $\mathbf{I}_3$ is the identity matrix of length 3. The R code for this can be found in Appendix 2. The sample means of monthly response times (equal to the maximum likelihood estimates) over the three months resulted in $\bar{\mathbf{y}}_A = (351.5, 349.7, 347.1)'$ for team A and $\bar{\mathbf{y}}_B = (332.2, 307.1, 280.8)'$ for team B.

The Gibbs sampler in Appendix 1 was used to get a sample of 1,000,000 posterior draws for the model parameters when using the noninformative Jeffreys' prior, the weakly informative prior, and the informative prior given in (9.8). The R code for this Gibbs sampler can be found in Appendix 2. Based on the posterior draws we estimated the posterior mean of each mean parameter and its 95 %-credibility interval. The results can be found in Table 9.1. As can be seen in the table, the Bayesian estimates based on the noninformative Jeffreys prior correspond to the sample means (this holds by definition). For the weakly informative prior the posterior means are very slightly shrunk towards the prior means of 350. For the informative prior this prior shrinkage is a bit stronger. Similar conclusions can be drawn when looking at the intervals estimates.

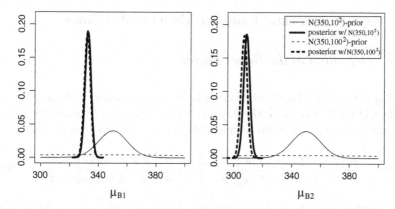

Fig. 9.1 Prior (*thin lines*) and posterior densities (*thick lines*) for μ_{B1} and μ_{B2} based on a normal prior with mean 350 and standard deviation 10 (*solid*) and a normal prior with mean 350 and standard deviation 100 (*dashed*). The sample mean of the response times in team B in the first month was equal to 332.2 and for the second month equal to 307.1

Figure 9.1 displays the weakly informative prior, $N(350, 100^2)$, and the informative prior, $N(350, 10^2)$, and the resulting posterior density estimates for μ_{B1} (left panel) and μ_{B2} (right panel). The posterior density estimates based on Jeffreys prior essentially coincided with the posterior density estimates based on the weakly informative prior and are therefore omitted in the Fig. 9.1. Note that the Jeffreys prior for μ_{B1} and μ_{B2} can be seen represented as a flat line over the whole unconstrained space $\mathbb{R}^1$. As can be seen the posterior densities based on the informative prior are slightly shrunk towards the prior mean of 350.

Overall we can conclude that the Bayesian estimates and the Bayesian credibility intervals are similar based on all three priors. This implies that the conclusions are quite robust to the choice of the prior. This is a consequence of the fact that the information in the data is relatively large, due to the sample size of $n_A = 114$ and $n_B = 86$, relative to the information in the prior. Consequently, even if the board is confident that the monthly response time means fall between 330 and 370 (with a prior probability of 95 % as in the informative prior), and we observe a monthly response time of 307.1 (for team B in the second month) which is well outside the expected range, the posterior mean of 309.0 is still close to the observed sample mean.

Finally note that the (interval) estimates in Table 9.1 already give some idea there is some evidence in these data in favor of the 'only positive time effect for the Mango users hypothesis' H_2 relative to the other hypotheses. This is clearly a consequence of the underlying model that was used to generate the data. In order to conclude that H_2 is indeed most supported by the data relative to the other hypotheses however a formal statistical test needs to be performed. In the next section it is motivated that the Bayes factor is exactly the right tool for this purpose.

9.3   Bayes Factors and Posterior Model Probabilities

9.3.1   Definition of the Bayes Factor

The Bayes factor is a Bayesian criterion for hypothesis testing that was originally developed by Jeffreys (1961). The Bayes factor for hypothesis H_1 against hypothesis H_2 is defined as the ratio of the marginal likelihoods under the hypotheses, i.e.,

$$B_{12} = \frac{p_1(\mathbf{Y})}{p_2(\mathbf{Y})} = \frac{\iiint p_1(\mathbf{Y}|\boldsymbol{\mu}_A, \boldsymbol{\mu}_B, \boldsymbol{\Sigma})p_1(\boldsymbol{\mu}_A, \boldsymbol{\mu}_B, \boldsymbol{\Sigma})d\boldsymbol{\mu}_A d\boldsymbol{\mu}_B d\boldsymbol{\Sigma}}{\iiint p_2(\mathbf{Y}|\boldsymbol{\mu}_A, \boldsymbol{\mu}_B, \boldsymbol{\Sigma})p_2(\boldsymbol{\mu}_A, \boldsymbol{\mu}_B, \boldsymbol{\Sigma})d\boldsymbol{\mu}_A d\boldsymbol{\mu}_B d\boldsymbol{\Sigma}}, \qquad (9.11)$$

where $p_t(\mathbf{Y}|\boldsymbol{\mu}_A, \boldsymbol{\mu}_B, \boldsymbol{\Sigma})$ denotes the likelihood under H_t and $p_t(\boldsymbol{\mu}_A, \boldsymbol{\mu}_B, \boldsymbol{\Sigma})$ denotes the prior under H_t, for $t = 1$ or 2. The Bayes factor quantifies how much more likely the data were generated under hypothesis H_1 relative to H_2. Therefore, the Bayes factor B_{12} can be interpreted as a measure of evidence in the data for H_1 relative to H_2. Thus if $B_{12} > 1$, there is more evidence for H_1 relative to H_2 and when $B_{12} < 1$ there is more evidence for H_2 relative to H_1. If $B_{12} = 1$, the evidence for H_1 is equal to H_2. Furthermore, a Bayes factor of, say, $B_{12} = 10$, implies that there is 10 times more evidence in the data for H_1 than H_2.

Note that expression (9.11) shows that there is a clear similarity between the Bayes factor and the likelihood ratio test statistic. The likelihood ratio between two hypotheses is the defined as the ratio of the likelihoods evaluated at their maximum likelihood estimates. The Bayes factor on the other hand can be seen as the ratio of integrated likelihoods weighted according to the priors under the hypotheses.

A direct consequence of the definition in (9.11) is that the Bayes factor has the following intuitive properties:

1. $B_{11} = 1$ (identity).
2. $B_{12} \geq 0$ (positivity).
3. $B_{12} = \frac{1}{B_{21}}$ (inverse).
4. $B_{12} = B_{13} \times B_{32}$ (transitivity).

For example, the transitivity relation implies that if the relative evidence for H_1 against H_3 is $B_{13} = 10$, and the relative evidence for H_3 against H_2 is $B_{32} = 5$, then the relative evidence for H_1 against H_2 is $B_{12} = B_{13} \times B_{32} = 50$. Furthermore, the inverse property implies that if H_1 is 10 times better than H_2, i.e., $B_{12} = 10$, then H_2 is 10 times worse than H_1, i.e., $B_{21} = 0.1$. Note that these intuitive properties are not shared by classical p-values.

9.3.2   Interpreting Bayes Factors

An important difference between a Bayes factor test and a p-value test lies in the interpretation. A p-value test results in a dichotomous decision: there is either enough or

Table 9.2 Guidelines for interpreting Bayes factors

B_{12}	Evidence in favor of H_1
<1	Negative (i.e., evidence for H_2)
$1-3$	Anecdotal
$3-20$	Positive
$20-150$	Strong
>150	Very strong

not enough evidence to reject the null hypothesis depending on whether the observed p-value is smaller or larger than a pre-specified significance level. For this reason conclusions such as "very significant" or "mildly significant" based on an observed p-value of 0.01 or 0.1, respectively, are not allowed. Note however that many researchers and practitioners tend to draw such conclusions. The problem is then that the p-value is misinterpreted as an error probability (For a discussion see Chap. 14 of this book or Hubbard and Armstrong 2006).

The outcome of the Bayes factor test on the other hand lies on a continuous scale. Based on a Bayes factor B_{12} we can make statements such as "little", "strong", or "decisive" evidence for H_1 against H_2, depending on its outcome. Default guidelines have been provided when interpreting Bayes factors (Jeffreys 1961; Kass and Raftery 1995). These are provided in Table 9.2. Note that these guidelines should be not be used as strict rules but more as a convenient starting point when interpreting Bayes factors.

9.3.3 Posterior Model Probabilities

Bayes factors can be used to update the prior odds between two hypotheses to obtain the posterior odds according to

$$\frac{\Pr(H_1|\mathbf{y})}{\Pr(H_2|\mathbf{y})} = B_{12} \times \frac{\Pr(H_1)}{\Pr(H_2)}, \tag{9.12}$$

where $\Pr(H_t)$ denotes the probability that hypothesis H_t is true *before* observing the data and $\Pr(H_t|\mathbf{y})$ denotes the probability that H_t is true *after* observing the data. Note that when using equal prior probabilities for the hypotheses, i.e., $\Pr(H_1) = \Pr(H_2)$, the posterior odds are equal to the Bayes factor. The posterior probability $\Pr(H_t|\mathbf{y})$ is often referred to as the posterior model probability of H_t.

When considering multiple hypotheses, say, $H_1, \ldots, H_T$, and we assume equal prior probabilities for the hypotheses, which is the default choice (i.e., $\Pr(H_1) = \ldots = \Pr(H_T) = \frac{1}{T}$), the posterior model probability for H_t can be computed via the Bayes factors according to

$$\Pr(H_t|\mathbf{y}) = \frac{B_{tT}}{\sum_{t=1}^{T} B_{tT}}, \tag{9.13}$$

for $t = 1, \ldots, T$. This follows automatically from (9.12).

It is important to note that posterior model probabilities differ fundamentally from p-values. The p-value quantifies the plausibility of observing the data $\mathbf{Y}$ conditional that H_0 is true. A p-value therefore does not quantify if the null hypothesis is true; it only quantifies if the data are unlikely under H_0. The posterior model probability of H_t on the other hand quantifies how plausible H_t is conditional on the observed data and other hypotheses under investigation. In our experience users find posterior model probabilities easier to interpret than classical p-values when testing statistical hypotheses. For an interesting discussion about the relation between Bayes factors and classical p-values we refer the interested reader to Sellke et al. (2001) and Wetzels et al. (2011).

9.3.4   Prior Specification When Computing Bayes Factors

The choice of the prior of the unknown parameters under each hypothesis plays an important role in a Bayesian hypothesis test. The reason is that the marginal likelihood $p_t(\mathbf{Y})$ quantifies how likely the data are to be observed under the chosen prior of H_t. Therefore one should not set the prior arbitrarily (vague). Also note that improper priors, such as the noninformative Jeffreys prior, cannot be used for the parameters of interest (Jeffreys 1961).

To illustrate the importance of the choice of the prior, let us consider a univariate data set of the differences between the response times of the first two months of team A. For simplicity let us assume that these data come from a normal distribution with unknown mean, δ, and known variance, say, $\sigma^2 = 10$. We are interested in testing whether there is a difference in the monthly response times in the population or not, i.e., $H_0 : \delta = 0$ versus $H_1 : \delta \neq 0$. Under H_0 we do not have to set a prior because there are no unknown parameters. The marginal likelihood under H_0 is then equal to the likelihood under H_1 evaluated at $\delta = 0$, i.e., $p_0(\mathbf{y}) = p_1(\mathbf{y}|\delta = 0)$. Under H_1 δ is unknown, so we have to set a prior for δ, denoted by $p_1(\delta)$. This prior quantifies which values for δ are expected under H_1 before observing the data. Because we are testing whether δ equals 0 or not, it is likely to expect that δ will be close to 0 if H_0 is not true. For this reason we could set a normal prior for δ under H_1 with mean 0, i.e., $p_1(\delta) = N(0, \sigma_0^2)$. Note that this implies that a positive effect is equally likely a priori as a negative effect under H_1 which seems a reasonable noninformative choice.

The prior variance σ_0^2 quantifies the effects that are expected if H_1 is true. A large (small) prior variance suggests that large (small) effects are anticipated if H_0 is not true. It is not recommended to set an arbitrarily large prior variance even though it may seem 'noninformative' as in the estimation problem. Setting an arbitrarily large prior variance implies that unrealistically large effects are likely under H_1. This has undesirable consequences. For example, when observing a 'medium' effect, which would suggest that H_0 is not true, the Bayes factor may prefer H_0 over H_1 because H_0, which assumes the effect is zero, may be a better and simpler explanation of the observed medium effect than H_1 with prior $p_1(\delta)$, which assumes that unrealistically large effects are expected. On the other hand it is also not recommendable to set a very small prior variance because then it will be very difficult to distinguish between the two hypotheses, either no effect (H_0) is expected or a very small effect (H_1) is expected. For this reason the prior variance should neither be too large nor too small.

Many different methods have been proposed to specify an automatic or default prior that satisfies this property. A well-known example is Zellner's g prior (with $g = n$), which contains the information of one observation, i.e., the unit information prior (Zellner 1986; Liang et al. 2008). Another possibility is to split the data in a training set that is used for constructing a proper prior and a testing set that is used for testing the hypotheses. The fractional Bayes factor (O'Hagan 1995) and the intrinsic Bayes factor (Berger and Pericchi 1996) are based on this approach. By choosing a training set of minimal size (referred to as a minimal training sample), maximal information is used for hypothesis testing. In a variation of this approach, Mulder et al. (2010) combined the idea of a minimal training sample with linear restrictions which ensure the prior is centered around the testing value of interest (which is 0 when testing $H_0 : \delta = 0$ versus $H_1 : \delta \neq 0$). This approach is illustrated in the following section.

9.4 A Bayesian T Test Using BIEMS

The software package BIEMS can be used for computing Bayes factors between competing hypotheses with equality and/or inequality constraints on the parameters of interest (Mulder et al. 2012). The package is freely downloadable from JORISMULDER.COM. The model that is implemented in BIEMS is the multivariate normal linear model. Special cases of this model are (multivariate) t-tests, (M)AN(C)OVA, (multivariate) regression, and repeated measures designs. Thus the hypotheses that were described in the introduction, with (in)equality constraints on the means in a MANOVA model, can be tested against each other using BIEMS. In this section we illustrate how the program works for a Bayesian t-test with multiple hypotheses.

9.4.1 Hypotheses

We consider the data of the 114 difference scores between the 1st and the 2nd month of team A and the 86 difference scores of team B. We focus on the mean difference of the response times between the 3rd and the 2nd month for team A and team B, separately. The difference scores are assumed to come from a normal distribution with unknown mean δ_A and unknown variance σ_A^2 for team A, and with unknown mean δ_B and variance σ_B^2 for team B. We are interested in testing whether there is 'no change' versus 'decrease' versus 'increase' in mean response times. This corresponds to the multiple hypothesis test of

$$H_0 : \delta_A = 0 \text{ versus } H_1 : \delta_A < 0 \text{ versus } H_2 : \delta_A > 0$$

for team A, and

$$H_0 : \delta_B = 0 \text{ versus } H_1 : \delta_B < 0 \text{ versus } H_2 : \delta_B > 0$$

for team B.

9.4.2 Prior Specification

In BIEMS the so-called encompassing prior approach is implemented for the unknown means and regression parameters (Klugkist et al. 2005). This means that an *unconstrained prior* is specified for δ_B or δ_B under an *unconstrained* hypothesis, denoted by H_u. Under H_u there are not additional constraints on the δ's, which implies that each δ can have any value on the real line. Subsequently, the priors for each δ under the one-sided hypotheses H_1 and H_2 are truncations of this unconstrained prior in their constrained regions. For example, the prior for δ_A under H_1 is truncated in the region where $\delta_A < 0$. Consequently prior specification comes down to specifying the unconstrained prior for each δ. In BIEMS a normal distribution is used by default. Furthermore, for the nuisance parameters, σ_A^2 and σ_B^2, the noninformative Jeffreys' prior is used.

The mean and variance in the unconstrained prior can be chosen automatically or manually. The automatic (or default) prior specification is based on the conjugate expected constrained posterior prior approach (Mulder et al. 2009, 2010, 2012). In this method the prior mean is set on the focal point of interest. In this example, the focal point is 0 because we are testing whether the population mean is equal to 0, smaller than 0, or larger than 0. For this reason the prior mean for δ_A and δ_B is set to 0. The prior variance is constructed using an automatic method based on minimal training samples (which contain the information of two observations). Consequently, the prior variance is a combination of the variation in the data and the observed effect. Thus more variation in the data or larger effects in the data result in a larger prior variance. This is an empirical Bayes approach where the prior adapts to the data. This methodology has proven to have good frequency properties (Hoijtink 2011). Therefore we recommend to use this default setting if prior information is weak or unavailable regarding the expected effect sizes if the null is not true.

For the data of team A and B, the sample mean and sample standard deviation were equal to $\hat{\delta}_A = -1.78$ and $\hat{\sigma}_A = 26.7$, and $\hat{\delta}_B = -25$ and $\hat{\sigma}_B = 31$, respectively. For the data of team A, BIEMS generated an automatic prior with a mean of 0 and a variance of 440 (with standard deviation 21), and for the data of team B, an automatic prior with mean 0 and a variance of 975 (with standard deviation 31) was generated. The default prior densities are displayed in Fig. 9.2. As can be seen the default prior variance for δ_A is smaller than the default prior variance for δ_A.

When prior information is available about the magnitude of the effect, the prior mean and prior variance under H_u can also be manually set in BIEMS. For example if the company is pessimistic about the actual effect if H_0 is not true, a small prior

Fig. 9.2 The unconstrained
default priors generated by
BIEMS for the two different
data sets of team A and B
and the resulting posteriors.
The default prior standard
deviations for the data of
team A and B are 21 and 31,
respectively. The
probabilities of $\delta_A > 0$ and
$\delta_B > 0$ are displayed as *grey*
areas

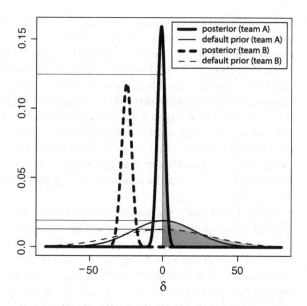

variance can be chosen. For example, a prior variance of 100 would imply that effects
of 10 s are anticipated by the company if H_0 is not true. On the other hand, if the
company is optimistic about the effect if H_0 is not true a larger prior variance can
be chosen. For example, a prior variance of 2500 would imply that an effect of 50 s
is expected if H_0 is not true. For this example we keep the prior mean equal to 0 to
ensure that a positive effect is equally likely a priori as a negative effect.

9.4.3 Bayes Factors and Posterior Model Probabilities

A consequence of the encompassing prior approach is that the marginal likelihoods
in (9.11) do not have to be computed directly. In this example the Bayes factors of
each constrained hypothesis H_0, H_1, and H_2 against the unconstrained hypothesis
H_u can be expressed as,

$$B_{0u} = \frac{p_u(\delta_A = 0|\mathbf{y})}{p_u(\delta_A = 0)} \tag{9.14}$$

$$B_{1u} = \frac{\Pr(\delta_A < 0|\mathbf{y}, H_u)}{\Pr(\delta_A < 0|H_u)} \tag{9.15}$$

$$B_{2u} = \frac{\Pr(\delta_A > 0|\mathbf{y}, H_u)}{\Pr(\delta_A > 0|H_u)}. \tag{9.16}$$

For a derivation see, for example, Klugkist et al. (2005) or Mulder (2014). For com-
pleteness we provided derivations of these expressions in Appendix 3. Hence, the
Bayes factor for the null hypothesis against the unconstrained hypothesis comes

down to the unconstrained posterior density of δ evaluated at 0 divided by the unconstrained prior density evaluated at zero, as can be seen in Eq. 9.14. This is known as the Savage-Dickey density ratio (Dickey 1971; Verdinelli and Wasserman 1995; Wetzels et al. 2010). Furthermore, the Bayes factor of a one-sided hypothesis against the unconstrained hypothesis is equal to the posterior probability that the inequality constraint holds divided by the prior probability that the constraint holds. The posterior probability that the inequality constraints hold can be interpreted as a measure of relative fit and the prior probability that the inequality constraints hold can be interpreted as a measure of relative complexity (both relative to the unconstrained hypothesis) (Mulder et al. 2010). In this example, $\Pr(\delta_A < 0, H_u) = \frac{1}{2}$, and therefore $H_1 : \delta_A < 0$ can be seen as half as complex as the unconstrained hypothesis $H_1 : \delta_A \in \mathbb{R}^1$.

Figure 9.2 displays the unconstrained default priors and the resulting unconstrained posterior distribution for δ_A and δ_B. As can be seen the unconstrained prior density for δ_A evaluated at 0 is approximately equal to 0.019 and the prior probabilities of $\delta_A < 0$ and $\delta_A > 0$ are both equal to 0.5. Furthermore, the unconstrained posterior density evaluated at 0 is approximately equal to 0.125, and the corresponding posterior probabilities of $\delta_A < 0$ and $\delta_A > 0$ are equal to 0.76 and 0.24, respectively. Following (9.14)–(9.16), the Bayes factors are then equal to $B_{0u} = \frac{0.125}{0.019} = 6.6$, $B_{1u} = \frac{0.76}{0.50} = 1.52$, and $B_{2u} = \frac{0.24}{0.50} = 0.48$. The transitive property of the Bayes factor can be used to compute the Bayes factor between two constrained hypotheses, e.g., $B_{01} = \frac{B_{0u}}{B_{1u}} = \frac{6.6}{1.52} = 4.3$. Thus there is 4.3 times more evidence for 'no effect' relative to a 'negative effect'. These Bayes factors can be converted to posterior probabilities that each hypothesis is true given the data according to

$$\Pr(H_t|\mathbf{y}) = \frac{B_{tu}}{B_{0u} + B_{1u} + B_{2u}},$$

where we assumed equal prior probabilities, $\Pr(H_0) = \Pr(H_1) = \Pr(H_2) = \frac{1}{3}$. The resulting posterior probabilities for the hypotheses based the default priors, the optimistic subjective prior, and the pessimistic subjective prior can be found in Table 9.3. By computing Bayes factors using different priors we get an idea how sensitive the results are when using different priors.

Table 9.3 Posterior probabilities of the constrained hypotheses for two different tests (and data) and different priors

	Team A			Team B		
	$\Pr(H_0|\mathbf{y})$	$\Pr(H_1|\mathbf{y})$	$\Pr(H_2|\mathbf{y})$	$\Pr(H_0|\mathbf{y})$	$\Pr(H_1|\mathbf{y})$	$\Pr(H_2|\mathbf{y})$
Default prior	0.767	0.177	0.056	0.000	1.00	0.000
Pessimistic prior	0.617	0.287	0.096	0.000	1.00	0.000
Optimistic prior	0.884	0.088	0.028	0.000	1.00	0.000

Table 9.3 shows that there is positive evidence that H_0 is true for team A. This implies that the data provide evidence that the mean response times remained stable between the first and second month for team A. The amount of evidence for H_0 varied for different priors with posterior probabilities varying between 0.617 and 0.884. To be able to draw a more decisive conclusion more data are needed. For team B there was clear evidence that H_1 is true with posterior probabilities of approximately 1. This implies that the sales representatives responded faster to their email in the second month in comparison to the first month.

9.5 Evaluation of the HCI Application

In this section we evaluate the six constrained hypotheses that were discussed in the introduction of this chapter using the Bayes factor. The Bayes factors are computed using BIEMS which comes with a graphical user interface. The interface allows users to specify the (in)equality constraints relatively easily.

In the first step the data are uploaded. Each row in the data matrix contains the three measurements of each sales representative in the first three columns followed by a group indicator to indicate whether the representative belong to team A or B. For the analysis team A was coded as 1 and team B was coded as 2. The R code for exporting the data to this format is provided in Appendix 2. When uploading the data in BIEMS, we need to specify that there are 3 dependent variables (corresponding to the three measurements) and 2 groups (corresponding to the two teams). A screen shot is provided in Fig. 9.3 (Upper left panel).

In BIEMS the constraints under each hypothesis must be specified separately. The separate constraints under each hypotheses are given by

'All positive effects ' H_1 :
$$\begin{cases} \mu_{A1} > \mu_{A2}, \ \mu_{A2} > \mu_{A3}, \\ \mu_{B1} > \mu_{B2}, \ \mu_{B2} > \mu_{B3} \\ \mu_{A1} > \mu_{B1}, \ \mu_{A2} > \mu_{B2}, \\ \mu_{A3} > \mu_{B3}, \end{cases}$$

'Only positive time effect for Mango users' H_2 :
$$\begin{cases} \mu_{A1} = \mu_{A2}, \ \mu_{A2} = \mu_{A3}, \\ \mu_{A1} > \mu_{B1}, \ \mu_{B1} > \mu_{B2}, \\ \mu_{B2} > \mu_{B3}, \end{cases}$$

'Positive team effect; no time effect' H_3 :
$$\begin{cases} \mu_{A1} = \mu_{A2}, \ \mu_{A2} = \mu_{A3}, \\ \mu_{B1} = \mu_{B2}, \ \mu_{B2} = \mu_{B3}, \\ \mu_{A1} > \mu_{B1} \end{cases}$$

'Positive time effect; no team effect' H_4 :
$$\begin{cases} \mu_{A1} > \mu_{A2}, \ \mu_{A2} > \mu_{A3}, \\ \mu_{A1} = \mu_{B1}, \ \mu_{A2} = \mu_{B2}, \\ \mu_{A3} = \mu_{B3} \end{cases}$$

'No effects' H_5 :
$$\begin{cases} \mu_{A1} = \mu_{A2}, \ \mu_{A2} = \mu_{A3}, \\ \mu_{B1} = \mu_{B2}, \ \mu_{B2} = \mu_{B3}, \\ \mu_{A1} = \mu_{B1}. \end{cases}$$

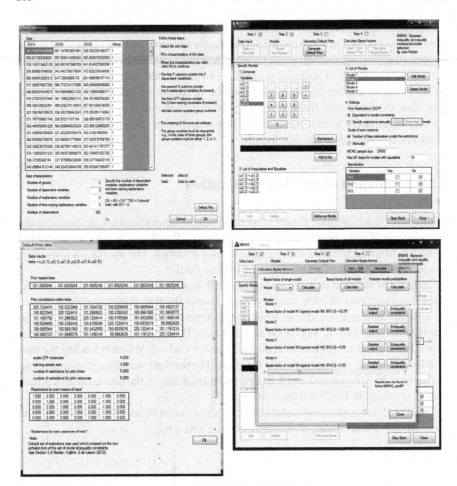

Fig. 9.3 *Upper left panel* Screen shot of BIEMS when uploading data with 2 groups (teams) and 3 dependent variables (measurements). *Upper right panel* Screen shot of BIEMS when specifying models (hypotheses). Hypothesis H_2 is displayed. *Lower left panel* Screen shot of default prior generated by BIEMS. *Lower right panel* Screen shot of resulting Bayes factors of each constrained hypothesis against the unconstrained hypothesis

A screen shot of this specification for H_2 is provided in Fig. 9.3 (Upper right panel). Note that the monthly response time mean μ_{B1} corresponds to $\mu(2, 1)$ in BIEMS (the first argument corresponds to the group number (1 or 2) and the second to the measurement occasion (1, 2, or 3)).

The automatic prior is generated by pressing the button "Generate default prior". A screen shot of the resulting automatic prior is given in Fig. 9.3 (Lower left panel). As can be seen the prior means for all μ's are approximately equal to 331. Furthermore, the prior variances are all equal to approximately 325 and the prior covariances are approximately equal to 100. Possibly one can manually set priors for the μ's depend-

ing on one's prior knowledge as discussed in Sect. 9.2.2. Here we shall continue with
the default (noninformative) setting.

Finally the Bayes factors of each constrained hypothesis against the unconstrained
hypothesis can be computed based on this unconstrained prior by pressing "Calculate
Bayes factors". Note that the unconstrained hypothesis contains no constraints on the
μ's. We can then compute Bayes factors between two constrained hypothesis via the
transitive relationship discussed earlier, e.g., $B_{12} = B_{1u}/B_{2u}$, where H_u denotes
the unconstrained hypothesis. A screen shot where all Bayes factors of each constrained hypothesis against the unconstrained hypothesis is computed is given in
Fig. 9.3 (Lower right panel). Note that "BF(2,0)" denotes B_{2u}, i.e., the Bayes factor of H_2 against the unconstrained hypothesis (so "0" reflects the unconstrained
hypothesis).

The Bayes factors of each constrained hypotheses H_1–H_5 against the unconstrained hypothesis using the default prior are presented in Table 9.4 (under the column default prior). As can be seen there is clearly no evidence that only a positive
team effect is present ($B_{3u} = 0$), no evidence that only a positive time team effect is
present ($B_{4u} = 0$), and no evidence that no effect is present ($B_{5u} = 0$). On the other
hand, the 'all positive effects hypothesis' H_1 received approximately 84 times more
evidence from the data than the unconstrained and the 'only positive time effect for
the Mango users hypothesis' H_2 received approximately 589 more evidence than H_u.
Using the transitive relationship of the Bayes factor we can compute the Bayes factors between the constrained hypotheses, e.g., $B_{21} = B_{2u}/B_{1u} = 7.01$, which implies
there is approximately 7 times more evidence that only there is only a positive time
effect for the Mango users instead that all effects are positive.

Based on these Bayes factors we can also compute the Bayes factor of the
'complement hypothesis' H_6 against the unconstrained hypothesis. Thus, similar
as in (9.15), the Bayes factor of H_6 against H_u is equal to the posterior probability
that none of the constraints of H_1 to H_5 hold divided by the prior probability that
none of the constraints of H_2 to H_5 hold. Because the hypotheses H_2 to H_5 contain
equality constraints which have zero measure, the posterior and prior probability that
the constraints of H_6 hold is equal to 1 minus the posterior and prior probability that
the order constraints of H_1 hold, respectively. Thus,

$$
\begin{aligned}
B_{6u} &= \frac{\Pr(\text{constraints of } H_1 \text{ to } H_5 \text{ do not hold}|\mathbf{Y}, H_u)}{\Pr(\text{constraints of } H_1 \text{ to } H_5 \text{ do not hold}|H_u)} \\
&= \frac{\Pr(\text{constraints of } H_1 \text{ do not hold}|\mathbf{Y}, H_u)}{\Pr(\text{constraints of } H_1 \text{ do not hold}|H_u)} \\
&= \frac{1 - \Pr(\text{constraints of } H_1 \text{ hold}|\mathbf{Y}, H_u)}{1 - \Pr(\text{constraints of } H_1 \text{ hold}|H_u)}
\end{aligned}
$$

Furthermore, the posterior and prior probability that the constraints of H_1 hold under
H_u can be found in the "detailed output" in BIEMS (Fig. 9.3, lower right panel)
under "estimated model fit" and "estimated model complexity" respectively. These
were equal to 0.582 and 0.00693, respectively, which explains the Bayes factor of

Table 9.4 Bayes factors of each constrained hypothesis against the unconstrained hypothesis and the corresponding posterior probabilities assuming equal prior probabilities and using different priors under the hypotheses

	B_{tu}	$\Pr(H_t\|\mathbf{Y})$
H_1: 'All positive effects'	84	0.124
H_2: 'Only positive time effect for team B'	589	0.875
H_3: 'Positive team, no time effect'	0	0.000
H_4: 'Positive time, no team effect'	0	0.000
H_5: 'No time, no team effect'	0	0.000
H_6: 'Complement'	0.42	0.001

$B_{1u} = \frac{0.582}{0.00693} = 83.95$ of H_1 against H_u (Fig. 9.3, lower right panel). Consequently, $B_{6u} = \frac{1-0.582}{1-0.00693} = 0.421$ (see Table 9.4).

Finally we can translate these Bayes factors to posterior model probabilities for the hypotheses which can be interpreted as the plausibility that a hypothesis is true after observing the data. The common default choice is to set equal prior probabilities for the hypotheses, i.e., $\Pr(H_1) = \ldots = \Pr(H_6) = \frac{1}{6}$. These prior probabilities are updated using the observed Bayes factors to obtain the posterior model probabilities using (9.13). The resulting posterior model probabilities can be found in Table 9.4. These posterior model probabilities tell the same story as the Bayes factors but because the posterior model probabilities add up to one they may be easier to interpret. From the posterior probabilities we can conclude that there is clear evidence for H_2 that team B (who use the Mango smart watch) respond faster to their email than team A (who don't use the smart watch) and that the response speed for team B increases over time while it remains stable over time for team A. This hypothesis received a posterior probability of 0.875. Furthermore, there was also some evidence for hypothesis H_1 that all effects are positive (with a posterior probability of 0.124), so we cannot yet completely rule out this hypothesis. In order to be able to draw a more decisive conclusion we need to collect more data.

9.6 Discussion

This chapter discussed a Bayesian data analysis of an application in HCI. Bayesian estimation and Bayesian hypothesis testing using the Bayes factor were considered. It was illustrated that Bayesian estimation often results in very similar results as classical estimation using maximum likelihood. The Bayesian approach to hypothesis testing on the other hand differs fundamentally from classical p-value tests. The main reason is that the Bayes factor, the Bayesian criterion in hypothesis testing, quantifies the relative evidence in the data between two hypotheses while the p-value quantifies how unlikely the data are under a specific null hypothesis. In our experience practitioners find Bayes factors (and the corresponding posterior model probabilities) easier to interpret than classical p-values. Furthermore, the Bayesian approach has the advantage that it can straightforwardly be used for evaluating multiple hypotheses with equality as well as order constraints on the parameters of interest.

The software package BIEMS was developed to evaluate constrained hypotheses using Bayes factors in a relatively easy manner. Because of the sensitivity of the Bayes factor to the prior, an automatic prior approach was implemented in BIEMS using an empirical Bayes approach. This default setting can be used when prior information regarding the magnitude of the effects is weak or unavailable. If prior information is available on the other hand, for example based on personal experience or published work, it is also possible to manually specify the prior. After the prior is specified Bayes factors and posterior model probabilities can be computed which provide a direct answer about the evidence in the data for each hypothesis under investigation relative to the other hypotheses.

Appendix 1: Gibbs sampler (theory)

We consider the general case of P repeated measurements. In the example discussed above, P was equal to 3. The following semi-conjugate prior is used for the model parameters,

$$p(\boldsymbol{\mu}_A, \boldsymbol{\mu}_B, \boldsymbol{\Sigma}) = p(\boldsymbol{\mu}_A) \times p(\boldsymbol{\mu}_B) \times p(\boldsymbol{\Sigma}) \tag{9.17}$$
$$\propto N_{\boldsymbol{\mu}_A}(\mathbf{m}_{A0}, \mathbf{S}_{A0}) \times N_{\boldsymbol{\mu}_A}(\mathbf{m}_{A0}, \mathbf{S}_{A0}) \times |\boldsymbol{\Sigma}|^{-\frac{P+1}{2}},$$

where $\mathbf{m}_{A0}$ and $\mathbf{m}_{B0}$ are the prior mean of $\boldsymbol{\mu}_A$ and $\boldsymbol{\mu}_B$, respectively, and $\mathbf{S}_{A0}$ and $\mathbf{S}_{B0}$ the respective prior covariance matrices of $\boldsymbol{\mu}_A$ and $\boldsymbol{\mu}_B$.

The data are stored in the $(n_A + n_B) \times P$ data matrix $\mathbf{Y} = [\mathbf{Y}'_A \ \mathbf{Y}'_B]'$, where the ith row of $\mathbf{Y}$ contains the P measurements of ith sales executive and the first n_A rows correspond to the responses of the executives in team A and the remaining n_B rows contain the responses of the executives of team B. The likelihood of the data can be written as

$$p(\mathbf{Y}|\boldsymbol{\mu}_A, \boldsymbol{\mu}_B, \boldsymbol{\Sigma}) = \prod_{i=1}^{n_A} p(\mathbf{y}_i|\boldsymbol{\mu}_A, \boldsymbol{\Sigma}) \times \prod_{i=n_A+1}^{n_A+n_B} p(\mathbf{y}_i|\boldsymbol{\mu}_B, \boldsymbol{\Sigma})$$
$$\propto N_{\boldsymbol{\mu}_A|\boldsymbol{\Sigma}}(\bar{\mathbf{y}}_A, \boldsymbol{\Sigma}/n_A) \times N_{\boldsymbol{\mu}_A|\boldsymbol{\Sigma}}(\bar{\mathbf{y}}_B, \boldsymbol{\Sigma}/n_B) \times IW_{\boldsymbol{\Sigma}}(\mathbf{S}, n_A + n_B - 2),$$

where $\bar{\mathbf{y}}_A$ and $\bar{\mathbf{y}}_B$ denote the sample means of team A and team B over the P measurements, the sums of squares equal

$$\mathbf{S} = (\mathbf{Y}_A - \mathbf{1}_{n_A}\bar{\mathbf{y}}'_A)'(\mathbf{Y}_A - \mathbf{1}_{n_A}\bar{\mathbf{y}}'_A) + (\mathbf{Y}_B - \mathbf{1}_{n_B}\bar{\mathbf{y}}'_B)'(\mathbf{Y}_B - \mathbf{1}_{n_B}\bar{\mathbf{y}}'_B),$$

and $IW_{\Sigma}(\mathbf{S}, n)$ denotes an inverse Wishart probability density for $\mathbf{\Sigma}$. Note that the likelihood function of $\mathbf{\Sigma}$ given $\boldsymbol{\mu}_A$ and $\boldsymbol{\mu}_B$ is proportional to an inverse Wishart density $IW(\mathbf{S}_{\mu}, n_A + n_B)$, where $\mathbf{S}_{\mu} = (\mathbf{Y}_A - \mathbf{1}_{n_A}\boldsymbol{\mu}_A')'(\mathbf{Y}_A - \mathbf{1}_{n_A}\boldsymbol{\mu}_A') + (\mathbf{Y}_B - \mathbf{1}_{n_B}\boldsymbol{\mu}_B')'(\mathbf{Y}_B - \mathbf{1}_{n_B}\boldsymbol{\mu}_B')$. These results can be found in most classic Bayesian text books, such as Gelman et al. (2004), for example.

Because the prior in (9.17) is semi-conjugate, the conditional posterior distributions of each model paramater given the other parameters have known distributions from which we can easily sample,

$$p(\boldsymbol{\mu}_A|\mathbf{Y}, \mathbf{\Sigma}) = N\left(\left(\mathbf{S}_{A0}^{-1} + n_A\mathbf{\Sigma}^{-1}\right)^{-1}\left(\mathbf{S}_{A0}^{-1}\mathbf{m}_{A0} + n_A\mathbf{\Sigma}^{-1}\bar{\mathbf{y}}_A\right), \left(\mathbf{S}_{A0}^{-1} + n_A\mathbf{\Sigma}^{-1}\right)^{-1}\right)$$

$$p(\boldsymbol{\mu}_B|\mathbf{Y}, \mathbf{\Sigma}) = N\left(\left(\mathbf{S}_{B0}^{-1} + n_B\mathbf{\Sigma}^{-1}\right)^{-1}\left(\mathbf{S}_{B0}^{-1}\mathbf{m}_{B0} + n_A\mathbf{\Sigma}^{-1}\bar{\mathbf{y}}_B\right), \left(\mathbf{S}_{B0}^{-1} + n_B\mathbf{\Sigma}^{-1}\right)^{-1}\right)$$

$$p(\mathbf{\Sigma}|\mathbf{Y}, \boldsymbol{\mu}_A, \boldsymbol{\mu}_B) = IW(\mathbf{S}_{\mu}, n_A + n_B).$$

We can use a Gibbs sampler to get a sample from the joint posterior of $(\boldsymbol{\mu}_A, \boldsymbol{\mu}_B, \mathbf{\Sigma})$. In a Gibbs sampler we sequentially draw each model parameter from its conditional posterior given the remaining parameters. The Gibbs sampler algorithm can be written as

1. Set initial values for the model parameters: $\boldsymbol{\mu}_A^{(0)}$, $\boldsymbol{\mu}_B^{(0)}$, and $\mathbf{\Sigma}^{(0)}$.
2. Draw $\boldsymbol{\mu}_A^{(s)}$ from its conditional posterior $p(\boldsymbol{\mu}_A|\mathbf{Y}, \mathbf{\Sigma}^{(s-1)})$.
3. Draw $\boldsymbol{\mu}_B^{(s)}$ from its conditional posterior $p(\boldsymbol{\mu}_B|\mathbf{Y}, \mathbf{\Sigma}^{(s-1)})$.
4. Draw $\mathbf{\Sigma}^{(s)}$ from its conditional posterior $p(\mathbf{\Sigma}|\mathbf{Y}, \boldsymbol{\mu}_A^{(s)}, \boldsymbol{\mu}_A^{(s)})$.
5. Repeat steps 2–4 for $s = 1, \ldots, S$.

In the software program R, drawing from a multivariate normal distribution can be done using the function 'rmvnorm' in the 'mvtnorm'-package and drawing from an inverse Wishart distribution can be done using the function 'riwish' in the 'MCMCpack'-package.

It may be that the initial values, $\boldsymbol{\mu}_A^{(0)}$, $\boldsymbol{\mu}_B^{(0)}$, and $\mathbf{\Sigma}^{(0)}$, are chosen far away from the subspace where the posterior is concentrated. If this is the case, a burn-in period of, say, 100 draws is needed. After the burn-in period convergence is reached and the remaining draws come from the actual posterior of the model parameters.

Appendix 2: Gibbs sampler (R code)

Conditional posteriors for μ_A, μ_B, and Σ.

```
require(mvtnorm)
require(MCMCpack)

#draw the measurement means of team A, muA, given the covariance matrix, Sigma.
draw_muA = function(ybarA,nA,nB,m0A,S0,Sigma){
  covPost = solve(solve(S0)+solve(Sigma/nA))
```

```
       meanPost = covPost%*%(solve(S0)%*%m0A+solve(Sigma/nA)%*%ybarA)
       muA = c(rmvnorm(1,mean=meanPost,sigma=covPost))
       return(muA)
}


#draw the measurement means of team B, muB, given the covariance matrix Sigma.
draw_muB = function(ybarB,nA,nB,m0B,S0,Sigma){
       covPost = solve(solve(S0)+solve(Sigma/nB))
       meanPost = covPost%*%(solve(S0)%*%m0B+solve(Sigma/nB)%*%ybarB)
       muB = c(rmvnorm(1,mean=meanPost,sigma=covPost))
       return(muB)
}


#draw the covariance matrix Sigma given the measurement means of team A and B
draw_Sigma = function(Ymat,nA,nB,muA,muB,S0,Sigma){
#the posterior is based on the Jeffreys' prior for Sigma
   muMatcurr = matrix(0,ncol=3,nrow=2)
   muMatcurr[1,] = muA
   muMatcurr[2,] = muB
   Xmat = matrix(c(rep(1,nA),rep(0,nB),rep(0,nA),rep(1,nB)),ncol=2)
   SSN = t(Ymat - Xmat%*%muMatcurr)%*%(Ymat - Xmat%*%muMatcurr)
   Sigma = riwish(nA+nB,SSN)
   return(Sigma)
}
```

Gibbs sampler

```
#MCMC sampler with sample size 1e4 by default
MCMC_HCI = function(Ymat,nA,nB,m0A,m0B,S0,samsize=1e4){

   MmuA = matrix(0,nrow=samsize,ncol=3)
   MmuB = matrix(0,nrow=samsize,ncol=3)
   MSigma = array(0,dim=c(samsize,3,3))

   #set ML estimates as initial values
   muA = c(apply(matrix(Ymat[1:nA,],ncol=3),2,mean))
   ybarA = muA
   muB = c(apply(matrix(Ymat[(nA+1):(nA+nB),],ncol=3),2,mean))
   ybarB = muB
   muMat = matrix(0,ncol=3,nrow=2)
   muMat[1,] = muA
   muMat[2,] = muB
   Xmat = matrix(c(rep(1,nA),rep(0,nB),rep(0,nA),rep(1,nB)),ncol=2)
   Sigma = t(Ymat - Xmat%*%muMat)%*%(Ymat - Xmat%*%muMat)/(nA+nB)

  #burn-in period of 100 draws
  for(ss in 1:100){
     muA = draw_muA(ybarA,nA,nB,m0A,S0,Sigma)
     muB = draw_muB(ybarB,nA,nB,m0B,S0,Sigma)
     Sigma = draw_Sigma(Ymat,nA,nB,muA,muB,S0,Sigma)
  }
  #actual draws from posterior
  for(ss in 1:samsize){
     muA = draw_muA(ybarA,nA,nB,m0A,S0,Sigma)
     MmuA[ss,] = muA
```

```
    muB = draw_muB(ybarB,nA,nB,m0B,S0,Sigma)
    MmuB[ss,] = muB
    Sigma = draw_Sigma(Ymat,nA,nB,muA,muB,S0,Sigma)
    MSigma[ss,,] = Sigma
  }
  return(list(MmuA,MmuB,MSigma))
}
```

Generate data matrix Y

```
#Set group size team A and team B
nA = 114
nB = 86
#Set true measurement means of team A and B over month 1, 2, and 3
muAtrue = c(350,350,350)
muBtrue = c(330,310,280)
muMat = matrix(0,ncol=3,nrow=2)
muMat[1,] = muAtrue
muMat[2,] = muBtrue
#Set true covariance matrix Sigma
Sigma = diag(3)*400
#Generate data matrix Y
Xmat = matrix(c(rep(1,nA),rep(0,nB),rep(0,nA),rep(1,nB)),ncol=2)
Ymat = rmvnorm(nA+nB,mean=c(0,0,0),sigma=Sigma) + Xmat%*%muMat
```

Compute classical estimates

```
#Compute maximum likelihood of the means
Bhat = solve(t(Xmat)%*%Xmat)%*%t(Xmat)%*%Ymat
#Compute unbiased least squares estimate of Sigma
SigmaHat = t(Ymat-Xmat%*%Bhat)%*%(Ymat-Xmat%*%Bhat)/(nA+nB-ncol(Xmat))
```

Set priors for Gibbs sampler

```
#Set prior hyperparameters
mn1 = 350
sd1 = 1e10
#Note that a very large values for sd1 essentially corresponds to the Jeffreys prior
m0A = mn1*rep(1,3)
m0B = mn1*rep(1,3)
S0 = diag(3)*sd1**2
```

Run Gibbs sampler

```
sampleSize = 1e4
out1 = MCMC_HCI(Ymat,nA,nB,m0A=m0A,m0B=m0B,S0=S0,samsize=sampleSize)
```

Compute descriptive statistics from Gibbs output

```
#Make trace plot for mu's
team=1 #team number A=1, B=2
dv=1    #which measurement 1, 2 or 3
plot(1:sampleSize,out1[[team]][1:sampleSize,dv],"l")
```

```
#density plot of posterior
plot(density(out1[[team]][1:sampleSize,dv]))

#Make trace plot for elements of Sigma
s1 = 1
s2 = 1
plot(1:sampleSize,out1[[3]][1:sampleSize,s1,s2],"l")
#density plot of posterior
plot(density(out1[[3]][1:sampleSize,s1,s2]))

#Compute posterior mean for mu
team=1 #team number A=1, B=2
dv=1    #which measurement 1, 2 or 3
mean(out1[[team]][,dv])

#Compute posterior mean for Sigma[s1,s2]
s1 = 1
s2 = 1
mean(out1[[3]][1:sampleSize,s1,s2])

#compute credibility intervals
team=1 #team number A=1, B=2
dv=1    #which measurement 1, 2 or 3
volgorde = order(out1[[team]][,dv])
percentage = 95
#upper bound
out1[[team]][volgorde,dv][round(sampleSize*((100/2+percentage/2)/100))]
#lower bound
out1[[team]][volgorde,dv][round(sampleSize*((100-percentage)/2)/100)]
```

Create data matrix for BIEMS

```
dataBIEMS = matrix(NA,nrow=nrow(Ymat),ncol=ncol(Ymat)+1)
dataBIEMS[,1:ncol(Ymat)] = Ymat
dataBIEMS[,ncol(Ymat)+1] = c(rep(1,nA),rep(2,nB))
write.table(dataBIEMS,file="dataBIEMS.txt",row.names=F,col.names=F)
```

Appendix 3: Derivation of the Bayes factor

The Bayes factor is derived for a one-sided hypothesis $H_1 : \delta < 0$ versus the unconstrained hypothesis $H_u : \delta \in \mathbb{R}$. In the encompassing prior approach, the prior under H_1, $p_1(\delta, \sigma^2)$, is a truncation of the unconstrained (or encompassing) prior under H_u, $p_u(\delta, \sigma^2)$, in the region where $\delta < 0$, i.e., $p_1(\delta, \sigma^2) = p_u(\delta, \sigma^2)I(\delta < 0)/\Pr(\delta < 0|H_u)$, where the prior probability $\Pr(\delta < 0|H_u) = \int_{\delta<0} p_u(\delta)d\delta$, where $I(\cdot)$ is the indicator function. Note that $\Pr(\delta < 0|H_u) = \frac{1}{2}$ if the unconstrained prior is centered at 0, such as $p_u(\delta) = N(0, \sigma_0^2)$. Also note that the likelihood under H_1 is a truncation of the likelihood under H_u, i.e., $p_1(\mathbf{y}|\delta, \sigma^2) = p_u(\mathbf{y}|\delta, \sigma^2)I(\delta < 0)$. For this reason we can omit the hypothesis index u in the likelihood functions in the derivation below. The Bayes factor of H_1 versus H_u can then be derived as follows

226   J. Mulder

$$B_{1u} = \frac{\iint_{\delta<0} p(\mathbf{y}|\delta,\sigma^2)p_1(\delta,\sigma^2)d\delta d\sigma^2}{\iint p(\mathbf{y}|\delta,\sigma^2)p_u(\delta,\sigma^2)d\delta d\sigma^2}$$

$$= \frac{1}{\Pr(\delta<0|H_u)} \iint_{\delta<0} \frac{p(\mathbf{y}|\delta,\sigma^2)p_u(\delta,\sigma^2)}{\iint p(\mathbf{y}|\delta,\sigma^2)p_u(\delta,\sigma^2)d\delta d\sigma^2} d\delta d\sigma^2$$

$$= \frac{1}{\Pr(\delta<0|H_u)} \iint_{\delta<0} p_u(\delta,\sigma^2|\mathbf{y})d\delta d\sigma^2$$

$$= \frac{\Pr(\delta<0|\mathbf{y},H_u)}{\Pr(\delta<0|H_u)},$$

which corresponds to (9.15), where $\Pr(\delta<0|\mathbf{y},H_u) = \iint_{\delta<0} p_u(\delta|\mathbf{y})d\delta d\sigma^2$ is the posterior probability that the constraints hold under H_u. For $H_2 : \delta > 0$ versus the unconstrained hypothesis $H_u : \delta \in \mathbb{R}$ we can follow the same steps to obtain (9.16).

For $H_0 : \delta = 0$ versus the unconstrained hypothesis $H_u : \delta \in \mathbb{R}$, the encompassing prior approach implies that $p_0(\sigma^2) = p_u(\sigma^2|\delta = 0)$. Consequently,

$$B_{0u} = \frac{\int p(\mathbf{y}|\delta=0,\sigma^2)p_0(\sigma^2)d\sigma^2}{\iint p(\mathbf{y}|\delta,\sigma^2)p_u(\delta,\sigma^2)d\delta d\sigma^2}$$

$$= \frac{\int p(\mathbf{y}|\delta=0,\sigma^2)p_u(\sigma^2|\delta=0)d\sigma^2}{\iint p(\mathbf{y}|\delta,\sigma^2)p_u(\delta,\sigma^2)d\delta d\sigma^2}$$

$$= \frac{1}{p_u(\delta=0)} \int \frac{p(\mathbf{y}|\delta=0,\sigma^2)p_u(\delta=0,\sigma^2)}{\iint p(\mathbf{y}|\delta,\sigma^2)p_u(\delta,\sigma^2)d\delta d\sigma^2} d\sigma^2$$

$$= \frac{1}{p_u(\delta=0)} \int p_u(\delta=0,\sigma^2|\mathbf{y})d\sigma^2$$

$$= \frac{p_u(\delta=0|\mathbf{y})}{p_u(\delta=0)},$$

which is equal to the Savage-Dickey density ratio in (9.14).

References

Akaike H (1973) Information theory and an extension of the maximum likelihood principle. In: Petrov BN, Csaki F (eds) 2nd International Symposium on Information Theory, Akademiai Kiado, Budapest, pp 267–281

Barlow R, Bartholomew D, Bremner J, Brunk H (1972) Statistical inference under order restrictions. John Wiley, New York

Berger JO, Pericchi LR (1996) The intrinsic Bayes factor for model selection and prediction. J Am Stat Assoc 91:109–122

Braeken J, Mulder J, Wood S (2015) Relative effects at work: bayes factors for order hypotheses. J Manage 41:544–573

Dickey J (1971) The weighted likelihood ratio, linear hypotheses on normal location parameters. Ann Stat 42:204–223

Gelman A, Carlin JB, Stern HS, Rubin DB (2004) Bayesian data analysis, 2nd edn. Chapman & Hall, London

Gu X, Mulder J, Decovic M, Hoijtink H (2014) Bayesian evaluation of inequality constrained hypotheses. Psychol Methods 19:511–527

Hoijtink H (2011) Informative hypotheses: theory and practice for behavioral and social scientists. Chapman & Hall, CRC, New York

Hubbard R, Armstrong J (2006) Why we don't really know what 'statistical significance' means: a major educational failure. J Mark Educ 28:114–120

Jeffreys H (1961) Theory of Probability, 3rd edn. Oxford University Press, New York

Kass RE, Raftery AE (1995) Bayes factors. J Am Stat Assoc 90:773–795

Kato BS, Hoijtink H (2006) A Bayesian approach to inequality constrained linear mixed models: estimation and model selection. Stat Model 6:231–249

Klugkist I, Laudy O, Hoijtink H (2005) Inequality constrained analysis of variance: a Bayesian approach. Psychol Methods 10:477–493

Liang F, Paulo R, Molina G, Clyde MA, Berger JO (2008) Mixtures of g priors for Bayesian variable selection. J Am Stat Assoc 103(481):410–423

Lynch SM (2007) Introduction to applied Bayesian statistics and estimation for social scientists. Springer Science & Business Media

Mulder J (In Press) Bayes factors for testing order-constrained hypotheses on correlations. J Math Psychol

Mulder J, Klugkist I, van de Schoot A, Meeus W, Selfhout M, Hoijtink H (2009) Bayesian model selection of informative hypotheses for repeated measurements. J Math Psychol 53:530–546

Mulder J, Hoijtink H, Klugkist I (2010) Equality and inequality constrained multivariate linear models: objective model selection using constrained posterior priors. J Stat Plan Inference 140:887–906

Mulder J (2014) Prior adjusted default Bayes factors for testing (in)equality constrained hypotheses. Comput Stat Data Anal 71:448–463

Mulder J, Hoijtink H, de Leeuw C (2012) Biems: a fortran 90 program for calculating Bayes factors for inequality and equality constrained model. J Stat Softw 46

O'Hagan A (1995) Fractional Bayes factors for model comparison (with discussion). J Roy Stat Soc Ser B 57:99–138

Robertson T, Wright FT, Dykstra R (1988) Order restricted statistical inference. Wiley, New York

Schwarz GE (1978) Estimating the dimension of a model. Ann Stat 6:461–464

Sellke T, Bayarri MJ, Berger JO (2001) Calibration of p values for testing precise null hypotheses. Am Stat 55(1):62–71

Silvapulle MJ, Sen PK (2004) Constrained statistical inference: inequality, order, and shape restrictions, 2nd edn. Wiley, Hoboken

Spiegelhalter DJ, Best NG, Carlin BP, van der Linde A (2002) Bayesian measures of model complexity and fit. J Roy Stat Soc Ser B 64(2):583–639

van de Schoot R, Hoijtink H, Romeijn J-W, Brugman D (2011) A prior predictive loss function for the evaluation of inequality constrained hypotheses. J Math Psychol 16:225–237

van de Schoot R, Hoijtink H, Hallquist MN (2012) Bayesian evaluation of inequality-constrained hypotheses in sem models using mplus. Struct Equ Model A Multi J 19:593–609

Verdinelli I, Wasserman L (1995) Computing bayes factors using a generalization of the savage-dickey density ratio. J Am Stat Assoc 90:614–618

Wagenmakers E-J (2007) A practical solution to the pervasive problem of p values. Psychon Bull Rev 14:779–804

Wetzels R, Grasman RPPP, Wagenmakers EJ (2010) An encompassing prior generalization of the Savage-Dickey density ratio test. Comput Stat Data Anal 38:666–690

Wetzels R, Matzke D, Lee M, Rounder JN, Yverson GJ, Wagenmakers EJ (2011) Statistical evidence in experimental psychology: an empirical comparison using 855 t tests. Perspect Psychol Sci 6:291–298

Zellner A (1986) On assessing prior distributions and Bayesian regression analysis with g-prior distributions, pp 233–243. Elsevier, Amsterdam, North-Holland

Part IV
Advanced Modeling in HCI

This final part of this book, consisting of 3 chapters, introduces a number of "advanced" statistical methods that are not generally covered in social science introductory courses. Each of these methods has experienced rapid developments in the past 20 to 30 years, mainly due to large improvements in computing power. Because of this, many numerical optimization methods needed to fit complex models are finally practically within reach.

This last part should not be seen as a definite overview of novel methods: there is much more happening in the large fields of research methods and statistics. Therefore, we have included (in addition to the extensive references provided by the authors) a number of pointers to both textbooks as well as recent articles to enable interested readers to find their ways.

Before introducing the chapters, we would like to make very explicit that the format of a book chapter obviously limits the depth in which methods can be discussed. As such, the authors have mostly chosen to present a high level introduction to the topic (accompanied by practical examples). However, for many methods, especially the very general frameworks such as latent variable models, this general introduction might not cover, in all detail, the pitfalls that come with powerful new methods: Each powerful method has its assumptions and drawback, and should not be used carelessly.

Chapter 10: Latent Variable Models

In this chapter Dr. A. Beaujean and Dr. G. Morgan introduce latent variable models, and specifically the lavaan [R] package for fitting these models. The chapter first explains the basic jargon and terminology used in the discussion of latent variable models, and subsequently focuses on using [R] to conduct confirmatory factor analysis and to fit structural equation models. Latent variable models provide a very flexible framework for modeling both experimental and observational data. However, the authors do add a word of caution; recently developed easy to use software to fit latent variable models might *"[...] allow the untrained analyst to specify models that exceed both their substantive knowledge as well as their ability to evaluate models critically"*. The authors point to an extensive discussion by Kline (2011) in the book *Principles and practice of structural equation modeling* which we feel should be a starting point for readers who wish to advance their use of latent variable models in HCI.

Chapter 11: Generalized Linear Mixed Models

In Chap. 10 Dr. M. Kaptein discusses generalized linear mixed models. The chapter starts with a discussion of relatively simple linear regression models with which we think most readers will be familiar. However, the chapter focuses on simulating datasets and plotting model predictions: a focus that is slightly different from the more common focus on null-hypothesis testing of model coefficients. After discussing simple linear models, and the use of [R] to fit these models, regularization and the bias-variance trade-off is discussed. The bias-variance trade-off is important when modeling sample data, but hardly discussed in social science courses (despite being an introductory topic in machine learning and AI).

After introducing regularization, the chapter introduces generalized linear models: by using link functions the well-known linear regression model can be altered to deal with more complex outcome variables (e.g., binary or count data). Then linear mixed models are introduced: these models allow the analyst to deal with complex (often nested) data structures.

Chapter 12: Mixture Models

In Chap. 11 Dr. D. Oberski discusses latent profile and latent class analysis. The author present a useful table positioning the different latent variable models and discusses both discrete and continuous mixture models. The author also discusses conceptually the EM algorithm that is used to fit the presented models: the EM algorithm is a widely used algorithm to fit all kinds of latent variable models (it is also often used for the generalized mixed models discussed in Chap. 10). The EM algorithm was also briefly touched upon in Chap. 4.

After providing an extremely readable didactic treatment of mixture models (which includes quite a bit of mathematical sophistication), the author discusses latent class analysis and provides several examples of the use of this method in HCI. For a more extensive introduction we would recommend, as also referred to by the author of the chapter, the book *applied latent class analysis* by Hagenaars and McCutcheon (2002).

Editor Suggestions

It is hard to determine where to start when recommending "novel" methods. However, there are a few books those generally interested should consult:

- The book *Pattern Recognition and Machine Learning* by Christopher Bishop (2007) provides an extensive overview of modern machine learning methods, often taking a Bayesian point of view.
- The book *The Elements of Statistical Learning: Data Mining, Inference, and Prediction.* by Trevor Hastie, Robert Tibshirani, and Jerome Friedman (2011) surveys methods of statistics learning and includes a large number of methods not generally covered in social science statistics curricula.

We would also like to point to novel books on a number of more specialized topics that we regretfully were unable to include in this book:

- *Causal inference*: a topic we regretfully have been unable to cover in this book. The books *Causal Inference for Statistics, Social, and Biomedical Sciences: An Introduction* by Guido Imbens and Donald Rubin (2015) and *Causality: Models, Reasoning and Inference* by Judea Pearl (2009) provide good starting points.
- *Network analysis*: An advanced topic that might also be of interest to readers is the analysis of network data; the book *Statistical Analysis of Network Data with R (Use R!)* by Eric Kolaczyk and Gabor Csardi (2014) provides an overview.
- *Bootstrapping*: An approach to inference that is "distinct" from frequentist NHST and Bayesian methods which can be useful in many situations where one would like to quantify uncertainty in the obtained estimates. *An Introduction to the Bootstrap* by Bradley Efron and Robert Tibshirani (1993) provides a good overview.
- *Optimal Design*: Usually not covered in methods courses are the (statistical) methods to design "maximally informative" experiments. The book *Optimal Design of Experiments: A Case Study Approach* by Peter Goos and Bradley Jones (2011) provides a starting point.
- *Sequential Decision making / Multi-armed Bandit problems*: Adaptive treatment selection the "sequential allocation of experiments" is interesting for its large number of applied uses. The book *Bandit problems: Sequential Allocation of Experiments* by Donald A. Berry and Bert Fristedt (2013) discusses the topic at length.

Obviously, many other interesting works and methods are not reviewed here. The fields of statistics, AI, and machine learning progress fast, and it takes time for theoretical advances to make their way into common practice.

Chapter 10
Latent Variable Models

A. Alexander Beaujean and Grant B. Morgan

Abstract Human-computer interaction research increasingly involves investigating psychological phenomena as latent variables. In this chapter, we discuss basic latent variable models using a path model approach. In addition, we given some examples of conducting a latent variable model analysis using the *lavaan* package in the R statistical programming language.

10.1 Introduction

The exploration of human-computer interaction (HCI) has grown to encompass practical uses in many areas of everyday life. Scholars have explored HCI and relations with various phenomena, such as simulation games in education (Gee 2005), computer-mediated communication (Maloney-Krichmar and Preece 2005; Haythornthwaite and Wellman 1998), engagement with avatar interaction (Norris et al. 2014), nursing training (Nehring and Lashley 2009), and customer experience with new product development (Robinson and Min 2002). These HCI studies all involve the examination of psychological phenomena, which are *latent variables* (LVs) and should be treated as such in the statistical analysis. A LV is one that is theorized to exist but cannot be directly measured (Bollen 2002). Instead, data are collected on a set of observed variables that are used as an indication or approximation of the underlying latent variable.

The use of LVs can be seen in several recent HCI studies. For example, Norris et al. (2014) used factor analysis to identify six factors (i.e., LVs) related to game player involvement, and van Schaik and Ling (2003) used factor analysis to investigate the quality of HCI in online surveys. Likewise, Schulenberg and Melton (2007) used factor analysis to gather construct validity evidence for the Computing Understanding and Experience Scale (Potosky and Bobko 1998).

A.A. Beaujean (✉) · G.B. Morgan
Baylor University, Waco, TX, USA
e-mail: Alex_Beaujean@baylor.edu

G.B. Morgan
e-mail: Grant_Morgan@baylor.edu

© Springer International Publishing Switzerland 2016
J. Robertson and M. Kaptein (eds.), *Modern Statistical Methods for HCI*,
Human–Computer Interaction Series, DOI 10.1007/978-3-319-26633-6_10

HCI scholars have employed LV techniques that go beyond traditional factor analysis. For example, Schmidt et al. (2002) used a special type of LV model for dichotomous items to investigate a 13-item survey instrument that measured aspects of upper-extremity student-role functioning. As another example, Nam et al. (2013) examined the predictive relations among LVs (i.e., structural equation model) in their study of the acceptance of assistive technology among special education teachers.

Given the inclusions of humans in HCI, many of the psychological phenomena of interest (e.g., engagement, competence, ease of use, technology acceptance) could be viewed as LVs. As such, statistical analyses uniquely developed for modeling LVs should be considered when conducting HCI research. The purpose of this chapter is to introduce basic LV modeling as an approach for studying psychological phenomena and provide worked examples using the R (**R** Development Core Team 2014) statistical programming language.

10.1.1 Data

To aid in our descriptions in this chapter, we use the System Usability Scale (SUS) data provided with this book. The SUS consists of 10 items with 7-point Likert-type scales. The dataset used for this chapter's examples consists of 86 responses on the SUS about the usability of the Mango Watch. While the original data contains responses across three time periods, we just use the data from the first time point.

10.2 Path Models

There are two non-mutually exclusive ways to introduce a *latent variable model* (LVM): matrix algebra and path models. We only focus on the path model approach in this chapter as it directly translates into the R package we use to demonstrate the latent variable analysis.[1] A *path model* is a pictorial representation of a theory of variable relations. Figure 10.2 shows an example of a path model using the SUS data with one latent variable .

10.2.1 Variables Types in a Path Model

There are two types of variables in path model: manifest and latent (see the top of Fig. 10.1). A *manifest variable* (MV) is one that is able to be measured directly. This differs from a LV, which can only be measured indirectly through other variables. In Fig. 10.2 there is one LV (*Usability*) and 10 MVs (SUS_1–SUS_{10}). In addition to

---

[1] Those interested in a matrix-based approach should see Bollen's (1989) classic text.

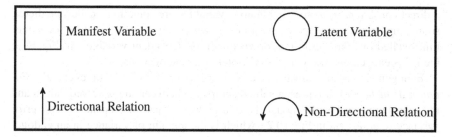

Fig. 10.1 Symbols used to create path model diagrams

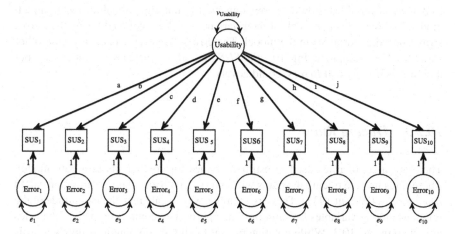

Fig. 10.2 Path model of System Usability Scale items using a single latent variable

variables, path models can also contain constants, which are scalar values used to specify intercepts and means. We do not discuss models that include constants in this chapter; those interested in such models should see Ployhart and Oswald (2004).

10.2.2   Variables Relations in a Path Model

There are two ways variables can relate to each other in a path model (see the bottom of Fig. 10.1). Single-headed arrows represent direct relations (e.g., regression, factor loading), while double-headed arrows represent non-directional relations (e.g., correlation, variance). A variable's variance is represented by a variable having a non-directional relation with itself. For example, in Fig. 10.2 the LV has a double-headed arrow that starts and ends with itself, representing the latent variance for Usability ($V_{Usability}$).

The variables involved in direct relations can be categorized into one of two types: those that are without a direct cause in the model (*exogenous*) and those with a direct cause (*endogenous*). Exogenous variables are sometimes called predictor, source, upstream, or independent variables, while endogenous variables are sometimes called outcome, criterion, downstream, or dependent variables. In Fig. 10.2, the LV is exogenous, while all the SUS items are endogenous.

Endogenous variables always have an attached *error* term (sometimes called *residual* or *disturbance*). It represents the discrepancy between the observed values and the values predicted by the model. The variability of these discrepancies is the error variance (e.g., e_1–e_{10} in Fig. 10.2), which is the amount of variance in an endogenous variable not explained by the other variables in the model. Because error represents something unexplained by the model, it has no direct cause and is exogenous. Endogenous variables should not be connected to non-directional arrows in a path model. The reason is that as all of their variance can be accounted for by their error terms and other variables in the model. The errors, however, can covary with other variables. For example, in Fig. 10.2 the SUS_1 and SUS_2 variables cannot covary; but their errors, $Error_1$ and $Error_2$, could covary.

10.2.3 Tracing Rules

There are a set of rules used to estimate values for coefficients in a path model. These rules involve tracing the paths within it (i.e., path analysis), so are often called *tracing rules* (Wright 1934). They are simply a way to calculate the magnitude of the relations among variables by summing the appropriate connecting paths. The rules are given in Fig. 10.3. While computers can do all the computations involved, it is useful to know the tracing rules in order to understand how all the variable relations are used to estimate the parameters. For some worked examples, see Beaujean (2014) or Boker et al. (2002).

- Trace all paths between two variables (or a variable back to itself), multiplying all the coefficients along a given path.
- You can start by going backwards along a single-headed arrow, but once you start going forward along these arrows you can no longer go backwards.
- You cannot go through the same variable more than once for a given path (i.e., no loops).
- At most, there can be one double-headed arrow included in a traced path.
- After tracing all the paths for a given relation, sum all the paths.

Fig. 10.3 Path model tracing rules

10.3 Latent Variable Models

A LVM is a broad class of statistical models that typically consists of two parts: the measurement model and the structural model. The structural model consists of regression-like relations among the variables. The measurement model forms any LVs used in the structural model. If the LVM contains both structural and measurement models, the LVM is often called a *structural equation model* (SEM); if the LVM does not contain a structural model, it is often called a *confirmatory factor analysis* (CFA). If there was not an a priori hypothesized set of relationships for the measurement model, then it would be an **exploratory factor analysis** (EFA). This chapter focuses largely on CFAs, although we do fit a very basic SEM at the end of the chapter. Beaujean (2013) demonstrated how to conduct an EFA in R.

The purpose of a CFA is to understand the underlying structure that produced relations among multiple manifest variables (i.e., covariance matrix).[2] The MVs that are directly influenced by the LV are the *indicator variables*. The idea behind factor analysis is that there are a small number of LVs within a given domain (e.g., disorientation, perceived ease of use, and intensity of flow; van Schaik and Ling 2003) that influence each of its many indicator variables, which subsequently produce the observed covariances. Thus, covariation in the indicator variables is due to their dependence on one or more LVs. LV modeling, then, involves identifying or confirming the number of the LVs that produce the observed covariation in the indicator variables as well as understanding the nature of those LVs (e.g., what they predict, what variables predict them).

One measure of the influence a LV has on MVs is the *factor loading*. These are akin to regression coefficients. The correlation between a LV and a MV is a *structure coefficient*. For models with one LV, factor loadings and structure coefficients have the same values. For models with more than one LV (e.g., Fig. 10.4), they will have different values unless all the LVs are uncorrelated with each other.

In Fig. 10.2, coefficients $a - j$ are all factor loadings. We can obtain something akin to a R^2 value for each MV using the tracing rules: find all the legitimate paths that go from a MV to the LVs and return back to the same MV. This value is called the *communality*. Conversely, the *uniqueness* is the amount of variance in the MV *not* explained by the model's LVs. For example, to find the communality for SUS_1 in Fig. 10.2, trace the path from it to Usability and then back to SUS_1. There is only one path that goes from SUS_1 to Usability that meets the tracing rules criteria, so the communality is $a \times v_{\text{Usability}} \times a$. Thus, the amount of SUS_1 variance that Usability explains is $a^2 \times v_{\text{Usability}}$. If the LV was standardized, then its variance would be one, the SUS_1's communality would be a^2, and its uniqueness would be $1 - a^2$.

---

[2]We assume that the LV is reflective (i.e., causes the MVs to covary). An alternative would be to have a formative LV, which are thought to result from the MVs' covariation. For more information on formative LVs, see Bollen and Bauldry (2011).

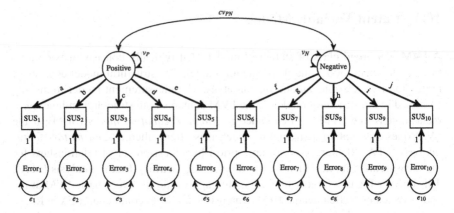

Fig. 10.4 Path model of System Usability Scale items using two latent variables

10.3.1 Identification of Latent Variable Models

To be able to estimate the parameters in a LVM, the MVs need to provide enough unique information to be able to estimate the required parameters. This is the issue of model *identification*. The amount of unique information in the data is the number of non-redundant variances and covariances in the variables used in the model. This can be calculated using Eq. 10.1.

$$\text{Unique Information} = \frac{p(p+1)}{2} \qquad (10.1)$$

where p is the number of MVs in the model.

If a model is *just identified*, then the number of parameters to estimate exactly equals the amount of unique information. If there are more parameters to estimate than the amount of unique information, then the model is *underidentified*. Conversely, if there is more unique information than parameters to estimate, then the model is usually *overidentified*.

If a model is underidentified, then it is not possible to find a single value for the model's parameters and most LVM programs will return an error message. If a model is over- or just-identified, there should be one "best" value for each parameter. For overidentified models, not only do they provide parameter estimates, but they can also provide measures of model fit. This is because they have *degrees of freedom* (*df*) greater than 0. In LVMs, *df* can be thought of as the number of unique pieces of information in the data minus the number of parameters to estimate.[3] Only overidentified models have *df* > 0.

Model identification can be tricky (Kenny and Milan 2012). Instead of going into all the complexities involved, we just provide some rules-of-thumb conditions

---

[3]For a more thorough explanation of the degrees of freedom concept, see Walker (1940).

that should work for typical LVMs. Meeting these conditions typically produces an overidentified LVM, or at least a just-identified LVM. It is atypical for the first two conditions not to be met, so we do not discuss them in any detail.

1. If there is more than one LV in the model, then for every pair of LVs, either there is at least one indicator variable per LV whose error variance does not covary with the error variance of the other LV's indicator variables, *or* the covariance between the pair of LVs is constrained to a specified value.
2. For every indicator variable, there must be at least one other indicator variable (of the same LV or a different LV) with which the error variances do not covary.
3. Every LV in a model has at least four indicator variables and none of their error variances covary.
4. The LVs' scales are set by constraining some parameter estimates.

If a LV cannot have at least four indicator variables, it can still be just-identified under any of the following conditions.

1. The LV has three indicator variables, and the error variances do not covary.
2. The LV has at least two indicators with non-covarying error variances *and* the indicator variables' loadings are set equal to each other.
3. The LV has one indicator variable, the directional paths are set to one, *and* its error variance is fixed to $(1 - r_{XX'})\sigma_X^2$, where $r_{XX'}$ and σ_X^2 are the indicator variable's reliability and observed variance, respectively.

The LVs' scales have to be set by the researcher because there are no inherent units by which to measure latent quantities. The two most common ways to set this scale are to standardize the LV or to use a marker variable. These different methods place the LVs on different scales, so the resulting parameter estimates will differ. The choice of scaling method will not alter how a model fits the data.

To standardize the LV, the LV's variance is constrained to one, which places the LV on a Z scale. Moreover, if there is more than one LV, then the covariance among the LVs becomes a correlation. If the indicator variables are standardized as well, the loadings can be interpreted the same as a standardized regression coefficient.

The marker variable method requires a single factor loading for each LV be constrained to an arbitrary value (usually one). The indicator variable whose loading is constrained is called the *marker variable*. With this method, the marker variable's variance defines the LV's variance.

10.4 Latent Variable Models in R

10.4.1 Entering Data

Both raw data and summary statistics can be used to fit most LVMs. Entering raw data into R is covered in Chap. 2 in this book, so we only focus on entering summary statistics and the book's SUS example data.

10.4.1.1 Summary Statistics

In some situations, there is not access to raw data but there is access to the covariance (or correlation) matrix. Since such matrices are symmetric, we can simplify the input using the *lavaan* package's `lav_matrix_lower2full()` function. The `lav_matrix_lower2full()` function requires entering the lower diagonal of the covariance matrix *by row*. The following syntax creates a correlation matrix named *example.cor* that consists of the correlations among four variables as well as a standard deviation (SD) vector named *example.sd* that consists of the SDs for the four variables. We name the variables using the native `rownames()`, `colnames()`, and `names()` functions. Last, we transform the correlations to covariances using *lavaan*'s `cor2cov()` function. It requires both a correlation matrix argument and a SD vector argument.

```
# load lavaan package
library(lavaan)
# name variables
example.vars <- c("Var1","Var2","Var3","Var4")
# input covariances
example.cor <- lav_matrix_lower2full(c(1,0.85,1,0.84,0.61,1,
                 0.68,0.59,0.41,1))
# name the rows and columns
rownames(example.cor) <- colnames(example.cor) <- example.vars
# enter the SDs
example.sd <- c(3.01,3.03,2.99,2.89)
names(example.sd) <- example.vars
# correlation matrix
example.cor
##       Var1 Var2 Var3 Var4
## Var1 1.00 0.85 0.84 0.68
## Var2 0.85 1.00 0.61 0.59
## Var3 0.84 0.61 1.00 0.41
## Var4 0.68 0.59 0.41 1.00

# convert correlations and SDs to covaraonces
example.cov <- cor2cov(example.cor,example.sd)
# covariance matrix
example.cov

##       Var1 Var2 Var3 Var4
## Var1  9.1  7.8  7.6  5.9
## Var2  7.8  9.2  5.5  5.2
## Var3  7.6  5.5  8.9  3.5
## Var4  5.9  5.2  3.5  8.4
```

Table 10.1 `lavaan` Syntax for specifying path models

Syntax	Command	Example
~	Regress onto	Regress B onto A: `B ~ A`
~~	(Co)variance	Variance of A: `A ~~ A`
		Covariance of A and B: `A ~~ B`
=~	Define latent variable	Define Factor 1 by A-D: `F1 =~A+B+C+D`
:=	Define non-model parameter	Define parameter u2 to be twice the square of u: `u2 := 2*(u^2)`
*	Label parameters (the label has to be pre-multiplied)	Label the regression of Z onto X as b: `Z ~b*X`

10.4.1.2 SUS Data

The SUS data is saved as a *Rdata* file, so we use the `load()` function to import it.

```
# load SUS data
load("SuSScaleData.rdata")
```

The dataset within the *SuSScaleData.rdata* file is named *scale*. For this analysis, we only want the data from Time 1, so we subset the original data and name this new dataset *scale.time1*.

```
# select data at time 1
scale.time1 <- scale[scale$Time == 1, ]
```

10.4.2 Specifying Models in Lavaan

There are multiple packages in R that can fit latent variable models, but we focus on the *lavaan* package (Rosseel 2012). *lavaan* (LAtent VAriable ANalysis) is designed for general latent variable modeling. Information and documentation about it can be found on the package's web page: http://www.lavaan.org.[4]

Estimating LVM parameters in *lavaan* is a two-step process. First specify the path model, then associate the model with a dataset and estimate the parameters. Specifying the model requires using the package's pre-defined model specification commands, many of which are shown in Table 10.1. As an example, the following syntax specifies the LVM shown in Fig. 10.2. Although not required, we label each parameter to match the figure's labels.

```
one.lv.model <- '
# define latent variable
```

---

[4]For examples of fitting LV models in R using a package other than `lavaan` see Fox et al. (2012).

```
usability =~  a*SUS1 + b*SUS2 + c*SUS3 + d*SUS4 + e*SUS5 +
f*SUS6 + g*SUS7 + h*SUS8 +  i*SUS9 + j*SUS10
# optional, label latent variance
usability~~v_lv*usability
# optional, label residual variance
SUS1~~e1*SUS1
'
```

The first line of the code above consists of the name of the model (one.lv. model), R's assignment operator ($<-$) and a single apostrophe ('). The apostrophe tells R that the subsequent syntax needs to be stored as text. Line 2 defines the part of the path model that has *Usability* as the LV and the SUS items as indicator variables. The LV is defined (=~) using all ten of the SUS items. We separate all the indicator variables for the same LV using the + sign before each variable after the first.

The last few lines are optional. By default, lavaan creates an error term for each endogenous variable and estimates its variance while constraining the path from the error term to one. So, the only contribution of the last lines is to label the latent variance and the error variance for SUS_1, respectively. The final line is another single apostrophe to indicate the end of R interpreting syntax as text.

Once the model is specified, use either the cfa() (for *C*onfirmatory *F*actor *A*nalysis), or sem() (for *S*tructural *E*quation *M*odel) function to fit the model. Either raw data or a covariance matrix (with accompanying sample size) are acceptable data to analyze. To input raw data, use the data argument; to input a covariance matrix and sample size, use the sample.cov and sample.nobs arguments, respectively.

For example, to estimate the parameters specified in one.lv.model using the raw SUS data, we use the following syntax:

```
one.lv.fit <- cfa (model = one.lv.model, data =scale.time1)
```

The first two arguments to the cfa() function are the model and data objects, which we previously defined. To use the variables' covariance matrix (named *scale.cov*) instead of the raw data, we would use the following syntax:

```
one.lv.fit <- sem(model=one.lv.model,
        sample.cov=scale.time1.cov,
        sample.nobs=81)
```

The third argument, sample.nobs, indicates the sample size from which the covariance matrix was calculated; it needs to be used every time summary statistics are used for input.

Both of the preceding lavaan calls will return nothing on screen because the results are stored in the *one.lv.fit* object. One option to produce the results from fitting the model is to use the summary() function.

summary(one.lv.fit)

```
## lavaan (0.5-18) converged normally after  22 iterations
##
##    Number of observations                                86
##
##    Estimator                                             ML
##    Minimum Function Test Statistic                  147.216
##    Degrees of freedom                                    35
##    P-value (Chi-square)                               0.000
##
## Parameter estimates:
##
##    Information                                     Expected
##    Standard Errors                                 Standard
##
##                    Estimate  Std.err  Z-value  P(>|z|)
## Latent variables:
##    usability =~
##      SUS1        (a)    1.000
##      SUS2        (b)    1.053    0.184    5.723    0.000

..<Output Omitted>..
```

By default, lavaan's `summary()` function returns: (a) a note indicating if the parameter estimation algorithm converged; (b) the sample size; (c) estimator; (d) fit statistic (χ^2) and its df and p-value; (e) the unstandardized parameter estimates; (f) the parameter estimates' standard errors; (g) the ratio of the parameter estimates to their standard errors (i.e., Wald statistic); and (h) the p-value for the Wald statistic.

The `summary()` function has these default specifications for its arguments: `standardized=FALSE`, `fit.measures=FALSE`, `rsquare=FALSE`, and `modindices=FALSE`. Setting `standardized=TRUE` will produce standardized estimates in the results, setting `fit.measures=TRUE` will produce fit indices in the results, setting `rsquare=TRUE` will produce the R^2 for each endogenous variable, and setting `modindices=TRUE` will produce modification indices.

Another option to produce the model results is to use the `parameter Estimates()` function. As with the `summary()` function, specifying `standardized=TRUE` produces both the unstandardized and standardized estimates. The unstandardized estimates (*Estimate*) use the raw score scales for the MVs and use the marker variable method to scale the LV. There are three types of standardized estimates returned. The first (*Std.lv*) standardizes the LV, but leaves the MVs in the raw score scale. The second (*Std.all*) standardizes both the LV and all the MVs. The third type (*std.nox*) standardizes all variables are except exogenous MVs.

```
parameterEstimates(one.lv.fit, standardized=TRUE)
```

```
##            lhs op        rhs  est     se std.lv std.all std.nox
## 1    usability =~      SUS1 1.00  0.000   0.68    0.72    0.72
## 2    usability =~      SUS2 1.05  0.184   0.71    0.69    0.69
## 3    usability =~      SUS3 0.94  0.170   0.63    0.66    0.66
## 4    usability =~      SUS4 1.05  0.186   0.71    0.68    0.68
## 5    usability =~      SUS5 1.08  0.190   0.73    0.69    0.69
## 6    usability =~      SUS6 0.40  0.160   0.27    0.29    0.29
## 7    usability =~      SUS7 0.55  0.148   0.37    0.44    0.44
## 8    usability =~      SUS8 0.52  0.188   0.35    0.33    0.33
## 9    usability =~      SUS9 0.49  0.172   0.33    0.34    0.34
## 10   usability =~     SUS10 0.59  0.168   0.40    0.41    0.41
## 11   usability ~~ usability 0.46  0.128   1.00    1.00    1.00
## 12        SUS1 ~~      SUS1 0.43  0.083   0.43    0.49    0.49
## 13        SUS2 ~~      SUS2 0.54  0.101   0.54    0.52    0.52
## 14        SUS3 ~~      SUS3 0.50  0.090   0.50    0.56    0.56
## 15        SUS4 ~~      SUS4 0.58  0.106   0.58    0.54    0.54
## 16        SUS5 ~~      SUS5 0.58  0.108   0.58    0.52    0.52
## 17        SUS6 ~~      SUS6 0.76  0.118   0.76    0.91    0.91
## 18        SUS7 ~~      SUS7 0.57  0.091   0.57    0.80    0.80
## 19        SUS8 ~~      SUS8 1.03  0.161   1.03    0.89    0.89
## 20        SUS9 ~~      SUS9 0.85  0.133   0.85    0.88    0.88
## 21       SUS10 ~~     SUS10 0.76  0.121   0.76    0.83    0.83
```

We can use the tracing rules and standardized parameter estimates to estimate the communality for SUS_1 in the one-factor model in Fig. 10.2. The standardized factor loading for SUS_1 is 0.72, making the communality $0.72^2 = 0.51$. This means that about half of the variance in SUS_1 can be explained by the latent variable.

In addition to the communality estimates, we can calculate the correlations implied by the model's parameter estimates, which we can then compare them to the actual correlations (i.e., residual correlations). Using the labels from Fig. 10.2, the relation between the SUS_1 and SUS_2 variables is defined by $a \times b$ since that is the only valid path from SUS_1 to SUS_2. Plugging in the values for a and b, the model-implied correlation is $0.72 \times 0.69 = 0.50$, which is similar to the sample correlation of 0.45. Hence, the model reproduces the observed correlation well. This is an indication of good model fit.

The `fitted()` function in `lavaan` returns all the model-implied covariances. A little manipulation of this output using R's `cov2cor()` function returns the implied correlations. We can then compare these to the actual correlations using the `residuals()` function with the additional `type="cor"` argument.

```
# model-implied covariances
fitted(one.lv.fit)$cov

# transform model-implied covariances to correlations
cov2cor(fitted(one.lv.fit)$cov)

# original correlations
cor(scale.time1[paste("SUS",1:10,sep="")])

# residual correlations
residuals(one.lv.fit,type="cor")
```

The `fitMeasures()` function returns measures of model fit. For more on interpreting model fit values, see West et al. (2012).

```
# fit of single-latent variable model
fitMeasures(one.lv.fit)
```

10.4.3   More Complex Models

There are alternative models we can fit to the SUS data other than the one in Fig. 10.2. We fit two of those alternative models. In the first model, we specify that there are two correlated LVs based on the SUS item types (positive vs. negative). In the second model, we fit a full SEM. We specify that a manifest *Positive* variable (created from the sum of SUS items 1–5) directly predicts the Negative LV. For examples of fitting more advanced LV models in R, see Beaujean (2014).

10.4.3.1   Model with Two Correlated Latent Variables

The model with two correlated LVs is shown in Fig. 10.4. The lavaan syntax for the model is similar to the original model, only now there are two LVs. Since the LVs are exogenous in this model, they are specified to correlate by default. For didactic purposes, we include the syntax allowing two variables to covary in our model specification.

```
# specify model with two latent variables
two.lv.model <- '
# define latent variables
positive =~  a*SUS1 + b*SUS2 + c*SUS3 + d*SUS4 + e*SUS5
negative =~  f*SUS6 + g*SUS7 + h*SUS8 + i*SUS9 + j*SUS10

# covariance between latent variables
positive~~cv_pn*negative
'


# fit model to SUS data
two.lv.fit <- cfa(two.lv.model, data=scale.time1)
```

10.4.3.2 Structural Equation Model

The structural equation model is shown in Fig. 10.5. Before fitting it, we first create
the composite Positive variable.

```
# create positive item set
pos.items <- c("SUS1","SUS2","SUS3","SUS4","SUS5")

# create composite score
scale.time1$pos.score <- rowSums(scale.time1[,pos.items])
```

The *lavaan* syntax for the model is similar to the model with two LVs, except that
we specify that the new Positive MV predicts the Negative LV. For more details on
how to interpret this model and its estimates please see Beaujean (2013) or Rosseel
(2012).

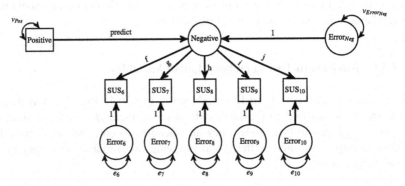

Fig. 10.5 Structural equation model of System Usability Scale items

```
# specify structural equation model
sem.model <- '
# define latent variable
negative =~  f*SUS6 + g*SUS7 + h*SUS8 + i*SUS9 + j*SUS10

# direct relation from composite positive to latent negative
negative~predict*pos.score
'

# fit model
sem.fit <- cfa(sem.model,data=scale.time1)
```

10.5   Cautions and Considerations in Using Latent Variable Models

Latent variable modeling has emerged as an incredibly popular and, in some respects, unifying framework for many types of statistical analysis commonly used in HCI research. Given the utility and flexibility of LVM, users must exercise considerable care and caution when making modeling decisions. This section highlights some of the cautions and consideration when using LVM.

To begin, much criticism has been offered regarding, for example, issues of the selecting a model among a set of competing models, model-data fit, and the ability to estimate causal relations within a LVM. The common theme in most of these criticisms is the role of substantive theory (or lack thereof). Each path specified in a LVM is an assertion of the researcher about the nature of the relation between two or more variables. As a result of this, some have criticized LVM for falsely allowing users to infer too strong of a causal relation from non-experimental data.

The nature of causal relationships is a centuries old interest of humans. The flexibility provided by the LVM framework allows researchers to model relationships in accordance with their guiding theory, even those that specify causation in the absence of experimental manipulation (e.g., Bollen and Pearl 2013). It is a combination of the guiding theory, nature of the collected data, and the method used to analyze the data that determines the strength of any causal inferences that can be inferred from a study (Antonakis et al. 2010). LVM as an analytic technique cannot overcome the absence of theory or a weak research design.

Another criticism of LVMs is the over-reliance on measures of model fit. Undoubtedly, the availability of many measures of model-data fit is a benefit to researchers using LVM as they assess their models. The problem comes when the fit measures are blindly interpreted or fit measure cutoff criteria are used uncritically. First, models that fit the data well may have underlying problems that are not reflected by the measures of fit. For example, Hancock and Mueller (2011) discussed a paradoxical relationship between poor measurement quality and model-data fit. They described a situation in which model-data fit was acceptable with a poorer quality measurement model, and fit was unacceptable with a high quality measurement model. Although the authors explained why this paradox may be observed, it provides evidence that poor models can produce acceptable model fit. Second, there are a theoretically infinite number of competing, or equivalent, models that fit at least as well as the ones being investigated. Reviews of published LVM studies have noted that researchers have often failed to explore other models, which is considered a type of confirmability bias (Kline 2011). Once again, researchers' guiding theory plays an essential role in model selection. If numerous models fit the data equally well, then researchers should rely on their theoretical expectations of the model relationships to identify the best approximating model among a set of competing models.

We should note that some of the criticisms leveled at LVMs have likely been exacerbated by the ever-increasing power of personal computers coupled with the growing ease of using LVM software packages (e.g., point-and-click type programs). For appropriately training researchers, these developments are welcomed, but they may also allow untrained analysts to specify models that exceed both their substantive knowledge as well as their ability to evaluate models critically. We agree with Kline (2011) that computers should make theoretically justified models easier to estimate, but not allow users to suspend their judgment as it relates to modeling decisions.

The bottom line is that the use of a LVM–in and of itself–is not sufficient to establish any sort of causal relationship. Researchers should only use LV modeling (or any other type of data analysis) in conjunction with a theory of how the variables should relate to each other as well as knowing any limitations of causal inference imposed on the data from the research design. While modern software and computer programs have made the estimation of LVMs much easier and more efficient now than at any point in history, this is not a substitute for rigorous training in the proper use and interpretation of LVMs.

10.6 Conclusion

Human-computer interaction research often involves investigating psychological phenomena that cannot be measured directly. In such studies, these LVs should be analyzed correctly using LV models. In this chapter, we showed how to analyze three relatively simple LVMs in the R language using the *lavaan* package. We concluded the chapter discussing some criticisms of LVMs as well as emphasizing that latent variable modeling (or any other type of data analysis) should always be conducted in the presence of some theory of how the variables should relate. Likewise, the accessibility that R provides to those wishing to analyze LVMs is not a substitute for proper training in their use and interpretation.

References

Antonakis J, Bendahan S, Jacquart P, Lalive R (2010) On making causal claims: a review and recommendations. Leadersh Quart 21:1086–1120

Beaujean AA (2013) Factor analysis using R. Pract Assess Res Eval 18(4):1–11

Beaujean AA (2014) Latent variable modeling using R: a step-by-step guide. Routledge, New York

Boker SM, McArdle JJ, Neale M (2002) An algorithm for the hierarchical organization of path diagrams and calculation of components of expected covariance. Struct Equ Model Multi J 9:174–194

Bollen KA (1989) Structural equations with latent variables. Wiley, New York

Bollen KA (2002) Latent variables in psychology and the social sciences. Annu Rev Psychol 53:605–634

Bollen KA, Bauldry S (2011) Three Cs in measurement models: causal indicators, composite indicators, and covariates. Psychol Methods 16:265–284

Bollen KA, Pearl J (2013) Eight myths about causality and structural equation models. Springer, Dordrecht, pp 302–328

Fox J, Byrnes JE, Boker SM, Neale MC (2012) Structural equation modeling in R with the sem and OpenMx packages. Guilford, New York, pp 325–340

Gee JP (2005) Learning by design: good video games as learning machines. E-Learning 2(1):5–16

Hancock GR, Mueller RO (2011) The reliability paradox in assessing structural relations within covariance structure models. Educ Psychol Measur 71:306–324

Haythornthwaite C, Wellman B (1998) Work, friendship, and media use for information exchange in a networked organization. J Amer Soc Inf Sci 49(12):1101–1114

Kenny DA, Milan S (2012) Identification: a nontechnical discussion of a technical issue. Guilford, New York

Kline RB (2011) Principles and practice of structural equation modeling, 2 edn. The Guilford Press, New York

Maloney-Krichmar D, Preece J (2005) A multilevel analysis of sociability, usability, and community dynamics in an online health community. ACM Trans Comput Hum Interact (TOCHI) 12(2):201–232

Nam CS, Bahn S, Lee R (2013) Acceptance of assistive technology by special education teachers: a structural equation model approach. Int J Hum Comput Interact 29:365–377

Nehring WM, Lashley FR (2009) Nursing simulation: a review of the past 40 years. Simul Gaming 40:528–552

Norris AE, Weger H, Bullinger C, Bowers A (2014) Quantifying engagement: measuring player involvement in human-avatar interactions. Comput Hum Behav 34:1–11

Ployhart RE, Oswald FL (2004) Applications of mean and covariance structure analysis: integrating correlational and experimental approaches. Organ Res Methods 7:27–65

Potosky D, Bobko P (1998) The computer understanding and experience scale: a self-report measure of computer experience. Comput Hum Behav 14:337–348

R Development Core Team (2014) R: a language and environment for statistical computing

Robinson WT, Min S (2002) Is the first to market the first to fail? Empirical evidence for industrial goods businesses. J Market Res 39(1):120–128

Rosseel Y (2012) lavaan: an R package for structural equation modeling. J Statist Softw 48(2):1–36

Schmidt LL, Amick BC III, Katz JN, Ellis BB (2002) Evaluation of an upper extremity student-role functioning scale using item response theory. Work: J Prev Assess Rehabil 19:105–116

Schulenberg SE, Melton AM (2007) Confirmatory factor analysis of the computer understanding and experience scale. Psychol Rep 100:1263–1269

van Schaik P, Ling J (2003) Using on-line surveys to measure three key constructs of the quality of human-computer interaction in web sites: psychometric properties and implications. Int J Hum Comput Stud 59:545–567

Walker HM (1940) Degrees of freedom. J Educ Psychol 31:253–269

West SG, Taylor AB, Wu W (2012) Model fit and model selection in structural equation modeling.
  Guilford, New York, pp 209–231
Wright S (1934) The method of path coefficients. Ann Math Statist 5:161–215

Chapter 11
Using Generalized Linear (Mixed) Models in HCI

Maurits Kaptein

Abstract In HCI we often encounter dependent variables which are not (conditionally) normally distributed: we measure response-times, mouse-clicks, or the number of dialog steps it took a user to complete a task. Furthermore, we often encounter nested or grouped data; users are grouped within companies or institutes, or we obtain multiple observations within users. The standard linear regression models and ANOVAs used to analyze our experimental data are not always feasible in such cases since their assumptions are violated, or the predictions from the fitted models are outside the range of the observed data. In this chapter we introduce extensions to the standard linear model (LM) to enable the analysis of these data. The use of [R] to fit both Generalized Linear Models (GLMs) as well as *Generalized Linear Mixed Models* (GLMMs, also known as random effects models or hierarchical models) is explained. The chapter also briefly covers *regularized* regression models which are hardly used in the social sciences despite the fact that these models are extremely popular in Machine Learning, often for good reasons. We end with a number of recommendations for further reading on the topics that are introduced: the current text serves as a basic introduction.

11.1 Introduction

(Generalized) Linear Models ((G)LMs) and (Generalized) Linear Mixed Models (GLMMs) are a basic building block of many advanced statistical and machine learning methods, and they are invaluable tools in the toolbox of anyone analyzing complex data. This chapter introduces the use of [R] to fit such models, with a focus on estimation and prediction rather than (the more standard) hypothesis testing; the rationale of which is discussed extensively in Chap. 13. Throughout the chapter we present the [R] code both to *generate* the data used in the examples and the the code

M. Kaptein (✉)
Artificial Intelligence, Radboud University, Nijmegen, The Netherlands
e-mail: maurits@mauritskaptein.com

© Springer International Publishing Switzerland 2016   251
J. Robertson and M. Kaptein (eds.), *Modern Statistical Methods for HCI*,
Human–Computer Interaction Series, DOI 10.1007/978-3-319-26633-6_11

used to *fit the models*.[1] We focus on the generation of data since this allows the analyst to create a dataset with known properties and hence provides a valuable method to evaluate the chosen analysis against a ground truth. The format of a chapter (with a fairly strict page-limit) is obviously too limited to discuss these very general methods in large detail, hence, the chapter ends with a number of pointers to both introductory texts on the topics as well as more advanced discussions.

11.2 Linear Models

Let's start by creating a simulated dataset containing $n = 100$ observations that might have originated from the Mango watch evaluation as introduced earlier in the book. Here we will start by focussing on the possible relationship between the age of 100 Mango watch users, and the time (in minutes per week) they spend using the watch. The data can be generated using the following [R] commands:

```
> # Set the number of subjects:
> n <- 100
> # Generate a randomly uniform age between 20 and 80:
> age <-  runif(n, 20, 80)
> # Model usage time as a quadratic function of age plus noise:
> time <- 320 + 25*age - .3*age^2+ rnorm(n,0,80)
> # Put everything together in a dataframe.
> data <- data.frame(n = 1:n, age = age, time = time)
```

Note in the passing that in the simulated dataset the Mango employees retire at a fairly late age. A quick overview of the generated data is given in Table 11.1.

Before analyzing our data we should always have a look at our data by plotting it.[2] In this chapter we will mainly use the [R] core plotting functions to do so (despite more versatile alternatives such as lattice or ggplot). The code presented above Fig. 11.1 creates a simple scatterplot of the data that we have just generated: each dot represents a user, and depicts her or his age and usage time. It is clear from the plot that the relationship between age and usage time can be described by a parabola,[3] although there is quite some noise present in the data. Now, let's start our analysis by fitting a linear model to this dataset.

---

[1] The practice of fitting GLMs is also briefly discussed in Chap. 6 as a method for dealing with non-normal dependent data.

[2] See also Chap. 3 of this volume for more on data visualization.

[3] This is quite obvious since in this particular case we generated the data using a second-order polynomial, $y = 320 + 25x - 0.3x^2 + \varepsilon$. However, in a real study one would not know the exact data generating model and visual inspection of the data will help to understand the data.

Table 11.1 Illustration of the simulated data recording the relationship between the age of Mango watch users and the time they use the watch

n	Age	Time
1	72.84	620.55
2	51.14	715.43
3	37.22	719.39
...	...	...
...	...	...
100	59.20	702.24

```
> # Make a call to the default plotting and provide labels:
> plot(data$age, data$time, xlab="Age", ylab="Usage time")
```

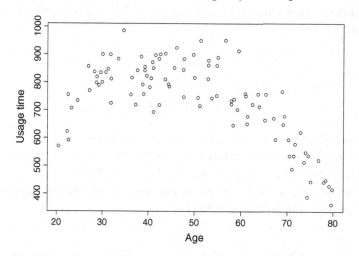

Fig. 11.1 Quick scatterplot of the relationship between the age of a user of the Mango watch and their usage time

11.2.1 Fitting a Line

One, informal, way to think of our aim when fitting linear (regression) models is that we are trying to find the line that "best" matches the observations, or the line that is "closest" to the observations.[4] In [R] the lm function allows us to find such "best" lines.

---

[4] More formally, finding the "best" of "closest" line can be (and is often) defined by minimizing the squared error $\sum_{i=1}^{n}(y - X\beta)^2$ where, using matrix notation, X is the $n \times k$ design *matrix*, and β the *vector* of coefficients of length k. For example, for model $M1$ ($\hat{y} = \beta_0 + \beta_1 x$, see body text), X is a $n \times 2$ matrix of which the first column contains only 1's (for the intercept) and the second column contains the values $x_{1,...,n}$ respectively. We are looking for the vector β that minimizes the square error which is relatively easy to do by taking the gradient (vector of first order partial derivatives) of the error function and setting it to 0. Minimizing the squared error gives the same solution for β

The function call has two primary arguments[5]: the first argument is the so called model formula, while the second (not required) argument specifies the data.frame from which the data is obtained. The code below uses the lm function three times to fit three possible models to our generated data:

```
> # Fit a "intercept only" model:
> M0 <- lm(time ~ 1, data=data)
> # Fit a model with an intercept and linear effect of age:
> M1 <- lm(time ~ 1+ age, data=data)
> # Add a column to the dataset containing age squared:
> data$age2 <- data$age^2
> # Fit a model with a linear and quadratic effect of age:
> M2 <- lm(time ~ 1 + age + age2, data=data)
```

The different model formulas used in the code above specify, in order, the following models:

$$\hat{time}_{M0} = \beta_0$$
$$\hat{time}_{M1} = \beta_0 + age\beta_1$$
$$\hat{time}_{M2} = \beta_0 + age\beta_1 + age^2\beta_2$$

where $\hat{time}_M$ denotes the predicted value of the time given model M.

We can now inspect the estimated parameter (vector) β for the models. Let us, for example, examine $M1$ by printing a summary of the model:

```
> # print a summary of M1 using xtable for fancy layout:
> print(xtable(summary(M1)))
```

	Estimate	Std. Error	t value	Pr(>|t|)
(Intercept)	1005.1836	35.3206	28.46	0.0000
age	−5.3098	0.6705	−7.92	0.0000

(Footnote 4 continued)

as *maximizing the likelihood* using a probabilistic framework. Likelihood maximization provides an estimation method that scales more easily to more complex models then the minimixation of the squared error. To use maximum likelihood estimation we would assume $y|X \sim \mathcal{N}(X\beta, \sigma^2)$ where σ^2 denotes the residual variance. Hence, in this model we assume the dependent variable y to be distributed normal conditional on X. The likelihood of the dataset, given that we assume our observations to be independent and identically distributed (*i.i.d*), is just the product over the likelihood for each datapoint. This we can maximize by taking its derivative and setting to zero. Often, for practical purposes, we take the derivative of the *log* of the likelihood which results in a summation over datapoints instead of a product and is thus easier to differentiate (For more info see, e.g., Gelman and Hill 2007; Millar 2011). In the case of simple linear models (LMs) an exact solution for β exists and is given, in matrix notation, by: $\hat{\beta} = (X^T X)^{-1} X^T y$.

[5]The call takes a number of additional arguments which are not discussed here. For more details one can always type ?lm into the [R] terminal and see the documentation.

This table gives an overview of the model estimates given that we are fitting a linear trend (which we know to not be correctly representing the data-generating model). It shows that the estimated intercept, the predicted usage time of the Mango watch for users of age 0 is high; $\beta_0 = 1005.18$. Furthermore, we find an effect of age that is negative: $\beta_1 = -5.31$. Thus, $M1$ would lead us to conclude that the older users get, the less time they will spend using the Mango watch (and, that newborns spend quite a lot of time using the Mango watch; this might be quite unrealistic). Note that in both cases the estimated coefficient β is significantly different from 0 evaluated using a t-test: the p-value, $Pr(>|t|)$, is smaller then 0.05 for both β_0 as well as β_1 (thus, the null hypotheses $H_0 : \beta_0 = 0$ and $H_0 : \beta_1 = 0$ are both rejected).

We can also easily compare the three models that we just fit using standard F-tests or fit measures such as the AIC or BIC:

```
> # Print an ANOVA (F-test) comparison table:
> print(xtable(anova(M0, M1, M2)))
```

	Res. Df	RSS	Df	Sum of Sq	F	Pr(>F)
1	99	1985256.47				
2	98	1210551.49	1	774704.98	162.64	0.0000
3	97	462041.28	1	748510.21	157.14	0.0000

```
> # Print the rounded AIC (or BIC()) value for each model:
> print(paste(round(AIC(M0)), round(AIC(M1)), round(AIC(M2))))
```

```
[1] "1277 1230 1136"
```

This analysis shows that the AIC of model $M2$, the model with a second order polynomial of age, is the lowest and is thus preferred. Also, $M2$ presents a significant increase in model fit compared to $M1$ and $M0$.[6]

The fact that the model including both a linear as well as a quadratic term of age is the best fitting model is easily seen by plotting the predictions. Figure 11.2 presents the predicted relationship between age and time for each of the three models.

11.2.2   *[R] Model Formulas*

The previous section has introduced basic linear model fitting using [R], and demonstrated the use of ANOVA F-tests to compare models. Also, we explicitly inspected model $M1$ by displaying its estimated coefficients, and using the standard t-test to test the null hypothesis $H_0 : \beta = 0$. Adding to this we also explored plotting (using base [R] plotting functions) the three models to graphically inspect model fit. Jointly

---

[6]Please be cautious using these types of comparisons: a "good" fit, does not mean the model is true. This chapter is too short to properly cover model selection methods. More on the topic of model selection can be found in (e.g., Bozdogan 1987).

```
> # Setup the scatterplot:
> plot(data$age, data$time, xlab="Age", ylab="Usage time")
> # Add the (horizontal) line for M0:
> abline(M0, lty=1)
> # Add the line for M1:
> abline(M1, lty=2)
> # Sort the data (necessary to add the line for m2):
> data <- data[order(data$age), ]
> # Add a line using age and the predictions from M2:
> # Note the use of the "predict" function.
> lines(data$age, predict(M2, data), lty = 3)
```

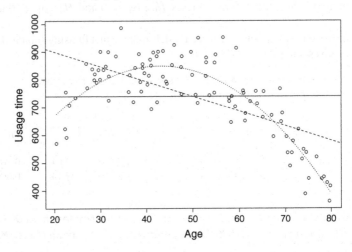

Fig. 11.2 Scatterplot of the relationship between the age of a user of the Mango watch and their usage time. Included are, using different line types, the predicted usage time values as derived from the three different models

this provides a brief overview of the basic linear regression methods used in the social sciences. It is however worthwhile to also inspect in a bit more detail the versatility of the [R] formula interface.

We have already seen how we can specify the dependent and independent variables, and how we can include higher order terms of an independent variable. The following uses are however also noteworthy:

- Specification of a model without an intercept requires explicit deletion of the intercept in the formula: y ~-1 + x + ... Omission of the "−1" in the formula will *by default* include an intercept.
- Specification of an *interaction* between two predictors in a formula can be done using the "*" sign: y ~x1 * x2 + ... Using a "*" includes both the interaction as well as the two main effects (by default). Including an interaction and *excluding* the main effects (which is often regarded bad-practice, but might be useful occasionally) can be done using the ":" sign: The formula y ~x1 : x2 + ... includes the interaction between $x1$ and $x2$, but does not include the main effects of $x1$ and $x2$.

- Independent variables of nominal or ordinal level—also sometimes called *categorical* predictors—can automatically be transformed to dummy coding using the as.factor() function. If (e.g.,) predictor x has four unique values then data$fact.x <- as.factor(data$x) will encode x as a "factor". Subsequently calling y ~fact.x + ... will fit a model with an intercept (default), and three dummy variables.[7] One can specify specific contrasts in [R] quite easily using the contrast or multcomp packages.

11.3   Regularization

The previous section introduced the usage of the lm function in [R] to fit linear models. While admittedly very condensed, we have introduced the standard methods of model fitting, model comparison, model building (using model formulas), testing of null-hypothesis, and dealing with nominal or ordinal predictors (see for a more elaborate introduction on linear models Gelman and Hill 2007).

In this section we introduce *regularized* linear models as a noteworthy and useful extension of the linear modeling framework. There are a number of arguments to motivate regularized regression approaches; an often used argument is the fact that in cases where the number of predictors k is larger then the number of observations n (thus $k > n$), the standard linear model cannot be fit (its solution is undefined) and in such situations we need alternative methods. While true, we think that the argument of *overfitting* when using models with large k (not necessarily larger then n) should already motivate interest for regularization methods (For more on overfitting see for example Hawkins 2004; Zou and Hastie 2005). The term overfitting loosely refers to the idea that the model that we might fit to the data (and use to draw substantive conclusions) might actually, in part, be modeling noise in the data that is not a genuine part of the true data-generating model. Thus, while we might believe our model fit improves by seeing the fit measures improve on the data we collected in actuality the fitted model would perform badly on new data: in the new data the noise will be different, and hence our "overfitted" model will not approximate the newly collected data very well.

To illustrate this idea, let's continue with our dataset describing the age and the time spend on the Mango watch. However, this time we fit a model using not just a quadratic function of *age*, but rather a polynomial of degree 30 (using the poly function)[8]:

---

[7]Note that analysis using only categorical predictors are often thought of in an ANOVA frame-work by most social scientist. However, the lm models and ANOVA models are mathematically the exact same, perhaps with a different choice of dummy encoding and different summary statistics that are of interest.

[8]Model $M0$ is a 0th order polynomial, $M1$ is a first order polynomial of age (the linear term), and $M2$ a second order polynomial of age (the quadratic term). The poly function easily generates higher order polynomial. The model we fit here thus looks as follows: $y = \beta_0 + \beta_1 age + \beta_2 age^2 + \cdots + \beta_{30} age^{30}$.

```
> # Create the scatterplot:
> plot(data$age, data$time, xlab="Age", ylab="Usage time")
> # Add the line predicted by model M3:
> lines(data$age, predict(M3, data), col = "red")
```

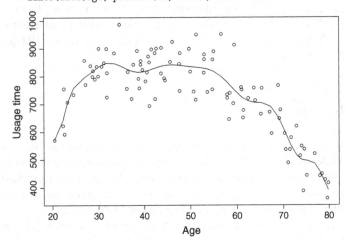

Fig. 11.3 Fit of a high order polynomial to the Mango watch data: Note that while the line is "close" to the observed data-points, it likely models, in part, noise that is present in the data as opposed to actual signal (we know for sure that this is true in this specific case, since we created the data using only a quadratic function)

```
> # Fit a high order polynomial to the data using poly:
> M3 <- lm(time ~ poly(data$age, 30, raw=TRUE), data=data)
```

Figure 11.3 shows the fit of this new model to the dataset. While the black line is fairly "close" to each of the individual datapoints, one can imagine that the line actually partially models a signal which should have been regarded as noise.[9] For example, the little jitter at $age = 75$ in the Figure seems to reflect the particularities of this dataset more then the actual relationship between age and time in the population.

Model $M3$ is a good example of a model that *overfits* the data. Often this is thought of a model having high variance and low bias, where variance is the error from sensitivity to small fluctuations in the sample (noise), while bias is the error that results from erroneous assumptions in the model (see for a more elaborate discussion of the Bias-Variance tradeoff Hastie et al. 2013). A classical challenge when modeling data is to decide how much bias or variance to introduce: Model $M2$ is a model with higher bias then $M3$, but with lower variance. In this case, since we created the data ourselves, we know that $M2$ fits the data generating process more closely than $M3$.

The idea of overfitting can also be illustrated by comparing the *within-sample* and *out-of-sample* prediction errors of the different models. We start by computing the within sample (so for the 100 datapoint is our dataset) mean squared prediction error

---

[9]Actually, in this specific case we know that $M3$ is modeling noise: we generated the data using only a 2nd order polynomial and some Gaussian noise.

$$Error = \frac{\sum_{i=1}^{n}(\hat{y}_i - y_i)}{n}. \tag{11.1}$$

for both M2 as well as M3 on our simulated dataset.

```
> # Compute predictions for model M2:
> # Note that the ``data'' term could have been omitted since
> # this is the default behavior of the predict function
> yhat.M2.in <- predict(M2, data=data)
> # Compute and print the mean squared error
> print(sum((data$time - yhat.M2.in)^2) / n)

[1] 29006.65

> # And similarly for M3
> yhat.M3.in <- predict(M3, data=data)
> print(sum((data$time - yhat.M3.in)^2) / n)

[1] 3939.105
```

The mean squared error is, as expected, (much) lower for $M3$ since the fitted line "matches" the observations better.

However, when creating a new dataset and subsequently using the estimated β's obtained on the original sample to predict scores *out of sample* we see:

```
> # Create a new dataset called data2
> # Note we use the same parameters as before (albeit a larger n):
> n <- 1000
> age <- runif(n, 20, 80)
> time <- 320 + 25*age - .3*age^2+ rnorm(n,0,80)
> data2 <- data.frame(n = 1:n,
+                     age = age,
+                     time = time)
> # Now we generate predictions for our new dataset (data2)
> # using the estimated coefficients in M2:
> yhat.M2.out <- predict(M2, data=data2)
> # And we print the mean squared "out of sample" error:
> print(sum((data2$time - yhat.M2.out)^2) / n)

[1] 37449.92

> # And similarly for M3:
> yhat.M3.out <- predict(M3, data=data2)
> print(sum((data2$time - yhat.M3.out)^2) / n)

[1] 38277.4
```

Note that on this new dataset the *out-of-sample* prediction error of model $M2$, containing more bias, is actually *lower* then that of $M3$. This indicates that $M3$ was indeed overfitting the data.[10]

While in this case we were fully aware of the *true* data generating model, this is often not the case. Thus, often in practice we do not know where to stop adding variance (e.g., including more predictors. A higher variance of the model will lead to increased *within* sample fit of the model, but realistically we would like to select a model that also performs well for new datasets: we want to prevent explicitly modeling the noise in the sample.

One method of addressing this problem is the addition of a so-called *regularization* term to the linear model: this additional (mathematical) term introduced in the problem of finding the "best" fitting line "punishes" extremely large values of β and essentially introduces bias in the model even if k is large.[11]

We can use the lm.ridge function in [R] to fit a *regularized* model: again, this is a model in which the size of the coefficients is penalized to introduce bias:

```
> # Use lm.ridge to fit a regularized regression model
> M4 <- lm.ridge(time ~ poly(data$age, 30, raw=TRUE),
+          data=data, lambda=.01)
```

The lambda argument controls the size of the penalty: when lambda= 0 the ridge regression and the standard linear model will give the exact same result since no penalty is introduced. The following table compares the first 5 coefficients of both the unpenalized polynomial model, as well as the ridge regression model using lambda = 0.1:

```
> # Extract the first five coefficients of M3:
> coefsM3 <- as.numeric(coef(M3))[1:5]
> # Similarly for M4:
> coefsM4 <- as.numeric(coef(M4))[1:5]
> # Add both to a fancy printed table:
> compare <- data.frame(M3 = coefsM3, M4=coefsM4)
> print(xtable(compare))
```

Note that the fitted values for the first few terms of the regularized model $M4$ are much closer to the true values, $\beta = \{320, 25, 0.3\}$, then fitted values in the large polynomial model ($M3$). Lambda is referred to as a tuning parameter and needs to be selected by the analyst. While several methods for choosing lambda exist, in most cases it is selected by inspecting the out-of-sample predictions of the model

---

[10]This procedure outlines the standard methods that are used to asses overfitting: by splitting up a dataset into a training-set and a test-set one can fit models on the training-set, and subsequently evaluate them on the test-set. If a model performs well on the training-set, but badly on the test-set (in terms of error), then the model likely overfits the data.

[11]Regularization changes the definition of "best" line to one in which we minimize a term that looks like $\sum_{i=1}^{n}(y - X\beta)^2 + \lambda f(\beta)$. Here, $f(\beta)$ is some function whose output grows as the size of the elements of β grow. Using the sum of the absolute elements of β for $f(x)$ is called the "Lasso", while using the L2 norm is called "ridge" regression. Here, λ is a tuning parameter which determines the magnitude of the penalty.

	M3	M4
1	14724907.77	155.42
2	−4489768.72	31.89
3	607555.30	−0.28
4	−47892.92	−0.00
5	2418.58	−0.00

and choosing a value of `lambda` that minimizes the out-of-sample error. In practice we often use a procedure called *cross-validation* (Cross validation is described in detail in Hastie et al. 2013): across multiple subsampled datasets from the original data the *out-of-sample* error is computed and `lambda` is "tuned" to obtain a low out-of-sample error.

Regularization can be a feasible solution in cases where the number of predictors k is large compared to the number of datapoints n. This often occurs in HCI when a large number of features can be measured (properties of the product and of the user), but it is costly to do a large experiment; in such cases the number of observations n is limited, but the number of possible predictors k is large. Also, regularization can be extremely useful when the focus of the modeling effort is on *out-of-sample* prediction instead of testing or estimating model coefficients. For example, in HCI, if we are interested in predicting task-completion times for new users, we might benefit in our predictions from the use of regularization.

11.4 *Generalized* Linear Models

Mathematically, we have up to now been assuming y to be (conditionally) normally distributed $y|X \sim \mathcal{N}(X\beta, \sigma^2)$. Practically, we were also assuming y to take on all the possible values on a real number line. However, what do we do for other types of observations? We often have observations in which people "yes" or "no" make a decision; for example, based on their age, users might decide to abandon using the Mango watch altogether. We would then have a dataset very similar to our previous example, but this time $y \in \{0, 1\}$. The following code simulates such a dataset:

```
> # Setup the number of people and generate random ages:
> n <- 100
> age <-  runif(n, 20, 80)
> # use a "inverse logit" function to compute the probability of usage:
> prob.adopt <- invlogit(320 + 25*age - .3*age^2
+ + rnorm(n,0,80) - 700)
> # Simulate usage from a Bernoulli(prob.adopt):
> adopt <- rbinom(n, 1, prob.adopt)
> # Create the new dataset
> data3 <- data.frame(n = 1:n, age = age, adopt = adopt)
```

Note that here we use first compute the probability of adopting the watch using a scheme very similar to our earlier discussion, but this time we use the inverse logit function in the `arm` package to "rescale" the outcomes which we obtained to fall within the range of 0 to 1 (probabilities). The `invlogit` function, $y = \frac{1}{1+e^{-x}}$

```
> # Quick plot of the invlogit function:
> plot(invlogit, xlim=c(-10,10), ylim=c(0,1))
```

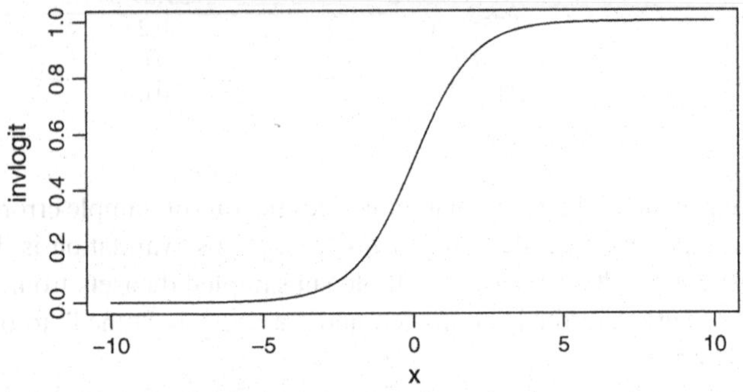

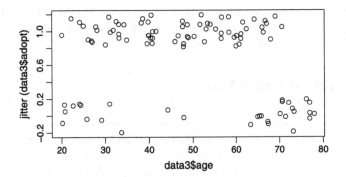

Fig. 11.4 Quick plot of the inverse logit function

```
> # scatter plot of the choice to adopt (0,1) of the Mango watch
> # as a function of age (note the call to "jitter()")
> plot(x=data3$age, y=jitter(data3$adopt))
```

Fig. 11.5 Quick plot of the generated data

is quickly plotted in Fig. 11.4. The `invlogit` function maps a range of values from $-\infty < x < \infty$ to $0 < y < 1$ using a continuous function. Thus, we end up with a dataset describing a (quadratic) relationship of age to the *probability* of adopting the mango watch. The line `adopt <- rbinom(n, 1, prob.adopt)` generates, from the predicted probabilities, the actual observations $y \in \{0, 1\}$.

Figure 11.5 provides a quick look at the data and shows that those with a "medium" age are likely to use the mango watch, while those who are either old or young are less likely to use the watch.[12]

---

[12]Note the use of `jitter` to display the values of adopt. Since these observations are $\in \{0, 1\}$, plotting the values directly would clutter the figure. The jitter command adds a slight random variation to the observed values.

Once we have simulated (or, in a real case, collected) a dataset denoting the age of users and their adoption of the watch, we could wonder how to best model the data. One choice could be to model the data using a (regularized) linear model; the models we have just discussed. However, next to a number of more technical issues[13] fitting a linear model would lead us to fit a model that would predict values that are unrealistic: the linear model would predict values for y anywhere on the real number line, while we know that y in reality only takes up values of 0 or 1. Hence, the standard linear model does not seem to work well for this type of data. This is a more general problem: for example, if we observe count data then we know the data has only integer values and is truncated at 0; none of these limitations would be included in the model if we used a linear model to model counts.

A very versatile method to deal with "non-normal" (conditionally) dependent data is to use a linear model in combination with a so-called *link* function: the link function can be thought of as a mapping of the values predicted by the linear model to values within the range of the expected value of the dependent variable. More technically, it links the *expected* value of the dependent variable, conditional on the predictors, to the linear part of the model. Models using link functions are called Generalized Linear Models (GLMs). So, while the linear model predicts the expected value of the outcome y given X directly:

$$E[y|X] = X\beta \tag{11.2}$$

GLMs use a link function $\mathscr{L}()$:

$$E[y|X] = \mathscr{L}(X\beta) \tag{11.3}$$

and clearly the linear model is a special case of the generalized linear model where $\mathscr{L}(x) = x$. Note that in the above formulas we used matrix notation, capital X and β, to denote the *linear* part of the model which allows us to write models using (possibly) a large number of predictors k in a concise way.

For the case of adoption of the Mango watch the *expected value of adoption* of the Mango watch is the probability of adopting the watch: $Pr(\texttt{adopt} = 1|X)$. Since probabilities run from 0 to 1, we need a link function that maps the continuous values produced by the linear part to a scale ranging from 0 to 1: indeed, the inverse logit function that we used to simulate the data is an often used choice (For a more elaborate discussion of link functions see, e.g., Gelman and Hill 2007). The full model specification of the so-called logit model (also known as the *logistic regression model*) then becomes:

---

[13]For example the fact that for the linear model, one of the assumptions—in the maximum likelihood framework—is the fact that the conditional expected value and the variance of the observed variable are unrelated: while this is true for normally distributed outcomes, it is not generally true for many other outcome types.

```
> # Create age squared in the new dataset:
> data3$age2 <- data3$age^2
> # Fit the Generalized Linear Model:
> GM <- glm(adopt ~ 1 + age + age2, data=data3, family=binomial(logit))
> # Make a scatterplot of the data:
> plot(data3$age, jitter(data3$adopt))
> # Add the predicted line to the plot:
> data3 <- data3[order(data3$age), ]
> lines(data3$age, predict(GM, data3, type="response"))
```

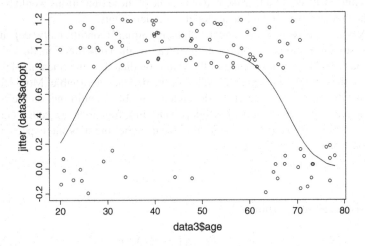

Fig. 11.6 Predicted probability of adopting the Mango watch as a function of age

$$E[y|X] = Pr(y = 1|X) = \mathscr{L}(X\beta) = \frac{1}{1 + e^{-X\beta}} \qquad (11.4)$$

As we did for our linear model, we can now look for a "best" fitting line as a function of β.[14] The following code uses the glm function in [R] to fit a generalized linear model to the data we have just created. Here, in the glm call we specify the link function using the family=binomial(logit) argument.

Next, we plot the raw data and superimpose a line depicting the expected value of y given the different values of age. Note that here we use type="response" in the predict function to indicate that we want to retrieve the expected values (by

---

[14]For more info on the actual methods of finding a "best" line in this context, using Maximum Likelihood estimation, see (Hastie et al. 2013).

default, predict gives the predictions of only the *linear* part of the model). For the code and output see Fig. 11.6.

Link functions provide a very versatile tool to model, using the basic ideas derived from linear models, all kinds of dependent variables. Note that we have only scratched the surface here of the use of generalized linear models. The logit link is useful for Bernoulli or Binomial distributed dependent variables, while many other links for (e.g.,) Poisson or Exponentially distributed dependent variables exist. Many of the standard methods of obtaining confidence intervals of the estimated β's, performing null-hypothesis significance tests, or comparing models are provided by [R] in a fashion that is very similar to these procedures in the case of linear models (See for more details Gelman and Hill 2007).

11.5 Linear *Mixed* Models

We have now (briefly) discussed methods to model observations both when these are assumed to be conditionally normally distributed (linear models), as well as for other types of distributions of the dependent variable (*generalized* linear models). In this section we introduce so-called "Mixed Models", which are provide another extension of the linear modeling framework. The main conceptual difference is that in GLMs we assumed the observations to be conditionally independent, while in mixed models (LMMs or GLMMs) we deal with data in which the outcome of interest has some dependency structure: for example, if we consider multiple observations within individuals, then it is likely that the observations within an individual are related. Also, when we conduct a usability study of educational software we likely observe multiple pupils per school class and the observations of pupils within the same class are likely related. Or, if we have observations of the usage of a device—for example the Mango watch—within different countries, then there might be relationships between the observations within a country.

To explain mixed models, we again simulate some data that could motivate the use of Mixed Models in a research context. The code below creates a dataset again describing the relationship between the age of a user (age), and the duration of usage of the Mango watch (time), but this time we also have information regarding the twenty different countries of origin of the user of the watch. Note that in each country the baseline usage duration (operationalized by the different *intercepts* of the model for each country in this case) is distinct.

```
> # Setup the independent variables
> n <- 100
> age <-  runif(n, 20, 80)
> # Specify the number of countries:
> countries <- 20
> # Generate a countrycode for each participant in "n":
> countrycode <- sample(1:countries, n, TRUE)
> # Create a data.frame with participant id,
> # countrycode, and age:
> data <- data.frame("id"=1:n, "country"=countrycode, "age"=age)

> # Setup the data generating model:
> # 1. Draw a random intercept for each country from
> # a normal distribution:
> intercepts <- rnorm(countries, 0, 100)

> # 2. Use the "ddply" function from "plyr" to generate the data:
> # ddply will run through participants form a distinct country in
> # batches of the country. We here thus generate a usage time
> # as a function of age using a different intercept for each country:

> data <- ddply(data, .(country), function(x, intercepts){
+         y <- intercepts[x$country] + 320 + 25*x$age - .3*x$age^2
+         + norm(length(x$age),0,20)
+           return(data.frame("id"=x$id, "country"=x$country,
+           + "age"= x$age, "time" = y))
+ }, intercepts=intercepts)
```

The call to ddply is quite involved so we will explain it in a bit more detail: ddply takes as first input argument a matrix (the 100×3 matrix of simulated datapoints in this case), and the second argument .(country) specifies that the original dataset should be passed to the third argument (a custom function in this case) in batches grouped by the different values of country. Hence, the function is executed 20 times, once for each country, and for each country it simulates the dependent variable y. Different from the earlier listings of simulation code, the intercept of the model, β_0 are different for each country.

After generating the data we can inspect the data by plotting it and see that while the overall trend is similar everywhere (a quadratic effect of age on usage time), the starting points (intercepts) for the country differ: some countries apparently use the watch longer then others. Figure 11.7 shows an overview of the data that we just generated. Note that (e.g.,) the country indicated by the solid dots has consistently lower values then most of the other countries.

We could now wonder how to analyze such a dataset. Since we are familiar already with linear models, we have two logical courses of action:

1. We fit a so-called *pooled* model: We ignore the country structure and simply fit a model that ignores the country variable.
2. We fit a so-called *unpooled* model: In effect, we fit different models for each country.

```
> # Use lattice for easy "group-by" plots:
> library(lattice)
> # Use only black and white:
> lattice.options(default.theme = standard.theme(color = FALSE))
> # Create a plot grouped by country:
> xyplot(time ~ age, data=data, groups=country)
```

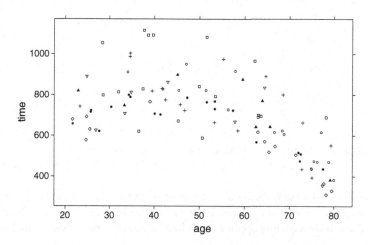

Fig. 11.7 Relationship between age and usage time in multiple countries. Plot created using package `lattice` for easy splitting based on the countries. The data in each country uses its own symbol

While these two approaches could both be sensible in some cases, they both suffer from a number of drawbacks. The most general drawback is the fact that at different "levels" of the data (e.g., within a country or between countries), the effect under study might differ.

To illustrate the latter, suppose we would collect a dataset like that depicted in Fig. 11.8, where we see simulated data of the relationship between x and y for five distinct groups. Clearly, fitting a pooled model—ignoring the groups—would lead us to conclude that x has a positive effect on y, while if we focussed on each group individually (unpooled), the effect in each case would be negative. This "reversal" of effects is generally known in statistics as *Simpson's paradox*, and should make one very cautious when dealing with grouped data. What is also often problematic about the above suggested approach is that for individual groups—when we are fitting *unpooled* models—the size of the data is often limited, leading to very noisy estimates of the parameters; often we only have a limited number of observations within a school class, individual, or country.

Mixed models can be though of as providing a way of modeling hierarchical (or otherwise dependent) data which is "in between" the two extremes of the pooled and the unpooled approach: within the mixed modeling framework we specify *batches* of parameters that we link together: For example, we might fit a model with a different intercept in each country of origin, but we do not use distinct dummies for each, but

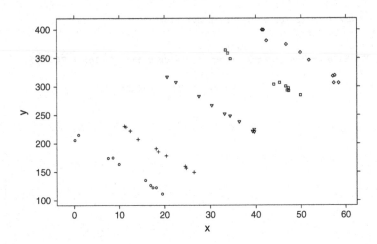

Fig. 11.8 Plot illustrating a possible reverse effect at different levels

rather we make a distributional assumption regarding the intercepts. We assume that the intercepts are *random* draws from a *distribution* of country level effects.

The mixed modeling approach can be illustrated using a more formal notation:

- In pooled models we fit a model of the following form $y = \beta_0 + \beta_1 age + \cdots$. We do not explicitly include the countries in the model.
- In an unpooled model we fit a model of the following form: $y = \beta_0 C_1 + \beta_1 C_2 + \beta_2 C_2 + \cdots + \beta_j age + \cdots$ where $C_1, \ldots, C_k$ would be (dummy) indicators for the countries. Hence each country has its own intercept. Note that we have to estimate this parameter for each country.[15]
- Using hierarchical models the model would be $y = \beta_{[k]} + \beta_1 age + \cdots$ where $\beta_{[k]} \sim \mathcal{N}(\beta_0, \sigma_C^2)$. Here, with the $\beta_{[k]}$ notation, we identify a *random* effect: we assume that the intercepts for each country themselves can be modelled as being drawn randomly from a normal distribution of country intercepts with mean β_0 and variance σ_C^2. Note that in this case we only estimate two parameters to model all the country intercepts.[16]

Effectively, the *assumption* that the country intercepts are drawn from a normal distribution[17] leads to estimates for each country that are "shrunk" together: large values of $\beta_{[k]}$ for individual countries are effectively penalized since these are less likely

---

[15]Often, in a complete unpooled approach, the analyst actually fits multiple, completely independent models. Then, the slopes would also differ per country. Here we focus only on the intercept for illustration purposes.

[16]From the above it can be seen why also more formally mixed models can be regarded "in-between" pooled and unpooled models: A pooled model is the special case of a mixed model where $\beta_{[k]} \sim \mathcal{N}(\beta_0, 0)$, and an unpooled model is the special case where $\beta_{[k]} \sim \mathcal{N}(\beta_0, \infty)$.

[17]The analyst could also include different distributional assumptions regarding the "batches" of coefficient. This however is outside the scope of this article.

given the normality assumption. This is very similar to the penalties we discussed for regularized models.

Intuitively the shrinkage can be motivated as follows: if a country has (a small number of) observations which are all (extremely) high compared to observations in other countries, then—assuming that the data contains noise—this country likely has a number of "upwards" errors: collecting more measurement for the country likely decreases its mean. The likely decrease is informed by the information that is "borrowed" from the other countries. In this sense mixed models introduce bias in the estimates of the country level intercepts, but this bias (as was the case for regularization), likely improves the out of sample predictions of the models (For more on shrinkage and the relationships to mixed models please see Morris and Lysy 2012).

11.5.1 Random Intercept Models

The lme4 package provides a convenient way of fitting mixed effect models. Lets quickly examine the simulated Mango watch dataset for different countries using a pooled, an unpooled (at least in the intercepts), and a mixed modeling approach. First, we focus on the pooled model. The estimated coefficients are presented in Table 11.2. In this model the possible differences between the countries are not modelled explicitly.

```
> # Add quadratic:
> data$age2 <- data$age^2
> # Fit the model:
> m.pooled <- lm(time ~ age + age2, data)
> # Print a summary of the model:
> print(xtable(summary(m.pooled)))
```

We then fit the unpooled model, and the estimated coefficients are presented in Table 11.3.

```
> # Fit the model:
> m.unpooled <- lm(time ~ -1 + as.factor(country) + age
+ + age2, data)
> # Print a fancy summary:
> xtable(summary(m.unpooled))
```

Table 11.2 Summary of the completely pooled model fit to the country dataset

	Estimate	Std. error	t value	Pr(>|t|)
(Intercept)	348.9431	113.6533	3.07	0.0028
age	22.5714	4.8881	4.62	0.0000
age2	−0.2739	0.0480	−5.70	0.0000

Table 11.3 Summary of the unpooled model fit to the country dataset. A number of the intercepts are omitted because of space limitations

	Estimate	Std. error	t value	Pr (>|t|)
as.factor(country)1	250.2092	82.1222	3.05	0.0032
as.factor(country)2	272.8883	87.2648	3.13	0.0025
as.factor(country)3	589.5119	85.4191	6.90	0.0000
as.factor(country)4	342.6736	89.2812	3.84	0.0003
...	...	...	...	...
as.factor(country)19	404.8110	74.1133	5.46	0.0000
as.factor(country)20	361.2721	87.7444	4.12	0.0001
age	20.5396	3.0617	6.71	0.0000
age2	−0.2555	0.0299	−8.54	0.0000

For comparison we can contrast with these fitted intercepts with the actual intercepts used when generating the data. The following commands print the standard deviations of the estimated and true intercepts:

```
> sd(intercepts)

[1] 116.5052

> sd(coef(m.unpooled)[1:10])

[1] 163.3219
```

Note that here the standard deviation of the estimated intercepts is too high; this is caused by the relatively low number of datapoints at the country level which results in overfitting of the model.

Finally, we can use the the `lmer` function from the `lme4` package to fit a *mixed* model:

```
> # Fit the model (note the similarity to (g)lm
> m.mixed <- lmer(time ~ age + age2 + (1 | country), data)
> # Print a summary of the model:
> summary(m.mixed)

Linear mixed model fit by REML ['lmerMod']
Formula: time ~ age + age2 + (1 | country)
   Data: data

REML criterion at convergence: 982.8

Scaled residuals:
     Min       1Q    Median       3Q      Max
-2.50655 -0.49838 -0.01547  0.60033  2.79736

Random effects:
 Groups    Name         Variance Std.Dev.
 country   (Intercept)  11602.5  107.71
 Residual                 414.3   20.35
Number of obs: 100, groups: country, 20

Fixed effects:
               Estimate Std. Error t value
(Intercept) 320.784312  29.962472   10.71
age          25.326697   0.778436   32.54
age2         -0.303246   0.007664  -39.57

Correlation of Fixed Effects:
     (Intr) age
age  -0.578
age2  0.552 -0.988
```

The term ...+ `(1 | country)` in the call to the `lmer` function indicates the fact that we want to fit a "random" effect for the intercepts of different countries. Using this syntax we are fitting a model in which the intercepts are assumed to be distributed normally around some mean β_0 with a variance σ_C^2.

In the output we find both the so called *fixed* effects as well as the *random* effects. The fixed effects provide the estimates of the coefficients β that are the same for all levels of the grouping factor (countries) in this case. Here we find that the overall intercept (the mean intercept over countries) is 320.78, and thus very close to it's actual value. Second, we find $\beta_1 = 25.33$ and $\beta_2 = -0.30$, again very close to the values we used to generate the data. Finally, the random effect for country estimates σ_C^2, and it thus quantifies the "spread" of the country level intercepts. The estimated standard deviation of the country level intercepts $\hat{\sigma}_C = 107.71$ is also fairly close to its true value $\sigma_C = 100$. The final random effect coined "Residual" provides an estimate of the error variance of the model (For more details see, e.g., Gelman and Hill 2007).

11.5.2 More Random Effect Specifications

The above provided an example of a very simple mixed model: here only the country level intercepts where assumed to be related. However, one could easily imagine the fact that the effect of age might also differ between countries, or that other types of grouping are present in the data (e.g., we do not only know the country of origin, but we also know the primary education of the user of the Mango watch; this would provide another grouping factor of the data—another dependency structure—that is not nested within the countries). The `lmer` function allows for a number of alternative specifications:

- Using `~x1 + x2 + ...+ (1 + x1 | country) + ...` would indicate not only random intercepts for different countries, but would also introduce random "slopes": now the effect of $x1$ on y can differ for different countries. Technically the intercepts and slopes are now assumed to be generated from a multi-variate normal distribution with mean vector (β_k, β_{x1}) and co-variance matrix Σ.
- Using `~x1 + x2 + ...+ (1 | country) + (1 | education) ...` would introduce not merely a random intercept for countries, but also a random intercept for education, the possible second grouping present in the Mango watch data. This latter model is often referred to as a crossed-random effects model.

The package `lme4` is very versatile, and one easily fits very complex models to the data. One should be careful not to overcomplicate the analysis. A recommended check after fitting models is to generate data from the model (again using the `predict` function) and comparing the predicted outcomes with the observed outcomes. However, despite possible complications, nested (or otherwise dependent) datastructures are omnipresent in HCI, and thus mixed models often provide a useful addition to our standard hierarchical modeling techniques.

11.5.3 Generalized Mixed Models

After discussing LMs, GLMs, and LMMs, a logical next step is the introduction of link functions when using mixed models. This leads to the use of so-called Generalized Linear Mixed Models. Conceptually the step from LMMs to GLMMs is the same as that from LMs to GLMMs: we can introduce a link function given specific distributional assumptions regarding the dependent variable. In [R] the function `glmer` which is also provided in the `lme4` package can be used to fit GLMMs. Here we can again use the `family=` argument to specify the link function.

11.6 Conclusions and Recommendations

In this chapter we have introduced the use of [R] for fitting LMs, GLMs, and GLMMs. We have tried to focus on simulation and plotting of the data (as well as inspection of model fit), as opposed to statistical testing since testing is heavily discussed in other chapters of this volume. GLMMs provide an extremely powerful framework for analyzing a large range of possible datasets. We have tried to illustrate cases where the data are dependent (the country example), or where the dependent data where not conditionally normally distributed (the adaptation of the watch "yes" vs "no" example using logistic regression).

We encourage readers to try out the here presented examples by themselves, and inspect the model objects in detail. But we would also like to refer interested readers to additional materials. We recommend the following:

- A more extensive guide to LMs, GLMs, and GLMMs and the use of [R] to fit these models can be found in Gelman and Hill (2007). This book is referenced throughout the Chapter; however, it is by no means the only book on the topic. We just regard this specific book a very good starting point before digging into the more theoretical discussions of (G)L(M)Ms.
- A Bayesian approach to many of the methods discussed here can be found in Gelman et al. (2013). The Bayesian framework—other then the frequentist framework used throughout the chapter—provides an often useful and more natural extension to the above presented modeling techniques. For introductions into the Bayesian "way of thinking" see also Chaps. 8 and 9 of this book.
- A more theoretical discussion on issues such as overfitting, the bias-variance trade-off can be found in (Hastie et al. 2013).
- A discussion of (G)LMs from a machine learning point of view can be found in (Bishop 2006).
- LMs, GLMs, and GLMMs are already being used routinely in HCI analysis. Examples are Kaptein and van Halteren (2012), who use GLMMs to analyze the outcomes of their experiments evaluating a persuasive technology, and (Kaptein and Eckles 2012), where the authors use a LMM to estimate the heterogeneity in the effects of persuasive messages.

References

Bishop CM (2006) Pattern recognition and machine learning. Springer

Bozdogan H (1987) Model selection and akaike's information criterion (aic): the general theory and its analytical extensions. Psychometrika 52(3):345–370

Gelman A, Hill J (2007) Data analysis using regression and multilevel/hierarchical models. Cambridge University Press

Gelman A, Carlin JB, Stern HS, Dunson DB, Vehtari A, Rubin DB (2013) Bayesian data analysis, 3rd edn, vol 1. CRC Press

Hastie T, Tibshirani R, Friedman J (2013) The elements of statistical learning: data mining, inference, and prediction, vol 11. Springer Science & Business Media

Hawkins DM (2004) The problem of overfitting. Journal Chem Inf Comput Sci 44(1):1–12

Kaptein MC, Eckles D (2012) Heterogeneity in the effects of online persuasion. J Interact Mark 26(3):176–188

Kaptein MC, van Halteren A (2012) Adaptive persuasive messaging to increase service retention. J Pers Ubiquit Comput 17(6):1173–1185

Millar RB (2011) Maximum likelihood estimation and inference: with examples in R, SAS and ADMB. Wiley, Chichester

Morris CN, Lysy M (2012) Shrinkage estimation in multilevel normal models. 27(1):115–134

Zou H, Hastie T (2005) Regularization and variable selection via the elastic net. J Roy Stat Soc: Ser B (Stat Methodol) 67(2):301–320

Chapter 12
Mixture Models: Latent Profile and Latent Class Analysis

Daniel Oberski

Abstract Latent class analysis (LCA) and latent profile analysis (LPA) are techniques that aim to recover hidden groups from observed data. They are similar to clustering techniques but more flexible because they are based on an explicit model of the data, and allow you to account for the fact that the recovered groups are uncertain. LCA and LPA are useful when you want to reduce a large number of continuous (LPA) or categorical (LCA) variables to a few subgroups. They can also help experimenters in situations where the treatment effect is different for different people, but we do not know which people. This chapter explains how LPA and LCA work, what assumptions are behind the techniques, and how you can use R to apply them.

12.1 Introduction

Mixture modeling is the art of unscrambling eggs: it recovers hidden groups from observed data. By making assumptions about what the hidden groups look like, it is possible to get back at distributions within such groups, and to obtain the probability that each person belongs to one of the groups. This is useful when:

- You measured one thing but were really interested in another. For example, how students answer exam questions is indicative of whether or not they have mastered the material, and how somebody you chat with online reacts to your messages is indicative of them being human or a bot;
- You fit a model but suspect that it may work differently for different people, and you are interested in how. For example, when designing the information given to vistors of a birdwatching site, putting up signs with just the Latin names of birds is helpful to some people and likely to annoy others. When investigating the effect of putting up such signs it might be helpful to take this into account.

D. Oberski (✉)
Tilburg University, Tilburg, The Netherlands
e-mail: D.L.Oberski@uvt.nl

© Springer International Publishing Switzerland 2016
J. Robertson and M. Kaptein (eds.), *Modern Statistical Methods for HCI*,
Human–Computer Interaction Series, DOI 10.1007/978-3-319-26633-6_12

Table 12.1 Names of different kinds of latent variable models

Observed	Models for means		Regression models	
	Latent		Latent	
	Continuous	Discrete	Continuous	Discrete
Continuous	Factor analysis	**Latent profile analysis**	Random effects	Regression mixture
Discrete	Item response theory	**Latent class analysis**	Logistic ran. eff.	Logistic reg. mix.

- You have a lot of different variables—too many to handle and interpret—and would like to reduce these to a few easily interpretable groups. This is often done in marketing where such groups are called "segments".

There are many other uses of mixture modeling—too many to explain here. Suffice to say that by understanding mixture modeling, you will make a start at understanding a host of other statistical procedures that can be very useful, such as regression mixture modeling, noncompliance in experiments, capture-recapture models, randomized response, and many more. Moreover, mixture models are popular tools in computer vision, such as face detection and hand gesture recognition (e.g., Yang and Ahuja 2001). While these applications go beyond the scope of this chapter, it may be helpful to keep in mind that they are extensions of the models we discuss here.

Mixture modeling is a kind of latent variable modeling: it helps you to deal with situations where some of the variables are unobserved. The specific thing about mixture modeling is that is concerns latent variables that are discrete. You can think of these as groups, "classes", or "mixture components"—or as categories of an unobserved nominal or ordinal variable. Depending on whether the observed variables are continuous or categorical, mixture models have different names. These names, together with the names of the other kinds of latent variable models, are shown in Table 12.1, in which the rows correspond to continuous or discrete *observed* variables, and the columns to continuous or discrete *latent* variables. The left part of the table concerns models in which the groups are based on differences in means, and the right part concerns models in which the groups are based on differences in regression-type coefficients. The two types of models dealt with in this chapter are indicated in bold: "latent profile analysis", which tries to recover hidden groups based on the means of continuous observed variables, and "latent class analysis", which does the same for categorical variables.[1] Some of the other models in the table are explained in other chapters.

A different name for latent profile analysis is "gaussian (finite) mixture model" and a different name for latent class analysis is "binomial (finite) mixture model". Its Bayesian version is popular in the computer science literature as "latent Dirichlet allocation". Here we will stick to the terminology LCA/LPA, which is more common in the social sciences.

---

[1]Confusingly, sometimes latent class analysis is used as a broader term for mixture models.

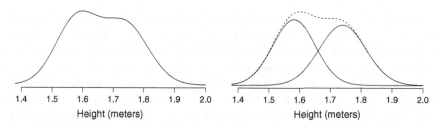

Fig. 12.1 Peoples' height. *Left* observed distribution. *Right* men and women separate, with the total shown as a *dotted line*

12.2   Mixtures of Continuous Variables: Latent Profile Analysis

For this chapter, I measured the height of every human being on the planet.[2] I then plotted the distribution of heights measured in Fig. 12.1 (right-hand side).

Interestingly, the height distribution on the left-hand side of Fig. 12.1 is clearly not normal. It has two peaks that look like they might come from two groups. Now, you may have happened to guess what these groups are: women and men. If I had recorded each person's sex, I could confirm this by creating my picture separately for men and women, as shown on the right-hand side of Fig. 12.1. Women differ in their height according to a normal distribution, as do men—it is just when you combine the two that the non-normal picture emerges.

Unfortunately, I forgot to record peoples' sex, and now it is too late. When you perform an experiment this might happen to you too—or it might have happened to the people who collected your data. For example, a usability test might omit peoples' handedness. Even more commonly, you may need information that is difficult or impossible to get at directly, such as an attitude, feeling, or socially desirable behavior. In all of these cases you will be in a similar spot as I am with the height data: I think there might be hidden groups, but I have not actually recorded them. Latent class analysis is concerned precisely with recovering such hidden ("latent") groups.

So how can we recover the picture on the right-hand side of Fig. 12.1? One idea is to split the sample on some guess about peoples' sex and make histograms within each guessed group. Unfortunately, it can be shown that this will never give the picture on the right (McLachlan and Peel 2004, pp. 26–28). Without extra information, the only way to get exactly that picture is to guess each person's sex correctly, but the only information I have to guess sex is height. And although a random man is likely to be taller than a random woman, inevitably people like Siddiqa Parveen, who is currently the world's tallest woman, and Chandra Bahadur Dangi, the shortest man, will cause me to count incorrectly, and create a picture that is at least slightly different from the "true" one on the right.[3]

---

[2]This is not true, but the rest of the chapter is.

[3]Apparently, Ms. Parveen is 213.4 cm and Mr. Dangi is 48.3 cm.

This is where mixture modeling comes to the rescue. Because it turns out that, while we will never know each person's sex for certain, we can still recover a picture very close to that on the right-hand side of Fig. 12.1. So we can discover the distributions of height for men and women without ever having observed sex! Even more astoundingly, as more and more data are gathered, we will more and more correctly surmise what the distributions for men and women look like *exactly*.

There is a well-known saying that "there is no such thing as a free lunch". I have personally falsified this statement on several—sometimes delicious—occasions. But while false in real life, in mathematics this statement is law. We will pay in unverifiable assumptions—on this occasion the assumption that height is normally distributed for men and women. This assumption is unverifiable from just the observed data because the problem is exactly that we do not know sex. So when faced with data that produce a picture like the one on the left-hand side of Fig. 12.1, we will need to simply assume that this picture was produced by mixing together two perfect normal distributions, without us being able to check this assumption.

The corresponding mathematical model is

$$p(\text{height}) = Pr(\text{man})\text{Normal}(\mu_{\text{man}}, \sigma_{\text{man}}) + Pr(\text{woman})\text{Normal}(\mu_{\text{woman}}, \sigma_{\text{woman}}),$$
(12.1)

which I will write as

$$p(\text{height}) = \pi_1^X \text{Normal}(\mu_1, \sigma_1) + (1 - \pi_1^X)\text{Normal}(\mu_2, \sigma_2).$$
(12.2)

So we see that the the probability curve for height is made up of the weighted sum of two normal curves,[4] which is exactly what the right-hand side of Fig. 12.1 shows. There are two reasons for writing π_1^X instead of $Pr(\text{man})$: first, when fitting a mixture model, I can never be sure which of the "components" (classes) corresponds to which sex. This is called the "label switching problem". Actually, it is not really a problem, but just means that X is a dummy variable that could be coded $1 = \text{man}, 2 = \text{woman}$ or vice versa. The second reason is that by using a symbol such as π_1^X, I am indicating that this probability is an unknown parameter that I would like to estimate from the data. Note that the superscript does not mean "to the power of" here, but is just means "π_1^X is the probability that variable X takes on value 1". This way of writing equations to do with latent class analysis is very common in the literature and especially useful with categorical data, as we will see in the next section.

Assuming that both men's and women's weights follow a normal distribution, the problem is now to find the means and standard deviations of these distributions: the within-class parameters (i.e. μ_1, μ_2, σ_1, and σ_2).[5] The trick to doing that is in starting with some initial starting guesses of the means and standard deviations. Based on these guesses we will assign a *posterior probability* of being a man or woman to each person. These posterior probabilities are then used to update our guess of the within-class parameters, which, in turn are used to update the posteriors, and so

---

[4] As can be gleaned from the figures, by "normal curve" I mean the probability density function.
[5] We also need to know the proportion of men/women π_1^X but I will ignore that for the moment.

Fig. 12.2 EM algorithm estimating the distribution of height for men and women separately without knowing peoples' sex

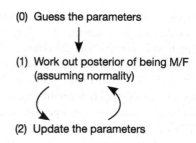

(0) Guess the parameters

(1) Work out posterior of being M/F
     (assuming normality)

(2) Update the parameters

Stop when parameters stop changing

Fig. 12.3 Tall woman or short man? The probability density of observing a person 1.7 m tall is a weighted sum of that for men and women separately

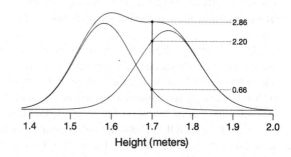

on until nothing seems to change much anymore. This algorithm, the "expectation-maximization" (EM) algorithm, is depicted in Fig. 12.2. The online appendix contains R code (`simulation_height.R`) that allows you to execute and play with this algorithm.

How can the posterior probabilities be obtained (step 1), when the problem is exactly that we do not know sex? This is where our unverifiable assumption comes in. Suppose that my current guess for the means and standard deviations of men and women is given by the curves in Fig. 12.3, and I observe that you are 1.7 m tall. What then is the posterior probability that you are a man? Figure 12.3 illustrates that this posterior is easy to calculate. The overall probability density of observing a person of 1.7 m is 2.86, which we have assumed (in Eq. 12.2) is just the average of two numbers: the height of the normal curve for men plus that for women. The picture shows that a height of 1.7 m is much more likely if you are a man than if you are a woman. In fact, the posterior is simply the part of the vertical line that is made up by the normal curve for men which is $2.20/(2.20 + 0.66) = 2.20/2.86 \approx 0.77$. So, if all I know is that you are 1.7 m tall, then given the current guess of normal curves for men and women, the posterior probability that you are a man is about 0.77. Of course, the posterior probability that you are a woman is then just $1 - 0.77 = 0.23$, since both probabilities sum to one.

Now for step (2) in Fig. 12.2. I apply my earlier idea: guess people's gender, and then count their height towards men's or women's means and standard deviations, depending on the guess. Recognizing that I am not 100 % certain about any one person's sex, however, instead of guessing "man" or "woman", I will use the posterior probabilities. For example, if a 1.7 m-tall person has a 0.77 posterior chance of being a man and (therefore) a 0.23 chance of being a woman, I will add $(0.77)(1.7)$ to my estimate of the mean of men but also $(0.23)(1.7)$ to that for women. So each person's observed value contributes mostly to the mean of the sex I guessed for them but also some to the other sex, depending on how strongly I believe they are a man or woman. If I have no idea whether a person is man or woman, that is, when the probability is 0.50:0.50, the height contributes equally to the guessed means of both. In Fig. 12.3 this occurs where the two curves cross, at about 1.65. By using the posterior probabilities as weights, I obtain new guesses for the means and standard deviations, which allow me to go back to step (1) and update the posteriors until convergence. Note that whereas earlier in the section this idea of guessing then calculating would not work, the assumptions allow me to get the posterior probabilities necessary to perform this step.

This section has shown how you might recover hidden groups from observed continuous data. By making assumptions about what the hidden groups look like, it is possible to get back at distributions within such groups, and to obtain a posterior probability that each person belongs to one of the groups. There are several software packages that can do latent profile analysis, including Mplus (Muthén and Muthén 2007) and Latent GOLD (Vermunt and Magidson 2013a). In R, this model could be fitted using the mclust library (Fraley and Raftery 1999):

```
library(mclust)
height_fit_mclust <- Mclust(height)
summary(height_fit_mclust, parameters = TRUE)
```

As mentioned above, you can play with this example using the online appendix (simulation_height.R).

With just one variable, we needed to pay a hefty price for this wonderful result: an unverifiable assumption. It is possible to do better by incorporating more than one variable at the same time; for example, not just height but also estrogen level. Both are imperfect indicators of sex but using them together allows me to guess the hidden group better. The next section gives an example of modeling with several categorical variables.

12.3   Mixtures of Categorical Variables: Latent Class Analysis

Latent class analysis (LCA) is similar to latent profile analysis: it also tries to recover hidden groups. The difference, as you can see in Table 12.1, is that LCA deals with categorical observed variables. Another difference between LCA and LPA is that no specific distribution is assumed for the variables: each of the observed variables' categories has an unknown probability of being selected without this probability following any particular functional form. But by retracting our assumption, we also retract the necessary payment to buy the possibility of estimating latent classes. In LCA, this payment is made, not by assuming that the variables are distributed in any particular way, but by assuming that *within each class, the observed variables are unrelated to each other*. This assumption is called "local independence", and tends to create classes in which the observations are similar to each other but different from those in other classes.

Typically, the researcher (1) determines the "best" number of latent classes K that sufficiently explain the observed data; and (2) summarizes the results. At times, researchers are also interested in (3) relating the most likely class membership to some external variables not used in the model. When performing this last task, however, the researcher should be very careful to account for the uncertainty in each observation's class membership: failure to do so will result in biased estimates of the class membership prediction. Modeling class membership while accounting for the uncertainty about it is called "three-step modeling" in the literature, and can be done in certain software packages such as Mplus and Latent GOLD. For more information, see Bakk et al. (2013).

Suppose there are three observed variables A, B, and C, all three categorical with six categories. The model for traditional latent class analysis is then typically written as

$$\pi_{abc}^{ABC} = \sum_x \pi_x^X \pi_a^{A|X} \pi_b^{B|X} \pi_c^{C|X}, \tag{12.3}$$

where X is the latent class variable, π_x^X the size of class x and, for example, $\pi_a^{A|X}$ is the probability that variable A takes on the value a in the latent class x. Equation 12.3 describes the probability of seeing any combination of values a, b, and c as depending solely on the differences in latent class sizes (π_x^X) combined with how different these classes are in terms of the observed variables. Within the classes, the variables are unrelated ("conditionally independent"), which is reflected in the product $\pi_a^{A|X} \pi_b^{B|X} \pi_c^{C|X}$.

Let's apply LCA as an exploratory technique to the SuSScale example data with 3 time points. As a reminder, some example answers to the 10 questions in the questionnaire are shown in Table 12.2. These 10 variables are moderately related

Table 12.2 Example data from the SUS questionnaire

	Time	V01	V02	V03	V04	V05	V06	V07	V08	V09	V10
1	1	4	3	5	4	3	4	3	2	2	3
87	2	4	5	3	5	5	5	5	4	5	5
173	3	3	3	2	4	3	2	3	2	2	3
2	1	3	2	3	3	3	3	4	3	3	2
...	...	...	...	...	...	...	...	...	...	...	...

Table 12.3 Fit of the latent class models with increasing numbers of classes

# Classes	Log-likelihood	AIC	BIC
1	–3753.32	7614.64	7806.50
2	–3441.70	7103.39	7494.22
3	–3327.72	6987.45	7577.24
4	–3245.73	**6935.46**	**7724.22**

The lowest AIC and BIC are shown in **boldface**

with an average correlation of 0.4. Our goal is to find K classes such that these relationships are small within the classes, where we still need to find out the best number of classes K.

Because the data are categorical, we apply a latent class model for polytomous variables to the 258 observations. This is done using the poLCA package in R (Linzer and Lewis 2011; Core Team 2012):

```
library(poLCA)
f <- as.matrix(dplyr::select(scale, starts_with("V")))~Time
M4 <- poLCA(f, scale, nclass=4, nrep=50)
```

Here, the first command loads the library; the second command constructs an R formula with all of the observed indicators (variables that measure the class membership) V01–V10 on the left-hand side, and the covariate Time on the right-hand side to control for any time effects. The last command fits the model with four classes. The nrep=50 argument tells poLCA to try out 50 different starting values so that we are certain that the best solution has been found. This is always recommended when performing latent class analysis.

We fit the model for a successively increasing number of classes, up to four: $K = \{1, 2, 3, 4\}$. With one class, the model in Eq. 12.3 simply says the variables are independent. Obviously if this one-class model fits the data well we are done already since there are no relationships between the variables in that case. The first order of business is therefore to evaluate how well the latent class models with different numbers of classes fit the data and to select one of them. There are many measures of model fit, the most common ones being the AIC ("Akaike information criterion") and BIC ("Bayesian information criterion"). These are shown for our four models in Table 12.3.

In Table 12.3, lower values of the fit measures are better. The best model appears to be the four-class model. We therefore pick that model as our preferred solution. This procedure of choosing the lowest BIC is the most used in LCA. However, this is an exploratory method: just as in exploratory factor analysis, it is therefore often also possible to pick a lower or a higher number of classes based on substantive concerns or ease of interpretation. We might only be interested in finding a small number of broad classes, for instance, and ignore any remaining distinctions within these classes (Fig. 12.4).

Fig. 12.4 Output of `poLCA` for the four-class model showing the estimated distribution of the ten observed variables V01–V10 within each of the four classes. The profile plot is easier to read

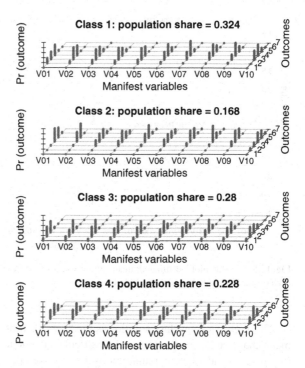

With the argument `graphs=TRUE`, `poLCA` produces graphs that show the estimated distributions of the observed variables in each latent class. These graphs can be very useful with fewer variables of nominal measurement level, but with ten variables having six categories each, this output is rather hard to read. Instead, I created a so-called "profile plot" for these variables in Fig. 12.5, which displays the estimated class means instead of their entire distribution. This plot is usually reserved for continuous variables, but with our six-point ordinal variables it still makes sense to display their means.

Figure 12.5 shows the profile plots for all four fitted models. In a profile plot, there is one line for each class. The lines represent the estimated mean of the observed variable on the x-axis within that class. So the profile plot for the two-class solution shows that the two classes separate people who give high scores on all of the questions (class 2) from people who give low scores on all of them (class 1). Note that the class numbers or "labels" are arbitrary. In the three-class solution, there is also a class with low scores on all of the variables (class 1). The other two classes both have high scores on the first five variables but are different from each other regarding the last five variables: class 2 also has high scores on these whereas class 3 has low scores. The four-class solution, finally, has "overall high" (class 2) and "overall low" (class 3) classes, as well as "V01–V05 but not V06–V10" (class 4) and its opposite (class 1).

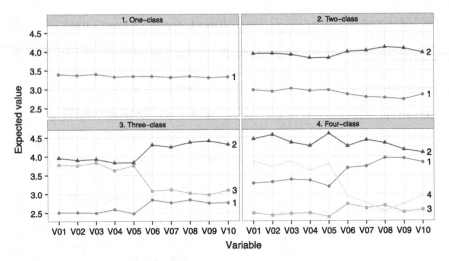

Fig. 12.5 "Profile plot": estimated means of the 10 observed variables in the SuSScale data within each of the K classes for $K = \{1, 2, 3, 4\}$

Although the four-class solution is the "best" solution, this does not necessarily mean that it is a good solution. In particular, if our local independence model is to provide an adequate explanation of the observed data, the relationships between the indicators after controlling for class membership should be small. An intuitive way of thinking about this is that the scatterplot between two indicators should show a relationship *before* conditioning on the class membership, but none *after* this conditioning.

Figure 12.6 demonstrates this with two example indicators, V01 and V10. To make the points easier to see in the figure they have been "jittered" (moved a bit). The top part of Fig. 12.6 is simply a scatterplot of V01 and V10 over all 258 observations. The shape of the points here corresponds to the most likely class membership of that point. For example, the upper-rightmost point is a triangle to indicate that its most likely class is the "overall high" class (class 2). It can be seen that there is a moderate relationship between these two indicators before accounting for the classes, with a linear correlation of 0.30. The bottom part of Fig. 12.6 splits up the same scatterplot by class, so that each graph contains only points with a particular shape. It can be seen that within each of the classes the relationship is almost non-existent. This is exactly what conditional independence means. Therefore the model fits well to the data for these two indicators. Graphs like Fig. 12.6 only make sense when the observed score (1–6 in our case) is approximately of interval level. For nominal variables, a different kind of fit measure is therefore necessary. One such measure is the "bivariate residual" (BVR), the chi-square in the residual cross-table between two indicators. At the time of writing, the BVR is not available in R but can be obtained from commercial software such as Latent GOLD (Vermunt and Magidson 2013b).

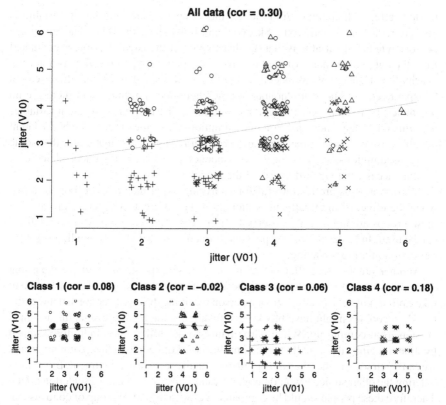

Fig. 12.6 *Top graph* the data with observed correlation 0.30 are modeled as a "mixture" of four classes (*circles, triangles, pluses,* and *crosses*). *Bottom graph* these classes are chosen such that the correlation between the variables is minimal within them

In this example we applied LCA as an exploratory method to artificial data that were generated according to a linear factor model. The profiles then recuperate the generated structure. In real data, there will often be additional classes. For example, if some respondents tend to use the extreme points of a scale ("extreme response style") while others use the whole scale, this will lead to an additional class in which the extremes are more likely to be chosen. Because this is a nonlinear effect, such a finding is not possible with linear models such as factor analysis.

12.4   Other Uses of Latent Class/Profile Analysis

While the traditional use of LCA/LPA is as an exploratory technique, latent class models can also be seen as a very general kind of latent variable modeling. Latent class models are then a type of structural equation modeling, factor analysis, or random effects (hierarchical/multilevel) modeling in which the latent variable is discrete rather than continuous (Skrondal and Rabe-Hesketh 2004). The advantage of a discrete latent variable is that the distribution of the latent variable is estimated from the data rather than assumed to have some parametric form, such as a normal distribution. Hence, several special cases of latent class models are sometimes called "nonparametric". The term "nonparametric" here does not mean that there are no parameters or assumptions; rather, it means that the distribution of the latent variables is estimated. In fact, the relaxation of assumptions about the distribution of the latent variables usually means that there are *more* parameters to estimate, and that some of the assumptions, such as local independence rather than just uncorrelatedness, become necessary to identify parts of the model.

Mixture models are also useful for analyzing experimental data. For example, when the effect of the treatment is thought to be different in different groups, but these groups are not directly observed: in this case "regression mixture modeling" can be used. In R, the `flexmix` package (Gruen et al. 2013) is especially useful for regression mixture modeling.

Another situation that often occurs in randomized experiments with people is that the people do not do what they are supposed to do. For example, a patient assigned to take a pill might neglect taking it, or a person receiving different versions of a website based on cookies might have blocking software installed that prevents the assigned version from coming up. When participants do not follow the randomly assigned treatment regime, this is called "noncompliance". For people in the treatment group, we can often see whether they did or did not actually receive the treatment. But simply deleting the other subjects would break the randomization, causing a selection effect. Therefore these people should be compared, not with the entire group of controls, but with a hidden subgroup of controls who *would have taken the treatment if they had been assigned to it*. The fact that we cannot observe this hypothetical hidden group leads to a latent class (mixture) model, and methods to deal with noncompliance in randomized experiments are special cases of the models discussed here. The Latent GOLD software contains several examples demonstrating how to deal with noncompliance. In R, a package containing some basic noncompliance functionality is `experiment` (Imai 2013).

12.5 Further References

An accessible and short introduction to latent class analysis and its variations is given by Vermunt and Magidson (2004). More background information and details on the various types of models that can be fitted is found in Hagenaars and McCutcheon (2002). A comprehensive introduction-level textbook is Collins and Lanza (2013). The manuals and examples of software that can fit these models, especially Mplus and Latent GOLD, are another great source of information. Some examples of applications of LCA and LPA to human-computer interaction are Nagygyörgy et al. (2013)

and Hussain et al. (2015). For an application to computer detection of human skin color, see Yang and Ahuja (2001, Chap. 4).

References

Bakk Z, Tekle FB, Vermunt JK (2013) Estimating the association between latent class membership and external variables using bias-adjusted three-step approaches. Sociol Methodol 43(1):272–311

Collins LM, Lanza ST (2013) Latent class and latent transition analysis: with applications in the social, behavioral, and health sciences, vol 718. Wiley, New York

Fraley C, Raftery AE (1999) Mclust: software for model-based cluster analysis. J Classif 16(2): 297–306

Gruen B, Leisch F, Sarkar D (2013) flexmix: Flexible mixture modeling. http://CRAN.R-project. org/package=flexmix. R package version, pp 2–3

Hagenaars JA, McCutcheon AL (2002) Applied latent class analysis. Cambridge University Press, Cambridge

Hussain Z, Williams GA, Griffiths MD (2015) An exploratory study of the association between online gaming addiction and enjoyment motivations for playing massively multiplayer online role-playing games. Comput Hum Behav 50:221–230

Imai K (2013) Experiment: R package for designing and analyzing randomized experiments. R package version 1.1-1

Linzer DA, Lewis JB (2011) poLCA: an R package for polytomous variable latent class analysis. J Stat Softw 42(10):1–29

McLachlan, G. and Peel, D. (2004). Finite mixture models. John Wiley & Sons, New York

Muthén LK, Muthén B (2007) Mplus user's guide. Muthén & Muthén, Los Angeles

Nagygyörgy K, Urbán R, Farkas J, Griffiths MD, Zilahy D, Kökönyei G, Mervó B, Reindl A, Ágoston C, Kertész A et al (2013) Typology and sociodemographic characteristics of massively multiplayer online game players. Int J Hum-Comput Interaction 29(3):192–200

R Core Team (2012) R: a language and environment for statistical computing. R Foundation for Statistical Computing, Vienna, Austria. ISBN 3-900051-07-0

Skrondal A, Rabe-Hesketh S (2004) Generalized latent variable modeling: multilevel, longitudinal, and structural equation models. Interdisciplinary statistics series. Chapman & Hall/CRC, Boca Raton

Vermunt JK, Magidson J (2004) Latent class analysis. The sage encyclopedia of social sciences research methods, pp 549–553

Vermunt J, Magidson J (2013a) LG-Syntax user's guide: manual for Latent GOLD 5.0 Syntax Module. Statistical Innovations Inc., Belmont

Vermunt JK, Magidson J (2013b) Technical guide for Latent GOLD 5.0: basic, advanced, and syntax. Statistical Innovations Inc., Belmont

Yang M-H, Ahuja N (2001) Face detection and gesture recognition for human-computer interaction. Springer Science & Business Media

Part V
Improving Statistical Practice in HCI

This book has tried to introduce a number of statistical methods that might be of use in HCI that are not covered, at least not extensively, in most social science methods curricula. Hence, we hope to have introduced novel options to readers, and we hope to have inspired readers to be critical regarding their own analysis, explore multiple options, and feel empowered to not merely stick to the defaults that are present in our field.

However, merely providing new methods will likely not change our practice, and it is worthwhile to consider whether our statistical practices should be improved, and how this might be done. If a change is needed (we somewhat feel it is, this partly inspired this book), we should be aware that the change will need to be made both by authors, as well as reviewers and editors.

This final part of the book consists of two discussion pieces, both aimed at critically evaluating our current analysis practice and introducing novel ideas.

Chapter 13: Fair Statistical Communication
In Chap. 13 Dr. P. Dragicevic discusses how we can move from the standard reporting on NHST methods, to what he coins "fair statistical communication." The chapter clearly illustrates the difficulties that NHST methods have, and, like Chap. 5, discusses effect sizes. However, the chapter subsequently focuses primarily on estimation: What do we want to know, and how do we quantify and visualize it? Dr. Dragicevic makes a strong argument in favor of adopting an estimation (as opposed to testing) approach: a view on fair statistical communication that is worthwhile for any author or reviewer to consider.

The chapter ends with a large number of practical pointers on how to improve our analysis and reporting in HCI. Although not every pointer might be applicable for your study at hand, we definitely recommend authors and reviewers to consider the tips. At http://www.aviz.fr/badstats Dr. Dragicevic maintains a collection of ideas and tips to improve statistical communication in HCI.

Chapter 14: Should We Improve?
This book ends with a final contributed chapter by the editors. In this chapter we try to wrap up the views presented in the book, and provide suggestions for the future. The chapter also tries to evaluate whether our current practice needs improvements by reviewing a number of the most cited quantitative works in our field.

Chapter 13
Fair Statistical Communication in HCI

Pierre Dragicevic

Abstract Statistics are tools to help end users accomplish their task. In research, to be qualified as usable, statistical tools should help researchers advance scientific knowledge by supporting and promoting the effective communication of research findings. Yet areas such as human-computer interaction (HCI) have adopted tools — i.e., p-values and dichotomous testing procedures — that have proven to be poor at supporting these tasks. The abusive use of these procedures has been severely criticized in a range of disciplines for several decades, suggesting that tools should be blamed, not end users. This chapter explains in a non-technical manner why it would be beneficial for HCI to switch to an *estimation* approach, i.e., reporting informative charts with effect sizes and interval estimates, and offering nuanced interpretations of our results. Advice is offered on how to communicate our empirical results in a clear, accurate, and transparent way without using any tests or *p*-values.

13.1 Introduction

A common analogy for statistics is the toolbox. As it turns out, researchers in human-computer interaction (HCI) study computer tools. A fairly uncontroversial position among them is that tools should be targeted at end users, and that we should judge them based on how well they support users' tasks. This applies to any tool. Also uncontroversial is the idea that the ultimate task of a scientific researcher is to contribute useful scientific knowledge by building on already accumulated knowledge. Science is a collective enterprise that heavily relies on the effective communication of empirical findings. Effective means clear, accurate, and open to peer scrutiny. Yet the vast majority of HCI researchers (including myself in the past, as well as researchers from many other disciplines) fully endorse the use of statistical procedures whose usability has proven to be poor, and that are not able to guarantee either clarity, accuracy, or verifiability in scientific communication.

P. Dragicevic (✉)
Bat 660 Université Paris-Sud, 91405 Orsay Cedex, France
e-mail: pierre.dragicevic@inria.fr

© Springer International Publishing Switzerland 2016   291
J. Robertson and M. Kaptein (eds.), *Modern Statistical Methods for HCI*,
Human–Computer Interaction Series, DOI 10.1007/978-3-319-26633-6_13

A distinguishing feature of these statistical procedures is their mechanical nature: data is fed to a machine called "statistics", and a binary answer is produced: either we can trust the data or not. The idea is that for the work to qualify as scientific, inference from data should be as objective as possible and human judgment should be put aside. Few HCI researchers see the contradiction between this idea and the values they have been promoting—in particular, the notion that "humans in the loop" are often more powerful than algorithms alone (Beaudouin-Lafon 2008). Similarly, researchers in information visualization (infovis) went to great lengths to explain why data analysis cannot be fully delegated to algorithms (Fekete et al. 2008): computing should be used to augment human cognition, not act as a substitute for human judgment. Every year infovis researchers contribute new interactive data analysis tools for augmenting human cognition. Yet when analyzing data from their own user studies, they strangely resort to mechanical decision procedures.

Do HCI and infovis researchers suffer from multiple personality disorder? A commonly offered explanation for this contradiction is that there are two worlds in data analysis: (i) exploratory analysis (see Chap. 3), meant to generate hypotheses, and where human judgment is crucial and (ii) confirmatory analysis, meant to test hypotheses, and where human judgment is detrimental. This chapter challenges the view that human judgment can be left out when doing confirmatory analysis.

By mechanical decision procedures I refer to a family of statistical procedures termed *null hypothesis significance testing (NHST)*. This chapter compares NHST with *interval estimation of effect sizes* (or *estimation* for short), an alternative approach that consists of reporting effect sizes with interval estimates and offering nuanced interpretations (Cumming 2013). The chapter skips many technical details, widely available elsewhere. The key difference between the two approaches lies in their usability, and it can be summarized by the illustration in Fig. 13.1.

NHST as it is typically carried out involves (i) computing quantities called p-values and then (ii) applying a cut-off to these p-values to determine "statistical significance". Section 13.2 focuses on the notion of p-value divorced from the notion of a cut-off. Confidence intervals, a particular type of interval estimate closely related to p-values, will be used as a baseline of comparison. Section 13.3 discusses the use of cut-offs to determine statistical significance and contrasts this approach

Fig. 13.1 If empirical knowledge was coffee and articles were coffee cups, experiments would be coffee machines and statistical tools would be coffee pots. Drawing inspired from Norman (2002)

with estimation. Section 13.4 offers practical advice on how to achieve fair (i.e., clear and truthful) statistical communication through estimation. Readers seeking practical advice can jump to Sect. 13.4, while those seeking for justifications can keep on reading.

13.2 *p*-Values, Effect Sizes and Confidence Intervals

Though the aim of this chapter is not to offer an introduction to statistics, it is useful to start by briefly reviewing a few basic concepts. This will make sure we understand the examples offered throughout this chapter, and will also clarify our assumptions.

13.2.1 *A Minimalistic Example and Quick Reminders*

Imagine you need to help your best friend decide whether or not she should buy an expensive pill for losing weight, and you find a scientific paper assessing the pill's efficacy. From the statistical report you gather the information in Fig. 13.2.

What can you conclude from this figure? How confident can you be? Where does the uncertainty come from, exactly?

Sample and population. There is uncertainty as to the true efficacy of the pill, partly because the pill has only been tested on a few volunteers. Ideally, these volunteers constitute a random *sample* from a *population* of interest (e.g., all overweight US citizens), to which we assume your friend belongs. The mean weight loss only informs us about the *sample*, but a much better measure would be the weight loss averaged across the entire *population*. Neither measure will tell for sure what will happen to your friend, but the population average would be a much better indication.

Statistical inference. Since the population average is a better measure of efficacy, we decide it is really our measure of interest, even though it can only be guessed. This guessing process about a hypothetical population is essentially what is meant by statistical "inference". It is only part of what we can do with statistics but it is central in HCI and other domains, and this is what this chapter focuses on. Note that other interpretations of statistical inference exist that are perhaps more accurate and realistic for HCI experiments (Frick 1998). However, random sampling is by far the most widespread and we will stick to it for simplicity.

Fig. 13.2 Results of an imaginary study on the effectiveness of a weight-loss pill

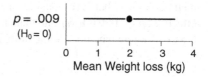

Replication. In statistics, a replication typically refers to a hypothetical sample that could have been obtained from the same (also hypothetical) population on a different experiment. For example, had the researcher above chosen a different set of randomly selected volunteers, the results would have been different. A concrete illustration of multiple replications will be provided in Sect. 13.2.4.4.

Point estimate. The black dot on the chart is the *point estimate* of the population-wise weight loss: it is our *best bet* on how much weight your friend will lose, in the absence of any other information. A simple method for computing the point estimate is to take the sample mean (for other methods see Sect. 13.4.3). Different replications would yield a different point estimate, hence the uncertainty.

Interval estimate. The bar on the figure is an *interval estimate*. It indicates the uncertainty around the point estimate. The most common type of interval estimate is the confidence interval. Let us assume that a 95 % confidence interval has been provided, as it is commonly the case. Strictly speaking, a 95 % confidence interval is an interval that is obtained from a procedure that satisfies a certain property, this property being that the intervals it generates capture the population mean 95 % of the time across many replications. In practice, it is simpler to think of a confidence interval as a *range of plausible values* for the population mean (Cumming 2012; Fidler and Loftus 2009; Schmidt and Hunter 1997). The point estimate is the *most plausible*, and plausibility *smoothly decreases* as we move away from it—in typical cases, the point estimate is about *seven times more plausible* than the confidence limits, i.e., the interval's upper and lower ends (Cumming 2013, p. 17). Plausibility does not suddenly drop when crossing the limits, as values outside are implausible but *not impossible*. This interpretation is an approximation and there is debate over whether it is a good one (more on this in Sect. 13.3.1), but for now let us trust it.

***p*-values**. The number to the left is the *p*-value for a *null hypothesis of no effect*. This null hypothesis is the devil's advocate claim that the pill yields exactly zero weight loss on average across the entire population. If this was true, any result would be caused by sampling error alone. However, not all results would be equally likely: a consistent and massive weight loss, for example, would be quite unlikely under the null hypothesis. This is what the *p*-value captures: it is the probability of observing results as extreme as (or more extreme than) what was actually observed if the null hypothesis was true. In practice, it is easier to think of a *p*-value as *a measure of strength of evidence against the null hypothesis*; The closer *p* is to 0, the more evidence that the pill has a some effect overall, or more specifically has a strictly positive effect, since here the point estimate is positive. This is how R.A. Fisher, who introduced *p*-values, thought we should understand them (Goodman 1999, p. 997; Gigerenzer 2004, p. 593). A different view will be given in Sect. 13.3.1.

There is no way of interpreting Fig. 13.2 that would satisfy all statisticians and methodologists, but a reasonable interpretation is that we can trust the pill to be effective ($p = .009$ is low), and that on average the weight loss is most likely between 0.5 to 3.5 kg, maybe not too far from 2 kg. Now let us see how useful *p* really is.

13.2.2 Choosing a Pill

Your friend has now decided to buy a pill to lose weight, but there are many options and she cannot make up her mind (this problem is inspired from Ziliak and McCloskey (2008, p. 2303)). As a proponent of evidence-based decision making, you search for publications online, find four different studies testing different pills, write down the results and compile them into a single chart, shown in Fig. 13.3.

Note that you *only have access to the four study reports*. So even if you can do statistics and would like to compute the *p*-values for all pairwise differences between pills, you cannot. This scenario is meant to illustrate to what extent *already published studies* can be used to inform decisions, depending on how results are *reported*. A researcher who writes a literature survey does not usually download all datasets to re-run analyses. Also, it does not matter whether the *p*-values are used to assess conditions individually (as it is the case here) or differences between conditions (as is more often the case in HCI). It may help to think of the reported weight losses as differences between pills and a common baseline, e.g., a placebo.

Any trained scientist will have immediately noticed the enormous amount of uncertainty in the data—except apparently for the first pill[1]—and should not feel compelled to draw any conclusion. But here you need to make a decision. Given the data you have, which pill would you recommend?

I have shown this problem to different audiences and most people would choose pill 4. This is indeed a sensible answer: it is reasonable to favor a pill that yields the maximum expected utility—here, weight loss. Recall that each point estimate shows your friend's most likely weight loss with that pill. For your friend, pill 4 is the best bet, and it is certainly a much better bet than pill 1.

Now suppose that pill 4 does not exist. Which pill would you pick among the remaining ones? Look at Fig. 13.3 carefully. With some hesitation, most people reply pill 3. Now also remove pill 3. More hesitation ensues: some people choose pill 2 while others choose pill 1. But the most reasonable choice is really pill 4, then 3, then 2, then 1. The expected weight loss with pill 1 is way lower than with any other. Unless your friend had bet her life that she will lose at least some weight (even one gram), there is no logical reason to favor pill 1 over any other.

13.2.3 How Useful Is the Information Conveyed by P?

Not very much. When presented with the pill problem, many researchers will ignore *p*-values, despite using them in their papers. This stems from a correct intuition: the *p*-values are not only largely irrelevant to the decision, but also redundant. If needed,

---

[1]The width of confidence intervals generally increases with the variability of observations and decreases (somehow slowly) with sample size (Cumming 2012). So either pill 1 has a much more consistent effect or the number of subjects was remarkably larger. It is not very important here.

Fig. 13.3 Chart showing the results from four (imaginary) studies on the effectiveness of different weight-loss pills. *Error bars* are 95 % confidence intervals and *p*-values assume a null hypothesis of no effect

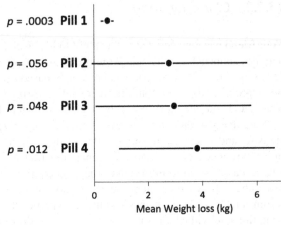

Table 13.1 The *p*-value for each pill

Pill 1	$p = .0003$
Pill 2	$p = .056$
Pill 3	$p = .048$
Pill 4	$p = .012$

a *p*-value can always be roughly inferred from a confidence interval by looking at how far it is from zero (Cumming and Finch 2005; Cumming 2012, pp. 106–108).

But suppose we get rid of all confidence intervals and only report the *p*-values (Table 13.1). Ranking the pills based on this information only yields a quite different outcome: pill 1 appears to give the most impressive results, with a hugely "significant" effect of $p = .0003$. Then comes pill 4 ($p = .012$), then pills 3 and 2, both close to .05. Such a ranking assumes that losing *some* weight (even a single gram) is the *only* thing that matters, which is absurd, both in research and in real-world decision making (Gelman 2013b). We should, at the very least, account for the point estimates in Fig. 13.3, i.e., our best bets.

13.2.3.1 The Importance of Conveying Effect Sizes

Broadly speaking, an effect size is *anything that might be of interest*[2] (Cumming 2012, p. 34). An effect size can be, e.g., the average completion time difference between two techniques. In our case, effect sizes are simply average weight losses.

p-values capture what is traditionally termed *statistical significance*, while effect sizes capture *practical significance* (Kirk 2001). For example, the effect of pill 1

---

[2]The term *effect size* is often used in a narrower sense to refer to *standardized effect sizes* (Coe 2002, see also Chap. 5). Although sometimes useful, reporting standardized effect sizes is not always necessary nor is it always recommended (Baguley 2009; Wilkinson 1999, p. 599).

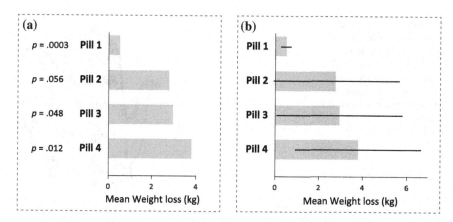

Fig. 13.4 Showing the most plausible effect sizes and their associated uncertainty using **a** *p*-values with point estimates of effect sizes (here shown as *bar charts*); **b** 95 % CIs around point estimates

can be said to exhibit a high statistical significance, but only a moderate practical significance compared to others.

Practical significance is our primary focus, both in research and in real-world decision making. Thus it is widely recognized that effect sizes should be reported (APA 2010). What methodologists generally mean by this is that we should report all *point estimates* of interest, or equivalently—assuming we are interested in simple effect sizes—all *sample means* of interest. But since a point estimate only conveys our best guess about the population, it is crucial to also convey information on uncertainty. Figure 13.4 shows two ways of doing this.

On the figure, each black dot has been replaced by a bar, but this is only a matter of presentation (see Fig. 13.9 in Sect. 4). The option *a* (left) follows the orthodoxy and the common recommendation to report *p*-values together with effect sizes (Thompson 1998). The option *b* (right) follows an estimation approach that consists of reporting point and interval estimates for effect sizes, without *p*-values (Cumming 2012). In the simplest cases, *a* and *b* are theoretically equivalent and convey the same information—readers can even learn to mentally convert from *b* to *a* (Cumming 2012, pp. 106–108). However, it seems harder to mentally convert from *a* to *b*, especially when confidence intervals are asymmetrical (e.g., confidence intervals on proportions, correlations, transformed data, or bootstrap confidence intervals). Regardless, the option *b* is clearly easier to read and more informative.

Methodologists who remain attached to *p*-values (APA 2010; Abelson 1995; Levine et al. 2008b) suggest reporting everything: *p*-values, point estimates of effect sizes, and their confidence intervals. No clear explanation has been offered on why *p*-values are needed, as the same information is already provided by confidence intervals. The recommendation to "complement" *p*-values with effect sizes and 95 % confidence intervals also misleadingly suggests that effect sizes and their associated uncertainty are secondary information.

Fig. 13.5 Merging a bad
design with a good design
does not necessarily yield a
good design. In statistical
communication, reporting
everything just in case can
produce unnecessary clutter
and prompt
misinterpretations

Some may still find it more rigorous to complement a confidence interval with
a *p*-value that captures accurately how far it is from zero. Later I offer arguments
against this idea, which can be summarized using the illustration in Fig. 13.5.

13.2.3.2   The Importance of Conveying Effect Similarity

The fictional chart in Fig. 13.6 shows the differences between three interactive information visualization techniques in terms of average number of insights. We can
safely say that *B* outperforms *A*. We can also say that *A* and *C* are similar in that
they may yield a different number of average insights across the population, but the
difference is likely less than 0.5. We have less information on *A* versus *D*, but we
can be reasonably confident that the mean population difference is less than 2.

Since the confidence interval for *C–A* is roughly centered at zero, its *p*-value is
quite high ($p = .66$). It is common knowledge that we cannot conclude anything from
such a high *p*-value: it tells us that zero is plausible, but says nothing about other
plausible values—the confidence interval could be of any size. In fact, the *p*-value
for *D–A* is exactly the same: $p = .66$. Knowing the sample mean in addition to the
p-value does not help, unless it is used to reconstruct the confidence interval (assuming it is possible). Had you only focused on *p*-values and effect sizes in your study,
you could have thrown almost all of your data away. Had you not tested technique
B, you probably would not have submitted anything.

Fig. 13.6 95 % confidence
intervals showing differences
between conditions

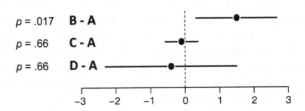

Knowing that two conditions are similar is very useful. In medicine, it is important to know when a drug is indistinguishable from a placebo. In HCI, if two techniques perform similarly, we want to know it. Medicine has developed equivalence testing procedures, but confidence intervals also support formal (Dienes 2014, p. 3; Tryon 2001) as well as informal (see above) inferences on equivalence.

We can often conclude something from a confidence interval. Arguably, if an experiment does not have enough participants and/or the effect is small (i.e., the experiment has *low power*), confidence intervals can be disappointingly wide as with D–A, making it hard to conclude anything really useful. Confidence intervals just reveal the uncertainty in the experimental data. This is crucial information.

13.2.4   Usability Problems with p-Values

So far we have mostly focused on the amount of exploitable information conveyed by p (i.e., its low *usefulness*), but a lot has been also written on how ineffective p is at conveying that information (i.e., its poor *usability*). Recall that the task is to communicate empirical findings clearly and accurately.

13.2.4.1   General Interpretation Difficulties

It is safe to assume that the general public can grasp confidence intervals more easily than p-values. Confidence intervals simply convey the uncertainty around an average, and they are used by the media, for example when reporting opinion polls (Cumming and Williams 2011). Another important difference is that confidence intervals have natural visual representations while p-values do not.

One issue specific to confidence intervals is their lack of standardization. They are visually represented by error bars, which are also used to show several other types of information, including standard errors (typically about half the size of 95 % CIs) and standard deviations. Researchers simply need to become more consistent and get used to clearly indicating what error bars refer to (Cumming et al. 2007).

As evidenced by numerous studies on statistical cognition (Kline 2004; Beyth-Marom et al. 2008), even trained scientists have a hard time interpreting p-values, which frequently leads to misleading or incorrect conclusions. Decades spent educating researchers have had little or no influence on beliefs and practice (Schmidt and Hunter 1997, pp. 20–22). Below we review common misinterpretations and fallacies. Because confidence intervals are theoretically connected with p-values, they can also be misinterpreted and misused (Fidler and Cumming 2005). We will discuss these issues as well, and why they may be less damaging.

13.2.4.2 Misinterpretations Regarding Probabilities

Again, p is the probability of seeing results as extreme (or more extreme) as those actually observed if the null hypothesis were true. So p is computed under the assumption that the null hypothesis is true. Yet it is common for researchers, teachers and even textbooks to think of p as the probability of the null hypothesis being true (or equivalently, of the results being due to chance), an error called the "fallacy of the transposed conditional" (Haller and Krauss 2002; Cohen 1994, p. 999).

As will be discussed in Sect. 13.3.1.2, stating that a particular 95 % confidence interval has a 0.95 probability of capturing the population mean is also generally incorrect. However, confidence intervals do not convey probabilities as explicitly as p-values, and thus they do not encourage statements involving precise numerical probabilities that give a misleading impression of scientific rigor despite being factually wrong (Fidler and Loftus 2009). Shown visually, confidence intervals look less rigorous, and do not prompt overconfidence when making inferences about data.

A lot has been written on the fallacy of the transposed conditional, but a widespread and equally worrisome fallacy consists in ascribing magical qualities to p by insisting on computing and reporting p-values as rigorously as possible, as if they conveyed some objective truth about probabilities. This is despite the fact that the probability conveyed by p is only a theoretical construct that does not correspond to anything real. Again, p is computed with the assumption that the null hypothesis is true — i.e., that the population effect size takes a precise numerical value (typically zero) — which is almost always false (Cohen 1994; Gelman 2013a).

Reasoning with probabilities is possible, using Bayesian statistical methods (see Chaps. 8 and 9). In particular, tools exist for computing confidence intervals that convey probabilities, as will be further discussed in Sect. 13.3.1.

13.2.4.3 Misinterpretation of High p-Values

Although strictly speaking, p-values do not capture any practically meaningful probability, we can use them, like Fisher, as an informal measure of strength of evidence against the null hypothesis (Goodman 1999, p. 997; Gigerenzer 2004, p. 593). The closer a p-value is to 0, the stronger the evidence that the null hypothesis is false. If the null hypothesis is the hypothesis of zero effect and p is very low, we can be reasonably confident that there is an effect. But unfortunately, the closer p is to 1 the less we know. As seen before (see Fig. 13.6), we cannot conclude anything from a high p-value, because it tells us that zero is plausible, but says nothing about other plausible values. Despite this, few researchers can resist the temptation to conclude that there is no effect, a common fallacy called "accepting the null" which had frequently led to misleading or wrong scientific conclusions (Dienes 2014, p. 1). Plotting confidence intervals such as in Fig. 13.6 eliminates the problem.

Fig. 13.7 *p*-values and 95%
confidence intervals obtained
by simulating replications of
an experiment (normally
distributed population with
$\mu = 10$ and $\sigma = 20$; $n = 20$;
statistical power 0.56). After
Cumming (2009a)

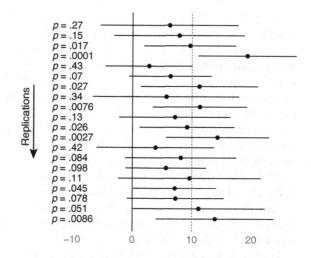

13.2.4.4   Misinterpretations Regarding Reliability

Many researchers fail to appreciate that *p*-values are unreliable and vary widely
across replications. This can be shown with simple simulations such as in the *dance
of p*-values video (Cumming 2009a), or in Fig. 13.7.

Running an experiment amounts to closing your eyes and picking one of the
p-values (and confidence interval) in this figure. With a statistical power[3] of about 0.5
[typical in both psychology (Rossi 1990) and HCI (Kaptein and Robertson 2012)]
about any *p*-value can be obtained. The behavior of *p*-values across replications
is well understood (Cumming 2008). Suppose an experiment yields $p = .05$ for a
t-test. If the experiment is repeated with different participants, there is a 20% chance
that the new *p*-value will fall *outside* the interval (.00008, .44). Even if the initial
experiment yielded an impressive $p = .001$, there is still a 20% chance that the new
p-value falls outside the interval (.000006, .22). *p* will remain appropriately low most
of the time, but with such a wide range of possible values, reporting and interpreting
p values with up to three decimal places should strike us as a futile exercise.

Many find it hard to believe that "real" *p*-values can exhibit such a chaotic behavior.
Suppose you run a real study and get a set of observations, e.g., differences in
completion times. You compute a mean difference, a standard deviation, and obtain
a *p*-value from a one-sample *t*-test. Now suppose you decide to re-run the same study
with different participants, again for real. Would you expect the mean and standard
deviation to come up identical? Hopefully not. Yet *p* is a function of the mean and the
standard deviation (and sample size, if not held constant). Thus the *p*-value obtained
would be different for the exact same reasons: sampling variability.

---

[3]Briefly, statistical power is the probability of correctly detecting an effect whose magnitude has
been postulated in advance. The more participants, the larger the effect size and the lower the
variability, the higher the statistical power (see also Chap. 5).

Any statistical calculation is subject to sampling variability. This is also true for confidence intervals, which "jump around" across replications (see Fig. 13.7). By definition (see Sect. 13.2.1), only 95 % of these will capture the population mean in the long run. Being fully aware of the dance of confidence intervals is certainly an important prerequisite for their correct use and interpretation. Watching replication simulations (e.g., from Cumming (2009a)) is enough to get a good intuition, and one can hardly claim to understand statistics without being equipped with such an intuition. *p*-values add another layer of complexity. It is easier to remember and picture a typical dance of confidence intervals (they are all alike) than to recall all possible replication *p*-intervals. Any single confidence interval gives useful information about its whole dance, in particular where a replication is likely to land (Cumming 2008, 2012, Chap. 5). Any single *p*-value gives virtually no such information. There are also likely perceptual and cognitive differences: confidence intervals, especially shown graphically, may not give the same illusion of certainty and truth as *p*-values reported with high numerical precision.

Here is the R code for Fig. 13.7 to help you play with your own simulations:

```
require(ggplot2)
require(plyr)

replications <- 20
sampleSize <- 20
populationMean <- 10
populationSd <- 20
plotRange <- c(-15, 35)

createReplication <- function(replication) {
  #set.seed(replication) # uncomment this to get the same results each time
  obs <- rnorm(sampleSize, populationMean, populationSd)
  ttest <- t.test(obs)
  data.frame(mean = mean(obs), ci.lower = ttest[4]$conf.int[1],
             ci.upper = ttest[4]$conf.int[2], pvalue = ttest[3]$p.value)
}

dance <- ldply(1:replications, createReplication)

format_p <- function(p) {
  paste("p =", substring(prettyNum(p, digits=2, scientific=FALSE), 2))
}

ggplot(data = dance, aes(x = 1:replications, y = mean, label=format_p(pvalue))) +
  geom_pointrange(aes(ymin=ci.lower, ymax=ci.upper), size=0.7) +
  geom_text(y=plotRange[1], hjust=0) +
  geom_abline(intercept = 0, slope = 0) +
  geom_abline(intercept = populationMean, slope = 0, lty = 2) +
  ylim(plotRange) + coord_flip() +
  theme_bw() + theme(
    axis.title = element_blank(),
    axis.text.y = element_blank(),
    axis.ticks = element_blank(),
    panel.grid = element_blank(),
    panel.border = element_blank(),
    text = element_text(size=17))
```

13.2.5 Conclusion

There rarely seems to be a good reason to report p-values in an HCI research paper, since confidence intervals can present the same information and much more, and in a much clearer, more usable manner. Perhaps the only remaining argument in favor of p-values is that they are useful for formally establishing statistical significance. But as we will now see, the notion of binary significance testing is a terrible idea for those who want to achieve fair statistical communication.

13.3 Null Hypothesis Significance Testing Versus Estimation

We previously mentioned that *statistical significance* can be quantified in a continuous manner with p-values. Roughly speaking, p-values tell us how confident we can be that the population effect size differs from some specific value of interest—typically zero. We also explained why this notion is less useful than the orthodoxy suggests. As if the current overreliance on p-values was not enough, a vast majority of researchers see fit to apply a conventional (but nonetheless arbitrary) cut-off of $\alpha = .05$ on p-values. If p is less than .05, then the "results" are declared significant, otherwise they are declared non-significant (the term "statistically" is typically omitted). This is a major component of null hypothesis significance testing (NHST).

13.3.1 A Few More Reminders

To put things in context and further clarify our underlying assumptions, let us recall a few under-discussed but important statistical ideas before proceeding.

13.3.1.1 Frequentist Statistics, Fisher and Neyman–Pearson

For the sake of simplicity let us equate the null hypothesis to the hypothesis of no effect. Suppose that (1) many replications of an experiment are carried out; (2) each time, the researcher concludes that there is an effect *iif* $p < \alpha$; (3) there is in truth no effect. In the long run, the researcher will be wrong $(100 \times \alpha)\%$ of the time. A known proportion of the time, she will be committing what is called a Type I error.

This way of interpreting p-values is termed *frequentist* because it involves long-run frequencies. Originally put forward by Fisher, it was formalized into a rigorous procedure by Neyman and Pearson (Goodman 1999, p. 998; Gigerenzer 2004, p. 590–591). According to this procedure, the researcher sets α before carrying out the experiment, and if $p < \alpha$, the researcher behaves as if there was an effect.[4] If all researchers were to apply this procedure and agree on, say, $\alpha = .05$, then only 5 % of all significance tests where there is in truth no effect would yield a Type I error.

Neyman and Pearson insisted that if $p < \alpha$, the researcher should *behave as if* there was an effect, and *nothing else*. The researcher should not only ignore p, but also refrain from reasoning or holding any belief (Gigerenzer et al. 1990, pp. 98–105). This view of statistics can be characterized as strictly frequentist and *behavioristic*. It seems well suited for automating repeated decisions (e.g., in quality control), but not so much for actual research practice. Fisher, who was an applied researcher, advocated an *epistemic* view of statistics, where the p-value brings knowledge about the data. Although he suggested in his earlier writings that conventional α cut-offs can be useful (see Chap. 5), he viewed p as a continuous measure of strength of evidence. He rejected the Neyman–Pearson procedure as "childish", "remote from scientific research", and intellectually "horrifying" (Gigerenzer 2004, p. 593). In turn, Neyman and Pearson criticized Fisher for lacking rigor and consistency. Although this may be true, fair statistical communication seems deeply incompatible with the Neyman–Pearson view of scientists as brainless decision machines.

Today no researcher uses a strict Neyman–Pearson procedure, since virtually any researcher carries out statistical analyses for *epistemic* reasons: for learning things, drawing conclusions and making arguments. Yet some aspects of the procedure crept into research practice and textbooks. Researchers report and often interpret p-values, but they also apply an α cut-off and use it to make dichotomous "decisions" about what we should believe. NHST as it is carried out today consists of this incoherent mix of Fisher and Neyman–Pearson methods (Gigerenzer 2004).

13.3.1.2　On Interpreting Confidence Intervals

Having covered frequentist statistics, it is now possible to discuss interpretation issues with confidence intervals. Perhaps surprisingly, confidence intervals were first introduced by Neyman. They were designed to be used within his strict frequentist and behavioristic framework: the researcher states that the confidence interval contains the population mean, and nothing else (Morey et al. 2015, p. 3). She does not reason or holds beliefs, only *behaves as if* this was true. If the confidence level is 95 %, in the long run she will be wrong about 5 % of the time.

There is another link between confidence intervals and Neyman–Pearson testing. Confidence intervals can be used to carry out statistical significance tests, since examining whether a $100 \times (1 - \alpha)\%$ CI contains the value v is the same as examining whether the p-value for $H_0 = v$ is lower than α. This can be verified in all previous figures for $\alpha = .05$ and $v = 0$. This use of confidence intervals is common practice but since it is essentially the same as NHST, it inherits all of its drawbacks.

---

[4]Strictly speaking, Neyman–Pearson's procedure involved choosing between the null hypothesis and an *alternative hypothesis* generally stating that the effect exists and takes some precise value. Accepting the null if the alternative hypothesis is true is a Type II error. Its frequentist probability is noted β, and power is defined as $1 - \beta$. These notions are not important to the present discussion.

Advocates of estimation reject both interpretations of confidence intervals and recommend instead the more nuanced epistemic interpretation offered in Sect. 13.2.1 (Schmidt and Hunter 1997, p. 13; Cumming 2012). This approach focuses on extracting as much useful information as possible from confidence intervals while recognizing that they cannot be fully trusted.

There is a caveat, though. Confidence intervals are defined in a frequentist way (see Sect. 13.2.1), and this definition is permissive enough to allow for many different types of confidence interval procedures, including absurd ones. For example, a random procedure that returns the real line ($\mathbb{R}$) 95 % of the time and the empty set ($\varnothing$) 5 % of the time is a valid 95 % confidence interval procedure. This challenges the notion that any given confidence interval will necessary capture the range of plausible values. Other pathologic cases are illustrated by Morey et al. (2015).

Bayesian interval estimates, or credible intervals (see Chaps. 8 and 9), are the only interval estimates for which the "range of plausible values" interpretation is formally correct (Morey et al. 2015). In addition, they produce more reasonable and more informative interval estimates if there is reliable *a priori* knowledge about the possible range of effect sizes (Gelman 2013a).

Nevertheless, there are practical reasons to use confidence intervals. In many common situations, confidence intervals agree with so-called *objective* credible intervals (Greenland and Poole 2013). This is true for exact confidence intervals (Bayarri and Berger 2004, p. 63) and bootstrap confidence intervals (Bååth 2015). In addition, confidence intervals are easier to compute than credible intervals, they are more widely used, and they are currently better supported by statistical tools. In the context of this chapter, their mathematical equivalence with statistical significance testing also allows us to clearly contrast estimation thinking with dichotomous testing. Confidence intervals can be seen as the "poor man's" credible intervals, and as a good bridge between mindless NHST and sophisticated Bayesian reasoning.

With these issues in mind, let us now compare significance testing as it is carried out today (i.e., using α as an epistemic tool) with estimation as it is done today (i.e., using confidence intervals as approximations to objective credible intervals).

13.3.2 How Useful Is the α Cut-Off?

The insights yielded by the use of an α cut-off can be assessed by returning to our first scenario and considering again the respective merits of our four pills Fig. 13.8.

As we saw previously, a sensible ranking scheme (shown to the right) would give a preference to pill 4, then pills 2–3 (whose results are almost identical), then pill 1. Nothing is certain and we may well be wrong, especially about pills 2, 3, and 4 for which the data is very unreliable. But since we need to decide we are forced to rank. In a scientific paper one would typically be much more conservative and would perhaps only comment on the likely superiority of pill 4 over pill 1. Regardless, doing statistical inference is always betting. There are good bets and bad bets.

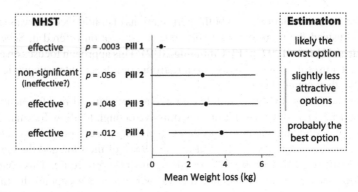

Fig. 13.8 The same four pills, ranked based on the outcome of statistical tests (*left*), and based on an examination of effect sizes and interval estimates (*right*)

Good bets require relevant information. The left part of Fig. 13.8 shows how our decision maker would have summarized the studies had the authors focused on NHST methods: pills 1, 3 and 4 had a statistically significant effect on weight loss ($p < .05$): they would have been presented as effective. Pill 2, on the other hand, would have been presented as having a non-significant effect[5] and despite textbook warnings against "accepting the null", the message would have almost certainly become that the pill may not be effective at all.

A large amount of information is thrown away by the use of a cut-off. Statistical significance in its continuous form—i.e., reporting exact *p*-values—already did not carry much useful information (compared to interval estimates). It is only logical to assume that statistical significance in its binary form cannot carry more.

13.3.3 More Usability Problems Brought by the α Cut-Off

Binary significance testing is based on *p*-values and therefore inherits their usability problems. The use of a binary decision rule based on a cut-off also introduces a range of additional usability problems that are discussed next.

13.3.3.1 Misjudgments of Uncertainty

p-values give a seductive illusion of certainty and truth (Cumming 2012, Chap. 1). The sacred $\alpha = .05$ criterion amplifies this illusion, since results end up being either "significant" or "non-significant". In a researcher's mind, significant results have passed the rigorous test of statistics and are declared "valid"—uncertainty almost ceases

---

[5]The sharp distinction between pills 2 and 3 is not a caricature. Due to Neyman–Pearson's heritage, even pointing out that a non-significant *p*-value is close to .05 is often considered a serious fault.

to exist, and sample means often end up being interpreted as being exact (Vicente and Torenvliet 2000, pp. 252–258; Hoekstra et al. 2006). For example, this amounts to saying that in Fig. 13.4a, each bar with $p < .05$ should be trusted fully. On the other hand, non-significant results are interpreted either as no effect or no information whatsoever, both of which are incorrect. Potential misjudgments abound and are easily dispelled by plotting confidence intervals, as in Fig. 13.4b.

The use of a cut-off on p is especially problematic in studies with low statistical power, given how widely p-values vary across replications (see Sect. 13.2.4.4). Thus many HCI experiments effectively amount to tossing a coin (Dragicevic et al. 2014).

13.3.3.2   Misinterpretations Regarding Comparisons

Few researchers are fully aware of the disturbing paradoxes yielded by the use of a cut-off when comparing findings. The results for pills 2 and 3, for example, appear very different despite being virtually identical (Fig. 13.8). In fact, pill 2 has close to a 50 % chance of ending up better than pill 3 on the next replication (remember the dance in Fig. 13.7). This paradox causes erroneous inferences both within studies and across studies. Within studies, two conditions can be wrongly interpreted as being different, simply because one happened to pass a test while the other one did not (Gelman and Stern 2006; Abelson 1995, p. 111). Across studies, research can appear inconsistent or controversial for the same reasons (Cumming 2012, Chap. 1).

Although it has been recognized that statistical significance cannot be used as a criterion for comparison (Gelman and Stern 2006), refraining from comparing entities that are given very different labels goes against the most basic human intuitions. The problem clearly lies not in researchers' minds, but in the design of NHST tools.

With estimation, results are labeled with confidence intervals, whose comparison is not always trivial (Cumming 2012, Chap. 6) but is certainly much less problematic. For example, instead of simply writing "we were not able to replicate previous work by Schmidt (2010) and John (2012) who found a significant improvement on task completion time", a conscientious researcher could write "our mean improvement of 1.9 s, 95 % CI [−0.7, 4.4] is consistent with the improvement of 3.1 s, 95 % CI [1.7, 4.7] reported by Schmidt (2010) but seemingly lower than the improvement of 5.2 s, 95 % CI [4.1, 6.6] reported by John (2012)".

13.3.3.3   Misinterpretations Regarding Type I Error Rates

Due to sampling error, any statistical analysis is error-prone. The idea that a researcher can take control over the likelihood of making false discoveries is very appealing, and so is the idea that among all published results a known proportion will be wrong. But Neyman–Pearson's Type I error rate captures neither of these, even remotely (Pollard and Richardson 1987; Colquhoun 2014). Like p (see Sect. 13.2.4.2), the Type I error rate is computed with the assumption that the null hypothesis is true. In many disciplines a Type I error is impossible, and one can only fail to detect the effect,[6] or commit sign errors and magnitude errors (Gelman 2004). In addition, the fact that not all results are published renders theoretical error rates mostly irrelevant for assessing research reliability (also see Sect. 13.3.3.5). The Type I error rate is only a theoretical convenience that captures an idealized situation. It is a useful and powerful thinking tool, but the current obsession with Type I error rates and insistence on maintaining them at a precise 5 % level sound more like a magical ritual than something that will necessarily guarantee reliable research.

13.3.3.4 Multiple Levels of Significance

A practice that has become less popular in HCI (although it is still sometimes advocated) is the use of multiple levels of significance by the way of "post-hoc" α values (.001, .01, .05, .1), stars (***, **, *), or codified significance terminology ("highly significant", "marginally significant", etc.). This categorical approach suffers from the same problems as binary approaches, and is inconsistent with both Neyman–Pearson's strict frequentist approach and Fisher's approach of using exact p-values as a measure of strength of evidence (Gigerenzer 2004). Few, if any, statistical methodologists recommend the use of multiple levels of significance.

13.3.3.5 Issues Regarding Publication Bias

Since statistical significance is a major criterion for publishing study papers, conference proceedings and journals give a very distorted image of reality. This issue, termed *publication bias* or the *file drawer problem*, is harming science's credibility (The Economist 2013; Goldacre 2012). In HCI, publication bias can hamper scientific progress because results on ineffective techniques are never published and those that are published because of statistical luck or flawed analyses are never disproved. By legitimizing negative and (to some extent) inconclusive results and making publication criteria more flexible (Anderson 2012), estimation can reduce publication bias, advance our knowledge of what does *not* work, and encourage replication (Hornbæk et al. 2014) and meta-analysis (Cumming 2012).

13.3.3.6 Issues Regarding p-Hacking

Another damaging consequence of the NHST ritual is the widespread use of "statistical convolutions [...] to reach the magic significance number" (Giner-Sorolla 2012). These include selectively removing outliers and trying different testing procedures until results are significant (Abelson 1995, p. 55). Such practices go by various

---

[6]Since computing β (or the probability of a Type II error) requires assigning a precise value to the population mean, β is also very unlikely to correspond to an actual probability or error rate.

names such as *p-hacking, torturing data, data dredging*, or *researcher degrees of freedom* (Nuzzo 2014; Lakens et al. 2014; Simmons et al. 2011; Brodeur et al. 2012; Gelman and Loken 2013). They differ from the legitimate practice of exploratory data analysis (Tukey 1980) because their goal is to obtain the results one wishes for, not to learn or to inform. Information obfuscation can also occur after *p*-values have been computed, e.g., by selectively reporting results (*cherry picking*), using post-hoc α cut-offs (Gigerenzer 2004), or elaborating evasive narratives (Abelson 1995, p. 55). NHST makes it easy to dissimulate unscientific practices under the appearance of objectivity and rigor. Since humans excel at unconsciously taking advantage of fuzzy lines between honest and dishonest behavior (Mazar et al. 2008), merely promoting scientific integrity is likely futile. To be usable, statistical tools should be designed so that they do not leave too much space for questionable practices and self-deception. Estimation approaches do not draw a sharp line between interesting and uninteresting results, and thus make "torturing" data much less useful. As I will discuss later, planned analyses are another very effective safeguard.

13.3.3.7   Dichotomous Thinking

Humans like to think in categories. Categorical thinking is a useful heuristic in many situations, but can be intellectually unproductive when researchers seek to understand continuous phenomena (Dawkins 2011). A specific form of categorical thinking is dichotomous thinking, i.e., thinking in two categories. Some dichotomies are real (e.g., pregnant vs. non-pregnant), some are good approximations (e.g., male vs. female, dead vs. alive), and some are convenient decision making tools (e.g., guilty vs. not guilty, legal vs. illegal). However, many dichotomies are clearly *false dichotomies*, and statistical thinking is replete with these. For example:

1. There is an effect or not.
2. There is evidence or not.
3. An analysis is either correct or wrong.[7]

Statistical testing promotes the second dichotomy by mapping statistical significance to conclusive evidence, and non-significance to no evidence. This dichotomy is false because the degree of evidence provided by experimental data is inherently continuous. NHST procedures also promote the first dichotomy by forcing researchers to ask questions such as "is there an effect?". This dichotomy is false because with human subjects, almost any manipulation has an effect (Cohen 1994).

There is a more insidious form of false dichotomy concerning effects. In HCI, researchers generally do not test for the mere presence of an effect, but instead ask questions such as "is *A* faster than *B*?". Since there is likely a difference, *A* can only be faster than *B* or the other way around. Thus the dichotomy is formally correct,

---

[7]For elements of discussion concerning this particular dichotomy, see Stewart-Oaten (1995), Norman (2010), Velleman and Wilkinson (1993), Wierdsma (2013), Abelson (1995, Chap. 1) and Gigerenzer (2004, pp. 587–588).

but it conceals the importance of magnitude. For example, if A takes one second on average and B takes two, A is clearly better than B. But the situation is very different if B takes only a millisecond longer. To deal with such cases, some recommend the use of equivalence testing procedures (e.g., Dienes 2014, p. 3; Tryon 2001). However, this does little more than turn an uninformative dichotomy into a false trichotomy, as there is rarely a sharp boundary between negligible and non-negligible effects.

Thinking is fundamental to research. A usable research tool should support and promote clear thinking. Statistical significance tests encourage irrational beliefs in false dichotomies that hamper research progress—notably regarding strength of evidence and effect sizes—and their usability is therefore low. Estimation seems much more likely to promote clear statistical thinking.

13.3.3.8 Misinterpretations of the Notion of Hypothesis

Although the term *hypothesis testing* may sound impressive, there is some confusion about the meaning of a hypothesis in research. Most methodologists insist on distinguishing between *research* (or substantive) *hypotheses* and *statistical hypotheses* (Meehl 1967; Hager 2002). Briefly, research hypotheses are general statements that follow from a theory, and statistical hypotheses are experiment-specific statements derived from research hypotheses in order to assess the plausibility of the theory. Juggling between theories and statistical hypotheses is a difficult task that requires considerable research expertise (Meehl 1967; Vicente and Torenvliet 2000, pp. 252–258; Gelman and Loken 2013).

Many research hypotheses are dichotomous: the Higgs boson either exists or not; the acceleration of a falling object is either a function of its mass or it is not; a pointing method either obeys Fitts' Law or some other (say, Schmidt's) law. Such dichotomies are justified: although there is the possibility that a pointing method follows a mix of Fitts' and Schmidt's laws, it is sensible to give more weight to the simplest models. In such situations, asking dichotomous questions and seeking yes/no answers can be sensible, and Bayesian approaches (rather than NHST) can be considered (see Chaps. 8 and 9). That said, in many cases choosing a hypothesis is a decision that is informed both by data and by extraneous considerations, so estimation methods (e.g., for goodness of fit) can still be beneficial in this context.

Regardless, the vast majority of HCI studies are *not* conducted to test research hypotheses. That technique A outperforms technique B on task X may have practical implications, but this information is far from having the predictive or explanatory power of a theory. Using the term "hypothesis" in such situations presents a mere hunch (or hope) as something it is not, a scientific theory that needs to be tested. It is sufficient to simply ask a question. Since the respective merits of two techniques cannot be meaningfully classified into sharp categories, it is preferable to ask questions in a quantitative manner, and use estimation to answer them.

13.3.3.9   End User Dissatisfaction

NHST has been severely criticized for more than 50 years by end users to whom fair statistical communication matters. Levine et al. (2008a) offer a few quotes: "[NHST] is based upon a fundamental misunderstanding of the nature of rational inference, and is seldom if ever appropriate to the aims of scientific research; "Statistical significance is perhaps the least important attribute of a good experiment; it is never a sufficient condition for claiming that a theory has been usefully corroborated, that a meaningful empirical fact has been established, or that an experimental report ought to be published". Some go as far as saying that "statistical significance testing retards the growth of scientific knowledge; it never makes a positive contribution" (Schmidt and Hunter 1997). Ten years ago, Kline (2004) reviewed more than 300 articles criticizing the indiscriminate use of NHST and concluded that it should be minimized or eliminated. Even Fisher—who coined the terms "significance testing" and "null hypothesis" in the 1920s—came to reject mindless testing. In 1956 he wrote that "no scientific worker has a fixed level of significance at which from year to year, and in all circumstances, he rejects hypotheses; he rather gives his mind to each particular case in the light of his evidence and his ideas." (Gigerenzer 2004). The damaging side effects of NHST use (publication bias and p-hacking in particular) have even led some researchers to conclude that "most published research findings are false" (Ioannidis 2005; Open Science Collaboration 2015).

13.3.4   Conclusion

Null hypothesis significance testing rests on important theoretical ideas that can help reflect on difficult notions in statistics, such as statistical power and multiple comparisons (briefly covered in the next Section). However, it is now widely understood that it is not a good tool for scientific investigation. I—as many others before—have pointed out a range of usability problems with NHST procedures. HCI researchers may think they can ignore these issues for the moment, because they are currently being debated. In reality, the debate mostly opposes strong reformists who think NHST should be banned (e.g., Loftus 1993; Schmidt and Hunter 1997; Lambdin 2012; Cumming 2013) with weak reformists who think it should be (i) de-emphasized and (ii) properly taught and used (e.g., Abelson 1995, 1997; Levine et al. 2008a, b). I have already given arguments against (i) by explaining that p-values are redundant with confidence intervals (Sect. 13.2). Concerning (ii), I suggested that the problem lies in the tools' usability, not in end users. This view is consistent with decades of observational data (Schmidt and Hunter 1997, pp. 3–20) and empirical evidence (Beyth-Marom et al. 2008; Haller and Krauss 2002; Fidler and Cumming 2005). There is no excuse for HCI to stay out of the debate. Ultimately, everyone is free to choose a side, but hopefully HCI researchers will find the usability argument compelling.

13.4 Fair Statistical Communication Through Estimation

What do we do now? There are many ways to analyze data without using NHST or
p-values. Two frequently advocated alternatives are estimation and Bayesian methods, although the two address different issues and can be combined. As we mentioned
in Sect. 13.3.1.2, there is a Bayesian version of estimation, and much of the justification and discussion of interpretation of CIs can be transferred to these methods.
Again, we focus here on estimation with confidence intervals because it is simple
and accessible to a wide audience of investigators and readers (thus it emphasizes
simplicity as discussed next). Keep in mind, however, that some Bayesians strongly
reject any kind of frequentist tool, including confidence intervals for the reasons
outlined in Sect. 13.3.1.2 (Trafimow and Marks 2015; Morey et al. 2015).

Confidence intervals have been studied extensively, and statistical packages like *R*
offer extensive libraries for computing them. However, there is a lack of pedagogical
material that brings all of these methods together in a coherent fashion. Currently
there is also a lack of guidance on how to use estimation in practice, from the
experiment design stage to the final scientific communication. Cumming (2012) is a
good place to start for those already familiar with NHST. Since this is a vast topic,
in this section we only discuss a few general principles and pitfalls of estimation.

13.4.1 General Principles

Adopting better tools is only part of the solution: we also need to change the way we
think about our task. Most research tasks require expertise, judgment, and creativity.
The analysis and communication of empirical findings is no exception. This task is
necessarily subjective, but it is our job as scientists to carry it out (Thompson 1999;
Lambdin 2012).

While we cannot be fully objective when writing a study report, we can give our
readers the freedom to decide whether or not they should trust our interpretations. To
quote Fisher, "we have the duty of [...] communicating our conclusions in intelligible
form, in recognition of the right of other free minds to utilize them in making their
own decisions." (Fisher 1955). This is the essence of fair statistical communication.
From this general principle one can derive a set of more basic principles:

Clarity. Statistical analyses should be as easy to understand as possible, because
as implied by Fisher, one cannot judge without understanding. The more accessible
an analysis is, the more the free minds who can judge it. Thus a study report should
be an exercise of pedagogy as much as an exercise of rhetoric.

Transparency. All decisions made when carrying out an analysis should be communicated as explicitly as possible, because the results of an analysis cannot be fairly
assessed if many decisions remain concealed (see *p*-hacking in Sect. 13.3.3.6).

Simplicity. When choosing between two analysis options, the simplest one should
be preferred even if it is slightly inferior in other respects. This follows from the

principle of clarity. In other words, the KISS principle (Keep It Simple, Stupid) is as relevant in statistical communication as in any other domain.

Robustness. A statistical analysis should be robust to sampling variability, i.e., it should be designed so that similar experimental outcomes yield similar results and conclusions.[8] This is a corollary of the principle of clarity, as any analysis that departs from this principle is misleading about the data.

Noncontingency. Ideally, no decision subtending an analysis should be contigent on experimental data, e.g., "if the data turns out like this, compute this, or report that". This principle may seem less trivial than the previous ones, but it follows from the principles of clarity, transparency and simplicity, because data-contingent procedures are hard to explain and easy to leave unexplained (Gelman and Loken 2013). It is also a corollary of the principle of robustness because any dichotomous decision decreases a procedure's robustness to sampling variability.

Precision. Even if all the above precautions are taken, a study report where nothing conclusive can be said would be a waste of readers' time, and may prompt them to seek inexistent patterns. High statistical *power* (Cohen 1990), which in the estimation world translates to high statistical *precision* (Cumming 2012, Chap. 13), should also be a goal to pursue.

13.4.2   Before Analyzing Data

Experiment design and statistical analysis are tightly coupled (Drummond and Vowler 2011, p. 130). Many textbooks provide extensive advice on how to conduct research and design experiments, and most of it is relevant to estimation research. Here are a few tips that are particularly relevant to estimation methods and can help ensure fair statistical communication.

Tip 1: Ask focused research questions. Ask clear and focused research questions, ideally only one or a few, and design an experiment that specifically answers them (Cumming 2012). This should result in a simple experiment design (see Tip 2), and make the necessary analyses straightforward at the outset (see Tip 5).

Tip 2: Prefer simple designs. Except in purely exploratory studies and when building multivariate models, complex experiment designs—i.e., many factors or many conditions per factor—are best avoided. These are hard to analyze, grasp and interpret appropriately (Cohen 1990). There is no perfect method for analyzing complex designs using estimation (Franz and Loftus 2012; Baguley 2012), and even NHST procedures like ANOVA that have been specifically developed for such designs are not without issues (Smith et al. 2002; Baguley 2012; Kirby and Gerlanc 2013, p. 28; Rosnow and Rosenthal 1989, p. 1281; Cumming 2012, p. 420). Faithfully communicating results from complex designs is simply hard, no matter which method is used. Best is to break down studies in separate experiments, each answering a

---

[8]The meaning of *robust* here differs from its use in *robust statistics*, where it refers to robustness to outliers and to departures from statistical assumptions.

specific question. Ideally, experiments should be designed sequentially, so that each one addresses the questions and issues raised by the previous one.

Tip 3: Prefer within-subjects designs. While not always feasible, within-subjects designs yield more statistical precision, and also facilitate many confidence interval calculations (see Tip 10).

Tip 4: Prefer continuous measurement scales. Categorical and ordinal data can be hard to analyze and communicate, with the exception of binary data for which estimation is routinely used (Newcombe 1998a, b). Binary data, however, does not carry much information and thus suffers from low statistical precision (Rawls 1998). For measurements such as task errors or age, prefer continuous metrics to binary or categorical scales.[9]

Tip 5: Plan all analyses using pilot data. It is very useful to collect initial data, e.g., from co-authors and family, and analyze it. This makes it possible to debug the experiment, refine predictions, and most importantly, plan the final analysis (Cumming 2013). Planned analyses meet the uncontingency principle and are way more convincing than post-hoc analyses because they leave less room for self-deception and prevent questionable practices such as "cherry picking" (see Sect. 13.3.3.6). An excellent way to achieve this is to write scripts for generating all confidence intervals and plots, then collect experimental data and re-run the same scripts. Pilot data should be naturally thrown away. If all goes well, the researcher can announce in her article that all analyses were planned. Additional post-hoc analyses can still be conducted and reported in a separate "Unplanned Analyses" subsection.

Tip 6: There is no magic number of participants. The idea that there is a "right" number of participants in HCI is part of the folklore and has no theoretical basis. One issue is statistical precision, and it will be discussed next. A separate issue is meeting statistical assumptions. Concerning statistical assumptions, about twenty participants put the researcher in a safe zone for analyzing about any numerical data (see Tips 13 and 14). Analyses do not suddenly become invalid below that—just possibly less accurate. If all scales are believed to be approximately normal (e.g., logged times, see Tip 12), exact confidence intervals can be used and the lower limit falls to *two participants* (Forum 2015; Norman 2010, p. 628).

Tip 7: Anticipate precision. It is important to achieve high statistical precision, i.e., narrow confidence intervals (Cumming 2012, Chap. 13). Therefore, when deciding on an appropriate number of participants, the most rudimentary precision analysis is preferable to wishful thinking. One approach consists in duplicating participants from pilot data (see Tip 5) until confidence intervals get small enough. How small is small enough? At the planning stage, considering whether or not an interval is at a safe distance from zero is a good rule of thumb. The $p < .05$ criterion has so

---

[9]There is considerable debate on how to best collect and analyze questionnaire data, and I have not gone through enough of the literature to provide definitive recommendations. Likert scales are easy to analyze if they are constructed adequately, i.e., by averaging responses from multiple question items (see Carifio and Perla 2007). If responses to individual items are of interest, it can be sufficient to report all responses visually (see Tip 22). Visual analogue scales seem to be a promising option to consider if inferences need to be made on individual items (Reips and Funke 2008). However, analyzing many items individually is not recommended (see Tips 1, 5 and 30).

much psychological influence on reviewers that it is not unreasonable to try to meet it. However, it is better to forget about it in the analysis stage.

Tip 8: Hypotheses are optional. Hypotheses have their place, especially when they are informed by a theory or by a careful review of the past literature. However, it is often sufficient to simply *ask* questions. Reporting investigators' initial expectations can benefit transparency (Rosenthal and Fode 1963; Rosenthal 2009), but expectations do not need to be called hypotheses. Expectations can also change, for example after a pilot study (see Tip 5)—this is part of the research process and does not need to be concealed. Finally, having no hypothesis or theory to defend departs from typical narratives such as used in psychology (Abelson 1995), but admitting one's ignorance and taking a neutral stance seems much more acceptable than fabricating hypotheses after the fact (Kerr 1998; Gelman and Loken 2013).

13.4.3 Calculating Confidence Intervals

About any statistical test can be replaced with the calculation of a confidence interval. The counterpart of a classic *t*-test is termed (a bit misleadingly) an *exact confidence interval* (Cumming 2012). There is not much to say about calculation procedures, as they are extensively covered by textbooks and on the Web. Here are a few tips that are not systematically covered by existing material. Some of them are at odds with orthodox practices as popularized by textbooks, but they are in better accordance with fair statistical communication and are supported by compelling arguments from the methodology literature. I have also tried to include common pitfalls that I have committed or observed while working with students.

Tip 9: As many observations as participants. Perhaps the only serious mistake that can be made when computing confidence intervals is by not aggregating data. Suppose you recruit 20 subjects, show them various conditions (e.g., technique × task type), and for each condition you ask them to perform 10 similar tasks. Multiple measurements can greatly help reduce statistical noise, but reporting confidence intervals based on all measurements ($n = 200$) would be wrong (Lazic 2010). This is because the purpose of statistical inference in HCI is typically to generalize data to a population of people (see Sect. 13.2.1), not of trials.[10] Measurements need to be aggregated (e.g., averaged) so that each participant ends up with a *single observation* before any confidence interval is computed. NHST has developed notations that make it possible for readers to spot such mistakes, but estimation has not. Thus it is good practice to mention the number of observations involved in the computation of confidence intervals, either in the text or in figure captions (e.g., $n = 20$).

Tip 10: Feel free to process data. As long as Tip 9 is observed, it does not matter how the per-participant observations were obtained. Raw measurements can be converted into different units and be aggregated in any way: arithmetic means, geometric

---

[10]Both types of inferences can be combined using hierarchical or multi-level models, and tools exist for computing hierarchical confidence intervals (see Chap. 11).

means, sums, or percentages. With within-subject designs, new data columns can be added to capture averages across several conditions, differences between conditions, differences between differences (i.e., interactions), or even regression coefficients for learning effects. There is nothing sacred about raw measurements (Velleman and Wilkinson 1993, pp. 8–9), and these can be processed in any way as long as the numbers reflect something *meaningful* about participants' performance, answer a relevant research question (Tip 1), and all calculations have been planned (Tip 5).

Tip 11: Avoid throwing data away. Data can be discarded for good reasons, e.g., when a researcher ignores certain effects to achieve a more focused analysis (Tip 1). But data can also be discarded pointlessly, e.g., by turning continuous measurements into discrete or binary values through binning (see Tip 4). This results in a loss of information, and therefore of statistical precision, and possibly biased results (Rawls 1998; MacCallum et al. 2002). Discarding observations beyond a certain value (*truncation*, see Ulrich and Miller 1994) or based on spread (*restriction*, see Miller 1991) can help eliminate spurious observations, but can also result in a loss of precision or in bias (Miller 1991; Ulrich and Miller 1994). Discarding observations based on rank (*trimming*, see Wilcox 1998, of which the *median* is a special case) can in some cases increase precision (Wilcox 1998), but for approximately normal distributions the mean outperforms all other measures (Wilcox 1998). In general there is disagreement on how to discard observations, and whether this should be done at all (see Osborne and Overbay 2004 for a favorable stance), but the simplicity principle would suggest to skip such procedures.

Tip 12: Consider the log transform. The log transform corrects for positive skewness in time measurements and gives less weight to extreme observations, thus rendering outlier removal unnecessary (Sauro and Lewis 2010). Another nice consequence is that it yields asymmetric confidence intervals, which better convey the underlying distributions and prevent the embarrassing situation where a confidence interval extends to negative values. The procedure consists in log-transforming all raw time measurements, performing all analyses as usual, then converting back (*antilogging*) the means and confidence interval limits at the very end, when they need to be presented numerically or graphically (Gardner and Altman 1986, p. 749). All means will indicate geometric (instead of arithmetic) means, and differences between means will become ratios (Gardner and Altman 1986, p. 750). As it turns out, ratios between completion times are easier to interpret than differences because they are unitless (Dragicevic 2012). No justification or test is needed for using a log transform on time measurements (Keene 1995) (see also Tip 14).

Tip 13: Consider bootstrapping. Bootstrapping is a very useful method that has not received enough attention (Kirby and Gerlanc 2013; Wood 2004, 2005). Briefly, it consists of generating many alternative datasets from the experimental data by randomly drawing observations with replacement. The variability across these datasets is assumed to approximate sampling error and is used to compute so-called *bootstrap confidence intervals*. This way of calculating confidence intervals is recent in the history of statistics because it requires computers, but it is very versatile and works for many kinds of distributions (Kirby and Gerlanc 2013). Also, since bootstrapping relies on a simple algorithm, the computer scientists in HCI may find it easier to intuitively grasp than the traditional analytical approaches (Ricketts and Berry 1994; Duckworth and Stephenson 2003). Bootstrap confidence intervals are generally accurate with about 20 observations or more (Kirby and Gerlanc 2013, p. 8), but tend to be a bit narrow with 10 or less (Wood 2005, p. 467).

Tip 14: Do not test for normality. The world is not sharply divided into normal and non-normal distributions. This false dichotomy has been largely promoted by NHST procedures for testing normality, which are logically and practically unsound (Wierdsma 2013; Stewart-Oaten 1995, p. 2002). When computing exact confidence intervals, departures from normality are not such a big deal: as with the t-test, the normality assumption does not concern the population distribution but the sampling distribution of the sample mean.[11] As per the central limit theorem, this distribution turns out to be approximately normal for almost any population distribution shape, provided that the sample size is large enough (Norman 2010, p. 628). One difficulty is that it is often unclear how large is large enough, as it also depends on how much the original population departs from a normal distribution. Another issue with exact confidence intervals is that they are necessarily symmetric, so they do not reflect skewed distributions very well and may cover impossible values. Thus there are merits to using alternative methods (see Tips 12 and 13) if there are reasons to think that the population distribution is not normal. Measurement scales that are strictly positive (e.g., time) or bounded (e.g., percents) cannot be normally distributed. Strictly positive scales are typically positively skewed and approximate a normal distribution once logged (Tip 12). When in doubt, use bootstrapping (Tip 13).

Tip 15: Report interval estimates for everything. Any statistic is subject to sampling variability, not only sample means. A report should complement *all* statistics from which inferences are made—including standard deviations, correlation coefficients, and linear regression coefficients—with interval estimates that convey the numerical uncertainty around those estimates. Many sources are available in textbooks and online on how to compute such intervals. Be aware, however, that not all confidence interval procedures are reliable, in the sense that in some special cases they may produce incorrect intervals (Morey et al. 2015).

13.4.4   Plotting Confidence Intervals

Confidence intervals can be conveyed numerically, or graphically by the way of error bars. There exists a standard numerical notation (APA 2010, p. 117), but no well-established standard for representing confidence intervals graphically. The tips I include here emphasize fair statistical communication and most of them are, I believe, based on common sense. As before, I have tried to include common pitfalls.

Tip 16: Prefer pictures. Graphic formats for confidence intervals effectively convey magnitudes and patterns (Fidler and Loftus 2009). Some would consider this

---

[11]For more on the important concepts of sampling distribution and the central limit theorem, see, e.g., Cumming (2013, Chap. 3) and the applet at http://tinyurl.com/sdsim.

as a disadvantage as many such patterns can be spurious, but plots do not lie—they just conceal less. For example, how different is 2.9 kg, 95 % CI [0.02, 5.8] from 2.8 kg, 95 % CI [−0.08, 5.7]? Or from 4.5 kg, 95 % CI [2.5, 6.5]? While this is not immediately clear with numerical data, the graphical representation in Fig. 13.3 makes comparison much easier. In addition, plots generally appear less precise than numbers, which likely reduces dichotomous thinking and overconfidence in results.

Tip 17: Use numbers wisely. If plots with confidence intervals are already provided, numerical values are not very useful and only produce clutter. However, because the numerical format is more compact, it can be used for reporting secondary results. A complete list of numerical confidence intervals can also be included as a table or in the accompanying material to facilitate comparison with future studies and meta-analysis. However, in the article itself, refrain from reporting an absurdly high number of significant digits, e.g., 2.789 kg, 95 % CI [−0.0791, 5.658].

Tip 18: Do not ignore conventions. When plotting confidence intervals, aim for simplicity and try to stick to the few existing conventions. Ideally, figures should be interpretable with as little contextual information as possible. Changing the level of confidence from the standard 95 % to 50 % or 99 % does not help. Similarly, do not use procedures that "adjust" or "correct" the length of confidence intervals unless there are good reasons to do so. Several such procedures have been described to facilitate visual inference or reinforce the equivalence with classical NHST procedures (Baguley 2012; Tryon 2001; Bender and Lange 2001), but their downside is that they change the meaning of confidence intervals and increase the amount of contextual information required to interpret them. Finally, do not show standard errors (SEs) in your plots. As Cumming and Finch (2005, p. 177) have pointed out, "if researchers prefer to publish SE bars merely because they are shorter, they are capitalizing on their readers' presumed lack of understanding of SE bars, 95 % CIs, and the relation between the two."

Tip 19: Be creative. The scarcity of graphical standards should be taken as an opportunity to explore custom visual designs, within the limits suggested by Tip 18. For example, there are many options for displaying error bars (Fig. 13.9): while the design (1) is widely used, (2) is a common alternative that has the advantage of

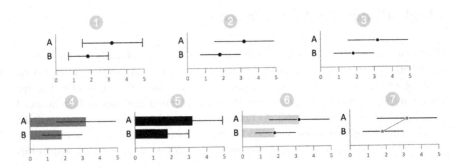

Fig. 13.9 Seven ways of plotting effect sizes with confidence intervals

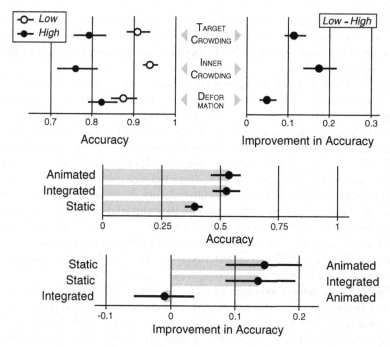

Fig. 13.10 *Top* the effects of three animation complexity metrics (one per row) on visual tracking accuracy. The *first plot* shows mean subject accuracy depending on whether animations are low or high on that metric, while the *second plot* shows mean within-subject improvement when switching from high to low (after Chevalier et al. 2014). *Bottom* the *upper plot* shows map reading accuracy for three terrain visualization techniques. On the *lower plot*, each row shows mean within-subject improvement when switching from the left technique to the right one (the scale has been magnified) (after Willett et al. 2015). All *error bars* are 95 % CIs, $n = 20$

de-emphasizing confidence limits; The variant (3) improves the legibility of point estimates; Error bars can also be combined with bar charts (4); Bars help compare magnitudes on a ratio scale (Zacks and Tversky 1999), but they introduce visual asymmetry (Newman and Scholl 2012; Correll and Gleicher 2014) and tend to de-emphasize error bars; This is evident in the so-called "dynamite plots" (5); The design (6) supports ratio comparison while maintaining emphasis on error bars; Finally, error bars can be combined with line charts (7) to convey temporal ordering (Zacks and Tversky 1999) or within-subject factors (Cumming 2012, p. 172).

Tip 20: Emphasize effects of interest. When choosing what to plot, focus on the effects that answer your research questions (Cumming 2012). These are typically differences between means, e.g., differences in average task average completion times between conditions. In within-subject designs, differences are typically computed on a per-participant basis, as with the paired t-test (Cumming 2012, pp. 168–175) (also see Tip 10). When comparing multiple conditions (see Tips 30 and 31), stick to the most informative pairs. For a nice example of informative pairwise comparisons, see the second experiment in (Jansen 2014, Chap. 5). Even though the individual means are rarely the researcher's focus, it can be very informative to show them alongside the differences (Franz and Loftus 2012). Doing so also has an explanatory value, and thus contributes to clarity. See Fig. 13.10 for two examples.

Tip 21: Aim for visual robustness. By *visually robust*, I refer to visual representations that are not overly affected by small changes in data,[12] and are thus resistant to sampling variability. See Dragicevic (2015) for illustrations. While it is hard to make a plot visually more robust without discarding information, there are many ways to make it less robust without adding any new information. One way consists of sorting conditions or pairwise comparisons by effect size. If effects are similar, every replication will lead to a different ordering—thus the plot misleads. Instead, choose a sensible ordering ahead of time. For similar reasons, boxplots (Wickham and Stryjewski 2011) lack visual robustness because they embed dichotomous decisions as to whether an observation should be considered as an "outlier". The resulting dots draw unnecessary attention to observations that just happen to be at the tails of the population distribution (Wickham and Stryjewski 2011, pp. 3–5). When designing a plot, always try to imagine how it could "dance" across replications.

Tip 22: Think beyond averages. Inferences about population means are an important but limited part of statistical analysis and communication. Distributions and individual differences can also be insightful (Vicente and Torenvliet 2000, pp. 250–253). Some empirical data—especially categorical or ordinal data like questionnaire responses—is also hard to faithfully capture with a single aggregated measure. As an alternative, such data can be conveyed without loss of information using compact visualization methods such as matrix displays (Perin et al. 2014). Showing individual observations next to error bars can also be informative and pedagogical (Drummond and Vowler 2011; Ecklund 2012). Finally, while confidence and credible intervals are useful for conveying uncertainty about population averages, alternatives such as *tolerance intervals* and *prediction intervals* may be better suited in some cases (Nelson 2011). Unfortunately, using interval estimates with very different meanings may exacerbate confusions surrounding the meaning of error bars.

13.4.5 Interpreting Confidence Intervals

Interpreting confidence intervals is a key aspect of estimation. It is hard to master, and it could almost be called an "art". Despite this, not much has been written on the topic. Here is a list of recommendations that can help interpret plots with confidence intervals, and since this is both an important and an error-prone task, some of the tips here will be developed more extensively than the previous ones.

---

[12]*Visual robustness* is related to the concept of *visual-data correspondence* recently introduced in infovis (Kindlmann and Scheidegger 2014). The counterpart of robustness (i.e., a visualization's ability to reveal differences in data) has been variously termed *distinctness* (Rensink 2014), *power* (Hofmann et al. 2012), and *unambiguity* (Kindlmann and Scheidegger 2014).

Tip 23: Build strong intuitions. The key to a correct interpretation of confidence intervals is a deep understanding of their relationship to sampling variability, and of sampling variability itself. Simulated replications like those created by Cumming (2009a) are a powerful tool for building this intuition, perhaps more so than mathematical formulas. Watch simulations over and over again, and run your own.

Tip 24: Know inference by eye. Cumming offers useful rules of thumb for doing statistical inference "by eye" (Cumming and Finch 2005; Cumming 2009b). The most basic rule follows from the equivalence between CIs and NHST, that is, if a certain value is outside a 95 % CI, it would be rejected as a null hypothesis at the $\alpha = .05$ level. This is only a convenient reference point, *not a hard rule* to be applied mindlessly (see Tip 25). Cumming also explains how to visually compare confidence intervals in between-subjects designs: if two error bars overlap by less than $1/4$ of their average length, then the difference is statistically significant at the $\alpha = .05$ level. This rule is also just a convenient rule of thumb, and should not be used in a binary way. In within-subject designs, the $1/4$ overlap rule is often (but not necessarily) conservative. Pairwise differences of interest thus need to be plotted and interpreted separately (Cumming and Finch 2005, p. 176) (see Fig. 13.10).

Tip 25: Ban dichotomous interpretations. Using confidence intervals to provide yes/no answers defeats the whole purpose of estimation: "It seems clear that no confidence interval should be interpreted as a significance test" (Schmidt and Hunter 1997, pp. 3–15); "CIs can prompt better interpretation if NHST is avoided" (Cumming 2013, p. 17). Plausibility does not suddenly drop when crossing the confidence limits (See Sect. 13.2.1). A confidence interval can be thought of as abstracting a continuous "plausibility" function (Cumming 2012, pp. 98–102, 2013, p. 17). While a recent study has explored alternatives to error bars that visually convey this continuity (Correll and Gleicher 2014), the classical error bar has the benefit of being visually cleaner and more economical in terms of space and data-ink ratio (Wainer 1984, p. 139). The edges of error bars offer visual reference points, whereas other representations such as color gradients may not.

Tip 26: Use vague language and hedges. We could say that Fig. 13.6 "provides good evidence that B outperforms A, whereas C and A seem very similar, and results are largely inconclusive concerning the difference between D and A." The terms "good evidence", "very similar" and "largely inconclusive" are *vague*. The use of vague language is necessary for acknowledging and honestly conveying the uncertainty present in effect size estimates. Vague language — which is not the same as ambiguous language — plays a key role in reasoning (van Deemter 2010). In the face of uncertainty and complexity, the only alternatives to vagueness are false clarity (van Deemter 2010, Chap. 1) and pseudo-objectivity (Thompson 1999). The term "seem" in the text above is a *hedge*, and hedges are also important in science communication (van Deemter 2010, Chap. 6). There are many ways Fig. 13.6 can be described using text, and different investigators will use different wordings. The subjective nature of this task should not make the researcher feel uncomfortable. It is important to be objective when performing planned analyses and turning them into numbers and plots, but after that one can afford to be subjective, knowing that no

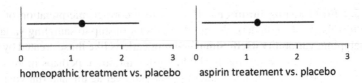

Fig. 13.11 Identical confidence intervals calling for different interpretations

reader is forced to accept one's conclusions. That said, wordings that misrepresent or exaggerate findings naturally tend not to give a good image of their authors.

Tip 27: Never say "no effect". Avoid suggesting that there is no effect, even using hedges (e.g., "results suggest that A has no effect on B"). Almost any experimental manipulation has *some* effect on human behavior (Cohen 1994), so an effet of exactly zero is highly implausible. Better wordings include "the direction of the effect is uncertain, but it is likely small", or "we were not able to measure an effect".

Tip 28: Use external information. A key part of empirical research consists of interpreting results in relation to externally available information. For example, the imaginary plot on Fig. 13.11 (left) shows the results of a study assessing the clinical efficacy of a homeopathic treatment. While the data speaks in favor of this treatment, the scientific consensus is that such treatments are ineffective, and thus the result should be interpreted with skepticism. Following the skeptical inquiry principle that "extraordinary claims require extraordinary evidence", perhaps the investigator should require that the confidence interval be much further from zero. In contrast, the right plot concerns a drug whose efficacy has been already firmly established, so one only needs to see it as a successful replication. The two results are *identical*, yet their interpretation is *very different*. Although Bayesian statisticians would typically attempt to incorporate such knowledge into the statistical analysis itself, not every reader needs to agree on the *a priori* plausibility of a result. Confidence intervals have both the drawback and the advantage of moving the burden of Bayesian reasoning to the investigator and the readers. The *cost of error* is also important. While HCI studies on safety-critical systems require cautious interpretations, excessive caution can slow down exploration and be detrimental to progress in studies that simply investigate new user interface technologies (i.e., most of HCI).

Tip 29: Use internal information. Individual confidence intervals should also be interpreted according to internal information, i.e., other pieces of information obtained from the same study. For example, in Fig. 13.12, there is nothing wrong

Fig. 13.12 In this plot, each confidence interval needs to be interpreted in relation to other confidence intervals

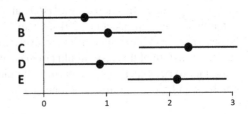

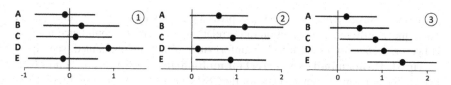

Fig. 13.13 Three possible sets of confidence intervals that can be tricky to summarize

with interpreting *A* as providing "only moderate evidence for an effect". However, it would be misleading to then interpret *B* as exhibiting "clear evidence for an effect". The principle of robustness requires that two similar results are interpreted in a similar way (also see Sect. 13.3.3.2 for the danger of not doing so). A less misleading way of describing Fig. 13.12 would be to group results, e.g., by stating that the figure provides evidence "for a small effect for A, B, D, and for a larger effect for C and E." Also see Tip 24 for information about how to read overlaps in confidence intervals. On the other hand, care must be taken *not* to suggest that the effects within each group are the same or similar — if pairwise differences are of interest, they should be reported and interpreted separately. Providing non-misleading interpretations of figures with confidence intervals requires judgment, and no mechanical decision procedure can carry out this job better than a thoughtful investigator.

Tip 30: Combine results very carefully. Drawing conclusions from a set of confidence intervals without any consideration for joint probabilities is particularly dangerous. Suppose that a person who purports to have extrasensory perception (ESP) abilities is subjected to testing sessions labeled *A–E* (Fig. 13.13-1). The investigator, observing that test *D* appears positive, may conclude that ESP is real. But even if ESP does not exist, the chances of observing *D* is about 5 %, already not particularly low. The chances of observing a similar deviation in *any* of the five tests is even higher: about 20 %. If 40 tests were conducted, the possibility of a false positive would be about 90 % — almost certain. An HCI researcher who concludes that a technique is promising because it succeeded in one out of five tasks commits the same fallacy. The converse fallacy (unsurprisingly less common) is also possible: a researcher observing Fig. 13.13-2 may conclude that the technique is imperfect because one task yields inconclusive results. However, such an outcome is likely to occur even if the technique is better in all respects (e.g., a consistent population difference of 1 for all tasks — see again the dance in Fig. 13.7).

Disjunctive (*or* operator) and conjunctive (*and* operator) logical combinations are best avoided when interpreting multiple results. Results should be *averaged*, or expressed with *buts* (Abelson 1995, Chap. 6): e.g., "results are inconclusive except perhaps for one task out of five", and "the technique seems consistently better, although possibly not for one out of the five tasks". Complex results should not be oversimplified in the paper's abstract or conclusion.

Finally, you may find on occasion a striking pattern, as in Fig. 13.13-3. Such a linear trend is unlikely to emerge from a dance of confidence intervals (unless conditions have been sorted, see Tip 21), so the investigator should not be shy to point it out. Nevertheless, it is best to express a pattern with a single number (e.g., a grand mean, difference, interaction or correlation) and report a confidence interval. However, such analyses are largely uninformative if they are unplanned (see Tip 5).

Tip 31: Do not mindlessly correct for multiplicity. Correction procedures (e.g., Bonferroni correction) that account for the ESP scenario in Tip 30 (Fig. 13.13-1) are part of the NHST ritual, and have been adapted to confidence intervals (Bender and Lange 2001; Tryon 2001). Such procedures are a powerful safeguard against fallacious reasoning, but they are too conservative in the many situations where results are not combined in a disjunctive manner. They also have the drawback of changing the meaning of error bars (Cumming 2009b, p. 209) (see Tip 18). Multiplicity correction procedures are far from having reached a consensus (Bender and Lange 2001) and there are strong arguments against their systematic use (Wilson 1962; Stewart-Oaten 1995, p. 2003). Between the fervent defenders and the strong opponents, estimation advocates tend to take a laissez-faire position (Cumming 2012, pp. 421–423; Cumming and Finch 2005, p. 177; Baguley 2012, pp. 173–174). The principle of simplicity provides an argument for skipping such procedures, while the principles of transparency and clarity requires that issues related to joint probabilities are kept in mind and pointed out if necessary. If a conclusion follows from a disjunctive combination of many confidence intervals, it can be useful to also report multiplicity-corrected confidence intervals. The best solution is to avoid reporting many confidence intervals by keeping experiments simple (Tip 2) and planning all analyses ahead of time (Tip 5) based on clear research questions (Tip 1).

Tip 32: Point out possibly spurious patterns. For a researcher who is committed to fair statistical communication, it is not enough to write an irreproachable analysis. Such a researcher should also anticipate possible misinterpretations of figures by statistically less sophisticated readers, and take the necessary precautions.

Tip 33: Defer judgment. NHST and the idea of statistical significance made us forget that no single study can provide conclusive evidence. Although this chapter focuses on uncertainty due to sampling error, there are many other sources of uncertainty (Brewer 2000; Meehl 1967; Rosenthal 2009; Vicente and Torenvliet 2000, pp. 264–266). According to Schmidt and Hunter (1997, pp. 3–16) "it is best for individual researchers to [...] refrain from attempting to draw final conclusions about research hypotheses." This echoes Fisher's belief that we should grant our readers the right to make "their own decisions". It is fine for a study to "provide strong evidence for X", but not to "show that X". Authors tend to be especially oversimplifying and brash in conclusions and abstracts, the very parts on which hurried readers (and journalists of course) tend to focus their attention. Using hedges as suggested in Tip 26 and providing nuanced conclusions as suggested in Tip 30 can help.

Tip 34: Share study material. Finally, sharing as much experimental material as possible (stimuli and data) is important as it greatly facilitates peer scrutiny and replication. Being able to run the experimental software and examine what participants saw (the techniques, tasks, instructions, and questions asked) is essential in order for other researchers to understand the details of a study and greatly facilitates replication. Similarly, experimental data (all data tables and possibly analysis scripts) is necessary for conducting re-analyses and meta-analyses. To be useful this material should be freely shared online upon paper acceptance.

For errata and updates, go to www.aviz.fr/badstats.

13.5 Conclusion

When assessing the quality of a statistical analysis in an HCI paper, reviewers often tend to exclusively focus on the rigorous application of statistical procedures. This reveals several misconceptions about statistics. One is the belief that there exists a set of "correct", universally-accepted statistical procedures, a myth largely cultivated by textbooks and introductory statistics courses (Gliner et al. 2002). Gigerenzer (2004, pp. 587–588) tells the story of a textbook author who was forced by his editor not to mention alternative methods in order to produce "the illusion that there is only one tool". Another belief is that statistical procedures can produce rigorous knowledge, just because they can output precise numbers. However, there is no such information in the data. Data is uncertain and messy, and so are statistics.

This chapter has introduced some basic principles of *fair statistical communication*, i.e., principles for conveying uncertainty in empirical data in a way that does not prompt misinterpretations, so that as-wide-as-possible an audience can judge and decide whether or not to trust the authors' conclusions. There are many questions this chapter does not address (e.g., what is a good research question? How to design experiments?) and it does not stand by itself as a guide to statistics — interested readers will need to go through some of the literature. Also, none of the tips offered in Sect. 13.4 should be taken as a dogma. Closely following guidelines will never be a necessary nor a sufficient condition for an article to merit publication. However, I do think that the general principles of fair statistical communication outlined in Sect. 13.4.1 should be given more consideration in peer reviewing.

Among the worst enemies of good statistical communication is dichotomous thinking. False dichotomies exist at many levels in current statistical practice, and have been greatly encouraged by NHST procedures. Judging articles based on the outcomes of such procedures reveals a deep misunderstanding of the purpose of statistics and is damaging to science, because it encourages questionable practices, information obfuscation, and publication bias. Dropping mindless statistical testing procedures and trying to achieve clarity and transparency while fully embracing the messiness of our data (Giner-Sorolla 2012) can not only benefit science, but can also make statistical analysis a much more exciting and rewarding experience.

Many issues outlined in this chapter are old and have been raised in many disciplines. But things seem to be changing — in the most recent edition of its highly influential "Publication Manual" (APA 2010), the American Psychological Association deemphasizes p-values and stresses the importance of reporting and interpreting effect sizes and confidence intervals (Fidler 2010). Meanwhile, high-impact psychology journals are starting to enforce the use of estimation (Eich 2014). Large collective initiatives, whose values overlap a lot with the idea of fair statistical communication, are also being started under the umbrella of the "open science" movement.[13] In parallel, more and more articles on bad statistics are being published in newspapers and blogs, raising the public's awareness of those issues. It may well be that statistical practice will be very different only a few years from now.

Since statistics are nothing but user interfaces meant to help researchers in their task of producing and disseminating knowledge, the fields of HCI and infovis can take a head start and show the way to other disciplines. HCI and infovis researchers also have the exciting opportunity to contribute new research, for example by studying new visual representations for communicating study results (Correll and Gleicher 2014; Perin et al. 2014). Such representations do not have to be static, and there are many ways computers, animation, and interactivity can be used to teach statistics and convey scientific evidence to a wide audience (Victor 2011).

Acknowledgments Many thanks to Elie Cattan, Fanny Chevalier, Geoff Cumming, Steven Franconeri, Steve Haroz, Petra Isenberg, Yvonne Jansen, Maurits Kaptein, Heidi Lam, Judy Robertson, Michael Sedlmair, Dan Simons, Chat Wacharamanotham and Wesley Willett for their helpful feedback and comments.

References

Abelson R (1995) Statistics as principled argument. Lawrence Erlbaum Associates

Abelson RP (1997) A retrospective on the significance test ban of 1999. What if there were no significance tests. pp 117–141

Anderson G (2012) No result is worthless: the value of negative results in science. http://tinyurl.com/anderson-negative

APA (2010) The publication manual of the APA, 6th edn. Washington, DC

Bååth R (2015) The non-parametric bootstrap as a Bayesian model. http://tinyurl.com/bayes-bootstrap

Baguley T (2009) Standardized or simple effect size: what should be reported? Br J Psychol 100(3):603–617

Baguley T (2012) Calculating and graphing within-subject confidence intervals for ANOVA. Behav Res Meth 44(1):158–175

Bayarri MJ, Berger JO (2004) The interplay of Bayesian and frequentist analysis. Stat Sci 58–80

Beaudouin-Lafon M (2008) Interaction is the future of computing. In: McDonald DW, Erickson T (eds) HCI remixed, reflections on works that have influenced the HCI community. The MIT Press, pp 263–266

Bender R, Lange S (2001) Adjusting for multiple testing: when and how? J Clin Epidemiol 54(4):343–349

Beyth-Marom R, Fidler F, Cumming G (2008) Statistical cognition: towards evidence-based practice in statistics and statistics education. Stat Educ Res J 7(2):20–39

Brewer MB (2000) Research design and issues of validity. Handbook of research methods in social and personality psychology. pp 3–16

Brodeur A, Lé M, Sangnier M, Zylberberg Y (2012) Star wars: the empirics strike back. Paris school of economics working paper (2012–29)

---

[13]see, e.g., http://centerforopenscience.org/ and https://osf.io/.

Carifio J, Perla RJ (2007) Ten common misunderstandings, misconceptions, persistent myths and urban legends about Likert scales and Likert response formats and their antidotes. J Soc Sci 3(3):106

Chevalier F, Dragicevic P, Franconeri S (2014) The not-so-staggering effect of staggered animated transitions on visual tracking. IEEE Trans Visual Comput Graphics 20(12):2241–2250

Coe R (2002) It's the effect size, stupid. In: Paper presented at the British Educational Research Association annual conference, vol 12. p 14

Cohen J (1990) Things I have learned (so far). Am Psychol 45(12):1304

Cohen J (1994) The Earth is round (p < .05). Am psychol 49(12):997

Colquhoun D (2014) An investigation of the false discovery rate and the misinterpretation of p-values. Roy Soc Open Sci 1(3):140, 216

Correll M, Gleicher M (2014) Error bars considered harmful: exploring alternate encodings for mean and error. IEEE Trans Visual Comput Graphics 20(12):2142–2151

Cumming G (2008) Replication and p intervals: p values predict the future only vaguely, but confidence intervals do much better. Perspect Psychol Sci 3(4):286–300

Cumming G (2009a) Dance of the p values [video]. http://tinyurl.com/danceptrial2

Cumming G (2009b) Inference by eye: reading the overlap of independent confidence intervals. Stat med 28(2):205–220

Cumming G (2012) Understanding the new statistics : effect sizes, confidence intervals, and meta-analysis. Multivariate applications series. Routledge Academic, London

Cumming G (2013) The new statistics: why and how. Psychol Sci

Cumming G, Finch S (2005) Inference by eye: confidence intervals and how to read pictures of data. Am Psychol 60(2):170

Cumming G, Williams R (2011) Significant does not equal important: why we need the new statistics. Podcast. http://tinyurl.com/geoffstalk

Cumming G, Fidler F, Vaux DL (2007) Error bars in experimental biology. J Cell Biol 177(1):7–11

Dawkins R (2011) The tyranny of the discontinuous mind. New Statesman 19:54–57

Dienes Z (2014) Using Bayes to get the most out of non-significant results. Front Psychol 5

Dragicevic P (2012) My technique is 20% faster: problems with reports of speed improvements in HCI. Research report

Dragicevic P (2015) The dance of plots. http://www.aviz.fr/danceplots

Dragicevic P, Chevalier F, Huot S (2014) Running an HCI experiment in multiple parallel universes. CHI extended abstracts. ACM, New York

Drummond GB, Vowler SL (2011) Show the data, don't conceal them. Adv Physiol Educ 35(2):130–132

Duckworth WM, Stephenson WR (2003) Resampling methods: not just for statisticians anymore. In: 2003 joint statistical meetings

Ecklund A (2012) Beeswarm: the bee swarm plot, an alternative to stripchart. R package version 01

Eich E (2014) Business not as usual (editorial). Psychol Sci 25(1):3–6. http://tinyurl.com/psedito

Fekete JD, Van Wijk JJ, Stasko JT, North C (2008) The value of information visualization. In: Information visualization. Springer, pp 1–18

Fidler F (2010) The american psychological association publication manual, 6th edn. Implications for statistics education. In: Data and context in statistics education: towards an evidence based society

Fidler F, Cumming G (2005) Teaching confidence intervals: problems and potential solutions. In: Proceedings of the 55th international statistics institute session

Fidler F, Loftus GR (2009) Why figures with error bars should replace p values. Zeitschrift für Psychologie/J Psychol 217(1):27–37

Fisher R (1955) Statistical methods and scientific induction. J Roy Stat Soc Ser B (Methodol): 69–78

Forum C (2015) Is there a minimum sample size required for the t-test to be valid? http://tinyurl.com/minsample

Franz VH, Loftus GR (2012) Standard errors and confidence intervals in within-subjects designs: generalizing Loftus and Masson (1994) and avoiding the biases of alternative accounts. Psychon Bull Rev 19(3):395–404

Frick RW (1998) Interpreting statistical testing: process and propensity, not population and random sampling. Behav Res Meth Instrum Comput 30(3):527–535

Gardner MJ, Altman DG (1986) Confidence intervals rather than p values: estimation rather than hypothesis testing. BMJ 292(6522):746–750

Gelman A (2004) Type 1, type 2, type S, and type M errors. http://tinyurl.com/typesm

Gelman A (2013a) Commentary: p-values and statistical practice. Epidemiology 24(1):69–72

Gelman A (2013b) Interrogating p-values. J Math Psychol 57(5):188–189

Gelman A, Loken E (2013) The garden of forking paths. Online article

Gelman A, Stern H (2006) The difference between significant and not significant is not itself statistically significant. Am Stat 60(4):328–331

Gigerenzer G (2004) Mindless statistics. J Socio Econ 33(5):587–606

Gigerenzer G, Kruger L, Beatty J, Porter T, Daston L, Swijtink Z (1990) The empire of chance: how probability changed science and everyday life, vol 12. Cambridge University Press

Giner-Sorolla R (2012) Science or art? how aesthetic standards grease the way through the publication bottleneck but undermine science. Perspect Psychol Sci 7(6):562–571

Gliner JA, Leech NL, Morgan GA (2002) Problems with null hypothesis significance testing (NHST): what do the textbooks say? J Exp Educ 71(1):83–92

Goldacre B (2012) What doctors don't know about the drugs they prescribe [TED talk]. http://tinyurl.com/goldacre-ted

Goodman SN (1999) Toward evidence-based medical statistics. 1: the p value fallacy. Ann Intern Med 130(12):995–1004

Greenland S, Poole C (2013) Living with p values: resurrecting a Bayesian perspective on frequentist statistics. Epidemiology 24(1):62–68

Hager W (2002) The examination of psychological hypotheses by planned contrasts referring to two-factor interactions in fixed-effects ANOVA. Method Psychol Res, Online 7:49–77

Haller H, Krauss S (2002) Misinterpretations of significance: a problem students share with their teachers. Methods Psychol Res 7(1):1–20

Hoekstra R, Finch S, Kiers HA, Johnson A (2006) Probability as certainty: dichotomous thinking and the misuse of p values. Psychon Bull Rev 13(6):1033–1037

Hofmann H, Follett L, Majumder M, Cook D (2012) Graphical tests for power comparison of competing designs. IEEE Trans Visual Comput Graphics 18(12):2441–2448

Hornbæk K, Sander SS, Bargas-Avila JA, Grue Simonsen J (2014) Is once enough?: on the extent and content of replications in human-computer interaction. In: Proceedings of ACM, ACM conference on human factors in computing systems, pp 3523–3532

Ioannidis JP (2005) Why most published research findings are false. PLoS med 2(8):e124

Jansen Y (2014) Physical and tangible information visualization. PhD thesis, Université Paris Sud-Paris XI

Kaptein M, Robertson J (2012) Rethinking statistical analysis methods for CHI. In: Proceedings of the SIGCHI conference on human factors in computing systems, ACM, pp 1105–1114

Keene ON (1995) The log transformation is special. Stat Med 14(8):811–819

Kerr NL (1998) HARKing: hypothesizing after the results are known. Pers Soc Psychol Rev 2(3):196–217

Kindlmann G, Scheidegger C (2014) An algebraic process for visualization design. IEEE Trans Visual Comput Graphics 20(12):2181–2190

Kirby KN, Gerlanc D (2013) BootES: an R package for bootstrap confidence intervals on effect sizes. Behav Res Methods 45(4):905–927

Kirk RE (2001) Promoting good statistical practices: some suggestions. Educ Psychol Meas 61(2):213–218

Kline RB (2004) What's wrong with statistical tests–and where we go from here. Am Psychol Assoc

Lakens D, Pigliucci M, Galef J (2014) Daniel Lakens on p-hacking and other problems in psychology research. Podcast. http://tinyurl.com/lakens-podcast

Lambdin C (2012) Significance tests as sorcery: science is empirical, significance tests are not. Theory Psychol 22(1):67–90

Lazic SE (2010) The problem of pseudoreplication in neuroscientific studies: is it affecting your analysis? BMC Neurosci 11(1):5

Levine TR, Weber R, Hullett C, Park HS, Lindsey LLM (2008a) A critical assessment of null hypothesis significance testing in quantitative communication research. Hum Commun Res 34(2):171–187

Levine TR, Weber R, Park HS, Hullett CR (2008b) A communication researchers' guide to null hypothesis significance testing and alternatives. Hum Commun Res 34(2):188–209

Loftus GR (1993) A picture is worth a thousand p values: on the irrelevance of hypothesis testing in the microcomputer age. Behav Res Meth Instrum Comput 25(2):250–256

MacCallum RC, Zhang S, Preacher KJ, Rucker DD (2002) On the practice of dichotomization of quantitative variables. Psychol Methods 7(1):19

Mazar N, Amir O, Ariely D (2008) The dishonesty of honest people: a theory of self-concept maintenance. J Mark Res 45(6):633–644

Meehl PE (1967) Theory-testing in psychology and physics: a methodological paradox. Philos Sci: 103–115

Miller J (1991) Short report: reaction time analysis with outlier exclusion: bias varies with sample size. Q J Exp Psychol 43(4):907–912

Morey RD, Hoekstra R, Rouder JN, Lee MD, Wagenmakers EJ (2015) The fallacy of placing confidence in confidence intervals (version 2). http://tinyurl.com/cifallacy

Nelson MJ (2011) You might want a tolerance interval. http://tinyurl.com/tol-interval

Newcombe RG (1998a) Interval estimation for the difference between independent proportions: comparison of eleven methods. Stat Med 17(8):873–890

Newcombe RG (1998b) Two-sided confidence intervals for the single proportion: comparison of seven methods. Stat Med 17(8):857–872

Newman GE, Scholl BJ (2012) Bar graphs depicting averages are perceptually misinterpreted: the within-the-bar bias. Psychon Bull Rev 19(4):601–607

Norman DA (2002) The Design of Everyday Things. Basic Books Inc, New York

Norman G (2010) Likert scales, levels of measurement and the laws of statistics. Adv Health Sci Educ 15(5):625–632

Nuzzo R (2014) Scientific method: statistical errors. Nature 506(7487):150–152

Open Science Collaboration (2015) Estimating the reproducibility of psychological science. Science 349(6251):aac4716+

Osborne JW, Overbay A (2004) The power of outliers (and why researchers should always check for them). Pract Asses Res Eval 9(6):1–12

Perin C, Dragicevic P, Fekete JD (2014) Revisiting Bertin matrices: new interactions for crafting tabular visualizations. IEEE Trans Visual Comput Graphics 20(12):2082–2091

Pollard P, Richardson J (1987) On the probability of making Type I errors. Psychol Bull 102(1):159

Rawls RL (1998) Breaking up is hard to do. Chem Eng News 76(25):29–34

Reips UD, Funke F (2008) Interval-level measurement with visual analogue scales in internet-based research: VAS generator. Behav Res Methods 40(3):699–704

Rensink RA (2014) On the prospects for a science of visualization. In: Handbook of Human Centric Visualization. Springer, pp 147–175

Ricketts C, Berry J (1994) Teaching statistics through resampling. Teach Stat 16(2):41–44

Rosenthal R (2009) Artifacts in behavioral research: Robert Rosenthal and Ralph L. Rosnow's Classic Books. Oxford University Press, Oxford

Rosenthal R, Fode KL (1963) The effect of experimenter bias on the performance of the albino rat. Behav Sci 8(3):183–189

Rosnow RL, Rosenthal R (1989) Statistical procedures and the justification of knowledge in psychological science. Am Psychol 44(10):1276

Rossi JS (1990) Statistical power of psychological research: what have we gained in 20 years? J Consult Clin Psychol 58(5):646

Sauro J, Lewis JR (2010) Average task times in usability tests: what to report? In: Proceedings of the SIGCHI conference on human factors in computing systems, ACM, pp 2347–2350

Schmidt FL, Hunter J (1997) Eight common but false objections to the discontinuation of significance testing in the analysis of research data. What if there were no significance tests. pp 37–64

Simmons JP, Nelson LD, Simonsohn U (2011) False-positive psychology: undisclosed flexibility in data collection and analysis allows presenting anything as significant. Psychol Sci 22(11):1359–1366

Smith RA, Levine TR, Lachlan KA, Fediuk TA (2002) The high cost of complexity in experimental design and data analysis: type I and type II error rates in multiway ANOVA. Hum Commun Res 28(4):515–530

Stewart-Oaten A (1995) Rules and judgments in statistics: three examples. Ecology: 2001–2009

The Economist (2013) Unreliable research: Trouble at the lab. http://tinyurl.com/trouble-lab

Thompson B (1998) Statistical significance and effect size reporting: portrait of a possible future. Res Sch 5(2):33–38

Thompson B (1999) Statistical significance tests, effect size reporting and the vain pursuit of pseudo-objectivity. Theory Psychol 9(2):191–196

Trafimow D, Marks M (eds) (2015) Basic Appl Social Psychol 37(1):1–2. http://tinyurl.com/trafimow

Tryon WW (2001) Evaluating statistical difference, equivalence, and indeterminacy using inferential confidence intervals: an integrated alternative method of conducting null hypothesis statistical tests. Psychol Methods 6(4):371

Tukey JW (1980) We need both exploratory and confirmatory. Am Stat 34(1):23–25

Ulrich R, Miller J (1994) Effects of truncation on reaction time analysis. J Exp Psychol: Gen 123(1):34

van Deemter K (2010) Not exactly: in praise of vagueness. Oxford University Press, Oxford

Velleman PF, Wilkinson L (1993) Nominal, ordinal, interval, and ratio typologies are misleading. Am Stat 47(1):65–72

Vicente KJ, Torenvliet GL (2000) The Earth is spherical (p < 0.05): alternative methods of statistical inference. Theor Issues Ergon Sci 1(3):248–271

Victor B (2011) Explorable explanations. http://worrydream.com/ExplorableExplanations/

Wainer H (1984) How to display data badly. Am Stat 38(2):137–147

Wickham H, Stryjewski L (2011) 40 years of boxplots. Am Stat

Wierdsma A (2013) What is wrong with tests of normality? http://tinyurl.com/normality-wrong

Wilcox RR (1998) How many discoveries have been lost by ignoring modern statistical methods? Am Psychol 53(3):300

Wilkinson L (1999) Statistical methods in psychology journals: guidelines and explanations. Am Psychol 54(8):594

Willett W, Jenny B, Isenberg T, Dragicevic P (2015) Lightweight relief shearing for enhanced terrain perception on interactive maps. In: Proceedings of ACM conference on human factors in computing systems. ACM, New York, NY, USA, CHI '15, pp 3563–3572

Wilson W (1962) A note on the inconsistency inherent in the necessity to perform multiple comparisons. Psychol Bull 59(4):296

Wood M (2004) Statistical inference using bootstrap confidence intervals. Significance 1(4):180–182

Wood M (2005) Bootstrapped confidence intervals as an approach to statistical inference. Organ Res Meth 8(4):454–470

Zacks J, Tversky B (1999) Bars and lines: a study of graphic communication. Mem Cogn 27(6):1073–1079

Ziliak ST, McCloskey DN (2008) The cult of statistical significance. University of Michigan Press, Ann Arbor

Chapter 14
Improving Statistical Practice in HCI

Judy Robertson and Maurits Kaptein

14.1 Introduction

So you have come to the end. You have, if all is according to plan, learned novel methods and have started to think fairly critically about the methods that are of common use in HCI. Perhaps you are convinced that we could, and should, improve our reporting practice. The previous chapter has highlighted, practically without reference to specific methods or choosing a "camp" (Bayesian or Frequentist), a large number of possible directions for improvements.

In this closing chapter we have two final aims. First, we strengthen the argument that HCI needs change, by reflecting critically upon some of the most highly cited quantitative studies in the HCI field. Referring back to the seven common fallacies in our current methods as introduced in Chap. 1, we examine how these fallacies are present, even in our most respected pieces of work. We do not aim to discredit the work done by the authors that we review here: in each case the paper is rightfully influential in the field. However, we do aim to strengthen the argument that continuous improvements of statistical methods can benefit the even the best in the field, and thus likely the field as a whole. To this end, we close with a series of recommendations to authors, reviewers, and editors for improving the quality of statistical methodology and reporting in HCI.

J. Robertson (✉)
Moray House School of Education, Edinburgh University, Edinburgh, UK
e-mail: judy.robertson@hw.ac.uk

M. Kaptein
Donders Centre for Cognition, Radboud University Nijmegen,
Nijmegen, The Netherlands
e-mail: maurits@mauritskaptein.com

© Springer International Publishing Switzerland 2016
J. Robertson and M. Kaptein (eds.), *Modern Statistical Methods for HCI*,
Human–Computer Interaction Series, DOI 10.1007/978-3-319-26633-6_14

14.2   Case Studies from the HCI Literature

Perhaps flaws which commonly occur in psychology or economics might not occur in HCI. Even though scholars in these neighbouring fields are clearly advocating a deviation from the procedural use of NHST methods, we might ourselves not be at risk. And, even if such flaws do occur in HCI, perhaps they do not practically matter much. To conclude this book, we decided to review highly cited (quantitative) papers from respected HCI publications to identify whether methodological "flaws" (or at least analysis and reporting practices that could be debated or strengthened) do get past reviewers within HCI, and if so, what impact these flaws could have. We also wished to document good practice which other researchers could adopt in the future. We conducted a literature search for the top 50 most cited article(s) matching the search terms "human computer interaction" OR "HCI" with no date restriction in the Scopus citation database.[1] Scopus was chosen based on Meho and Rogers (2008) conclusions that the coverage of Scopus is superior to Web of Science and is sufficiently good that it can be used as the "a sole data source for citation-based research and evaluation in HCI" (p1).

Of the 50 most highly cited HCI articles, 8 (16 %) reported the results of quantitative analysis using t-tests or analysis of variance (ANOVA), tests which are commonly misapplied in other fields. We use the methodologies of these papers as case studies in this section.

It is worth noting that the proportion of this sort of quantitative articles in the most highly cited papers in a field is likely to be lower than the proportion within all published papers in a field, as theories, review and meta-analysis papers are likely to attract high numbers of citations. Within our 8 papers, the least cited had 143 citations, and the most cited had attracted 250 citations. The articles were published in reputable journals such as *Human Computer Interaction* and *Computers in Human Behaviour.* Topics ranged across the spectrum of HCI from emerging technology (human-robot interaction) to documenting user behaviour with established technology (patterns of internet usage) to exploring facets of user satisfaction (such as the relationship between usability and aesthetics). Table 14.1 shows the 8 articles that were selected based on the publication counts including the references use below to identify the different papers (e.g. **P1, P2,**... etc.). In the remainder of this section we first briefly summarize these top scoring 8 quantitative papers, after which we will examine these paper for common misconceptions as introduced earlier.

P1, the first of our 8 reviewed papers, surveyed college internet users in order to assess incidence of pathological internet usage (PIU) and to investigate the characteristics of those users who did exhibit PIU. Only 27 % of users showed no symptoms of PIU. Users whose Internet usage was considered pathological were more likely to be male, technologically sophisticated and to play internet games. Given the alarmingly high proportion of users who displayed some characteristics of PIU, it is not surprising that this paper is highly cited (250 citations). In **P2**, the authors investigated status effects in electronic communication compared to face to face communication. They

---

[1] The search was carried out in Sept 2013.

Table 14.1 Overview of the 8 highly cited quantitative HCI articles used in the review of HCI's statistical practices

ID	Reference	Citation count
P1	(Morahan-Martin and Schumacher 2000)	250
P2	(Dubrovsky et al. 1991)	248
P3	(Tractinsky et al. 2000)	241
P4	(Kanda et al. 2004)	180
P5	(Schumacher and Morahan-Martin 2001)	160
P6	(Endsley and Kaber 1999)	153
P7	(Claypool et al. 2001)	152
P8	(Hassenzahl 2004)	143

found that status and expertise were less influential in email, thus make contributions more equal across group members.

In **P3** the authors explored the relationship between the aesthetics and usability of interfaces in a study in which 132 participants used an ATM simulation. Pre-test and post-test measures indicated a strong correlation between aesthetics and usability. Based on a multivariate analysis, the authors observed that "the results suggesting interface aesthetics has a major effect on priori perceptions of ease of use, and perhaps more importantly on post-facto evaluations of usability may come as a surprise to those versed in the field of HCI" (p140). Hassenzahl's 2004 paper (**P8**) on usability and aesthetics which discusses **P3** at length is also one of our case studies. **P8** reports two studies on the interplay of beauty, goodness, and usability in interactive products. The authors conclude that beauty is related to self-oriented and hedonic attributes of a product, while goodness is related to goal-oriented and pragmatic attributes. This latter paper thus nuances the conclusions drawn in **P3**.

P4 explored the potential for robots to form relationships with children and whether children might learn English from them. The authors report that interaction with the robots during the second of week of the study predicted scores in the post-test. The paper suggested that robots may have been more successful when they had something common with their users.

P5 explores whether internet and computer experiences, skills, and attitudes are related. It does so over two time points (1989/90 and 1997). The study is survey based, and studies freshman college students. In the analysis the authors focus on trends over time in internet use, computer experience, and attitudes towards computers as well as on gender differences. The study shows that the overall competency and comfort towards computers and the internet increase over the 7 years. Finally they show that on a number of measures gender differences exist and that females report higher levels of incompetence and discomfort than males do.

The next paper we examined, **P6**, examines the effects of automation on performance, situation awareness and workload in a dynamic control task. The authors

J. Robertson and M. Kaptein

examine how different levels of automation—e.g. handing more control over to a computer in a task that is completed jointly by a computer and a human—influences several aspects of the joint task. Thus, the article examines the fundamental question of how much automation is feasible in control tasks. The authors conclude that under normal operation some specific types of automation, namely that of the implementation portion of the task, should be preferred in terms of performance.

We also examined **P7** by Claypool et al. (2001). Taken from a different area of HCI, this highly cited paper examines how implicit interest indicators compare to explicit interest indicators. The authors discuss explicit interest rating as (e.g.) product ratings that users provide to train a recommendation engine. Implicit ratings would be other indicators of interest for the product which are not provided by the users, but rather are derived from the browsing behaviour of the customer. The authors conclude that the time that users spend on a page and the amount of scrolling people perform strongly relate to explicit interest indicators.

All of these eight studies clearly examine questions that are important to HCI researchers. In the following sections we discuss the good and poor practices adopted in these papers in terms of the six commonly occurring methodological flaws we previously discussed in Chap. 1.

14.2.1 Misinterpretations of the p-Value

Our first examination of the above eight papers concerns the interpretation of p-values. As described earlier it is fairly common for researchers to misinterpret the p-value in two basic ways: first, rejection of the null hypothesis is often interpreted as strong evidence in favour of the alternative hypothesis, despite the fact that the specific alternative is often not tested. Second, a failure to reject the null is often interpreted as evidence in favour of the null hypothesis while this need not be the case. In **P5** this second erroneous interpretation of the p-value is striking: the researchers combine the survey results of two subsequent years (89 and 90) since there is no statistically significant difference between the two (although from the description it is somewhat unclear which dependent variables are actually used in this analysis). Next, the researchers compare 89/90 with 97 and describe trends over time. Despite the non-significant difference for the first 2 years the researchers could have modelled the 89/90 difference explicitly in their subsequent analysis and perhaps had obtained different results. Without a discussion of power (which is not present) assuming a null result as proof for "absolutely no effect" is a threat to the validity of the conclusions. The first interpretation error is also present in **P5** albeit less prominently: Despite directional expectations arising from previous work the authors only test the null against its rather uninformative alternative (not null) instead of testing explicitly for directions of the differences.

A similar mistake was made in **P3**, where the authors write *"...most surprising is the fact that post-experimental perceptions of usability were affected by the interface's aesthetics and not by the actual usability of the system"* p140. That is, no differences were *detected* in perceptions of usability according to the actual usability of the system; the authors are taking a large p-value as evidence in favour of the null, without a discussion of how Type II errors were controlled. **P4** also appears to misinterpret *p*-values, confusing a non-significant *p*-value with lack of an effect (confirmation of the null hypothesis) "The amount of time children spent with the robot during the 1st week also had no effect on their improvement in English by the 2nd week" (p.77). Again, power is not discussed.

A misinterpretation of *p*-values in one way or another, albeit not always explicit, is present in each of the eight papers we reviewed. This is consistent with the questionnaire study by Oakes (1986) and with examinations in economics by Ziliak and McCloskey (2008): Even the top authors in our field occasionally misunderstand (or misrepresent) one of our most highly regarded numerical quantities. HCI is no exception in this regard.

14.2.2   The Fallacy of the Transposed Conditional

The second issue concerns an extension to the misinterpretation of p-values in which a low p-value is interpreted as a high probability that the alternative hypothesis is true, or a high p-value is interpreted as large evidence in favour of the null hypothesis. If no prior probabilities for either of the hypotheses being true are specified, such a claim is hard to defend.

A small chance that the data would have occurred given that no differences exist in the population seems sufficient evidence within HCI to accept (e.g.) directional conclusions about hypothesis. Conversely, a large probability to observe the data given the data comes from a null hypothesis population (see also the next section) is often interpreted as decisive evidence in favour of the null. To consider two specific examples, in **P6** the authors find an "extremely significant F value" (p 477), incorrectly suggesting a connection between the size of the F ratio and actual strength of evidence. This latter use of the F value as a comparison to other F-values would only be possible if n and s are equal.

In **P4**, the authors write: *"However, this analysis did show that sixth graders learned more English than first graders (p <0.01), and that first graders benefited slightly more from interaction with the robot in the 1st week (p < 0.08)."* p78. Here, although the *p*-value is above the standard alpha value of 0.05, it is incorrectly used to quantify differences in benefits between groups, suggesting that the authors equate *p*-value with strength of evidence for hypotheses.

It is surprising to see that the evidence in favour of the hypothesis that researchers are testing is not discussed in *any* of the 8 papers that we reviewed. None of the papers employed Bayesian analysis techniques despite that fact that for several papers— most noticeably **P5** and **P8**—prior knowledge in explicit quantified form is available to direct hypothesis. It may be, however, that appropriate Bayesian methods were unavailable to the authors at the papers were published. It would be interesting to apply the techniques discussed in Chap. 9 to these datasets to see what new insights may be gained.

14.2.3 A Lack of Power (Type II Errors)

We have discussed a lack of power as one of the threats to validity, especially when interpreting null results: when power is low a null result is hardly informative. It is striking to see that *none* of the case study papers report the results of power calculations or even discuss this issue. Hence, it is clear that type II errors, in comparison to type I errors, are not necessarily subject of our scrutiny.

In particular, **P5** should have discussed power at several places since within the paper the authors actually build on the null result comparing 89/90. Despite the fact that due to their large sample sizes power is unlikely to actually be an issue, such a discussion given the estimated effect sizes would be worthwhile and strengthen the reader's confidence in the validity of merging the results for the 2 years.

P8 uses a fairly small sample size (33 and 10, albeit with repeated measures) compared to the sheer number of tests (>30 for experiment 1 alone) that is reported upon. Power is however not discussed at all, despite the fact that the authors could have made informed guesses about effect sizes a priori (given previous literature on the topic) and thus could have performed explicit power calculations. The lack of power in **P8** becomes especially troublesome when, on several occasions, null effects—for example with regard to the effect of beauty—are explicitly interpreted and contrasted (a) to findings previously reported in the literature, and (b) to findings earlier in the paper. To be explicit, the second study reported in **P8** with a sample size of 10 would, with reasonable limits (e.g. alpha 0.05, and beta 0.20) only "find" correlations that are larger than 0.78 (see Chap. 5 to see how to perform this calculation). These are extremely high correlations in our field. Any correlations smaller than 0.78 for which a NHST is rejected will not be very informative. It is hard to decide whether it indicates no relation or simply too little data to make a decision. We argue that **P8** study 2 has too few observations to draw any meaningful conclusions from null-results.

Interestingly, the converse of a lack of power also plagues the validity of some of the studies. Out of all our reviewed papers, **P6** reports the most extreme p-values—and it reports many of them. However, for a number of the reported tests it is largely unclear how many observations were used (and whether these were treated as dependent or independent) due to the rather complex setup of the experiment. A more thorough discussion of the experimental setup and the data-treatment in the analysis stage would aid readers in their understanding of the reported results. Here, more advanced methods, like those discussed in Sect. 4 of this book (Chaps. 10–12) might be of use.

14.2.4   Confusion of p-Values and Effect Size Estimates

None of the papers include effect size predictions in their hypotheses, or quantify the size of effects found in the literature. There is only one standardised measure of effect reported in one section of one paper (Cohen's d), although some papers do report descriptive statistics sufficiently well to enable the reader to compare raw differences in means and draw their own conclusions. The authors by and large do not attempt to interpret the real world significance of the effect magnitudes they found. An example of a paper with clearly reported large effects is **P2** where the authors report the percentages of participants who were first advocates of an idea—the first person to propose an idea which was eventually adopted by the group—in face to face discussions compared to email discussions. There is a 42 % point difference between face to face and electronic discussions, indicating a more equal participation structure in the electronic medium. The authors, however, correctly resist the temptation to over interpret the results, cautiously concluding *"In sum, although we were able to use the experimental technique to study a small piece of the technology-participation link, we cannot generalise very far"* (p141).

In **P3** the authors do not interpret the effect size but a consideration of raw differences in scores between the experimental results does make the findings less compelling. This paper examines the relationship between the aesthetics and usability of interfaces in a study in which 132 participants used an ATM simulation. Pre-test and post-test measures indicate a strong correlation between aesthetics and usability. Based on a multivariate analysis, the authors observe that "the results suggesting interface aesthetics has a major effect on priori perceptions of ease of use, and perhaps more importantly on post-facto evaluations of usability may come as a surprise to those versed in the field of HCI." (p140). There were *statistically* significant differences in usability between interfaces of difference aesthetic quality, but were these differences practically significant? It is difficult to establish this because the necessary descriptive statistics are not clearly reported. However, figures are provided for the changes in perceived usability between pre and post test, which relate to one of the paper's most surprising findings: "the fact that post-experimental perceptions of system usability were affected by the interface's aesthetics and not by the actual usability of the system" (p140). The changes in perceptions of usability between pre and post test were around 0.5 on a scale between 1 and 10. Does this magnitude of improvement make a difference to real world interface designers? The answer to that is not obvious to us, and the authors do not argue the point either way.

P4 is a clear example where full interpretation of the effect size and consideration of practical issues should have made a difference to the conclusions of the study. This paper explores the potential for robots to form relationships with children and whether the children might learn English from them. The authors report that interactions with the robots during the second of week of the study predict scores in the English language post-test. The authors also suggest that robots may be more successful when they had something common with users. However, when the results are examined more closely it becomes apparent that these claims are misleading. The average raw difference in test scores before and after the experiment is in the order of tenths of a percentage point. The lack of convincing effect is not entirely surprising given that the children chose to interact with the robots for only a total of around 3 min in the second week of the study (the time period during which interactions predicted scores). It is unlikely that 3 min per week of instruction of any sort will make an impact on language learning. To their credit, the authors do acknowledge that "the benefits may be still too small to justify practical applications" (p81). However, this caveat is not prominent in the abstract and conclusions, leading to the possibility that the 180 authors who cited this work could have taken the headline claims at face value. This paper has further methodology flaws which can explain the significant statistical results which appear to challenge common sense, as discussed in the next section.

In **P5** the authors discuss several differences between years and gender. By giving percentages of (e.g.) internet use amongst their surveyed respondents they allow for interpretation of the effects that they find on a number of important metrics. However, while the percentages of use are intuitively clear and easy to interpret, the authors do not interpret the sizes of the differences uncovered on the other scales that they use. For example, table 8 of **P5** gives the differences between internet competent and internet incompetent users on a number of variables. Each is measured on a 4 points scales (of which interpretation as ratio (Kaptein et al. 2010) is debatable) and differences in means are presented. It is however not clear whether a mean difference on this scale of 0.24 points is important in practice.

Interestingly, **P7** (which we have hitherto not discussed as it conducts few inferential statistics) does a very good job at communicating unstandardized effect sizes. The authors present box-and-whiskers plots that are split according to the relationships that they wish to examine. Presented this way, readers have an almost full account of the collected data and can make up their own conclusions about the importance of the findings (although we would argue that providing some inference would make this much easier for the readers). Next, the authors explicitly try to interpret differences in median scores on the implicit ratings. The authors also provide a check of how well the implicit ratings (within sample) predict the explicit ratings: this gives a fairly good idea of the usefulness of implicit ratings when taking the explicit ratings a gold standard.

To conclude, this error is most definitely present in HCI work. A number of the eight papers we reviewed do focus on statistical significance rather than effect sizes or real-world importance. This leads to conclusions which might grossly overstate the importance of an effect—when measured with high precision—or understate the importance—when measurement error is large.

14.2.5 Multiple Comparisons (Type I Errors)

The case study papers are variable in the extent to which they successfully controlled Type 1 errors. There are some examples of good practice for reducing Type I errors among the case studies. **P1** for example controlled the likelihood of Type 1 errors by clearly specifying hypotheses in advance, and therefore not relying on multiple post-hoc tests. **P3** corrected for multiple post-hoc comparisons by using the Scheffe test, and **P6** applies Tukey's HSD correction. Hence it is clear that these authors considered the multiple comparisons problem and have tried to address it.

Not all papers however address the issue: In **P1**, which was cited by 250 subsequent papers, some of the discussion points no longer hold once Bonferroni corrections[2] to multiple post-hoc comparisons are made. For example, in the analysis of the reasons the participants gave for using the internet, the authors carried out nineteen follow up ANOVAs on dependant variables without any corrections. Once Bonferroni corrections are applied (assuming an intended alpha value of 0.05), four of the eleven previously significant results are no longer significant. The authors also performed follow up tests on 25 dependent variables about people's Internet behaviour. If Bonferroni corrections are applied, ten of the eighteen originally significant results no longer hold. The conclusions of the paper would remain broadly the same, but there are four occasions where the discussion makes potentially misleading points based on results which are not significant once corrections are performed.

P4 is a more extreme case where researcher degrees of freedom inflated Type 1 error rates. For example, the authors write *"Because we found significant improvement in English learning after 2 weeks, we examined whether there was any evidence of improvement after first week with the robot."* Although there were no initial hypotheses relating to the time period, the authors conducted some unplanned tests, which should be corrected. Because the reported p-values are close to the alpha value, if a Bonferroni correction were applied, even the headline finding from the abstract relating to the interaction time with robot in second week would not be deemed true. This not only highlights the threat to validity of a failure to correct for multiple comparisons, but it also highlights the arbitrariness of the NHST cut off points for significance. **P5** does not discuss the issue of multiple comparisons. This poses a threat to the validity of the conclusions since a large number of tests is reported (over 50) and it is thus unclear how many reported significant differences are due to chance. Given that the total number of test that were done (and the possibility of those which were conducted but were not reported upon in the paper) it is hard for the reader to assess whether or not the researchers are capitalizing on chance in their discussion.

Besides over testing, of the eight case studies, only three reported that they had checked whether the assumptions for the use of the statistical tests were reasonably met. The other papers may be thus be using statistical tests for which the assumptions have not been met, therefore possibly increasing the Type I error rates.

In sum, while we resort to NHST testing methods as an objective standard, we find that in many cases its assumptions are stretched or its basic ideas are not respected. This introduces subjectivity in our analysis, and raises the spectre of Ioannidis (2005)

---

[2] Other types of corrections may be more suitable given the intentions of the original research team: this is merely an illustrative example.

proposition: are these published research findings wrong? Were these findings merely quirks of randomness, something the NHST was supposedly guarding us against?

14.2.6 Researcher Degrees of Freedom

None of the papers reported stopping rules for data collection, the importance of which to NHST is highlighted by Dienes (2008), Kruschke (2011) and Simmons et al. (2011). **P4**, **P5**, and **P8** indicate the time period for data collection, in some cases implying that the stopping rule was time related but do not explicitly state it. For the other papers it is unclear why the number of subjects was chosen as is, and it is unclear whether this was done in advance.

P5 —similar to most survey studies—allows for a large number of researcher degrees of freedom. The authors posses a large number of measurements and can construct a large number of possibly interesting indictors. The authors focus in their discussion on changes of the effect of gender over time. It is however unclear whether other differences (e.g. ethnicity, socio-economic status, etc.) are measured or examined. Likely with these types of large scale surveys a multitude of comparisons *could* have been carried out and researchers have many opportunities to pick those tests that "work": e.g. produce statistically significant results. We are not implying dishonesty on the part of the authors, merely that explicit reporting along the lines of Simmons et al. (2011) recommendations removes ambiguity. On the other hand—in fairness to the authors of **P5**—the consistency of the findings presented over a multitude of dependent measures strengthens the confidence that the reported upon differences are indeed meaningful.

In **P4**, the researchers decided post-hoc to control for the presence of friends and initial pre-test score in analyses of learning gains in the human-robot interaction study. Both of these researcher degrees of freedom could have increased the likelihood of false positives. **P6**, due to its very large number of measurements, conditions, and tasks also allows for many different analysis methods. It is unclear how much this freedom has been exploited in this paper—perhaps none—but a more specific account of the initial plans, would have removed any doubt that might be cast on the validity of the reported results.

In general, many studies contain researcher degrees of freedom in one way or another. Post experiment removal of outliers (see **P7**) for example can have large effects on the presented results: such practice should only be undertaken if outlier criteria are identified a priori. Over testing, post-hoc re-classification, selection of "interesting" dependent variables based on p-values are other examples of researcher degrees of freedom which are—regrettably—all present within the body of the eight papers that we have reviewed.

14.3 What Do We Know Now?

Despite the common errors, it is important to review what we might have learned from the eight reviewed papers. Are the errors so severe that they hamper the validity of the results? In this section we try to address one by one the severity of the statistical errors on the validity of the conclusions in each of the eight reviewed papers.

P1 reports an alarmingly high rate of Pathological Internet Usage among their participants, and proposed a model of the characteristics associated with PIU. The paper reports a large number of post-hoc comparisons which are not corrected for. When corrections are applied, 14 of the results are no longer significant, although we do believe that the broad conclusions remain the same. So despite some caution, we would say that the authors provide sufficient evidence in favour of their conclusions. It is however unclear what the practical value for HCI and wider fields of the uncovered differences actually is since effect sizes are not reported. Hence, while we feel the general conclusion of the paper is warranted, more elaborate reporting, using (e.g.,) an estimation approach as advocated in Chap. 13, would have strengthened the impact of the work.

The analysis in **P2** was well conducted and the conclusions are appropriately careful. Their contribution about the equalisation of group members when using electronic communication have large effect sizes, and are likely to be reliable, assuming that the assumptions of the tests were met. This is an example of carefully planned and reported analysis.

P3 reported some surprising results regarding aesthetics and usability: users' post-test perceptions of a system were affected by aesthetics and not by usability. However, although these results were statistically significant, the effect sizes are very small and it is not obvious what impact this size of effect might have on designs in the real world. Hassenzahl (**P8**) also set out to study the relationship of beauty and usability; due to the lack of power in the experiments, however, we do not think the faith in the null effect—as advocated in the discussion—is warranted. While the Hassenzahl data might add to our belief that the effects of beauty on usability are typically not very large, concluding that they are zero is erroneous. This paper would have benefited from a Bayesian approach (Chaps. 8 and 9), which could have helped to authors quantifying evidence in favour of the null hypothesis. Thus, while the interplay of beauty and usability is of high interest—interesting enough to be the subject of two of the 8 most cited quantitative works in our fields—we feel that the actual relationship has not at all been fleshed out. This is a typical example in which methods matter, and better methods should be used to answer this important question. Again, the estimation approach advocated in Chap. 13 would also be an interesting way to widen the debate.

P4's results seem not very reliable due to problems with researcher degrees of freedom, and multiple comparisons. The effect sizes are very small. A key recommendation from the paper is that "we need to study long-term interactions to learn how to create effective partner robots" (p79). While this may be true, it does not follow from the experimental results reported in the paper. So despite the fact that one of the conclusions is sensible, the actual data presented hardly justifies the conclusions.

P5 is of interest party due to the trends it describes, but also partly due to the estimates of internet use that are contained within. The paper has been referenced for both. Regarding the trends described—and the explicit focus on gender differences—it is possible that many of the reported differences might have been due to chance. As discussed above the study permits many researcher degrees of freedom and the authors could have more explicitly discussed other possible covariates. For the estimates of internet use the study provides a very poor basis (partly because this was obviously not the intent of the authors) for generalisation beyond the American college in which the study took place.

P6 motivates how and when we should automate tasks: an extremely important topic. The work presented is nuanced, which is warranted given the complex experimental design. However, power is not discussed, nor are real world effect sizes discussed: the latter despite the fact that the topic begs for such a discussion. Thus, while this work surely contributes to our understanding of automation, it leaves us oblivious to the real world importance of the uncovered differences.

Lastly, **P7** while not at all standard in its reporting, actually raises the least objections: the authors' discussion of the importance of implicit ratings seems highly valid, and never are the results overstated. Although studies using other experimental groups for increased generalizability are feasible, we believe the paper poses no threats to its own conclusions.

To conclude, there were "flaws" in the analysis sections of our eight case study papers that were published in reputable HCI journals. These papers have been cited in a total of over 1300 other papers. This demonstrates that also HCI as a field is not immune to challenges in its statistical and methodological practice. We hope this book contributes to addressing these challenges.

14.4 Recommendations for Improving Statistical Methodology

It is clear from the above discussion, the six frequently occurring problems with respect to NHST also occur in HCI. These problems threaten the validity of some of the highest cited works in the field. By explaining the problems, highlighting them, and presenting above some examples of good practice, we hope to circumvent some of the problems and to have motivated researchers to analyse and report their quantitative data differently and more informatively. However, to further improve our reporting of quantitative studies, we recommend the following changes, adapted and extended from our previous recommendations in (Kaptein and Robertson 2012) according to our analysis of the eight case study papers.

1. Firstly, consider whether quantitative methods are actually appropriate for the type of research questions under consideration. If the research aims to richly

document the experiences of only a few key users, qualitative methods may be more appropriate. If the questions are exploratory in nature, hypothesis testing might best be deferred until descriptive (possibly quantitative) results from initial analysis have been published. Visualization (Chap. 3) and estimation techniques (Chap. 13) will be a good place to start.

2. A more specific hypothesis yields more information when it is falsified than a vaguely specified hypothesis. For this reason, researchers should be bolder about predicting the direction and magnitude of effects rather than choosing the "safe" null that there is no difference between conditions. Bayesian techniques (See Chap. 9) can be used to quantify evidence in support of competing hypotheses.

3. When planning an experiment, researchers should predict the size of the effect they are likely to find, based on previous findings from related studies if possible. Predictions can also be used to construct prior probabilities for Bayesian analysis (See Chap. 8).

4. Deciding on power, significance criterion (alpha value), and effect size in advance enable the researcher to calculate the number of participants they require to detect an effect of practical or theoretical importance. Power calculations can also be used to specify a stopping rule for data collection. Following Simmons et al. (2011) it is recommended that authors should collect at least 20 observations in each cell if NHST is to be used or provide a justification of why this was not possible on grounds of the cost of collecting the data. A more through discussion of stopping rules can be found in (Frick 1998). Chapters 5–7 of this book have discussed effect sizes details of the NHST framework extensively.

5. To increase the number of observations in cells, researchers should consider reducing the complexity of experimental design. For example, instead of comparing multiple versions of an interface in a single study, the researchers could run a comparison between two versions, and decide whether to pursue additional studies in the future to test further versions if the results warrant it. While the real-world is often complex and thus researchers should not avoid complexity per-se, researchers should be cautious about increasing the number of cells in their experiments without also increasing their power leading to results that are too ill informed by the data to derive any conclusions. If complex experimental designs are adopted, research should consider using more elaborate analysis methods such as those presented in Chaps. 10–12 of this book.

6. If there are practical difficulties in recruiting enough participants, research teams should consider collaborating for multi-site experiments. Power can also be increased by careful choice of valid and appropriate measurement instruments. Furthermore, analysing the results of multiple studies into the same topic (meta-analysis) can, through collaboration, strengthen our beliefs.

7. Researchers should consider using Bayesian analysis to calculate the probability of the hypothesis given the data instead of "orthodox" significance testing (see Chaps. 8 and 9). This analysis method enables researchers to build on the body of knowledge in the field by incorporating previous results as prior probabilities, and avoids the fallacy of the transposed conditional. It also enables the quantification of strength of evidence for a hypothesis without misinterpreting the p-value.

8. When making data collection and analysis decisions, authors should attempt to mitigate problems arising from researcher degrees of freedom by following the recommendations of Simmons et al. (2011) about reporting stopping rules, all variable collected, all experimental conditions, complete results of testing with and without covariates and how outliers are processed. Careful consideration of techniques for handling missing data are also important, as discussed in Chap. 4.

9. Researchers, reviewers, programme chairs and journal editors should work towards raising the standard of reporting statistical results in order that future researchers can use this information to inform their own hypothesis generation, effect size estimates and prior probabilities in Bayesian analysis. The guidelines in the 6th edition of the APA publication manual (American Psychological Association 2009) are helpful in this regard. At the very least, the mean and standard error should be reported to enable future researchers to calculate standardized effect sizes.

10. And, last but absolutely not least, researchers should interpret the magnitude of the effects in terms of real world significance. Here, unstandardized effect sizes need to be reported and interpreted. The mere reporting of standardized effect-sizes (such as Cohen's d, R2, etc.) as suggested by the APA is not sufficient: the measures also combine both signal and noise into a single estimate. Ultimately designers need to know the extent to which design decisions will impact their users to make cost benefit decisions and the certainty of these estimates.

The above recommendations should help researchers when discussing the results of their quantitative studies. In all cases however, there is no "single best answer". While NHST conveniently provides such a single-best answer procedure, it does so at great cost. NHST should be only one of many tools available to quantitative researchers, and perhaps it should not be singled out as the most important one. We would like to stress that we do not believe that there is a single best way to analyse data given the experimental setup: one can approach the data in a multitude of ways, examining descriptive statistics, running the appropriate (and planned) tests, and fitting models. However, as Box said: "All models are wrong, some are useful" (Box 1979). We are looking for a useful interpretation of our quantitative results that furthers our field. We are not merely seeking small p-values. This should be a note not just to authors, but perhaps even more prominently to reviewers.

14.5 Closing Remarks

So, do methods matter? We argue that they do; the above case studies suggest that lack of rigour in quantitative methods in HCI research has in the past led to the publication of possibly misleading findings in well-respected journals. We will now aim to place this argument in the context of the contemporary HCI community by examining some current debates among researchers and practitioners. As informal yet revealing debates currently often take place online, we will characterise points of view with quotes from recent calls for papers, panel discussion and HCI blogs and blog commenters.

Our intention is not to dissuade colleagues from using quantitative methods. Nor do we intend to imply that our own work is perfect in this regard (far from it!). According to the blog post of a CHI Associate Chair, hundreds of CHI conference papers are annually rejected on the basis of their statistical conclusion validity (including many of the errors described in this paper), even although the topic of the paper is timely and important.[3] It would be much better for the field if the authors could overcome these barriers and present their important work in front of their peers. Another CHI associate chair blogged that although *"poor rigor is seldom a winning recipe for publication …some flaw or compromise in the rigor can be found in most papers… the issue is how seriously to judge that flaw as a part of the whole contribution."*[4] While this is a reasonable consideration, based on the case study papers we examined above, our position is that flawed statistical analysis can seriously undermine the quality of a contribution and that therefore reviewers, editors and chairs should be able to confidently identity when the findings are not supported by the evidence as presented in the analysis.

We argue that methodological rigour is increasingly important, given important current trends within the HCI community: research in the wild (as discussed at a DIS 2012 workshop), longitudinal research (as discussed at the "Theories, methods and case studies of longitudinal HCI research" workshop at CHI 2012), and replication (see the Replichi panel at CHI 2011 and the more recent workshops stemming from it). A 2012 ToCHI call for papers on a special issue entitled "The Turn to the Wild"[5] reads: *"Whereas the burning question in HCI used to be "how many participants do I need?" the hotly debated question now is "how long should my study run for?" Some say a few weeks, others argue for months while some even suggest years are needed to show sustainable and long-term effects."* As the call for papers notes, in the wild research, particularly longitudinal work, can be extremely costly. While we acknowledge that not all in wild research will be quantitative, some such work will benefit from statistical methods. It is simply too expensive in terms of researchers' and users' time to run in the wild studies which aim to make quantitative claims but are inadequately designed or suffer from problems with data collection and analysis. The recommendations about transparent statistical reporting in Chap. 13 and Simmon's et al. advice (2011) on researcher degrees of freedom are particularly relevant here. Years of research effort could be wasted, thus raising the ethical question of whether the long-term intrusion into users' lives is warranted for compromised research findings.

There is a laudable move towards replication, as demonstrated by the replichi group, who ran a workshop at CHI 2014. Replication of quantitative research findings can only be done if the experimental reporting of the original work is clear

---

[3] See http://oulasvirta.posterous.com/86113982 for this discussion.

[4] Quote retrieved from: http://interactionculture.wordpress.com/2012/01/27/a-position-on-peer-reviewing-in-hci-part-1/.

[5] See http://cs.swansea.ac.uk/turntothewild/.

and complete. This relates to recommendations 4 and 9 which refer to basing power calculations on reported effect sizes from the literature and adopting the APA guidelines for clear reporting. For the replichi[6] movement to succeed, higher standards of reporting must be applied consistently (see also Chap. 13, Sect. 13.2.2).

At a deeper level, the replichi cause exemplifies debate about the very nature of HCI research, which will perhaps also concern critics of this book. In an extended abstract for CHI 2011, the replichi group writes: *"The replication of, or perhaps the replicability of, research is often considered to be a cornerstone of scientific progress. Yet unlike many other disciplines, like medicine, physics, or mathematics, we have almost no drive and barely any reason to consider replicating the work of other HCI researchers. Our community is driven to publish novel results in novel spaces using novel designs, and to keep up with evolving technology."*[7]

For some members of the community, the alignment of HCI with science is unwelcome.[8] Some consider HCI closer to engineering.[9] A somewhat cynical blog comment reads: *"I think that HCI is attempting to assume the mantle of science *because* science is 'practically the only measurable form of progress in the 20th century'; it's a legitimacy ploy"*[10] James Landay blogs: *"I think we have been blinded by the perception that "true scientific" research is only found in controlled experiments and nice statistics."*[11] Our position closely matches that of another blog commenter who wrote: *"Is HCI a science?—I don't care other than that I rarely find such discussions worthwhile other than as distractions. Can science be used to better HCI? Absolutely! Can someone ignorant of science be an effective HCI practitioner (without supervision of someone who's not ignorant)? Extremely unlikely."*[12] This captures our viewpoint in the sense that we believe that the scientific method using statistical analysis is a substantial and important tool in the toolkit of HCI researchers. We should therefore aspire to a state where all authors and reviewers who use these methods know how to do so competently and report them clearly in such a way that the results can be replicated. We hope this book is a contribution towards this goal.

Consistent with previous studies of statistical methods within the field of HCI (and our neighbouring fields), our examination of eight of the most highly cited quantitative papers from reputable HCI publications indicates that there is considerable room for improvement in our statistical methodologies. We believe that quantitative methods are important for some types of HCI research, and that we should continue to use them for hypothesis testing in confirmatory research. Broadly speaking we believe

---

[6] The first replichi special interest group can be found at: http://chi2012.acm.org/program/desktop/Session25.html.

[7] From http://www.cs.nott.ac.uk/$\sim$mlw/pubs/RepliCHI-panel_CR.pdf.

[8] For a detailed discussion of this see Stuart Reeve's blog at http://notesonresearch.tumblr.com/.

[9] Comment on http://web.archive.org/web/20100914113440/http://unraveled.com/archives/2003/10/hci_as_science.

[10] Comment on http://web.archive.org/web/20100914113440/http://unraveled.com/archives/2003/10/hci_as_science.

[11] See: http://dubfuture.blogspot.co.uk/2009/11/i-give-up-on-chiuist.html.

[12] Comment on http://web.archive.org/web/20100914113440/http://unraveled.com/archives/2003/10/hci_as_science.

that there are two issues which we as a field need to improve: *(a)* identifying cases where null hypothesis significance testing (NHST) tells us what we need to know and those cases where alternative analysis methods (e.g. Bayesian) might be more suitable and *(b)* eliminating common errors in carrying out NHST which potentially lead to errors in interpreting results, thus misdirecting future research effort. Such improvements will serve practitioners and users better by enabling us to quantify the outcomes of experiments in a real world context. We need to be confident both that most of our research findings are not false, but also that they are actually useful.

References

American Psychological Association (2009) Publication Manual of the American Psychological Association, 6th edn, p. 272

Box GEP (1979) Robustness in the strategy of scientific model building, Technical summary rept. University of Wisconsin

Claypool M, Le P, Wased M, Brown D (2001) Implicit interest indicators. In: Proceedings of the 6th international conference on intelligent user interfaces—IUI '01. ACM Press, New York, pp 33–40

Dienes Z (2008) Understanding psychology as a science: an introduction to scientific and statistical inference, 1st edn, p 150. Palgrave Macmillan

Dubrovsky V, Kiesler S, Sethna B (1991) The equalization phenomenon: status effects in computer-mediated and face-to-face decision-making groups. Human-Comput Interact 6(2):119–146

Endsley MR, Kaber DB (1999) Level of automation effects on performance, situation awareness and workload in a dynamic control task. Ergonomics 42(3):462–492

Frick RW (1998) A better stopping rule for conventional statistical tests. Behav Res Methods Instrum Comput 30:690–697

Hassenzahl M (2004) The Interplay of beauty, goodness, and usability in interactive products. Human-Comput Interact 19(4):319–349

Ioannidis JPA (2005) Why most published research findings are false. In: Jantsch W, Schaffler F (eds) PLoS Med 2(8):e124

Kanda T, Hirano T, Eaton D, Ishiguro, H (2004) Interactive robots as social partners and peer tutors for children: a field trial. Human-Comput Interact 19(1):61–84

Kaptein MC, Nass C, Markopoulos P (2010) Powerful and consistent analysis of likert-type rat-ingscales. In: Proceedings of the 28th international conference on human factors in computing systems—CHI '10. ACM Press, New York, pp 2391–2401

Kaptein MC, Robertson J (2012) Rethinking Statistical Methods for HCI. In: Proceedings of the 2011 annual conference on human factors in computing systems, CHI 212. ACM Press, New York, pp 1105–1114

Kruschke JK (2011) Bayesian assessment of null values via parameter estimation and model comparison. Perspect Psychol Sci 6(3):299–312 (May 2011)

Meho LI, Rogers Y (2008) Citation counting, citation ranking, and h-index of human-computer interaction researchers: a comparison of scopus and web of science. J Am Soc Inform Sci Technol 59(11):1711–1726

Morahan-Martin J, Schumacher P (2000) Incidence and correlates of pathological internet use among college students. Comput Hum Behav 16(1):13–29

Oakes M (1986) Statistical Inference: a commentary for the social and behavioural sciences. Wiley, p 196

Schumacher P, Morahan-Martin J (2001) Gender, internet and computer attitudes and experiences. Comput Hum Behav 17(1):95–110

Simmons JP, Nelson LD, Simonsohn U (2011) False-positive psychology: undisclosed flexibility in data collection and analysis allows presenting anything as significant. Psychol Sci 22(11):1359–1366

Tractinsky N, Katz A, Ikar D (2000) What is beautiful is usable. Interact Comput 13(2):127–145

Ziliak S, McCloskey D (2008) The cult of statistical significance: how the standard error costs us jobs, justice and lives. University of Michigan Press, Ann Arbor

Printed in the United States
By Bookmasters